BLACK FLAGS, BLUE WATERS

Caca Fogo.

Black Flags, Blue Waters

THE
EPIC HISTORY OF
AMERICA'S MOST
NOTORIOUS
PIRATES

Eric Jay Dolin

LIVERIGHT PUBLISHING
CORPORATION

A Division of W. W. NORTON & COMPANY

Independent Publishers Since 1923

NEW YORK • LONDON

FIRST EDITION

For information about permission to reproduce selections
from this book, write to Permissions, Liveright Publishing Corporation,
a division of W. W. Norton & Company, Inc.,
500 Fifth Avenue, New York, NY 10110

For information about special discounts for bulk purchases,
please contact W. W. Norton Special Sales
at specialsales@wwnorton.com or 800-233-4830

Manufacturing by LSC Communications Harrisonburg
Book design by Barbara M. Bachman
Production manager: Anna Oler

ISBN 978-1-63149-210-5

Liveright Publishing Corporation
500 Fifth Avenue, New York, N.Y. 10110
www.wwnorton.com

W. W. Norton & Company Ltd.
15 Carlisle Street, London W1D 3BS

2 3 4 5 6 7 8 9 0

To
Jennifer, Lily, and Harry

Ships are but boards, sailors but men:
there be land-rats, and water-rats,
water-thieves, and land-thieves;
I mean pirates.

—WILLIAM SHAKESPEARE, *The Merchant of Venice*

Contents

Author's Note

THE ARCHAIC AND OFTEN MYSTIFYING SPELLINGS OF WORDS that appeared in some quotes have been changed (modernized) for easier reading and comprehension.

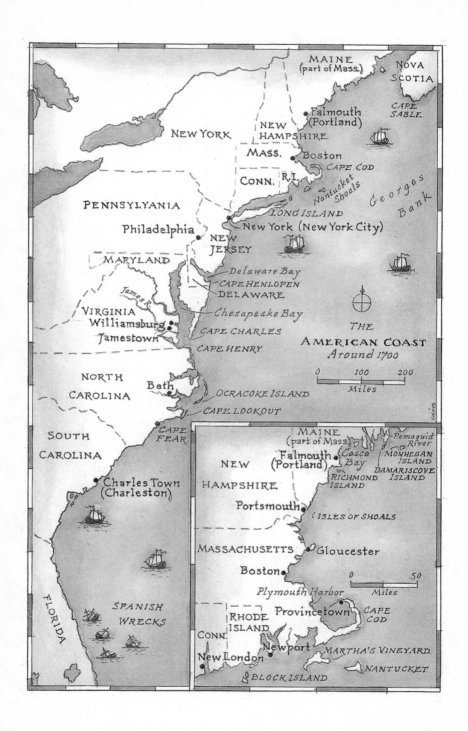

MAINE
(part of Mass.)

NOVA
SCOTIA

CAPE
SABLE

NEW YORK

NEW
HAMPSHIRE

Falmouth
(Portland)

MASS.

Boston

CAPE COD

CONN. R.I.

Nantucket
Shoals

Georges
Bank

PENNSYLVANIA

LONG ISLAND

Philadelphia

New York (New York City)

NEW
JERSEY

MARYLAND

Delaware Bay

CAPE HENLOPEN
DELAWARE

James R.

Chesapeake Bay

VIRGINIA
Williamsburg
Jamestown

CAPE CHARLES

CAPE HENRY

THE
AMERICAN COAST
Around 1700

NORTH
CAROLINA

Bath

OCRACOKE ISLAND

CAPE LOOKOUT

0   100   200
Miles

SOUTH
CAROLINA

CAPE
FEAR

MAINE
(part of Mass.)

Pemaquid
River

NEW

Falmouth
(Portland)

Casco
Bay

MONHEGAN
ISLAND

DAMARISCOVE
ISLAND

HAMPSHIRE

RICHMOND
ISLAND

Charles Town
(Charleston)

Portsmouth

ISLES OF SHOALS

MASSACHUSETTS

Gloucester

Boston

0   50
Miles

Plymouth Harbor

FLORIDA

SPANISH
WRECKS

RHODE
ISLAND

Provincetown

CAPE
COD

CONN.

Newport

MARTHA'S VINEYARD

New London

NANTUCKET

BLOCK ISLAND

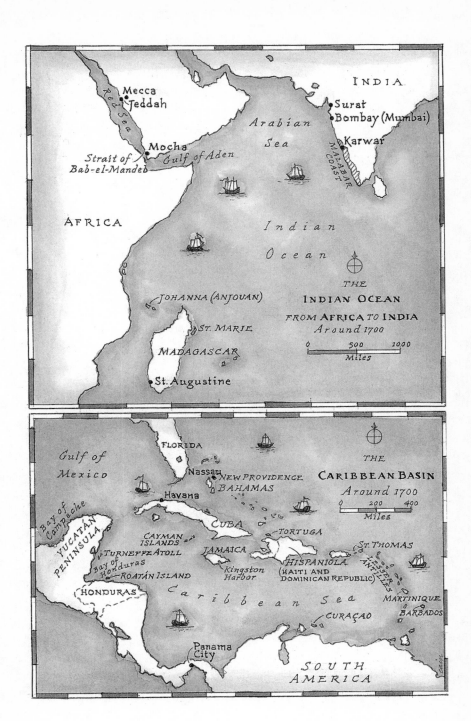

INDIA

Red Sea
Mecca
Jeddah

Arabian
Sea

Surat
Bombay (Mumbai)

Mocha
Strait of
Bab-el-Mandeb
Gulf of Aden

Karwar

MALABAR COAST

AFRICA

Indian

Ocean

THE
INDIAN OCEAN
FROM AFRICA TO INDIA
Around 1700

JOHANNA (ANJOUAN)

ST. MARIE

MADAGASCAR

0   500   1000
Miles

St. Augustine

Gulf of
Mexico

FLORIDA

Nassau
NEW PROVIDENCE
BAHAMAS

THE
CARIBBEAN BASIN
Around 1700

Bay of
Campeche

Havana

0   200   400
Miles

YUCATÁN
PENINSULA

CAYMAN
ISLANDS

CUBA

TORTUGA

ST. THOMAS

Bay of
Honduras
TURNEFFE ATOLL

ROATÁN ISLAND

JAMAICA

Kingston
Harbor

HISPANIOLA
(HAITI AND
DOMINICAN REPUBLIC)

LESSER ANTILLES

HONDURAS

Caribbean Sea

MARTINIQUE

BARBADOS

CURAÇAO

Panama
City

SOUTH
AMERICA

Introduction

*An early twentieth-century representation of
Blackbeard the pirate fighting against British Naval
Lieutenant Robert Maynard onboard the sloop* Jane
in late November 1718.

AT THE END OF APRIL 1726, CAPTAIN JOHN GREEN WAS FINALLY
ready to leave. The last of the food, water, and supplies had been
hoisted aboard the *Elizabeth*, which was tied to a wharf in Jamaica's

capacious Kingston Harbor. Green and his sixteen-man crew were about to sail across the Atlantic to Africa's Guinea Coast to pick up a cargo of slaves, the main labor source for the island's cruel economy. Jamaica's vast and lucrative sugar plantations brutally employed tens of thousands of slaves to do the backbreaking work of harvesting and processing sugar cane so that an ever-increasing number of people throughout the British Empire could sweeten their tea, coffee, and cakes—most of these consumers blissfully unconcerned about the horrors perpetrated to delight their palate. The death rate was so high on these plantations that the owners needed to continually replenish their supply of slaves to keep up with the growing demand for sugar. Without the services of men like Green and his crew, Jamaica's economy would eventually grind to a halt.

Not long after the *Elizabeth* departed from Jamaica's crystal blue waters, the trouble began. Captain Green, and his first mate, Thomas Jenkins, quickly earned the enmity of the majority of the crew, who claimed that the two men had subjected them to "bad usage," and treated them "barbarously . . . like dogs." Twenty-seven-year-old boatswain William Fly channeled this anger and began plotting a mutiny. In the dead of night on May 27, when the *Elizabeth* was hundreds of miles from the American coast, Fly and his coconspirators decided it was time to strike.

Just after one in the morning, Fly, who was standing watch, gave the signal. Tense with anticipation of the violence to come, he and four others strode across the main deck and approached Morrice Cundon, who was manning the helm. Fly leaned in close and whispered menacingly in Cundon's ear, "Damn you, if you stir hand or foot, or speak a word, I'll blow your brains out." To drive his threat home, Fly lifted his shirt to expose the gun tucked into his trousers. Petrified, Cundon watched as Fly climbed down the companionway to the captain's cabin below, with crewman Alexander Mitchell following closely behind.

Violently rousing the startled Captain Green from his bed, the two mutineers hauled the struggling officer to the main deck. As they were about to pitch him into the sea, he screamed, "For God's sake, boatswain, don't throw me overboard, for if you do I shall go to hell." Relishing his new position of power, Fly coolly ordered the captain to repeat after him, "Lord have mercy upon my soul," and then Fly, Mitchell, and a crewman named Winthrop threw Green over the rail. Reluctant to accept his fate, in a last-ditch effort the struggling captain grabbed hold of the mainsheet* with a vise-tight grip. It was, however, only a momentary reprieve. As Green dangled above the waves, Winthrop swung a cooper's broadax in a mighty arc, bringing it down on the hapless captain's wrist, severing his hand and launching him into the deep.

Their bloodlust still raging, the mutineers now searched for their next victim—Jenkins. Quartermaster Samuel Cole yelled to the mate, "Come out of your cabin you dog." But Jenkins, who had heard Green struggling with his executioners just moments before, would not budge. Instead he pleaded, "For the Lord's sake, save my life." The mutineers hauled Jenkins out to the main deck, where Winthrop shattered his shoulder with his now bloody broadax, shouting, "He should go over after his commander!" as he threw the first mate overboard. Bobbing in the water, Jenkins called out, "For God's sake, throw me a rope." But there would be no help. The mutineers controlled the vessel, rechristening it *Fame's Revenge*. Their reign as pirates had begun.

AFTER ELECTING FLY CAPTAIN, the pirates set a new course for the American coast in search of prey. *Fame's Revenge*, a two-masted, square-rigged vessel called a snow, was not particularly formidable, boasting just four cannons and two mounted swivel guns, but it was powerful enough to fulfill its crews' criminal designs. Over the next few weeks, Fly and company, boastfully calling themselves "Gentlemen of Fortune," plundered three merchant vessels between North Carolina and New Jersey, taking a number of prisoners along the

---

* A rope attached to the boom or lower corner of the mainsail and used to adjust the angle of the sail to the wind.

way. The most important prisoner was William Atkinson, the former captain of the merchantman *Bonetta*, who had been hitching a ride to Boston on one of the now-captured vessels. Since Atkinson was quite familiar with the local waters, Fly gave him a choice— either pilot *Fame's Revenge* to New England or the pirates would "blow his brains out."

A reluctant Atkinson took up the task, and around June 12, Fly ordered him to direct the snow to Martha's Vineyard, where the pirates hoped to get water and wood. Atkinson, however, had other plans. He purposely missed the Vineyard, and *Fame's Revenge* was well past Nantucket before Fly realized they were off course. Incensed by Atkinson's deception, Fly threatened to kill him but thought better of murdering his best pilot. Instead, he let Atkinson continue, ordering him to set a new heading for the waters off Nova Scotia, where the New England fishing fleet was gathered. If everything went according to plan, once there, Fly would be able to discard *Fame's Revenge*, a sluggish sailer, and upgrade to a better vessel, one that offered greater speed and agility.

Even before he had intentionally veered off course, Atkinson had been scheming. He was eager for a chance to take the snow, and he had shared his inchoate plan with a few of his fellow prisoners. In fact, Atkinson had often thought about what he would do if pirates took one of his own ships, and he had vowed that if he were captured, he would "humor" the pirates "till he could see his opportunity to rise upon them." All Atkinson needed was an opening.

By the morning of June 23, *Fame's Revenge* was on Browns Bank, about sixty miles south of Nova Scotia, and a favorite haunt of New England fishermen in search of the mighty cod. With their black flag—the universal symbol of pirates—raised aloft, Fly and his men quickly overtook the *James*, a fishing schooner out of Marblehead. But Fly wanted a faster vessel, so when another promising schooner hove into view, he placed the bulk of his crew on the *James* to hunt it down.

Fly's zeal for a faster vessel proved to be his undoing. Just three of his men remained on *Fame's Revenge*, and only one of them was fit for duty; another was in irons on suspicion of mutiny, while the third had gotten into the liquor and was three sheets to the wind. At the same time, there were fifteen prisoners aboard, a few of whom were unshackled.

Not long after the *James* departed on its piratical errand, Atkinson, who was at the bow of *Fame's Revenge*, informed Fly that he saw another fishing vessel in the distance. Thinking that this might be the opportunity he was waiting for, Atkinson then pretended to see a few more vessels, and he excitedly told Fly that he would soon "have a fleet of prizes." When Fly, who was on the quarterdeck near the stern, protested that he only saw one vessel through his spyglass, Atkinson bade him to come forward to take a closer look. In a move that proved Fly was neither a great pirate nor a good judge of men, he left his two loaded guns and sword on the quarterdeck as he joined Atkinson at the bow. Suspecting nothing, Fly sat on the windlass and took out his spyglass to scan the horizon.

While Fly's attention was thus engaged, Atkinson grabbed the unsuspecting and feckless pirate lord, pinioning his arms behind him. At that moment, two other prisoners, who had also committed themselves to rise up when the time was right, rushed forward and took hold of Fly, while Atkinson sprinted aft to retrieve one of Fly's guns. When Atkinson rushed back to the bow, he pointed the weapon at Fly, coolly informing him that "he was a dead man if he did not immediately submit himself [to be] his prisoner."

Hearing the commotion, the only other pirate fit for duty rushed up the ladder and onto the main deck. Atkinson spun around, struck him on the head with the butt of the gun, and subdued the man with the help of another prisoner. Fly and his followers were soon in chains. With that, Fly's short, bloody, and almost farcical career as a pirate captain came to an abrupt end.

Atkinson immediately set a course for Boston. Meanwhile, the pirates on the *James*, shocked to see *Fame's Revenge* leaving, chased it into the night. But the skilled sailor Atkinson was able to lose his pursuers in the covering darkness. Over the next few days, the men aboard *Fame's Revenge* were subjected to Fly's incessant ranting. He "cursed himself, and her that bore him,' as well as "the very heavens, . . . the God that judged him, [and] all rovers that should ever give quarter to [or spare] Englishmen," rather than put them to death upon capture. He also wished that "all the devils of hell would come and fly away with the ship"—a fate that he no doubt thought was better than that which awaited him in port.

ON JUNE 29, *Fame's Revenge* docked in Boston, the largest and most vibrant port in the American colonies. The shackled pirates were thrown into the town jail, a gloomy stone edifice with walls three feet thick and a massive oak and iron door, the keys to which were more than a foot long. The speedily convened Special Court of Admiralty ruled on July 5 that Fly and two of his men should be hanged for piracy, while the fourth, the drunkard and, as it turns out, a simpleton, was granted a reprieve.

For a week after sentencing, the pirates were the talk of the town, and the intense focus of Cotton Mather's ministrations. A third-generation Puritan preacher, and arguably the most famous man in the American colonies, Mather visited the condemned men and pleaded with them to renounce their crimes and repent before God. That was the only way, Mather argued, that they could "escape the Damnation of Hell" after their date with the gallows.

The following Sunday, Mather preached a sermon at Boston's Christ Church (the modern-day Old North Church), decrying the pirates' heinous acts and glorifying the rule of an all-powerful and merciful God. Two of the pirates, who had succumbed to Mather's entreaties and repented, were on hand to listen and serve as objects of pity for the parishioners filling the church's pews. Fly, however, refused to attend, declaring that "he would not have the mob to gaze upon him." Fly also cheekily told the earnest but long-winded Mather that he couldn't repent and disavow the actions he had taken because he had no remorse, and would not "go out of the World with a lie in my mouth."

Two days later, a cart was brought to the jail to transport the

"A South East View of the Great Town of Boston in New England in America," circa 1736. This image, which is based largely on an earlier engraving, depicts Boston much as it looked when William Fly and company were tried for piracy.

condemned to the place of execution at the harbor's edge. Despite the fact that Fly, in a "sullen and raging mood," had refused to eat for nearly a week, taking only an occasional drink, he was surprisingly energetic. According to a witness, "Fly briskly and in a way of bravery jumped into the cart," while his two fellow convicts solemnly climbed aboard. Thousands of people lined the streets, eager to witness the procession of shame. Fly, Mather said, was intent to die "a brave fellow." Holding a nosegay in his hand, Fly even complimented some of the spectators along the route. He "nimbly mounted the stage" set up under the gallows, and smiled at the assembled throng. Then, his bravado fully on display, "he reproached the hangman for not understanding his trade," and proceeded to retie the noose so that it would function properly.

Three local ministers offered prayers, and each of the pirates was given a chance to share his last words. Two of them took the time to pray and warn the spectators to avoid the sinful temptations they succumbed to, such as cursing, drunkenness, and Sabbath-breaking.

When it came time for Fly to speak, Mather hoped he would finally admit his failings before God. But that hope was in vain. With the noose around his neck, Fly defiantly looked out upon his audience and said he "would advise the masters of vessels to" treat their men well, or risk having them mutiny like he had done. Despite Fly's failure to accept responsibility for his actions, and his lack of remorse, Mather still had a small sliver of satisfaction. Just before Fly was to be sent swinging to face the "judgment to come," he noticed that the pirate's hands and knees were trembling. As well they should be, Mather must have thought, for the unrepentant soul has much to answer for in the next world.

After the execution, the pirates' bodies were rowed out to Nix's Mate,* a small island in Boston Harbor about five miles from the town, where Fly's two associates were buried. But Fly, the director of this sad and tragic story, was "hung up in irons, as a spectacle for the warning of others, especially seafaring men."

THE WARNING WAS HARDLY NECESSARY. Fly's spectacular, bloody, and brief piratical campaign was the last gasp of the so-called Golden Age of Piracy, which started in the late 1600s. This was the most dramatic era of maritime marauding the world has ever known, when pirates wreaked havoc across the Atlantic and the Indian Oceans. It produced such iconic characters as Captain William Kidd and Blackbeard, along with thousands of other pirates whose names are less familiar, but whose despicable deeds are often just as riveting. So powerful is the pull of the Golden Age that, in most people's minds, it is virtually synonymous with piracy.

Much has been written about that time period, and this book adds to that literary lineage, but with a twist. Rather than focusing broadly on this era, *Black Flags, Blue Waters* zeros in on the history

---

* Nix's Mate, a respectable, albeit very small, island at the time of the hanging, is today just a square pedestal of granite topped by a pyramidal day beacon that helps guide ships in and out of the harbor.

of the pirates who either operated out of America's English colonies or plundered ships along the American coast. From the early 1680s to 1726, these pirates had an exceedingly close, often tempestuous, and frequently deadly relationship with the colonies. While this arrangement began with a warm and financially lucrative embrace, it eventually ended in a bloody war against pirates punctuated by scores of hangings from Boston to Charleston. *Black Flags, Blue Waters* explores the fascinating origins and nature of this volatile relationship, and in so doing reveals one of the most gripping stories of the American experience.

Of course, America's connection to piracy did not abruptly end in 1726 with the execution of Fly. Most notably, in the early to mid-1800s the United States vanquished both the Barbary pirates who harassed American ships off the coast of North Africa, and Spanish pirates who waylaid American shipping throughout the Caribbean and off the East and Gulf Coasts of North America. More recently, twenty-first-century Somali pirates have seriously disrupted not just American, but the world's maritime commerce, by overpowering ships within striking distance of Somalia and holding them for ransom. The exploits of these and other pirates with an American connection, however fascinating, are beyond the scope of this book. Instead, what follows is a narrative and chronological history of America's pirates during the Golden Age.

At the core of *Black Flags, Blue Waters* are the pirates themselves, who made the fateful choice to attack and plunder on the high seas. But before one can talk about pirates, it is necessary to define the term and differentiate it from *privateer*. The word *pirate* first appeared in the fourteenth century and derives from the Greek, *peiratēs*, and the Latin, *pīrāta*, both of which broadly mean "to attempt, attack, assault." More specifically, in the maritime context, pirates are people who steal at sea; they are the oceanic equivalent of land-based robbers.

For as long as people have taken to the sea, there have been pirates. Every culture and country whose ships have dipped a paddle or oar into the salty brine, or raised a sail to harness the wind, has contended with what the Greek poet Homer called "sea-wolves raiding at will, who risk their lives to plunder other men." Captain John Smith, the controversial English explorer and one of the founders of the Jamestown Colony in Virginia, had it right when he remarked, "As in all lands where there are many people, there are some thieves, so in all seas much frequented, there are some pirates." And almost two thousand years before Smith, Roman historian and statesman Dio Cassius wisely observed, "There was never a time when piracy was not practiced, nor may it cease so long as the nature of mankind remains the same." Ancient and modern history is replete with stories about the path of ruin that pirates left in their wake.

Privateers, in contrast, are men who sailed on armed vessels owned and outfitted by private individuals who had government permission to capture enemy shipping during times of war. That permission was embodied in a "letter of marque," a formal legal document issued by the government that gave the bearer the right to capture vessels belonging to belligerent nations, and claim those vessels and their cargoes as prizes. The proceeds from the auction of these prizes were, in turn, usually split between the privateers, the investors in the operation, and the issuing authority. Typically, governments used privateers as a means of amplifying their power upon the seas, especially when their navies were not strong enough on their own to wage war. More specifically, by attacking and hobbling the enemy's maritime commerce and its naval forces, privateers could inflict a savage economic and military blow designed to help ensure victory. In a nod to both the legality of privateering, and its more than passing resemblance to piratical behavior, some have called it "licensed" piracy.

As numerous historians and writers have observed, the line between pirates and privateers is often exceedingly thin, to the point of sometimes being undetectable. Letters of marque can be of questionable legitimacy, and, by the same token, those people labeled as pirates might think that they are nonetheless acting in accord with the wishes, implied or stated, of the nations for which they are ostensibly fighting. Muddling matters further is the issue of perspective. Just as beauty is often in the eye of the beholder, one person's pirate may be another person's privateer. For example, while a privateer with proper papers is viewed as legitimate by the sponsoring nation, those on the receiving end of the privateer's attacks might well view the privateer as a pirate, the pejorative label only adding to the purportedly ignominious nature of the act.

This book is about pirates, not privateers, although there is no doubt that some readers will argue that in a few cases the distinction is improperly drawn in one direction or the other. Nevertheless, the focus will be on what famed English jurist and politician Sir Edward Coke (1552–1634) called *hostis humani generis*, or the "enemy of mankind," those ocean-borne outlaws who pillaged merchant vessels, usually without regard for the nationality of their victims, breaking the law and blazing a trail of terror on the high seas for private gain.

At its most elemental, *Black Flags, Blue Waters* is about men acting like oceanic gamblers, playing the risky and sometimes fatal game of preying on merchant ships in search of treasure. Most pirates failed to achieve great financial success, and had brief careers that often ended in violent death. But that was not always the case. There were some, especially those operating out of the colonies prior to 1700, who were able to retire from piracy with their riches.

This book is also a history of intimidation and, at times, extreme brutality. Pirates were almost always able to rely on the threat of force to get their victims to submit without violence, but when that approach failed, pirates were willing to fight for what they coveted. The bloodiest encounters, however, were generally not between pirates and their victims, but rather between the pirates and the forces sent to destroy them.

This is likewise a story of political intrigue and collusion. In the late 1600s, many colonists heartily encouraged and supported pirates, though such activities flouted English law. Those colonists viewed pirates not as dangerous raiders, but as commercial angels, and as friends and family, who enabled the colonies to obtain the goods and money they so desperately desired despite the onerous trade restrictions put in place by the mother country. Some colonial governors went so far as to accept bribes and issue privateering licenses to pirates to give them the veneer of official respectability, even though the governors knew full well that the pirates had no intention of going after England's enemies, but instead were heading to the Indian Ocean to loot ships carrying the riches of the Muslim world, and bring that wealth back home.

Finally, *Black Flags, Blue Waters* is about crackdowns, punishment, and eradication. Reacting to the growing problem of piracy in the late 1600s, England launched political, legal, and naval initiatives that had considerable success in countering the pirate threat. But in the mid-1710s, piracy experienced a resurgence, and the number of pirates exploded. More than ever before they focused their depredations on British ships traveling along the coast of the American colonies. Once viewed by many colonists and their official representatives in a favorable light, pirates were now increasingly viewed as mortal enemies who posed a grave threat to trade. Through a combination of legal, political, and military means, pirates were virtually eliminated by the middle of the 1720s, when Fly and his compatriots swung from the gallows.

Aside from their actions, *Black Flags, Blue Waters* explores the question of why pirates pursued such a dangerous and violent life so far outside the legal and social norms of society. Pirates' motivations are often difficult to discern, especially since we know little of most pirates' early lives, and almost none of them put their thoughts on paper. Yet, the records of the era, complemented by modern scholarship, are rich enough to make for an absorbing analysis of what drove these men to sail "under the banner of King Death."

IN THE FOLLOWING PAGES, the reader will meet a rogues' gallery of maritime plunderers. In addition to the infamous Kidd and Blackbeard, there is Dixie Bull, America's first pirate; buccaneer extraordinaire Henry Morgan; Thomas Tew, whose success electrified the colonies; gentleman pirate Stede Bonnet, a man out of place; Edward Low, who relished torture and murder; and Samuel Bellamy, who acquired and then lost a treasure worthy of Midas.

Pirates, however, are not the only dramatis personae who bring this story to life. They are joined by many others, including Edward Randolph, the acerbic English colonial administrator who viewed the pirate-supporting colonies with disdain; "King" Adam Baldridge, who served as ringleader of Madagascar's most notorious pirate haunt; New York's money-grubbing governor, Benjamin Fletcher; Lieutenant Robert Maynard, the man who proved that Blackbeard was not invincible; America's "Robinson Crusoe," Philip Ashton; and Captain Peter Solgard, who captured thirty-six pirates off Block Island in the summer of 1723.

Pirates have long been among the most colorful and memorable celebrities in popular culture. Much of this has to do with the impact of books and movies that use pirates as a motif, such as Robert Louis Stevenson's *Treasure Island*, and the 1935 film *Captain Blood*, which launched Hollywood idol Errol Flynn's career. More recently, Disney's *Pirates of the Caribbean* movie franchise, starring the flamboyant, sassy, and charismatic Johnny Depp as Captain Jack Sparrow, has generated a new pirate-mania, further cementing the hold that pirates have on the human psyche. No wonder, then, that pirate costumes are among the most popular donned on Halloween night, and International Talk Like a Pirate Day is observed by legions of devoted fans every September 19.

Many people view pirates in a romantic light, but there was absolutely nothing romantic about them, other than the legends woven about their exploits after they were gone. That is not to say that pirates were boring. Far from it. While the pirates in the pages that follow can't compete with the magnetic charms and witty repartee of Captain Jack Sparrow, they are compelling characters nonetheless. And the real story of America's pirates is even more astonishing and fascinating than any fictional pirate adventure ever written or cast on the silver screen.

BLACK FLAGS, BLUE WATERS

CHAPTER 1

Small Beginnings

Title page from the original Dutch edition of
The Buccaneers of America
by Alexander Olivier Esquemelin (1678).

PHILIP III, THE KING OF SPAIN AND PORTUGAL (REIGN 1598–1621), warily eyed the budding English colony at Jamestown, Virginia, which was founded in May 1607. While the English claimed they were only interested in colonization, Philip believed they had an ulterior motive. Having only recently concluded a peace treaty with England in 1604 after many years of intermittent fighting, he was not sanguine about the trustworthiness of his new "friend." Sharing his suspicions with a member of his Council of State in July 1608, Philip wrote that he had "been advised that the English are attempting to procure a foothold on the Island of Virginia, with the end [in mind] of sallying forth from there to commit piracy." Given all the riches that Philip was trying to protect, it is no wonder that he was worried.

In the sixteenth century, at the dawn of European expansion into the New World, Spain hit the mother lode of silver and gold when its conquistadors ruthlessly conquered two of the greatest native civilizations in the Americas. Hernando Cortés's savage overthrow of the Aztec Empire in 1521 launched the flow of precious metals into the Spanish economy. This became a flood when Francisco Pizarro routed the Incas in 1532, and then the following year killed the Incan emperor Atahualpa *after* he had paid a ransom of roughly twenty tons of gold and silver intended to secure his release.

At first, the Spanish mining towns that sprang up within the boundaries of the former Aztec and Incan empires shipped silver and gold bullion back to Spain. Later, mints transformed much of the bullion into coins. The most productive mint was established in 1575 in the Incan city of Potosí (in modern-day Bolivia), at the foot of what the Spanish called *Cerro Ricco*, or Rich Mountain. The nearly 16,000-foot peak, also appropriately dubbed Silver Mountain, contained one of the largest silver deposits ever discovered, inspiring the common saying, and most fervent wish the world over, "to be rich as Potosí."

The mints produced copious quantities of coinage for the Spanish

*A 1707 engraving of the Spaniards strangling to death
Incan Emperor Atahualpa in 1533.*

A 1553 engraving of Potosí, also known as Rich or Silver Mountain.

*The front and the back of an extremely rare piece of eight struck in 1683
at the Spanish mint located at the base of* Cerro Ricco, *or Rich Mountain,
in Potosí. Sold at auction in 2015 for $18,800.*

empire, including gleaming gold escudos,* and most importantly,
eight-reale coins (royals), those so-called pieces of eight,† or Spanish
silver dollars, which became the "first truly global currency." By the
end of the 1500s, Spanish America annually produced more than
3,000 tons of bullion and coinage, an explosion of wealth the likes
of which the world had never seen before. But these riches came at
a terrible cost. The Andean natives whom the Spanish forced to do
the backbreaking and dangerous work in the mines died in such
prodigious numbers that *Cerro Rico* became known as the "mountain
that eats men."

Long trains of pack mules transported bullion and coins from
the interior through dense jungles, over treacherous mountains, and
down rivers to waiting ships along the coast that routed the valuable cargo either across the Atlantic to Spain, or across the Pacific

---

* The two-escudos coin was also called a doubloon.

† They were called pieces of eight because they were worth eight reales. These coins
were often cut into eight pieces to make smaller denominations or change. Since the
American dollar was based on the Spanish silver dollar (or eight-reale coin), and there
were eight pieces in one dollar, two pieces were the equivalent of a quarter dollar. Thus,
"two bits"—or two pieces of a dollar—became a slang term for a quarter.

to Spain's colony in the Philippines. The grandest of these treasure ships were the so-called Manila Galleons that traveled the nearly nine thousand miles between modern-day Acapulco, Mexico, and Manila. Heavily armed with scores of cannons, and manned by hundreds of the empire's best sailors and soldiers, the galleons were massive ships whose hulls were made of teak and lanang, tropical woods so dense that cannon balls often harmlessly bounced off them. Sailing from Acapulco, galleons carried silver and gold to Spanish traders in Manila, who used it to purchase the luxury goods of Asia, including lustrous silks from China, cotton fabric from India, and spices from the Moluccas or Spice Islands. Those goods were then sent back to Acapulco, transported overland to Mexico's east coast, and placed on treasure ships bound for Spain. Contemporaries referred to the legendary galleons heading to Manila as "the prize of all the oceans."

While this influx of silver, gold, and exotic goods made Spain incredibly wealthy, and the leading imperial power, it infuriated other Europeans, who eyed Spain's prosperity with envy. Exacerbating their anger was the fact that Spain had claimed an enormous swath of the Americas, leaving few, meager territorial pickings for other European powers intent on exploiting the riches of the New World. Part of Spain's claim to territory was based on colonizing areas after its conquistadors had brutally subjugated native populations. Its claim also rested on the Treaty of Tordesillas, an agreement signed in 1494 between Spain and Portugal. The heart of this treaty was a geographic line of demarcation drawn on the world map by Pope Alexander VI that ran north to south. Spain was given the right to all lands lying to the west of that line that weren't already controlled by a Christian ruler, while Portugal had rights to similar lands to the east of the line. This essentially gave everything in North and South America, minus part of eastern Brazil, to Spain. Of course, other European countries, which had their own imperial ambitions, rejected the treaty and refused to abide by it. But for the Spanish, it meant that virtually all of the Americas was rightfully theirs.

Rival European powers, however, had their own means of

Illustration by Howard Pyle (1921) titled "An Attack on a Galleon."

assuaging their anger over Spain's massive land grab—they could steal from the Spanish. Since so much of Europe was embroiled in wars during the sixteenth and early seventeenth centuries, pitting Spain against a wide variety of foes, there were plenty of opportunities for countries to launch privateers in search of Spanish treasure ships to pillage. At the same time, many European pirates sailed with the same aim. While Dutch and French privateers and pirates constituted a major threat to Spanish ships, it was the Eng-

Engraved portrait of Sir Francis Drake, circa 1583.

lish who scored some of the biggest prizes. And the most successful of these Englishmen was Francis Drake.

RAISED IN THE COMPANY of pirates and privateers and schooled in the art of battle, Drake was a skilled mariner who gained renown for his circumnavigation of the world from 1577 to 1580. The first English expedition to achieve this goal, it was second only to Ferdinand Magellan's voyage that accomplished the same feat for Spain between 1519 and 1522. The motivation behind Drake's voyage, however, was not navigational glory, but money. His secret orders from Tudor Elizabeth I, the "Virgin Queen," whose forty-five-year reign (1558–1603) witnessed a renaissance of

The Cacafuego,
*or "Shitfire" (on
the left), being
attacked by
Francis Drake's*
Golden Hind.

culture and political power in England, were to plunder Spanish possessions in the Pacific, even though England and Spain were then nominally at peace. Harboring long-simmering resentment of the Spanish and a particular animosity toward her brother-in-law King Philip II (reign 1556–1598), whom she claimed had caused her "diverse injuries," Elizabeth wanted to punish the Spanish and appropriate their riches for England.

Drake delivered more than Elizabeth could have possibly hoped for. Attacking multiple Spanish towns and ships along the western coast of South America, Drake soon amassed a fortune in silver and gold. His most impressive conquest was the ship *Nuestra Señora de la Concepción*, which the Spanish sailors had colorfully nicknamed *Cacafuego*, or "Shitfire." Although it was but a coastal transport ship, and not one of the famed Manila Galleons, it carried a king's ransom. Onboard were eighty pounds of gold bars and so many tons of silver bullion that they were used as ballast instead of the cobblestones usually employed for that purpose. Adding to the riches were numerous chests of silver coins, as well as a quantity of precious jewels.

Drake's ship, the *Golden Hind*, returned in triumph to England, anchoring in Plymouth Harbor on September 26, 1580. While the infuriated Philip II labeled Drake a pirate, which he undoubtedly was, the English from that point on preferred to view him as a privateer and a hero—lending support to poet and literary critic Samuel Taylor Coleridge's trenchant observation some 250 years later that "no man is a *pirate*, unless his contemporaries agree to call him so."

Drake's illustrious status was confirmed on April 4, 1581, when Queen Elizabeth, in the course of a sumptuous banquet onboard the *Golden Hind*, knighted him. Rather than tap Drake on the shoulder with her gilded sword, she had the French ambassador do the honors, which some have interpreted as her rather flimsy attempt to make it appear that the Crown did not formally condone Drake's actions, though everyone knew it did. After all, Drake had not only presented lavish gifts of diamond- and emerald-studded jewelry to the queen, but he had also punished the Spanish at her bidding, and in the process brought back so much treasure that Elizabeth's half-share exceeded the Crown's annual income.*

IT WAS BECAUSE OF the attacks on Spanish treasure ships by Drake and other English "sea dogs," as Elizabeth's maritime raiders were called, that King Philip III, Philip II's son and successor, could easily picture Jamestown, Virginia, as a foothold for English piracy—that, and the fact that many of Jamestown's backers were

---

* In September 1618, the English explorer Sir Walter Raleigh reportedly said to Sir Francis Bacon, "none were called pirates for millions, but only for small things." Drake's treatment seems to bear this out. See "Notes by Sir T. Wilson, of his conversation with Raleigh (September 28, 1618)," *Calendar of State Papers, Domestic Series, The Reign of James I, 1611–1618*, vol. 9, ed. Mary Anne Everett Green (London: Longman, Brown, Green, Longmans, & Roberts, 1858), 577.

Captain John Smith's map of Virginia, engraved by William Hole in 1612.
Unlike for a typical map, in this one geographic north is to the right,
not toward the top of the map. The slender body of water that nearly
cleaves the land in two is Chesapeake Bay.

self-professed privateers, who were nothing more than pirates to the Spanish. The Spanish king's fears were reinforced when he heard back from Don Diego de Molina, the commander of a Spanish caravel, whom Philip had sent to spy on the Jamestown settlement.

Instead of spying on the colonists, Molina was captured by them in the summer of 1611 and imprisoned. A few years later, he had help smuggling a letter out of Jamestown that made it to the Spanish ambassador in London, and then on to Philip. In it, Molina warned "his majesty" that with respect to Virginia it was essential "to stop the progress of a hydra in its infancy." If left to develop, he felt, the colony would become a "gathering place of all the pirates of Europe," and would ultimately destroy the Spanish colonies in the Americas, seizing all of their riches in the process. Given Spain's dominant international role, and England's ambitions to knock

Spain from its perch, Philip took this threat to his lucrative American colonies very seriously.

PHILIP AND MOLINA'S FEARS about Virginia becoming a major launching point for pirate raids were clearly reasonable, but in the end they were largely unrealized. The struggling colony could barely sustain itself, much less threaten the Spanish. Its main focus was survival, and developing merchantable products like tobacco that would create a foundation for further growth and help anchor England's territorial claims in the New World. Nevertheless, Virginia did have one brush with piracy in these early years.

In early 1619, Daniel Elfrith, captain of the English ship *Treasurer*, sailed from Jamestown to plunder Spanish shipping in the Caribbean. Technically, the *Treasurer* was a privateer, since its owner, the Earl of Warwick, had purchased a commission from the Duke of Savoy, giving his ship permission to attack the Spanish. The governor of Virginia, who was a friend of Warwick's, accepted the commission's validity, and wished Elfrith good luck.

In the Gulf of Campeche, off the Mexican coast, the *Treasurer* teamed up with a Dutch vessel, the *White Lion*, attacked the Spanish slaver *São João Bautista*, and commandeered its human cargo. When the two ships returned to Jamestown later that year, the colonists bartered food in exchange for twenty of the slaves, among the first Africans to arrive in English North America (several had been brought to Bermuda a few years earlier). The fate of the twenty is hotly debated by historians and far from certain, but it appears that a few might have continued on as slaves, owned by the governor, while others became indentured servants who gained their freedom after laboring for a number of years on tobacco plantations.

The political situation in Virginia, however, had changed while the ships were away. The new colonial governor took a jaundiced view of Elfrith's "privateering," calling it piracy instead. This stance was in line with Crown policy, since England was at peace with Spain, and King James I, Elizabeth's successor and the first Stuart king, had outlawed any form of privateering, whether sponsored by English subjects or foreign governments. Harboring a significantly different opinion than his Tudor cousin, James viewed privateers as indistinguishable from pirates, whom he regarded as "lewd and ill disposed persons accustomed and habituated to spoil and rapine." The High Court of the Admiralty agreed with the governor and the Crown, forcing Warwick to defend Elfrith's actions. In the end, Warwick's political connections enabled him to avoid any significant backlash. But the leaders of the Virginia Company of London, which sponsored the colony, sent an unambiguous message to the governor ordering him to ensure that Virginia did not offend any of England's "friends," including the Spanish. Specifically, he was to prohibit pirate ships from leaving the colony, and keep pirates from retiring in the colony, unless they were "severely punished and their goods confiscated."

Although Virginia can lay claim to being the first American colony with a connection to pirates—albeit a tangential one—it is not the first to confront piracy in its own coastal waters. To see where that took place, it is necessary to travel farther up the coast, and further into the heart of the seventeenth century, as the English empire secured a stronger foothold in the New World.

IN THE EARLY 1630S, English colonist Dixie Bull* immigrated to New England, where beaver pelts were the most valuable commodity. Gathered by the Indians† and traded to the colonists for ironware,

---

* Some sources spell his name either Dixy or Dixey.

† In writing this book I had to decide whether to use the term *Indian* or *Native American* when referring broadly to the native inhabitants of North America. I chose *Indian* in large part because many of the authors I admire use that term, and it is the term with which I am most comfortable. Thus, I was glad to read in David Hackett Fischer's book *Champlain's Dream* that when he asked a gathering of Indian leaders what they preferred to be called, they gave two answers. If one is referring to a specific nation, then they said that the name of the nation should be used, e.g., Mohawk. But, if one is referring to "all of them together," then they said that the term Indian "was as good as any other," and that "they used it with pride." I will follow that advice. See David Hackett

*"American Beaver" by John James Audubon. These fascinating rodents were
the lifeblood of the colonial economy for many years.*

cloth, wampum, and various trinkets, the lustrous pelts were transported to England, where their fur was used to produce fashionable,
waterproof, and very expensive beaver hats that were all the rage in
Old World Europe. The sale of pelts was a crucial enterprise for the
few thousand Plymouth and Massachusetts Bay colonists, providing
them with their main source of income for purchasing supplies and
paying off their debts to the merchant adventurers who had subsi-
dized their voyage to America. Like many enterprising colonists who
tried their luck in the unforgiving American colonies, the ambitious
Bull hoped that procuring beaver pelts would make him rich.

Bull was trading with Indians along the coast of Maine when
disaster struck. In summer 1632, a small group of Frenchmen stole
his vessel, which was loaded with trading goods and pelts. Enraged,
Bull hastily commandeered a vessel and gathered a force of fifteen
armed men to exact revenge on the French. Having no luck in that
pursuit, and short on supplies, Bull resorted to piracy when he ran-

Fischer, *Champlain's Dream, The European Founding of North America* (New York: Simon
& Schuster, 2008), 636n26.

sacked two English vessels. Then, for reasons that are not clear, Bull convinced his band to set their predatory sights on Fort Pemaquid, at the mouth of the Pemaquid River, a few miles northeast of modern-day Boothbay Harbor.

Established in 1630 by Abraham Shurte, Fort Pemaquid was more trading post than fort—a gathering place for traders, around which about five hundred English colonists and fishermen had settled. Sometime in the fall, Bull led a raid on the fort and surrounding homes, stealing £500 of goods and provisions—this at a time when a captain of a merchant vessel earned about £24 per year, and a house in Cambridge, Massachusetts, with six acres of arable land, and another five acres of meadow, could be purchased for around £10. As the raiders were weighing anchor, preparing to leave with their loot, a well-aimed shot from the fort killed one of Bull's men. This sent a deathly chill through Bull's ranks, and they were, according to a contemporary account, "filled with fear and horror."

News of the unprovoked attack on the fort quickly filtered throughout New England, spreading alarm all along the coast. Toward the end of November, Captain Walter Neale of the Piscataqua Plantation (located in the vicinity of modern-day Portsmouth, New Hampshire) wrote to John Winthrop, the famed governor of the Massachusetts Bay Colony, telling him what had happened. Winthrop immediately convened a council, which agreed to send twenty men on the colony's bark, *The Blessing of the Bay*, to hunt down the pirates. But the extreme cold and snowy weather delayed the work necessary to prepare the bark for sailing. In the meantime, Winthrop learned that Neale had already sent out four vessels with forty armed men in pursuit of Bull—making this the first military naval action undertaken by the colonies. As a result, Winthrop and the council deferred "any further expedition against the pirates till they heard" back from Neale. When word finally arrived in early December, the news was discouraging. Neale's men had turned up nothing.

Over the next few months, there were periodic sightings of Bull and his men, who apparently had renounced piracy in fear of the

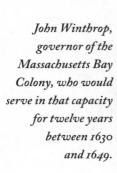

John Winthrop, governor of the Massachusetts Bay Colony, who would serve in that capacity for twelve years between 1630 and 1649.

fatal punishment that awaited them if they were caught. According to Winthrop, "They had been at some English plantations, and taken nothing from them but what they paid for." Winthrop also heard "that they had made a law against excessive drinking," and they would occasionally "assemble upon the deck, and one sing a song, or speak a few senseless sentences." To make it clear that they wanted no more trouble, Bull and his men sent a letter to the governors of all the English colonies and plantations "signifying their intent not to do harm to any more of their countrymen, but to go to the southward, and to advise them not to send against them; for they were resolved to sink themselves rather than be taken." At one point, they seized a Salem, Massachusetts, man and ship's captain named Anthony Dicks, but when they tried to force him to pilot them to Virginia, he resisted and ultimately escaped. Back on land, Dicks told a friend that his captors were so terrified of being captured "that they were afraid of the very rattling of the ropes."

In May 1633, Winthrop sent "a pinnace* after the pirate Bull,"

---

* A small boat with sails, typically used as a tender to a larger vessel.

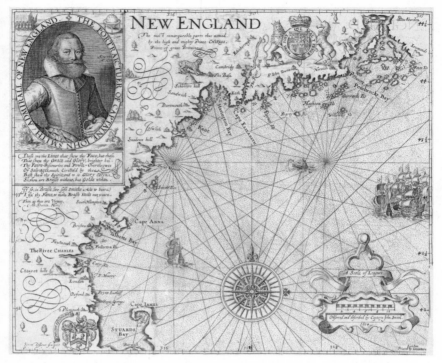

John Smith's map of New England, 1616. This entire region was on high alert as a result of Dixie Bull's brief tenure as a pirate.

but after two months of fruitless searching, it returned to Boston. Bull was never heard from again, and what happened to him remains a mystery to this day. One contemporary account claimed that Bull's crew "fled eastward," most likely to French settlements in Canada, "and Bull himself got into England; but God destroyed this wretched man." Others believe Bull joined the French, or that Indians killed him.

Despite causing some alarm in the colonies, and vexing Winthrop, Dixie Bull was not really much of a pirate, and his brief dalliance with debauchery spawned few imitators. In fact, over the next fifty years, up until the early 1680s, hardly any pirates plundered ships off the coast of the American colonies. This was primarily because the most tempting treasure, and the real action, was far to the south, in the Caribbean, which was fast becoming a pirate paradise.

DURING THE LATE 1500S and on into the early 1600s, most pirates who attacked Spanish ships and towns along the coast of Latin America swooped in, took what treasure they could grab, and quickly returned to their home bases in Europe. By the mid-1600s, however, an increasing number of pirates were operating out of haunts in the Caribbean. They were called buccaneers, a term that has its roots on the island of Hispaniola, today's Haiti and the Dominican Republic.

Around 1630, an amalgam of mainly French, as well as English, Dutch, and Portuguese refugees, settled on Hispaniola. Among their ranks were men who had survived wrecks, jumped ship, escaped indentured servitude on tobacco and sugar plantations in the West Indies, or been harried from other Spanish colonies in the region. For sustenance, these men hunted the island's numerous cattle and hogs, descendants of animals introduced by Christopher Columbus

Buccaneer from 1744 French edition of Esquemelin's
The Buccaneers of America.

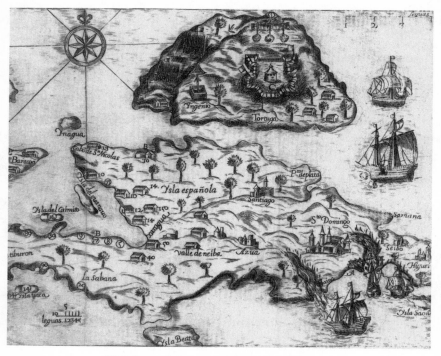

Map from 1658 showing the island of Tortuga
just to the north of Hispaniola.

on his second, more ambitious, voyage to the New World in 1493. The local Taíno population taught these men how to cure the meat by cutting it into strips and hanging it from frames of green wood perched over smoldering fires. The location where the curing took place was called a *boucan*, and the process of curing, *boucanier*, which translated from French means to smoke. Thus, these men were called *boucaniers* or, in English, buccaneers.

Initially, the buccaneers were peaceful men, content to hunt and sell their cured meat to passing ships and have little else to do with the outside world. But the Spanish were angered by this burgeoning settlement, viewing the men as interlopers in their domain. This led Spain to launch a series of vicious assaults on the buccaneers, forcing them to retreat to a small and more easily defended island off the northwest coast of Hispaniola called Tortuga, the Spanish word for *turtle* or *tortoise*, a reference to the island's unusual shape. When the buccaneers persisted in hunting on Hispaniola, the Spanish attacked Tortuga, slaughtering many of its defenders and scattering the rest. But the roughly three hundred survivors regrouped on Tortuga, built a fort, improved their defenses, and decided to hunt a new prey— Spaniards. Thus, the buccaneers became pirates pure and simple.

The heavily armed buccaneers first took to canoes and small boats, sallying forth from the island to the nearby shipping channels, where they attacked Spanish ships transporting goods and treasure from the continent to Spain. The success of these raids enabled the buccaneers to obtain larger vessels that allowed them to go farther afield in search of spoils. By the mid-1600s, the buccaneers' numbers had swelled across the Caribbean, and they developed a loose society called the "Brethren of the Coast," whose members were united by their hatred of the Spanish, loyalty to one another, and a set of rules by which they lived.

Unique in their methods, and dramatically out of step with the top-down governing ethos of the day, buccaneers opted for democ-

Buccaneers swarming onto a ship by Frederick Judd Waugh, circa 1910.

racy in organizing themselves. When a buccaneer captain wanted to commence a piratical foray, he issued a call, and volunteers grabbed their swords, guns, powder, and shot, and boarded his ship. In setting their course, buccaneers relied on a majority vote to determine where they would go in search of plunder. They also prepared an agreement, or set of articles, in democratic fashion, signed by all, that established how prizes would be divvied up. A typical contract, for example, might award a specialized crewman, such as a carpenter, 150 pieces of eight, and a surgeon, 250. The articles also laid out a rudimentary form of medical insurance, or workers' compensation, providing 600 pieces of eight, or six slaves, for the loss of a right arm, 300 or five slaves for a left arm, and 100 or one slave for the loss of an eye. Once all of these expenses were paid, any leftover prize money would be distributed, with the captain receiving the largest portion for the use of his ship and for himself, while the rest of the crew split the shares uniformly, with boys getting half a man's share.

Buccaneers were often quite cruel to those they captured. Popular tortures included tying a person down and beating him with sticks, or using ropes to spread-eagle the unlucky victim, while placing lit fuses between their fingers and toes. One particularly gruesome torture involved placing a cord around a person's head, and twisting it so tightly that "his eyes protruded like eggs." While some buccaneers tortured their prisoners for sport, or to elicit information, others were more calculated in their barbarity, using torture as a strategic ploy. They knew that if their mere presence spread genuine fear through the ranks of their intended victims, they would be that much more likely to give up without a fight. That way, the buccaneers wouldn't have to risk their own lives to get what they wanted. By occasionally resorting to torture, therefore, buccaneers maintained what in modern parlance would be called their threatening brand identity.

Of all the seventeenth-century buccaneers, none was more vicious than Frenchman François L'Ollonnais, who began his childhood in the Caribbean as an indentured servant and, after gaining his freedom, pursued the life of a buccaneer. His deep hatred of the Spanish

"The Cruelty of Lolonois." Engraving from the 1684 English edition of
Esquemelin's The Buccaneers of America *showing François L'Ollonnais*
taking a heart he has just cut out of one man's chest and shoving it in the face of
another prisoner from whom he is trying to extract information.

drove his sadism. Once, after capturing a Spanish ship, he forced the
captain and crew into the hold, and then ordered them to come up
the ladder to the main deck one at a time. As soon as the prisoners
cleared the hatch, L'Ollonnais cut them down, the arc of his sword
nearly severing their heads. Another time, after defeating Spanish troops who had tried to ambush him in a jungle, L'Ollonnais

Dutch map, circa 1652, showing North America,
Central America, and some of South America.

asked his Spanish prisoners if there was another road to his destination that would avoid similar attacks. When the men said no, L'Ollonnais flew into a rage. According to a contemporary account, he "ripped open one of the prisoners with his cutlass [sword], tore the living heart out of his body, gnawed at it, and then hurled it in the face of one of the others, saying, 'show me another way, or I will do the same to you.'" Not long after this brutal scene played out, L'Ollonnais himself was murdered in a manner reminiscent of his own barbarity, when he was hacked to death by natives in Panama, who severed his limbs and roasted them.

OVER TIME, BUCCANEERS SPREAD beyond Tortuga, and by the 1660s their favorite haunt was the island of Jamaica, which had been captured by the English in 1655. Buccaneers gravitated to the growing community of Port Royal, located on the tip of a ten-mile-long sand spit at the southeastern end of the island. They soon discovered that their skill set was of great value to Jamaica's governors, and a mutually beneficial relationship between the pirates and the colony was launched. Although the English had conquered Jamaica with a powerful fleet of ships, within a few years all of them had departed; at the same time a large number of the soldiers who had settled the island died from tropical diseases or returned back home. This left the colony relatively defenseless and surrounded by outposts of England's nearly perpetual enemy, Spain. To protect Jamaica from attack, the governors enlisted the buccaneers' support. After all, the buccaneers hated the Spanish, and they constituted a powerful fighting force.

From the 1660s through the 1670s, Jamaican governors issued letters of marque to numerous buccaneers, transforming them into privateers with the mere stroke of a pen. Not only did these privateers prey on Spanish shipping and settlements, but they also helped defend Jamaica. Even though the privateering commissions were issued at times of both peace *and* war between England and Spain and, therefore, were often of dubious legality, that didn't concern the Jamaican governors. Separated from the Crown by an entire ocean, they generally subscribed to the notion that there was to be "no peace beyond the line [established by the Treaty of Tordesillas]." And all the loot that the buccaneers-turned-privateers brought back pumped up the local economy and filled the colony's and the Crown's coffers.

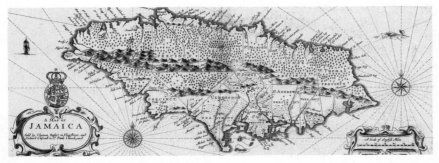

Map of Jamaica, circa 1676. Port Royal is located on the southeastern coast.

Arguably the wealthiest English city in the New World by 1680, with many stately brick homes and a population approaching three thousand, one-third of which were slaves, Port Royal's veneer of sophistication could not hide its decidedly sleazy underbelly. This is when Port Royal gained the well-earned reputation as the "wickedest city in the world," and the "Sodom of the West Indies." An unsavory mélange of buccaneers and privateers prowled Port Royal's streets and alleyways in search of liquid and carnal pleasure. As one buccaneer said of his peers,

> Whenever they have got hold of something they don't keep it for long. They are busy dicing, whoring, and drinking so long as they have anything to spend. Some of them will get through a good two or three thousand pieces of eight in a day—and next day not have a shirt to their back. I have seen a man in Jamaica give 500 pieces of eight to a whore, just to see her naked. . . . My own master used to buy a butt of wine and set it in the middle of the street with the barrelhead knocked in, and stand barring the way. Every passer-by had to drink with him, or he'd have shot them dead with a gun he kept handy.

Thus it is no wonder that Port Royal boasted an unusually high concentration of bars and brothels. Mary Carleton, one of the most notorious prostitutes in the city, had a particularly strong work ethic. "A stout figure she was," wrote one of her contemporaries, "or else she never could have endured so many batteries and assaults. . . . she was as common as a barber's chair: no sooner was one out, but another was in."

The most famous privateer operating out of Jamaica was Henry Morgan, although most will know him better for the brand of rum that is his namesake. Other than the fact that he hailed from Wales, Morgan's early life is shrouded in mystery. Conflicting stories recount how he ended up in Jamaica, but they all agree that he made it to the island about the same time that the English forces took it over in 1655. Once in Jamaica, Morgan joined a number of

Captain Henry Morgan depicted in the 1704 English edition of The Buccaneers of America.

buccaneering and privateering expeditions, but his greatest claim to fame was his blood-soaked privateering raid in 1671 on Panama City, the central depot for silver and gold emanating from Potosí and the mines in Peru.

With a fleet of fifty ships, and nearly two thousand men under his command, Morgan landed at Chagras, on the east coast of the Isthmus of Darien (modern-day Panama), destroyed a Spanish fort, and then slogged his way across the isthmus to Panama City, where the Spanish, alerted by scouts of the impending invasion, were waiting for him. These motley and poorly armed defenders, however, were no match for Morgan's battle-tested troops, many of whom had honed their fighting skills as buccaneers. In the end, six hundred Spanish defenders lay dead, with many more wounded, while Morgan lost only fifteen men.

But Morgan's hopes for a truly enormous haul of treasure were dashed. Before the attack, Don Juan Pérez de Guzmán, Panama's president, had much of the city's treasure transferred to ships waiting offshore. He also ordered his soldiers to place kegs of gunpowder in strategic locations with the understanding that, should the invaders breach the city limits, the fuses to those kegs would be lit. So, when Morgan's men marched in, the city exploded in flames, and much of the treasure that had been placed on ships simply sailed away. The next day, where thousands of buildings had once stood were only charred timbers and ashes. Recalling the scene of devastation later, Morgan wrote, "thus was consumed the famous and ancient city of Panama, which is the greatest mart for silver and gold in the whole world."

Still, for more than three weeks, in between torturing the city's

Captain Henry Morgan, standing before the city of Panama in flames, as portrayed in the 1726 edition of Johnson's A General History of the Pyrates.

inhabitants to find out where they hid their treasure, and raping captive women, Morgan's men sifted through the rubble to find melted concretions of silver, gold, and gems, and they scoured the countryside for spoils. The Spanish ships that hadn't escaped were also looted, adding to the booty. Estimates of the treasure thus obtained range from a high of more than 400,000 pieces of eight to a low of 140,000, with most of the available evidence supporting the lower amount. Fully cognizant of the vast fortune that had slipped through their hands, Morgan and his men were distraught contemplating what might have been.

Morgan was warmly received as a conquering hero by the public on his return to Jamaica in April 1671, but Sir Thomas Modyford, the governor who had given Morgan his commission, was worried. Nearly a year earlier, in July 1670, the Treaty of Madrid had been signed, establishing peace between the English and the Spanish in the Americas. Under the terms of the treaty, Spain recognized England's American possessions, including Jamaica, while both countries agreed to outlaw privateering and clamp down on piracy. Word of the treaty, however, did not make it to Jamaica until after Morgan had left on his expedition to Panama City. With the treaty's shake-up of the political landscape, Modyford feared that Morgan's depredations would be seen as a brutal, piratical attack on an English ally, rather than the sweet defeat of a hated enemy.

Modyford's concerns were not unwarranted. The Spanish government, viewing Morgan as a pirate, and reeling from the destruction at the heart of their American empire, demanded that heads roll. In an effort to appease Spain's King Charles II, England's King Charles II replaced Modyford and had him arrested, brought back to England in chains, and thrown into the Tower of London. Six months later, with England still eager to soothe the Spaniards, Morgan, too, was arrested, but when he returned to England he was allowed to wander free while the king considered his options.

In the end, all was forgiven, and then some. Modyford was released from the Tower in two years' time, and his name was restored. Three years after returning to London under a dark cloud, Morgan was not only absolved of all wrongdoing, but was knighted and sent back to Jamaica as the deputy governor with orders to eliminate piracy around the island. A number of factors likely contributed to Morgan's surprising resurrection. His successful attack on Panama City made him a hero in his own land, bringing back glorious memories of Drake's great triumphs, and giving the English a new cause for celebration. King Charles, too, got caught up in the hero worship. His majesty soon grew fond of the hard-charging, bawdy, liquor-loving Morgan, which made sense since Charles himself, the "Merry Monarch," was cut from much the same hedonistic cloth. At the same time, Charles became less enamored with his Spanish ally, who, he firmly believed, would soon be an enemy once again. Finally, there was the loot. With the sacking of Panama City and his earlier exploits, Morgan had greatly improved the monarchy's finances, and as is almost always the case, money absolves a great many sins.

Following the Treaty of Madrid, various Jamaican governors, including Morgan, attempted to banish pirates from the island through a combination of measures, among them royal pardons, punitive laws, trials, and hangings. The growing Jamaican merchant class applauded these actions. While they had formerly welcomed buccaneers as protectors of the island, the merchants now looked far less favorably on their activities since the threat of Spanish attack had been greatly reduced, in part because of the successful raids of Morgan and his fellow "privateers." Those merchants also wanted to erase Jamaica's infamous reputation as a pirates' retreat, and rebrand it as a welcoming place for colonization and the expansion of the booming slave-fueled sugar economy.

Eliminating pirates, however, proved to be a daunting task. As Sir Thomas Lynch, who served three terms as governor of Jamaica between 1663 and 1684, observed, "This cursed trade [piracy] has been so long followed, and there" are so many pirates, "that like weeds or hydras they spring up as fast as we can cut them down." Even so, by the time the fifty-three-year-old Morgan died on

August 25, 1688, a victim of a full-throttle, alcohol-soaked life, the number of pirates and privateers in Jamaica was much reduced, and the island was considerably less wicked, debaucherous, and raucous than it once had been.

THE FLUIDITY OF THE COLONIES' maritime network necessarily meant that England's northern colonies, from South Carolina to Massachusetts, were not completely divorced from Caribbean piracy. In fact, from the 1640s up through the 1680s, the colonies' relationship with piracy became ever stronger, a situation that, for the most part, benefited the pirates and the colonists alike.

CHAPTER 2

Welcomed with Open Arms

A view of New Amsterdam (New York) in 1673.

THE MOST IMPORTANT CONNECTION BETWEEN CARIBBEAN pirates and the colonies was financial. Colonial merchants sent numerous ships to the Caribbean, where they traded with pirates, and in turn, many pirates brought their treasure to the northern colonies, spending it on food, drink, prostitutes, and provisions for their next voyage. One of the earliest and most significant examples of pirate money filtering into the colonies occurred in 1646, when Captain Thomas Cromwell returned to New England.

Cromwell had been a "common seaman" in Massachusetts in the 1630s, but in the early 1640s he joined the Earl of Warwick's gang of "privateers" who attacked Spanish vessels in the Caribbean during times of peace, which in effect made him a pirate. In May, he sailed into Plymouth Harbor with three ships full of plunder and crewed by eighty "lusty" and "unruly" men, as Plymouth's governor, William Bradford, called them. The financially flush visitors remained in Plymouth for a month, spending "liberally." At first, their behavior consisted of getting drunk, fighting, and generally acting "like mad men," a hell raising that scandalized many of the colony's more prim and proper Puritan citizens. Toward the end of their stay, however, the pirates became "more moderate and orderly," and "gave freely to many of the poorer sort." John Winthrop, the former lawyer, and the deeply pious governor of the Massachusetts Bay Colony, viewed the pirates' visit to Plymouth in a religious light, asserting that "divine providence" brought them there to share their money, so as to "comfort and help" the town.

Other pirates followed in Cromwell's footsteps, spreading the wealth. In 1684, for example, Jamaican governor Lynch noted that the northern colonies "are now full of pirates' money." The numbers were astounding. Pirates had, Lynch claimed, carried the equivalent of £80,000 into Boston alone, a city that one English official labeled as "the common receptacle of pirates of all nations." To get an idea of the magnitude of this loot, consider that at the time a common male laborer in the colonies earned about £10 per year (a woman got roughly half of that), while the captain of a merchant vessel pulled down £72. According to one estimate, "at least half of the coins in colonial America were Spanish" pieces of eight, and most of them likely came from pirates.

In addition to coins, pirates brought silver bullion to Boston's mint, the first in English America, established in 1652. There the silver was transformed into the colony's famed pine tree shillings, aptly named for the image of a white pine tree stamped into the coin to

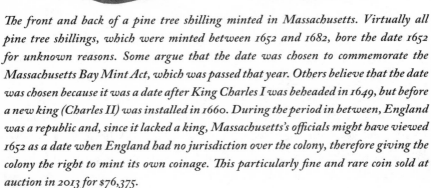

The front and back of a pine tree shilling minted in Massachusetts. Virtually all pine tree shillings, which were minted between 1652 and 1682, bore the date 1652 for unknown reasons. Some argue that the date was chosen to commemorate the Massachusetts Bay Mint Act, which was passed that year. Others believe that the date was chosen because it was a date after King Charles I was beheaded in 1649, but before a new king (Charles II) was installed in 1660. During the period in between, England was a republic and, since it lacked a king, Massachusetts's officials might have viewed 1652 as a date when England had no jurisdiction over the colony, therefore giving the colony the right to mint its own coinage. This particularly fine and rare coin sold at auction in 2013 for $76,375.

symbolize the important role that the tall, straight, and thick trunks of the mighty pines played in providing sturdy masts for England's growing navy and merchant marine. As a contemporary English official observed, the mint "encouraged pirates to bring their plate [silver] hither, because it could be coined and conveyed in great parcels undiscovered to be such." That it was for most of this period illegal for any American colony to mint coins didn't bother either the pirates or the colonial minters one bit. Another creative alternative was to bring the bullion to silversmiths, who acted as fences, melting down the precious metal and using it to make forks, knives, and spoons. Such domestic items could then be melted down for coinage at a later date, when the owner required money to pay debts.

Pirates also brought a great variety of goods to the American colonies, such as indigo, cloth, and sugar, all of which was eagerly swept up into the local economies. In addition, they brought Afri-

can slaves. Indeed, an increasing number of pirates not only supplied treasure, goods, and slaves, but they also put down roots in the
colonies. In 1688, a colonial official observed that recently "several"
pirates in New York and New London "have bought houses and
lands [and] are settled here bringing in £1,000 or £1,500 a man"—an
amount that was equal to, or a little bit more than, what a "good
substantial merchant" would be worth at the time. One of the most
dramatic instances of such a pirate-turned-citizen was Captain
Thomas Paine.

IN 1682 PAINE WAS cruising the Caribbean in the *Pearl*, preying
on Spanish vessels, when Jamaica's governor Lynch offered him a
deal in exchange for not being prosecuted for piracy. If Paine would
"bring in or destroy" pirates, all would be forgiven. Paine agreed,
and he was awarded a privateer's commission to do just that. But his
true nature revealed itself. Shortly after leaving Jamaica, Paine set
sail for the Bahamas, where, instead of carrying out his charge, he
joined forces with a few pirate captains. This band of brothers sailed
under false French colors to the Spanish settlement at St. Augustine,
Florida, where, to their dismay, they found the residents on full alert.
Instead of attacking the city, they plundered the surrounding areas,
terrorizing the Spanish inhabitants. The pirate flotilla now split up,
whereupon Paine and his men visited a Spanish wreck to dive for silver. After that, they sailed to Rhode Island, arriving in Newport in
the summer of 1683, where the considerable treasure Paine brought
with him was welcome indeed.

As soon as Boston's deputy customs collector Thomas Thacker
learned of Paine's arrival, he went to seize the ship. But William
Coddington Jr., the governor of Rhode Island, blocked the initiative,
and told Thacker they could address the issue the following morning. Thacker was convinced that this delaying tactic was employed
to warn Paine and give his men "time to arm themselves against
arrest." When morning came, Paine, Thacker, and Coddington, as
well as Governor Edward Cranfield of New Hampshire and Gover-

nor Thomas Dongan of New York, both of whom were in town on colonial business, met to hash over the situation. Paine presented his commission, at which point Thacker, Cranfield, and Dongan argued that it was a forgery, claiming that the signature was not Lynch's and that he was identified incorrectly as a gentleman of the King's Bedchamber, rather than the Privy Chamber. Since Paine in fact had an authentic commission from Lynch—which he was supposed to have used to attack pirates, not the Spanish!—these claims of forgery were almost certainly false, and likely leveled because the accusers knew that Paine had gone rogue. Coddington, however, accepted the commission's validity and refused to seize the ship, even after Thacker pointed out that the *Pearl* had "been on a piratical cruise" and had pillaged Spanish settlements in the vicinity of St. Augustine.

Now free and clear, Paine settled in Newport, but within a year's time, William Dyer, the customs collector for New York, came calling. In September 1684, he ordered Paine's arrest, labeling him the "arch-pirate." Dyer also charged Coddington with harboring a pirate, and for not assisting Thacker in seizing Paine and his ship. But nothing came of all this, and Paine was soon released. A few years later, he married the daughter of a prominent local judge and future governor of the colony, and became an upstanding member of the community.

Paine came to Rhode Island from the Caribbean, but the connection between pirates and the American colonies went both ways, with some pirates using the colonies as their home base and heading south in search of spoils. When Englishman Edward Randolph was sent to America in 1676 to inquire into the colonial trade practices and resolve land claims, he was shocked to learn how involved colonists were in promoting pirate ventures. "I observed that they fitted out vessels of 60 or 70 tons* a piece very well manned whom they call privateers, and sent them without commission to the Spanish West Indies, where they committed all acts of violence

---

* The tonnage is a measure of the cargo-carrying capacity of a vessel.

upon the inhabitants, and brought home great quantities of silver and coins and bullion, with rich copes [ceremonial robes], church plate, and other riches."

THE ACCEPTANCE OF PIRATES in the American colonies alarmed England. Piracy was considered a serious crime—a felony—by the authorities in the mother country, punishable by death, and they expected the colonies to fight pirates, not harbor them. Under English law, pirates were supposed to be shipped to London for trial, but the great time and expense of doing so meant that almost no pirates were sent across the Atlantic to face justice. And while some colonies did use local courts to try pirates, that was more often the exception rather than the rule. Even so, the antipiracy laws adopted by many of the colonies were filled with so many loopholes that they were virtually meaningless.

On those rare occasions when the colonies held piracy trials, they were usually sham affairs. In 1687, an enraged King James II wrote a letter to New York's governor Dongan, illustrating the problem. He said that he and parliament had received frequent reports from the colonies that showed that "instead of due prosecution of pirates . . . an unwarrantable practice hath been carried on," in which the pirates were immediately brought to trial "before any evidence could be produced against them," or the juries that heard the cases were partial, favoring the pirates. Either way, acquittal was the result, and the pirates were allowed to "continue their accustomed piracies to the great detriment of trade."

Even getting to the point of holding a trial assumed that one could bring pirates in to face charges, but there were often obstacles to doing so, chief among them being opposition from merchants who stood to gain from piracy. A particularly egregious example of this occurred in September 1684 when Dyer, the same New York customs collector who had failed to collar Paine, attempted to seize a French pirate ship, *La Trompeuse* (the Trickster), captained by Michel Landresson.

In August 1684, *La Trompeuse*, fresh from a successful cruise in the Caribbean, appeared at the mouth of Boston Harbor. Bostonians viewed the arrival of the pirate ship as a godsend, especially given reports that the treasure onboard was so great that each crewman's share came to £700—money that the pirates undoubtedly would soon be lavishly spending at the city's grog shops and other establishments. Samuel Shrimpton, one of Boston's wealthiest merchants, even dispatched a pilot to escort the ship to the harbor's Noddle's Island,* which he happened to own. A few weeks later, Dyer sailed into Boston and declared that he was seizing *La Trompeuse* in the name of the king, and that all who had aided and abetted Landresson, whom he called a pirate "of the first magnitude, famous in bloodshed and robberies," would be held to account.

But announcing the seizure and actually seizing the ship were two very different things. Writing to one of the king's advisors, Dyer said of Landresson, "I have moved for justice against him but have been delayed, and much discouraged and severely threatened by many, and more especially by one Mr. Samuel Shrimpton, . . . to have my brains beat out," or to be stabbed for attempting to confiscate the ship. Dyer complained that Shrimpton had taken the ship into custody on Noddle's Island, "the place and receptacle of all piratical" goods, including "great quantities of their gold, silver, jewels, and cacao." Making matters worse, the merchant boasted that he would defend the ship with force, and said he was planning to fit it out for another voyage. In the end, all Dyer could do was fume. Nobody was brought to justice. Shrimpton refitted *La Trompeuse*, and Landresson soon left Boston in search of other victims.

MANY REASONS CONTRIBUTED TO the colonies' welcome of pirates with open arms. Heading the list was the money that pirates provided, a chronically scarce resource. This was not surprising since,

---

* Noddle's Island is no longer an island, and instead is part of East Boston, adjacent to Logan Airport.

under the mercantile laws of the day, the balance of trade always favored England, and colonists typically had to use specie, or coin, when purchasing manufactured goods from the mother country. The fact that England suffered through a series of coin and bullion shortages in the mid- to late 1600s only made the monetary situation in the colonies more precarious. As Cotton Mather noted in 1691, "*Silver in New-England* is like the water of a *swift running river*; always coming and as fast going away."

Pirates helped keep this river from running dry. So valuable was pirate silver that a number of the colonies competed with one another to inflate the value they placed on foreign coins because pirates often chose to go to those colonies with the highest values, where they literally got the most bang for their bucks. The leaders in such manipulation were Massachusetts, Pennsylvania, New York, East and West Jersey (later New Jersey), and South Carolina, all of which, not coincidentally, had some of the highest concentrations of pirates visiting their ports and settling within their borders.

Colonial governors valued pirate money not only for the benefits that accrued to the local economy, but also for more selfish reasons. Since gubernatorial salaries were often paltry, some governors used their positions as a means to enhance their personal fortunes. Those who came from distinguished families that had fallen on hard times—a not uncommon occurrence—were especially likely to become speculators. And the fact that some governors had to personally subsidize their colony's defense only made their financial situation worse. Given all of this, it is perhaps not surprising that there were governors who accepted and encouraged kickbacks and bribes from pirates, a few so blatant or aggressive about it that they were ultimately forced to step down.

The goods that pirates brought with them furnished another reason for their warm reception. England's Navigation Acts required European goods coming into the colonies to be transported on English ships manned predominantly by Englishmen, and first to be transshipped through England, where steep customs duties had to be paid, which further increased the price of the already expensive imported items. Colonists hated the restrictive Navigation Acts, and pirates offered a golden opportunity to circumvent them. By purchasing goods directly from pirates, thus avoiding the middleman, merchants and their fellow colonists obtained the merchandise they wanted more cheaply than they could through legal traders.

Such cheap goods, combined with the valuable coins and bullion, often created a powerful and supportive constituency for pirates, which included the governor, legislators, merchants, and colonists, all of whom benefited from their ill-gotten gains. In those colonies where the governor might have wanted to adhere to Crown policy and act against pirates, there were often strong countervailing forces that kept him from doing so. As historian Mark G. Hanna notes, many governors had long-standing relationships with area merchants before being appointed or elected to their position, and "even if individual governors wished to shun piracy, pressure from this mercantile elite that thrived on the pirate market cowed them into compliance." Such pressure didn't come solely from the "mercantile elite." One contemporary chronicler argued that government officials would be "hardly safe in their persons or estates, if by a due and vigorous execution of the law against pirates or illegal traders, they should incense the people against them."

Pirates also offered protection. The Crown paid scant attention to the military needs of the colonies, often forcing them to fend for themselves, and that could be a rather slender reed to rely on since most colonial militias and naval forces were inadequate because of a lack of financial resources. Pirates helped fill the protection void by providing men who could fight. The versatile Captain Paine provides a good example of pirate-turned-protector.

IN THE SUMMER OF 1690, three French privateers appeared off the coast of New England, panicking the region. This was in the midst of the Nine Years' War (1688–1697), known as King William's War in the colonies, which arrayed most of Europe against the French.

The privateers had already attacked Nantucket, Martha's Vineyard, Fishers Island, and Block Island, where they ransacked houses, killed livestock, commandeered vessels, and whipped residents to get them to divulge where they had hidden their valuables. Word of the atrocities soon spread to the mainland, where the people of Newport, Rhode Island, were sure they would be next. The governor's council met in emergency session and commandeered the *Loyal Stede*, a Barbadian sloop* moored in Newport Harbor, with ten cannons and a crew of sixty. All they needed was someone to captain the vessel, and since there was no one in the colony who knew more about naval warfare than Captain Thomas Paine, he was chosen to lead.

Along with another sloop manned by thirty men, Paine sailed out of Newport Harbor, heading toward Block Island. Upon learning from the locals that the French had set off for New London, Paine went in pursuit, sighting the enemy vessels soon thereafter. For two-and-a-half hours the battle raged. Early on, the captain of one of the French sloops, "a very violent, resolute fellow," poured himself a glass of wine, and declared that it would "be his damnation if he did not board" one of the English vessels immediately. It proved a hollow boast. As he raised the glass to his lips, a bullet ripped into his neck, killing him instantly. Before darkness brought an end to the fighting, another Frenchman lay dead, along with an Indian who had fought with the English.

The contestants anchored for the night a short distance apart. Paine was sure that the fight would recommence in the morning, but shortly before dawn, the French vessels sailed away. A contemporary account claims that the Frenchman in charge of the fleet had been a privateer with Paine in an earlier war, and when he learned "by some means" that he was up against his old captain, he said that he "would as soon choose to fight with the devil as with him." Whether he fled for this reason or some other, the French were gone, and Paine and his men returned to a hero's welcome in Newport.

_____

* A one-masted sailing vessel with a mainsail and jib rigged fore and aft.

———

ALTHOUGH THE NUMBER OF pirates visiting and settling in the colonies was relatively small, they had an outsized impact on colonial life because the colonies themselves were sparsely populated. In 1690 there were just over 190,000 American colonists, along with about 17,000 slaves, thinly spread out along the eastern edge of the continent, with most people living within a few miles of the coast. Even the largest port in the colonies, Boston, had only 7,000 residents. Consequently, the considerable amount of money, goods, and muscle provided by the pirates was enough to make them a significant economic, social, and military force.

Just as pirates benefited the colonies, the colonies offered pirates valuable resources and opportunities in return. Colonial ports were places where pirates purchased supplies, sold stolen goods, recruited men, sought medical help, enjoyed liquid and libidinous entertainment, and settled down at the end of their piratical career, assuming they survived long enough to enjoy retirement. As important was the chance for pirates to careen their vessels.

Over time a vessel's hull became fouled with all manner of organisms, from seaweed to barnacles, which not only increased drag and slowed the vessel down, but also caused serious damage.

Although this image is from the mid-1800s, it is a good representation of careening—in this case, the vessels being careened are the two French corvettes La Astrolabe *and* La Zélée.

The worst were the Teredo worms (*Teredo navalis*), a form of mollusk that burrows into wood, creating tunnels and turning it into a pulpy mess that has a passing resemblance to Swiss cheese. Careening— essentially tipping the vessel on its side with the help of ropes to expose parts of the hull that are usually underwater—allowed the men to scrape the hull clean, replace rotted or riddled wood, recaulk leaky seams with oakum, and recoat the hull with an oily mixture of tar, sulfur, and tallow, thereby extending the life and improving the performance of the vessel. Specialized wharves in larger ports enabled pirates to careen their vessels, and if such wharves were lacking, careening could be done in sheltered coves or embayments along the coast.

By offering all of these benefits, the colonies provided pirates with a beachhead that enabled them to pursue their disreputable designs. Without such support, pirates couldn't have survived, much

*Teredo worms (*Teredo navalis*) make quick work of destroying submerged wood, boring holes throughout. The white structures are calcareous tube linings secreted by these most unusual mollusks.*

less thrived. Therefore, the colonies were, in a very real sense, the pirates' partners in crime.

The acceptance and support of pirates by the colonies was not absolute. While pirates were welcomed when they provided money, goods, and protection, they were not embraced when they practiced their "profession" in coastal waters, as the case of Thomas Pound reveals.

IN THE EARLY MORNING of August 9, 1689, Pound and twelve armed associates sailed a small sloop out of Boston Harbor, their ultimate goal being to reach the Caribbean and prey on the French. But first they needed a better vessel, and more men, food, arms, and ammunition. The next day, they overpowered a fishing ketch* called *Mary* out of Salem, captained by Halling Chard. Pound's men took the ketch, thereby officially launching their piratical voyage, and sent Chard and two of his crew away on the sloop, while another of Chard's men, John Darby, voluntarily remained behind—a rather strange, selfish, and rash decision, as he was leaving behind his wife and five children in Marblehead. Pound and his men next headed to Casco Bay, where they stole a calf and three sheep from one of the bay's many islands, and then moored off Fort Loyal, a small garrison located in what is today Portland, Maine.

Darby went ashore with two other men. While the men got water, Darby introduced himself to Silvanus Davis, the garrison's commander, who asked where they had come from. Darby said they had been fishing off Cape Sable when a French privateer attacked them, stealing their bread and water before letting them go. Being familiar with the *Mary*, Davis asked why Captain Chard hadn't come to the fort. He hurt his foot, Darby responded, adding that all they wanted was water, and for the local doctor to visit the ketch to tend to the captain. That, of course, was a lie. Pound's real intention was to convince the doctor to join his southern venture, since medi-

---

* A two-masted, fore-and-aft rigged sailing vessel with a main mast forward and a smaller mizzen aft.

cal expertise was in high demand on pirate ships, where injury was an occupational hazard, and going ashore to find a willing practitioner was rarely an option.

Darby's answers put Davis on alert. His suspicions heightened when his men visited the *Mary* and reported that it contained a far larger crew than a typical fishing vessel, and Captain Chard was nowhere to be seen. Davis began to fear that the visitors might be "rogues." Nevertheless, Davis allowed the doctor to be ferried to the ketch, but when he returned to shore—unconvinced by Pound's pleadings to sign on—the mystery deepened. The doctor seemed nervous, and kept changing his story about how many men were on the ketch, causing Davis to think that the doctor was involved in some wicked plot. Most likely shaken from the encounter with Pound, it wasn't the doctor that Davis should have been worried about. Unbeknownst to him, two of the soldiers who had visited the *Mary* earlier that day had agreed to join Pound, promising to enlist other soldiers as well.

That evening, Davis set armed guards around the fort and told them to keep a "good watch" on the "water side." At midnight, seven soldiers who had decided to cast their lot with Pound rose up and trained their guns on their fellows. Gathering all the arms, ammunition, and clothes that they could carry, the traitors took the fort's boat out to the *Mary*, and soon thereafter Pound set a course for Cape Cod.

A day later, off the highlands of the Cape (modern-day Truro), Pound captured the sloop *Goodspeed* and traded up once again, transferring his men, and sending off the *Goodspeed*'s crew in the *Mary*. He also sent a message. Pound told the *Goodspeed*'s crew to tell the authorities in Boston that if the government's sloop "came out after them," it would "find hot work," for every last one of his men would die "before they would be taken."

As it turned out, acting on intelligence provided by Captain Chard, the colonial government had already sent out an armed vessel to search for the pirates, and it would send out another after the *Mary* sailed into Boston Harbor. Both ultimately came up empty.

Meantime, Pound and his men traced a circuitous route. They stopped on the Cape and Martha's Vineyard to get more livestock and water, and on August 27 at Holmes Hole (modern-day Vineyard Haven), they robbed a brigantine* of food, rum, and tobacco, and then released it. Next, a ferocious storm forced them to Virginia, where they sheltered in the York River for eight days, picking up two more men and a slave. When calm seas returned, they headed back to Tarpaulin Cove, on Naushon Island, just off Martha's Vineyard. Over the next few weeks, Pound sailed between the Cape and the Vineyard, unsuccessfully chasing one vessel, and capturing two, one of which was plundered for food. At the end of September, the peripatetic pirates returned to Tarpaulin Cove to wait for good weather to sail to Curaçao.

Massachusetts governor Simon Bradstreet, alarmed by these continued depredations, ordered Pound's former ketch, the *Mary*, to be manned by twenty soldiers and sent to bring the "pirates" to Boston to face justice, using deadly force to "subdue" them if necessary. Captain Samuel Pease was put in charge, and he embarked on his mission from Boston Harbor on September 30, looping around the outstretched forearm of Cape Cod, then heading west toward Vineyard Sound. On October 4, Pease spied a canoe coming from Woods Hole into the channel. A man in the canoe said that "there was a pirate in Tarpaulin Cove," and upon hearing that, Pease's men "gave a great shout" and made ready for battle.

Not long thereafter, Pease saw the *Goodspeed* in the distance and ordered his men to bring their ketch in close. The pirates tried to flee but the *Mary* was a better sailer and quickly closed the gap. Once the *Goodspeed* was within range, the King's Jack was raised up the *Mary*'s mainmast, and cannon and musket shots were sent across the *Goodspeed*'s bow as a warning. Defiant, Pound's men raised their own "bloody [red] flag," which signaled that no quarter would be given, and arrayed themselves on the main deck, ready to fight.

---

* A two-masted sailing vessel with a square-rigged foremast and a mainmast rigged fore and aft.

Pease demanded that the pirates "strike to [the] King of England," but Pound was not cowed. Standing on his quarterdeck, he flourished his sword, and barked across the water, "Come aboard you dogs, and I will strike you presently." No sooner had Pound issued this bellicose invitation than the shooting began. Pound took a ball to the arm, and one just under the ribs, while Pease was struck in the arm, the side, and the thigh. Both men were then taken below. The soldiers repeatedly implored the pirates to give up, telling them that they would be given "good quarter," but the pirates scorned the offer. "Ye dogs," they yelled, "we will give you quarter." An hour after the first shots were fired, the soldiers swarmed onto the *Goodspeed*, getting off one good volley, and then using the butts of their muskets to mercilessly beat the pirates into bloodied submission. When the smoke cleared, four pirates were dead, and most of the rest were wounded, while five of the soldiers were injured. Among the dead pirates was John Darby, whose wife and children back in Marblehead were left to fend for themselves.

With the pirates secured, the *Mary* and the *Goodspeed* sailed to Rhode Island, where the wounded were taken to lodgings on the mainland and treated by doctors from Newport. But there was little they could do for Pease, who died of his wounds on October 12. A week later, the ships sailed into Boston, and the pirates were kept in the city jail under heavy lock and key.

The men of the *Goodspeed* were brought to trial in 1690 on charges of piracy and murder, and although fourteen of them were found guilty and sentenced to hang, that never happened. For reasons that are not entirely clear, a number of substantial citizens of the colony urged Governor Bradstreet to be lenient. Among the pleaders were a few "women of quality," and Waitstill Winthrop, the grandson of former governor John Winthrop and one of the magistrates who conducted the pirates' trial. Bradstreet complied, the result being that only a single pirate was hanged. The sentences for all of the rest, except for Pound, were remitted. For one of those set free, the pardon came at the penultimate moment, just as he was on the scaffold ready to swing. According to a member of the governor's council, this sudden turn of events caused "great disgust to the people," who were hoping for a show. As for Pound, his sentence was only reprieved, and he was sent back to England in the spring of 1690, where again, for reasons that remain unknown, all charges were dropped.

AROUND THE TIME THAT Pound was on the loose, a dramatic shift was taking place in the annals of piracy. Although pirates continued to terrorize the Caribbean, their numbers were declining as tropical hunting grounds became far less attractive to would-be marauders. Spanish treasure fleets were being more heavily guarded to protect against attack. Government crackdowns on piracy in Jamaica and elsewhere in the region were making the lives of pirates more difficult as well. Furthermore, even though the flow of silver and gold coming from Spain's possessions in the New World was still considerable, it was far less than it had been in former years.

As if to provide a fiery and dramatic symbol marking this decline, on June 7, 1692, just before the noon hour, a devastating earthquake struck Jamaica. In the pirate haven of Port Royal, buildings toppled and the streets were transformed into rolling rivers of liquefied earth that sucked people under and then crushed them to death when the shaking stopped and the soil solidified. Some of those trapped had only their heads sticking above ground, which roving packs of starving dogs gnawed upon in the ensuing days. When it was all over, nearly two-thirds of the landmass of Port Royal had slipped beneath the waves, and the death toll, including those who later succumbed to injuries and disease, approached five thousand—many of them buccaneers. In the gruesome aftermath, hundreds of dead and bloated bodies could be seen floating on the surface of the harbor, and washed up on the shore, where they became, according to one eyewitness, "meat for fish and fowls of the air." A local minister who survived called the earthquake a "terrible judgment of God" that was brought down upon the heads of the "most ungodly debauched people" in the world.

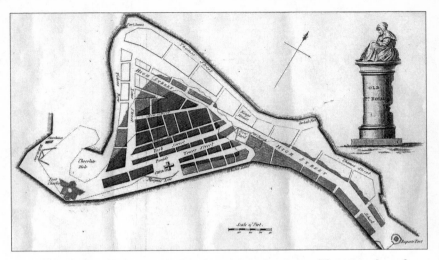

Port Royal as it appeared before the earthquake in 1692. The outer edges of the map are the borders of the old Port Royal, while the darkly shaded area toward the bottom and middle depicts the boundary of the city after the earthquake. The rest of the city was consumed by the sea.

Just as pirates' Caribbean prospects were dimming, a new venue of opportunity arose. Halfway around the world, on poorly defended ships in the Indian Ocean, the riches of Asia—fine silks, precious gems, sturdy calicoes, exotic spices, and tons of silver and gold jewelry and coins—offered a tempting target that pirates couldn't resist. Many pirates sailed for the Indian Ocean from American ports, with the enthusiastic support of colonial officials. And together, they inaugurated the most lucrative period of piracy in American history.

CHAPTER 3

"Where the Money Was as Plenty as Stones and Sand"

Piratical Station—Isle of Madagascar.

A pirate and a native woman on
Madagascar (1837 engraving).

IN THE SPRING OF 1689, THREE PIRATE SHIPS MOORED IN St. Augustine's Bay on the southwestern coast of Madagascar, the fourth largest island in the world. The ships, two English and one Dutch, were a sight to behold. "Almost useless and unfit for navigation," their hulls were riddled with wormholes and coated with a thick layer of marine life accumulated over many months at sea, while their canvas sails were so "worn and weather-beaten" that they had been replaced with doubled-over silk fabric. Despite the pathetic condition of these vessels, the men aboard were exultant. They were wealthy beyond their wildest dreams, having stolen "rich booty" from ships belonging to the powerful Mughal Empire, which ruled most of India and Pakistan from the early sixteenth through the mid-eighteenth century. Their silken sails were evidence of their plunder, as were the silver and gold in the ships' holds. On shore, the pirates spent their loot freely on "expensive European liquors . . . [and] noble wines," and boasted that "one of their small ships with but twenty men aboard" could easily overpower the largest Mughal vessel afloat.

These pirates were not the first to attack Mughal ships. For decades, European pirates had been pillaging in the Indian Ocean, seeking out these rich prizes. The stream of trading ships sailing between India and the Arabian ports of Jeddah and Mocha on the Red Sea provided an abundance of targets carrying coins, textiles, and other exotic East Indian* goods to the west, and then returning home with equally valuable cargoes. But it was the pilgrimage ships that were most seductive to thieving pirates. During the Haj, the annual Muslim pilgrimage to Mecca, Mughal ships were not only fitted out for trade, but they also carried throngs of pilgrims who brought with them their finest clothes and jewels, as well as plenty of money on these holiest of voyages.

News of the vast riches transiting the Indian Ocean ricocheted throughout the West. At grog shops over tankards of ale and rum, and on busy wharves serving as the crossroads for the world, mariners talked passionately about the allure of Mughal treasure. In America, pirates who had cut their teeth in the Caribbean chasing

---

* "East Indian" was a catchall phrase used at the time that typically included India, China, Japan, and the rest of the Far East.

*Detail of a 1656 map of the east coast of Africa from Somalia to the
Red Sea. The large body of water near the top of the map
("Mer De La Mecque") is the Red Sea. The pinch-point at the bottom
of the Red Sea is the Strait of Bab-el-Mandeb.*

Spanish treasure, and seamen who dreamed of a big strike, cast their
covetous gaze toward the waterborne golden highway in the East.
They were soon to find a unique way of pursuing those riches, courtesy of King William's War (1688–1697).

Just as it had in earlier wars, England relied on privateers to supplement its navy and assault the enemy, which in this particular conflict was the French. Across the British Empire, letters of marque
were duly issued, and many of the newly appointed privateers complied with their commission, pursuing the French. In America,
however, letters of marque often served a different purpose. For a

fee, more than a few governors knowingly bestowed letters on men who had no intention of fighting the French, but instead planned to attack Mughal ships in the Indian Ocean, using the letters as cover to give their voyages the semblance of legitimacy. If the phony privateers were stopped at sea for any reason, they could claim that they were on an officially sanctioned mission. Since England was not at war with the Mughal Empire, however, attacks on Mughal shipping were, by definition, pure piracy. This fact didn't bother colonial governors in the least. They not only lined their pockets when issuing letters of marque, but they, as well as any investors in the "privateering" cruise, also expected the pirates to return to the colony from which they departed to share the treasure and pay off debts.

THE FIRST KNOWN AMERICAN ship to go to the Indian Ocean in search of Mughal riches was the *Jacob*, captained by William Mason, which left Rhode Island in late 1690 *without* a letter of marque to serve as cover. For a year and a half the would-be pirates failed to make a capture, at which point dissension among the crew caused it to split up. Mason and nineteen followers left on another ship, while Edward Coates took over as captain of the *Jacob*. Then the *Jacob*'s luck changed. Over the next six months, Coates and his men plundered four Mughal ships, relieving them of enough silver coins, gold, and various East Indian goods to enrich each crewmember by £800. Sated by this bonanza, Coates and his men decided to return to America to enjoy their spoils.

They sailed to New York because its governor, Jacob Leisler, had a reputation for welcoming pirates and their booty from the Caribbean, and it was assumed that he would be similarly disposed toward pirates and wealth coming from the Indian Ocean. But by the time the *Jacob* arrived off the coast of New York in April 1693, the political landscape had shifted—Leisler was out, and Benjamin Fletcher was in—a change in administration that Coates likely learned of from a ship at sea. Instead of heading into New York harbor and an uncertain reception from Fletcher, Coates sailed the *Jacob* to Southold at the tip of Long Island, an area known to be quite friendly to pirates, so that he could safely mull over his next move. Coates sent his fellow pirate Edward Taylor to shore to confer with William Nicoll, a local politician, and the two of them then journeyed to New York City to meet with Fletcher to see whether he would grant permission for the *Jacob* to enter the harbor, and also shield the crew from legal action.

An eighteenth-century historian bitingly described Fletcher as "a man of strong passions and inconsiderable talents, very active, and equally avaricious." Like many colonial governors, he viewed his position as a means of feathering his own nest. One of his peers called him "a poor beggar" who "seeks nothing but money and not the good of the country," while another said he took "a particular delight in having presents made to him." Therefore, it was no surprise that when Taylor and Nicoll walked into his office, Fletcher was eager to deal.

If the pirates would pay him and Nicoll each £700, then Fletcher would allow the ship to enter New York's harbor. Taylor agreed, but since so many of the pirates had already dispersed with their shares, Coates had a difficult time collecting the money. Instead, he simply gave the *Jacob* to Fletcher, and scrounged another £200 for Nicoll. This outcome was even more advantageous for Fletcher, who promptly sold the *Jacob* for £800. In addition, Fletcher extracted £100 each from those pirates who came to the city, in exchange for leaving them alone. Fletcher's wife and daughter, too, benefited from the transaction, receiving from the pirates a selection of gold chains, jewels, and lustrous silks. Having made out so well from this venture, the grasping Fletcher was eager to partner with other would-be pirates intent on raiding Mughal ships. His first opportunity to do so was provided a little more than a year later in the shape of Captain Thomas Tew.

A RHODE ISLANDER BY BIRTH, Tew was in Bermuda in 1691 when he accepted a commission from that island's governor for a privateering venture to Africa to take the French fort located on the Gambia River at Gorée. Captaining the seventy-ton sloop *Amity*, with eight guns and a compliment of sixty men, Tew left Bermuda in the late fall of 1691 in consort with another vessel similarly tasked. On the way across the Atlantic, the two ships were separated during a violent storm. This gave Tew an opening. He had been a pirate in his earlier years, and now that he was on his own, he exhorted his crew to turn pirate too, urging them to head to the Indian Ocean, where there were plenty of rich Muslim ships to rob.

Tew, or the clarion call of Mughal treasure, proved persuasive. Around the Cape of Good Hope they sailed, and then on to the Strait of Bab-el-Mandeb, which connects the Red Sea with the Gulf of Aden, and through which all ships going to and from Jeddah and Mocha must pass. There, Tew spied a Mughal ship heading into the Red Sea. Although it was much larger than the *Amity*, and had many guns and more than three hundred soldiers aboard, Tew emboldened his men by promising them that despite the apparently overwhelming odds, they could take it. And take it they did, achieving a quick and bloodless victory. Tew's men ransacked the ship searching for silver, gold, jewels, and other riches. So plentiful was the bounty that they could only take part of the gunpowder they discovered, not having enough space on the *Amity* for the rest. Estimates of each man's share of the treasure ranged from £1,200 to £3,000.

Tew had planned to return to Bermuda, but when he and his men finally left the Indian Ocean in late 1693, violent gales in the Atlantic damaged the *Amity*'s main mast and blew it off course, forcing it to put in at Newport, Rhode Island, in April 1694. Tew's reception was electric. Rhode Islanders marveled at the treasure their native son had amassed, which, by one account, was worth as much as £100,000. Tew auctioned off some items, gave a generous present to Rhode Island's governor Caleb Carr, and sent word to the *Amity*'s backers in Bermuda informing them how they could obtain their cut of the loot, which amounted to fourteen times what they had invested in the venture.

Newport's newest celebrity openly discussed his exploits. When John Graves, an old friend of Tew's, ran into him on the wharf in Newport, the stories flowed. "He was free in discourse with me,"

Graves said, "and declared that he was last year in the Red Sea, that he had taken a rich ship belonging to the Mughal," leaving him with "twelve thousand odd hundred pounds" to split between himself and the ship's owners.

Tew was intent on retiring and enjoying his wealth, but he was soon pulled back into the pirates' fold. Many of his men had squandered their shares on drink and women, and they soon came round begging their former captain to embark on another trip so that they could recoup their losses. Tew, interested in helping his crew, and further enriching himself, finally relented. But before leaving, he wanted to obtain a privateering commission that would serve as cover for his voyage to the Indian Ocean. To that end, he headed to New York, and to Benjamin Fletcher.

TEW HAD BEEN TO New York before, selling purloined Mughal jewels, and while there he had met Fletcher. What the two men said to each other is not known, but it is clear that Tew had an inkling that Fletcher would provide the commission he sought, and that is why he found himself back in New York in October 1694. On the cobbled streets of the bustling port city, whose population had recently passed four thousand, Tew cut a dashing figure. Small in stature, and around forty years old, he sported a blue cap encircled by a silver ribbon, and a blue velvet jacket festooned with gold lace and oversized pearl buttons that shimmered with iridescence as the light played on their surface. Linen pants and ornately embroidered stockings added to his sartorial ensemble, which was topped off with finely wrought chain of Arabian gold hanging about his neck, and a gleaming dagger, "its hilt set with the rarest of gems," tucked neatly into the mesh of his knitted belt. Such bright and showy attire was not uncommon for pirates of the day, who relished flouting restrictive sumptuary laws and customs that kept most colonists' wardrobes in check, displaying their success through their dress. At local taverns and on the street, Tew let slip his plans to return to the Indian Ocean. Fletcher, seeing a man with whom he could do business, graciously welcomed him to the city, and gave him the privateering commission he desired in exchange for £300.

Years later, when home officials questioned him on his support of piracy, Fletcher claimed that he hadn't known Tew or anything about his background before he arrived in the city at the end of 1694. Tew, he said, "came as a stranger, and came to my table like other strangers who visit the province. He told me he had a sloop well manned, and gave bond to fight the French at the mouth of Canada [St. Lawrence] River, whereupon I gave him a commission and instructions accordingly." Fletcher added that Tew seemed to be "a man of courage and activity . . . a very pleasant man." The two

A meeting between pirate Thomas Tew (left) and New York governor Benjamin Fletcher, illustrated by Howard Pyle (1921), and titled "He had found the captain agreeable and companionable."

sometimes went on late afternoon walks to amiably discuss various matters, and Fletcher tried mightily to convince Tew to break his loathsome habit of swearing, and to give up the demon drink. To encourage Tew to pursue a straight and narrow path, Fletcher presented him a book on gentlemanly manners on which to model his deportment. To further cement their friendship, Fletcher presented Tew with a gun, and in return received a gift that Fletcher described as "a curiosity, though in value not much."

Not to put too fine a point on it, this was pure nonsense, and nothing more than a self-serving attempt to cover his tracks. Fletcher knew very well who Tew was and what he was after, and he was thrilled to have a paying customer on his hands. As Peter Delanoy, the former mayor of New York (1689–91), noted, Tew was "highly caressed by" Fletcher, and taken through the streets of the city for all to see, in the governor's "coach and six horses, and presented with a gold watch to engage him to make New York his port at his return. Tew retaliated the kindness with a present of jewels." Fletcher was absolutely certain that Tew was not heading to the St. Lawrence River to fight the French, but instead was going to the Indian Ocean for Mughal treasure. As one contemporary observer noted, "It was public and notorious that" Tew was a pirate.

Commission in hand, Tew returned to Newport in early November, where the *Amity* was being readied for the voyage. Word of Tew's plans had spread far and wide, in no small measure because of his boasting, and a great array of men flocked to the wharf to sign on as crewmembers, brilliant images of treasure no doubt firing their imaginations. They all wanted "to go to the Red Sea," according to a contemporary account, "where the money was as plenty as stones and sand. . . . [G]reat was the commotion . . . servants from most places of the country coming from their masters, sons from their parents, and many had their . . . relations going against their wills." Not just prospective crew, but entire ships full of would-be pirates wanted in on the action, and a few vessels, including ones from Boston and Pennsylvania, joined the venture.

By the end of November, the *Amity* and its consorts set sail on their voyage to the Indian Ocean.

Tew should have quit while he was ahead. When he attacked a Mughal ship quite capable of defending itself near the mouth of the Red Sea the following year, the Amity—and Tew—got the worst of it. According to one account, a cannon ball ripped into Tew's mid-section, disemboweling him. After he fell to the deck, dead, his men gave up the chase and sailed to Madagascar. With the *Amity* in bad shape, and a slow sailer even under the best of conditions, the crew set off down the coast, where they found another vessel and commandeered it. These remnants of the *Amity*'s crew continued their pirating, never again returning to New York. In this way, Fletcher's bet on Tew failed to pay off.

FLETCHER'S MISS WITH TEW was counterbalanced by a number of hits, in which he doled out privateering commissions, pocketing the fee and any other emoluments that came his way when the pirates returned after a successful voyage. His typical exaction from pirates hoping to enter the city was what he charged Coates and his men— £100 each—and for that he offered them what was commonly referred to at the time as "protection." This money was necessary, claimed a pirate, "to prevent their being put to trouble." By one account, during his tenure, Fletcher offered protection to hundreds of pirates.

Despite the evidence pointing to his collusion with pirates, Fletcher steadfastly maintained his innocence. When confronted with the fact that many of the men to whom he had granted privateering commissions had veered directly into piracy, he unconvincingly asserted, "It may be my misfortune, but not my crime, if they turn pirates: I have heard of none yet that have done so." During his nearly six years in office, it is estimated that Fletcher pocketed an astounding £30,000 beyond his gubernatorial salary. While he was notorious for taking kickbacks from military officials and merchants, as well as for embezzling government funds, much of that wealth came from his connections to piracy.

Of course, Fletcher wasn't the only New Yorker who profited from piracy. The royal customs collector Chidley Brooke took bribes from pirates to let them be, as did the local sheriff. And prominent New York merchants, including titans Stephen Delancey and William "Tangier" Smith, invested heavily in pirate ventures, which only added to their fortunes. According to historian Gary B. Nash, such entrepreneurial activity was "an early American version of white-collar crime." One New York merchant, however, settled on a different business plan. Rather than investing in pirate ventures, Frederick Philipse decided to trade with the pirates instead.

A DUTCHMAN BY BIRTH whose given name was Fredryck Flypsen, Philipse came to America in the 1650s. He landed in New Amsterdam, the teeming capital of the Dutch colony of New Netherland, located at the southern tip of the island of Manhattan. A carpenter by trade, Philipse worked for the governor—"old peg leg" Peter Stuyvesant—building many structures throughout the city, including the twelve-foot-tall wall after which Wall Street was named, and which was intended to keep invaders at bay. Ambitious and shrewd, Philipse soon branched out into trading, and in 1662 his prospects brightened considerably when he married Margaret Hardenbroeck de Vries, the widow of shipping magnate Pieter Rudolphus de Vries. With Margaret's substantial inheritance and her business acumen now at his disposal, Philipse had big plans, but they were gravely threatened in August 1664, when four English warships arrived at the mouth of the Hudson and, without firing a shot, took control of the Dutch colony, renaming the flourishing port city as New York.

The enterprising Philipse, not to be deterred by the shifting political winds, turned this potential catastrophe into an opportunity. Like many of his fellow Dutch residents, he accepted the generous English terms of surrender and pledged his allegiance to the Crown, thereby becoming a loyal English subject. To further his civic transformation, he also anglicized his name. The dramatic expansion of his shipping

A tobacco merchant in New Amsterdam, circa the mid-1600s,
around the time that Frederick Philipse's merchant career was
starting to take off. Notice the slaves laboring in the background.

empire in the ensuing decades, along with his investments in wampum manufacturing and flour mills, made him one of the richest men in the colony. Philipsburg Manor, his sprawling ninety thousand–acre estate on the Hudson River, lying just to the north of the city, served as the ultimate symbol of his social standing and great wealth.

Philipse's entrée into the world of pirates came through slaves. In the late 1600s New York was the hub of the colonial slave trade, and with seven hundred in bondage, it had more black slaves than any other city on the North American mainland. Philipse dipped his toe into this abominable trade in the 1680s, but his involvement dramatically increased in the 1690s after receiving a letter from Adam Baldridge, a resident of St. Marie (or Nosy Boraha), a sliver of an island off the northeastern coast of the Madagascar mainland.

THOUGH LITTLE IS KNOWN about Baldridge's early life, reports circulated of his fleeing Jamaica in 1685 to avoid accusations of murder, and then turning pirate soon thereafter. Whatever his past might have been, when Baldridge arrived at St. Marie in January 1691 aboard the *Fortune*, he jumped ship to settle on the island. This wasn't a rash decision, but rather a calculated move. Baldridge planned to become a slave broker.

Madagascar was an especially promising place for an aspiring slave trader to settle for two reasons, first and foremost being their availability. England's Royal African Company had a monopoly on the extensive slave trade with West Africa, but its reach did not extend to the Indian Ocean. And although the English East India Company had the monopoly on trade in the Indian Ocean and the rest of the East Indies, it showed virtually no interest in the slave trade. This meant that there was nothing to stop English traders from obtaining slaves on Madagascar and shipping them to the American colonies. The second reason for Madagascar's attractiveness was price. A single West African slave cost a trader six to eight times more than a Malagasy slave, which meant that their traffickers could reap higher profits from selling them in the Western colonies.

By the time Baldridge arrived at St. Marie, English slavers had been engaged in their appalling business on Madagascar for nearly twenty years, and Baldridge hoped to become one of their trading partners. To ingratiate himself with the natives, he joined them in their seemingly never-ending wars against rival clans. This not only cemented his relationship with the locals but also was an avenue for obtaining slaves in the form of captured foes. In addition to acquiring slaves through battle, Baldridge planned to barter for them with area tribes. Baldridge's success as a military leader attracted other Malagasies to join him on St. Marie, where he built a modest fort, and he was soon being referred to as "King Baldridge."

How Baldridge learned of Philipse's slave-trading activities is not known, but in September 1691 he used that knowledge to send the New York merchant a business proposition, offering to send him two hundred slaves at thirty shillings each. But it didn't end there. With an increasing number of pirates using St. Marie as their base of operations in the Indian Ocean, Baldridge had easy access to desirable

East Indian goods. Should Philipse want to purchase any of them, Baldridge said that he would be happy to act as his agent, obtaining the goods from the pirates on his behalf. And if Philipse wished to sell the pirates any merchandise, Baldridge could do that too.

Philipse sensed a brilliant prospect, and soon dispatched the *Charles*, which arrived at St. Marie in August 1693. At the bazaar that ensued, Baldridge displayed Philipse's goods, including speckled shirts and breeches, stockings, shoes, casks of Madeira wine, cases of rum, grindstones, saws, whale oil, iron pots, gunpowder, garden seeds, hoes, and two Bibles. It was almost as if a New York City market had been plunked down in Madagascar. The pirates, many of whom had originally sailed from the American colonies, were pleased with the wide selection, and eagerly handed over their money. The markup was phenomenal. A gallon of rum purchased in New York for two shillings sold in St. Marie for fifty, while a pipe of wine (126 gallons), which cost £19 in the city, was scooped up by the pirates for £300.

Baldridge, however, didn't keep his end of the bargain. Instead of two hundred slaves, he sent back only thirty-four—fifteen of them being children under three years old—along with 1,100 pieces of eight, fifteen head of cattle, and fifty-seven bars of iron. Philipse was crestfallen with the paltry return on his investment. Slaves were, he said, his "chiefest profit," with healthy adults selling for upwards of £30 a head in the colonies. Had Baldridge supplied the full complement of slaves, Philipse ruefully noted, that would have added roughly £4,000 to his bottom line.

Determined to recoup his losses, Philipse dispatched another ship, and urged Baldridge to make good on his promise. Apparently he did, for in subsequent years, Philipse continued his long-distance trade with St. Marie, relying on Baldridge as his primary slave broker and salesman, and in the process becoming the largest slave importer in New York. The flow of slaves and currency pleased Philipse, as did the great array of East Indian goods, which were sold in New York and England. An additional profit center proved particularly lucrative. Charging each passenger a fee of one hundred pieces of eight, plus the cost of food, Philipse's ships gladly ferried many homesick pirates back to America. Although Philipse was the undisputed leader of the New York–Madagascar trade, his success spawned imitators, and quite a few of his fellow New York merchants grew rich sponsoring round-trip trading, slaving, and transporting voyages to St. Marie.

With the likes of Fletcher and Philipse taking leading roles, New York was so intimately associated with piracy that it became, in historian Robert C. Ritchie's words, "notorious as a pirate haven and the center for supplying the Indian Ocean pirates," and while it "was not quite as outrageous as Port Royal in its heyday, it enjoyed a similar reputation." After years roaming the Indian Ocean in search of victims, pirates were eager to spend their hard-earned, ill-gotten lucre. At the city's waterfront, in grog shops and brothels, and along its winding streets and alleyways, they engaged in bacchanalian orgies that scandalized the New York's more proper citizenry.

ALTHOUGH NEW YORK WAS arguably the epicenter for piratical activity in America throughout much of the 1690s, it was hardly the only colony to support and welcome pirates. Many others, foremost among them Rhode Island, Massachusetts, Pennsylvania, and South Carolina, were quite friendly to the pirates who participated in what was called the "pirate round," sailing to the Indian Ocean and back, typically stopping at Madagascar one or more times during their voyage. Such pirates were commonly referred to as Red Sea Men since their piracy focused on treasure-laden Mughal ships that sailed to and from that magnificent body of water.

By one estimate, during the 1690s nearly forty ships sailed to the Indian Ocean from America and/or returned to America from there. And virtually all of those ships' captains "held a [privateering] commission, signed by a governor, to fight the 'king's enemies.'" But in reality, almost none of them pursued the French; instead, most turned to piracy.

The attraction of this line of "work" was almost irresistible. "The vast riches of the Red Sea and Madagascar," noted one contem-

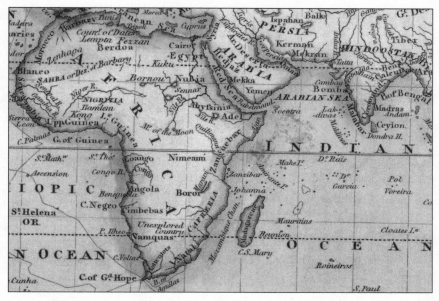

Detail from an 1814 map of the world, showing the Indian Ocean, and the relative locations of Africa, Madagascar, the Red Sea, and India.

porary observer, "are such a lure to seamen that there's almost no withholding them from turning pirates." After all, this was a time when the average legitimate mariner earned only one to two pounds per month, while a pirate could clear a hundred or even a thousand times that amount if he were lucky.

Few, if any, pirates had qualms about attacking Muslim ships and stealing their treasure. As Nathaniel Coddington, a clerk in Rhode Island's admiralty court, observed in 1699, the men who sailed to the Indian Ocean viewed the Muslims as "infidels & it was no sin to kill them." In a similar fashion, a pirate who was tried in London about this time for plundering Mughal vessels claimed, "he had not known but that it was very lawful to plunder ships and goods belonging to the enemies of Christianity," which he perceived the Muslims to be. This general disdain for the people of the Mughal Empire was certainly shared by most of the colonists in America, who were overwhelmingly Christian, and to a great degree rather dismissive of many other cultures and religions, not just Muslims.

Many colonists, government officials, and merchants up and down the Atlantic Seaboard embraced the Red Sea Men for the same reasons that they embraced the pirates who operated out of the Caribbean in earlier decades. Pirates pumped money into the colonies and, by skirting the Navigation Acts, they made East Indian goods readily available to eager merchants and their customers at prices that were far less than what would have to be paid to acquire the same items legally from England—that is, if those items could even be obtained lawfully in the colonies at all. Despite their high cost, East Indian goods, such as lustrous silks and delicate porcelain, were in such high demand in London that the best examples were quickly snapped up, leaving only the less desirable objects available for export to America. Pirates eliminated this bottleneck and kept all types of East Indian goods flowing at bargain basement prices. Pirate money and goods were especially welcomed because King William's War had placed a stranglehold on trade and greatly depressed colonial economies.

In welcoming pirates, the colonists, government officials, and merchants were acting in their own self-interest, the laws and desires of parliament and the Crown be damned. This latter point is quite important. Even at this time, long before the American Revolution, many Americans were already feeling somewhat separate—and one could argue, independent from the mother country—and did not always feel constrained by its dictates. As the Massachusetts General Court declared in 1678, "The laws of England are bounded within the four seas, and do not reach America. The subjects of his majesty here being not represented in Parliament, so we have not looked at ourselves to be impeded in our trade by them." Such an attitude made it easier for the colonists to accept pirates in their midst.

Making it easier still was the fact that many pirates sailing from the colonies were accepted and much-beloved members of those same places. They were sons, fathers, and brothers who chose to better their lives, and the lives of their families, by robbing "infidels" halfway around the world. Most of these pirates planned to pursue this endeavor only until they had accumulated enough wealth to return to their communities as wealthy men. And, as wealthy men with strong local connections, they knew that they would find a warm reception. Furthermore, few, if any, of their peers viewed them as lawbreakers. Instead, they were seen as upstanding members of their communities who were helping their neighbors survive, and even thrive, in the difficult terrain of the New World. Indeed, many colonists didn't view the Red Sea Men as pirates at all, but referred to them as privateers, a semantic distinction that was not supported by the facts but nevertheless provided the colonists with a "legal" justification for these men's actions.

Yet another reason why pirates were welcomed into the fabric of colonial society, rather than shunned and turned over to the Crown for prosecution, was that local officials were, as Hanna points out, "protecting their own hides." If pirates were prosecuted for their crimes, colonists would likely be forced to provide testimony about their intimate connections with the accused. Given how intricately interwoven piracy was with colonial society, colonists had a vested interest in preventing "depositions proving that they had harbored pirates or purchased their goods"—or were even related to them. Therefore, by safeguarding pirates and keeping them from being tried for their crimes, the colonists avoided self-incrimination.

With such an inviting environment, the colonies became magnets for pirates. In 1693, Sir William Beeston, the lieutenant governor of Jamaica, noted that "several privateers and pirates 'that go under the notion of this Island' have found their way into the Red Sea, where they have committed unheard of piracies, murders and barbarities. These are now returned with vast wealth to most of the northern plantations in America where they quietly enjoy their ill-gotten riches." Another time, he complained that after bringing their plunder to the American colonies, the pirates "are pardoned and fit out for a fresh voyage, which makes all kinds of rogues flock to them."

Although many colonial officials were happy to welcome Red Sea Men and profit from their activities, a few were of a different mind. Francis Nicholson, a former lieutenant in the army, and the governor or Maryland (1694–1698), was, as one English official admiringly noted, "really zealous to suppress piracy and illegal trade . . . and was very severe to those who were even suspected of countenancing pirates." Despite Nicholson's best efforts, though, the pirates still flocked to the colony. In 1695, he noted that pirates, who had been coming to Maryland from the Red Sea and bringing "£1,000 or £1,500 a man," were enticing mariners with the promise of similarly large sums to abandon their merchant vessels and return with them to the Indian Ocean. "I fear," said Nicholson, that only "one or two ships will be left behind in this province by reason of their men running away, though I have used all possible means to prevent them, but the country is so open, that it is almost impossible to hinder them. I do not doubt that at least a hundred men have run thither from the Virginia and Maryland fleet, for they are now building twelve or fourteen sloops, brigantines and other vessels in order to manage their [piratical] trade."

AT THE SAME TIME that Red Sea Men were influencing the colonies, they were also significantly impacting St. Marie. Just as Tortuga and Jamaica had served as the home base for buccaneers, and the American colonies did the same for many pirates, so, too, was St. Marie the home base for the Red Sea Men while they were operating in the Indian Ocean. They used it as a place to careen and repair their ships, offload cargo, divvy up loot, and reprovision for future voyages, taking advantage of Madagascar's plentiful drinking water and bounty of cattle, poultry, citrus, and rice. And, of course, for those who stayed on the island for an extended period, it was in fact their home away from home.

King Baldridge was certainly the highest profile Western resident of the island, but he was hardly alone. A visitor in early 1697 reported that there were about 1,500 pirates on the island living in the vicinity of the "commodious harbor," which was sheltering seventeen vessels, some of which were armed with as many as forty guns. Other accounts cast great doubt on the pirate community ever being nearly so large, but it was certainly considerable at times, and it fluctuated wildly as pirates, predominantly English, came and went. Baldridge, who was charged with being the "head of a disorderly rabble of Europeans and natives," built a small fort—perhaps nothing more than mounded dirt or a low palisade—near the mouth of the harbor, with an array of roughly twenty cannons facing the harbor's mouth in case any unwanted visitors showed up. The pirates lived in unimposing huts, or retreated to their ships at night.

Although St. Marie was a four- to six-month sail from America, the pirates maintained a steady correspondence with friends and family back home, their letters being transported back and forth on slave-trading and pirate ships alike. All types of news was shared, ranging from reports of deaths in the family, to a wife's concern about making ends meet, and estimates of how long it might be before the absent pirate might come home. One woman wrote to her husband, saying that she longed for his return, and she ended the letter with these sweet sentiments: "I have not more to enlarge, but only true love to you with daily wishes for your company is the continual longing desire of your true and loving wife." Far from being misanthropic loners with anger issues, most of these pirates had lives that were intimately intertwined with the communities from which they came, and to which they one day hoped to return to enjoy their spoils. They viewed piracy as a job, not a lifestyle.

First-person observations of everyday life on St. Marie are sparse, but it is clear that there was a lot of drinking, boasting, and sex with Malagasy women. Gambling was also a favorite pastime, with fortunes won and lost. A single toss of the dice earned a lucky pirate from New York 1,300 pieces of eight. And there were plenty of fights. In one brawl, fourteen pirates who were bitterly unsatisfied with the amount of loot they had accumulated during their recent trip decided to split into two groups of seven and fight to see which side would walk away with the treasure. According to a New Englander who arrived on St. Marie a few weeks after this battle royal, "The whole of one seven were killed and five of the other, so that two men enjoyed the whole booty."

The bloodiest episode in the history of the pirate colony at St.

Marie took place during the summer of 1697. In June of that year, Baldridge bought part ownership in the brigantine *Swift*, and sailed from St. Marie on a trip to expand his trading empire to other Madagascar locales. A little more than a week later, St. Marie's natives rose up and killed about thirty pirates who were on the island. Baldridge and his men learned of the massacre from a passing vessel on their way back to the island, and, rightfully fearing for their lives, wisely opted to sail for New York, where Baldridge, a wealthy man, retired to a life of leisure.

Baldridge later insisted that the uprising resulted from pirates abusing the natives, but other, more persuasive, testimony lays the blame squarely on him, claiming that he had crossed the line by selling the locals into slavery, instead of restricting his slave traffic to Malagasies obtained through battle or trade. Meanwhile, back on St. Marie, the natives settled down. A man named Edward Welch, who had come to Madagascar from New England years earlier when just a boy, assumed Baldridge's middleman role on the island, and the pirate colony carried on much as before.

BY THE END OF the seventeenth century, English officials in the mother country were well aware of the significant increase in piracy both in the American colonies and the Indian Ocean. A growing swell of correspondence from colonial governors highlighted the problem, as did communiqués from employees of the Bombay-based East India Company, which ran England's trade with the Mughal Empire. The single most damning report on the growing pirate menace, however, came not from a colonial governor or an East India Company employee, but from Edward Randolph, who was the surveyor general of customs in America.

Randolph, a dyspeptic and arrogant bureaucrat in his mid-sixties who had held a number of administrative positions in America going back to the 1670s, was almost uniformly critical of the colonists and their governments. A staunch supporter of the Crown and centralized authority, he viewed the colonies like wayward teenagers who had rebelled against their parents and refused to take direction or follow the rules. Everywhere Randolph looked, he found the colonists and their appointed officials flouting English law when it benefited them. In his eyes, their most heinous offense was disregarding the Navigation Acts and engaging in illegal trade, which included smuggling and piracy.

Despite his jaundiced view, Randolph was a keen observer, and he painted a strikingly accurate portrait of colonial malfeasance, focusing a harsh spotlight on piracy, which not only circumvented the Navigation Acts but was also a capital crime. In May 1696, he submitted a report to government authorities in England that exposed, in broad strokes, the scope of the problem. He claimed that piratical activity was rife throughout the colonies, with governors "permitting pirates of all nations to be masters & owners of all vessels," which only served as a "great encouragement to the illegal trade." His list of the "chief places where pirates resort & are harbored" included South Carolina, North Carolina, Rhode Island, Massachusetts, and Pennsylvania, where he asserted that "the governor entertains several pirates who carry on an illicit trade with Curaçao and other places." Oddly enough, Randolph didn't mention New York, even though he knew full well it was a major sponsor of and haven for pirates.

Randolph's report, in combination with the news from America and the Indian Ocean, caused considerable consternation in the halls of government in England. Proclamations and acts were issued, requiring colonial governors to clamp down on piracy, but lacking effective enforcement, such calls to action were worth little more than the paper on which they were printed. As such, the colonies, by and large, didn't change their ways. The tide, however, was just about to turn, in part because of the actions of one of the most enigmatic and successful pirates, Henry Avery.

CHAPTER 4

Crackdown

Avery's Fancy *engaging a Mughal ship (1837 engraving).*

THE MEN ABOARD THE *CHARLES II* WERE FURIOUS. THE ship was part of a four-vessel expedition to the West Indies sponsored by English investors, the goal of which was to attack French outposts, salvage treasure from Spanish wrecks, and trade with Spanish settlements. The convoy had left Gravesend, England, in August 1693, and then sailed to La Coruña, Spain, to receive documentation from the Spanish government allowing them to proceed. After many delays, the convoy arrived in early 1694, whereupon months of waiting for the required documents began. Making the situation increasingly unbearable was the fact that, other than a small advance, none of the sailors had been paid, despite petitions imploring the investors to cover their salaries so that they could support themselves and their families back home. Finally, in May 1694, nearly ten months after leaving Gravesend, the crew had had enough, their anger boiling over. They approached first mate Henry Avery* and asked him to lead a mutiny.

Avery was about forty years old and battle hardened, having served as a midshipman, mate, and chief mate on Royal Navy warships prior to signing on to the *Charles II*. He was described by a contemporary as being of average height, plump, daring, and "of a gay and jolly complexion," but "unforgiving to the last degree" if he was crossed. As it turned out, he was the perfect man for the job. He quickly consented, and soon the bulk of the men aboard swore allegiance to the plan, which was set in motion on the night of May 7.

While Captain Charles Gibson lay in his cabin reeling from a high fever, crewmembers from the *Charles II* rowed a boat over to the nearby *James*, one of the other vessels in the convoy, to collect sailors who had asked to join the mutineers. In the process of retrieving the recruits, an alarm was raised, which forced Avery to act immediately. He and his followers quickly overpowered the remaining crewmembers of the *Charles II* and then prepared the ship to sail. Despite being fired upon by the *James* and the nearby Spanish fort, the *Charles II* made it out of the harbor unscathed, and then headed south.

When Gibson woke up the following morning, he was surprised to see Avery and other crewmembers crowded around his bed. Realizing that they were underway, Gibson demanded to know what was going on. "I am a man of fortune, and must seek my fortune," Avery began, as he explained to Gibson that they were headed to the Indian Ocean to be pirates, and that he could remain captain if

---

*   Henry Avery is the most common name by which he is known, but other contemporary sources identify him as Henry Every, Long Ben, John Avery, and Captain Bridgeman.

he joined the venture. Stunned by this betrayal, Gibson refused, and he, along with about fifteen other men who opposed the change, were mercifully sent off in one of the ship's boats to make their way to the nearest land.

No doubt feeling a bit cheeky, Avery promptly renamed the ship *Fancy*, and he and his men spent the next eight months raiding their way down the African coast, plundering ships and making off with brandy, fabrics, anchors, gold dust, and other items. After rounding the Cape of Good Hope, the *Fancy* reprovisioned and careened at Madagascar, where Avery added to his crew. He then sailed a few hundred miles to the northwest to the small island of Johanna (modern-day Anjouan, part of the Comoro archipelago). There, the band of pirates stocked up in anticipation of launching a raid on Mughal shipping near the Strait of Bab-el-Mandeb.

Before leaving Johanna in late February 1695, Avery penned a calling card of sorts. Addressed to "all English commanders," he let them know that the *Fancy* was a formidable foe, with forty-six guns and 150 men. To put the commanders' fears to rest, however, he told them that as long as he was in charge he would not attack any English ships. To gain his forbearance, he instructed English captains who were unsure as to the identity of an approaching vessel to ball up their ensign, or flag, and raise it to the top of the mizzenmast, which is just aft of the main mast. Avery promised to do the same, and then leave the English vessel alone. Like all pirates, however, he was aware that his control over his crew was not absolute. "My men are hungry, stout, and resolute," he noted, "and should they exceed my desire I cannot help myself." The letter ended with the congenial, "As yet an Englishman's friend." Avery's hope was that by focusing solely on Mughal ships, and steering clear of English ones, he would avoid angering the East India Company. That proved to be a major miscalculation.

As soon as Avery's note was relayed to East India Company offices in Bombay in the late spring of 1695, company officials began to worry. For much of the seventeenth century, the company had carried on an exceedingly profitable trade with the Mughal Empire

Henry Avery in the foreground, and the Fancy *in the background taking a Mughal ship.*

CAP.ᵗ AVERY and his Crew taking one of the GREAT MOGUL'S...

that had transformed it into an economic and political powerhouse. Needless to say, piracy threatened this trading relationship. Past pirate attacks had infuriated Mughal officials, and since English ships were the main offenders, most of the ire was directed at the East India Company, even though it was not involved. In some instances, provincial Mughal governors had retaliated against the company by placing embargos on trading and imprisoning its officials within their factories (offices). Now, with every expectation that Avery was heading to the Red Sea, the company feared the worst. If he attacked Mughal ships, it would result in "infinite clamors" at the Mughal court, and the company would certainly suffer.

IN MID-SUMMER, THE *FANCY* arrived off the desolate island of Perim, in the Strait of Bab-el-Mandeb, but it was not alone. It had been joined along the way by a bevy of ships, all of which were "privateers" from the American colonies intent on pursuing the same goal. The roll call included Captain Want's vessel, the *Dolphin*, fitted out in Lewes, Delaware (which was then part of Pennsylvania); Thomas Tew's *Amity* from New York; the *Susannah* out of Boston, commanded by Thomas Wake; and two entries from Rhode Island—the *Portsmouth Adventure*, captained by Joseph Faro, and Captain William Muse's *Pearl*. They all agreed to serve under Avery's lead, and wait for the Mughal ships to leave Mocha and sail for India. When the ships passed by Perim, the pirates would pounce.

After more than a week of waiting, the pirates got a rude surprise when men on a passing ketch told them that the twenty-five-ship convoy had sailed by the night before, just two miles from where the pirates were moored. Wasting no time, the pirates began their pursuit, setting a course for Surat, the convoy's destination. The *Dolphin*, being a poor sailer, was soon burned, and its crew transferred to the *Fancy*, which was already towing the *Pearl* behind. The *Portsmouth Adventure* stayed near the *Fancy*, but the *Amity* couldn't keep up, and not long after disappearing from sight, it chanced upon the Mughal ship whose spirited defense robbed Captain Tew of his life.

In early September, after covering nearly two thousand miles, the pirates sighted the *Fath Mahmamadi*, a three-hundred-ton ship with six guns, owned by Abdul Ghafar, the richest trader in Surat. Like the other ships in the convoy, it was returning from the Haj with hundreds of pilgrims aboard. With the *Fancy* at the lead flying the Union Jack, the pirates bore down on their intended prey. The *Fath Mahmamadi* got off three shots to no effect before being overrun. The pirates slaughtered a few of the men aboard, tortured others, and took £50,000 to £60,000 in silver and gold.

With the *Fath Mahmamadi* in tow, the pirates continued their pursuit. A few days later they hit the jackpot about one hundred miles from Surat. The *Gang-i-Sawai*, or *Gunsway* at it became known in English, was no ordinary Mughal ship. It was owned by Emperor Aurangzeb (reign 1658–1707), and was the largest ship in

Pirate captain Henry Avery and his men taking Mughal treasure aboard the Fancy *(1837 engraving).*

his fleet, carrying nearly one thousand pilgrims, eighty guns, and four hundred rifles, and as many soldiers to defend it.

For two hours the pirates' ships and the *Gang-i-Sawai* battled, with heavy casualties on both sides. Despite the *Gang-i-Sawai*'s overwhelming manpower and firepower, its soldiers were no match for the pirates. After a well-placed cannon ball shattered the *Gang-i-Sawai*'s mainmast, and one of its cannons exploded, killing four and wounding others, the Muslim defenders surrendered. One account claimed that as the pirates swarmed the ship, its captain, Muhammad Ibrahim, ran below decks and, in a last-ditch effort, armed a group of concubines he had brought back from Mecca, urging them to fight, to no avail.

The pirates plundered the ship for several days, torturing passengers for confessions of where the treasure was hidden. When they weren't gathering loot, the pirates engaged in an animalistic and vile orgy, viciously raping numerous women. A few of the intended victims, unable to bear the humiliation of having their families and friends see them ravished and defiled, killed themselves with daggers or jumped into the ocean to their death. One of the pilgrims subjected to such barbarous treatment was an elderly relative of the emperor and wife of a high-ranking court official.

The *Gang-i-Sawai* was a magnificent haul, worth at least a few hundred thousand pounds sterling. When all of the treasure from the two Mughal ships was finally divided among the pirates, each one received £1,000, with captains and first mates getting a double share, and a share and a half, respectively. After that, the pirates quickly dispersed. The *Pearl* headed for Ethiopia, the *Susannah* to St. Marie, and the *Portsmouth Adventure* to an unknown destination; all of them, apparently, hoping to capture other prizes. Avery, on the other hand, had had his share of piracy, and was looking forward to retiring. He ultimately made his way to New Providence in the Bahamas, surviving an attempted mutiny on the journey, and scattering rebellious crewmembers at various places along the way.

Upon arriving at New Providence in April 1696, Avery sent a note to the Bahamian governor, Nicholas Trott, asking for permission to bring the *Fancy* into the harbor, and requesting protection for him and his men while in port. To sweeten the deal, the pirates promised to give the governor the ship and all its contents, as well as twenty pieces of eight and two pieces of gold per pirate, with Avery throwing in double that amount. Trott, a man cut from the same cloth as New York's governor Fletcher, was extremely pleased with the arrangement, and he laid out the welcome mat for his honored guests. The pirates soon split up, with about half of them, including Avery, heading back to England and Ireland, and the rest sailing for the Carolinas.

WHEN NEWS OF AVERY'S attacks reached East India Company officials in Bombay, they dashed off a fevered report to company headquarters in London. "All this will raise a black cloud at [the Mughal] court," the report ominously noted, "which we wish may not produce a severe storm." Despite this wish, an epic storm ensued. As soon as the *Fath Mahmamadi* and the *Gang-i-Sawai* arrived in Surat, and

*Mughal Emperor
Aurangzeb.*

word of the theft and the atrocities spread, people spilled into the streets calling for blood. They surrounded the East India Company factory, whose walls protected scores of Englishmen inside just long enough for local soldiers to arrive to keep the rioters from breaching the compound and killing all within. The soldiers, however, were not there to liberate the Englishmen from vigilante justice, but to imprison them. Company officials were shackled, and boards were placed over the factory's windows. An Englishman being escorted by soldiers back to the compound was beaten so severely by the mob in the streets that he died of his injuries three days later.

The ultimate fate of not only the officials imprisoned in Surat, but also of all company operations in India, rested with Aurangzeb. Not surprisingly, he flew into a rage when he heard what had taken place. It was bad enough when pirates attacked run-of-the-mill Mughal traders, but this time they had struck one of his ships and the ship of a very important merchant, and both were carrying religious pilgrims performing one of the holiest rites in the Muslim religion.

Much more than a commercial disaster, this was a political disaster, and a sacrilegious blow aimed right at the heart of Islam.

Aurangzeb's first inclination was to wage war on the East India Company and banish them from India, but cooler heads prevailed. For nine months the factory remained a prison, and trade was halted, while behind the scenes negotiations between the company and the emperor's representatives attempted to resolve the standoff. In the end, hefty bribes and the company's commitment to provide an armed escort for pilgrimage convoys traveling to and from the Red Sea proved satisfactory. In June 1696 the gates of the Surat factory were reopened, and trade resumed soon thereafter.

AVERY'S BLOODY ACTS FORCED the East India Company to confront the unthinkable—that they would be permanently shut out of the lucrative Indian trade. Realizing the critical importance of showing Aurangzeb that the company was doing everything it could to fight piracy, the company petitioned England's Privy Council to take action against Avery and his men. Since the English government benefited mightily from the revenues brought in by the company, and so wished to protect its interests in India, the council issued a proclamation on July 17, 1696, labeling Avery and his crew pirates, and ordering colonial officials as well as all officers at sea to seize them so that they could be brought to justice. To improve the odds of getting their men, the council turned pirate against pirate by promising to pardon any of Avery's men who helped capture their captain or one of their peers. When the council members balked at offering a reward for such captures, the company stepped forward with £500 for Avery's apprehension, and £50 for any of his underlings. This unprecedented call for action, in effect an international wanted poster, launched what historian Douglas R. Burgess Jr. called "the first worldwide manhunt in recorded history." The results, however, were disappointingly meager.

Upon leaving the Bahamas, Avery made his way to Donegal, on the north coast of Ireland, and then simply vanished. In subsequent years the mythology surrounding him and his exploits transformed him into a legendary, even heroic, figure in many people's eyes. Pamphlets, books, and ballads were written about him, as well as a satirical play called *The Successful Pyrate*, which had a profitable run in London's Theatre Royal, Drury Lane. In one of the more preposterous accounts of his later life, Avery was said to have become the king of a fabulously wealthy, and completely fictitious, pirate society on Madagascar, and to have taken for his bride one of Aurangzeb's granddaughters, whom he had purportedly abducted from the *Gang-i-Sawai*.

As for Avery's crew, only a relatively small number were arrested, and most of them were not tried. One of the most intriguing captures was credited to a nosy maid. Soon after one of the pirates checked into a boarding house about thirty miles from London, the maid rifled through his belongings. Inspecting his coat, she found roughly £1,000 worth of gold coins sewn into the lining. More honest than avaricious, she alerted the local authorities, who impounded the money and promptly threw the pirate in prison.

The trial of six of the purported pirates commenced on October 19, 1696, in the Old Bailey, an imposing brick building in the western part of London, named after the street on which it was located, and also known as Justice Hall and the Central Criminal Court. Dr. Henry Newton, the king's counsel, launched the prosecution by outlining for the jury the great stakes involved. "For suffer pirates, and the commerce of the world must cease, which this nation has deservedly so great a share in, and reaps such mighty advantage by." If the pirates went unpunished, Newton continued, the result might be war with India, and "the total loss of the Indian trade, and thereby the impoverishment of this kingdom." In other words, the consequences of a merciful ruling could be economic catastrophe. Despite the overwhelming weight of the evidence and the damning testimony of some of Avery's men, who aided the prosecution in exchange for clemency, the jury returned with six not-guilty verdicts.

The government and the East India Company officials were thunderstruck. They were certain that the pirates would be found guilty, ensuring their date with the hangman. Indeed, the image of those pirates dangling from ropes was going to be used to prove to Aurangzeb that England was serious about cracking down on piracy, thereby helping repair the frayed relationship between the company and the Mughal Empire. Instead, the jury's stunning decision gave new life to the widely and long-held belief that England was "a nation of pirates." In that view, Avery was just another in a long line of Englishmen reaching back to the glory days of Drake and his fellow sea dogs who committed robbery on the high seas. The reasons for the jury's decision are unknown since there are no records of their deliberations, although some have mused that the jury might have viewed crime against Muslims—or "heathens" as they were typically viewed in the West—as no crime at all, despite the fact that such piracy posed a serious threat to the English economy.

Whatever the reasons, the government quickly decided that the verdicts must be nullified, but how? To solve that problem, Sir Charles Hedges, the chief judge of the High Court of the Admiralty, and one of the greatest legal minds in England, was called in. He proposed trying the six men again—not for piracy, but rather for the mutiny on the *Charles II*.

The second trial began on October 31, and Hedges, as lead prosecutor, framed the argument for the jury just as starkly as Dr. Newton had done in the first trial. "Since foreigners look upon the decrees of our courts of justice as the sense and judgment of the whole nation," Hedges said, the jury must take a strong and decisive stand against lawlessness. If they don't, "the barbarous nations will reproach us as being a harbor, receptacle, and a nest of pirates; and our friends will wonder to hear that the enemies of merchants and of mankind, should find a sanctuary in this ancient place of trade."

With what must have seemed like the weight of the entire English government and the East India Company bearing down on them, the jury this time found all six defendants guilty. The presiding judge in the case, breathing a sigh of relief, thanked the jury, stating that they had "done very much to regain the honor of the nation and the city." The pirates were hanged on November 25, 1696, at Execution Dock at Wapping, along the bank of the Thames River about a mile below the Tower of London, where a simple gallows had been in use since the early 1400s to send a vast number of maritime criminals into the great beyond. One of the condemned men, just before the noose was placed around his neck, "expressed a due sense of his wicked life, in particular the most horrid barbarities he had committed" upon the Indians who he had "so inhumanely rifled and treated so unmercifully." Even though he considered those Indians no better than "heathens and infidels," he declared "that his eyes were now open to his crimes, and that he justly suffered death for such inhumanity."

AS HARD WON AS they were, the guilty verdicts didn't go very far in assuaging Aurangzeb. After all, only six of the pirates were brought to justice, and the biggest prize, Avery, got away. Furthermore, the trial and convictions changed nothing on the water. In Avery's wake, and in part encouraged by his success, other English pirates scoured the Indian Ocean, waylaying a number of Mughal ships, as well as a few European ones. A letter from the East India Company's Bombay factory in early 1697 highlighted the growing threat. "So alluring is the gain of piracy, and what it will amount to in a little time, if care be not taken to suppress these villains, God knows . . . what place they will seize or fortify to make their rendezvous." The two trials, nevertheless, did have one major impact. They further exposed the intimate relationship between the American colonies and pirates, which caused the English government to refocus its attention on this controversial issue.

Just six months prior to the trials, Edward Randolph submitted his report detailing widespread colonial support for pirates, and the testimony at the trials only added credence to Randolph's devastating claims. The Board of Trade took this damning intelligence about piracy quite seriously. Established in May 1696, the Board of Trade replaced the Lords of Trade and Plantations, which had done a relatively poor job of overseeing colonial administration, monitoring compliance with English law, and advising the home government on combating piracy. The Board of Trade, in contrast, was a more professional group with deeper knowledge of the situation in the colonies, and from its inception it made fighting piracy a top priority.

A few months after Avery's men were hanged, the Board of Trade sent a flurry of letters to various colonies imploring them to mend their ways. A letter sent to Massachusetts governor William Stoughton in January 1697 reminded him that King William III (reign 1689–1702) had ordered that governors "do their utmost to repress piracy," and added that at "the trial of Avery's crew there was too frequent mention of New England as the place from which pirates are fitted out and where they are entertained." The colonies of Rhode Island, South Carolina, and Pennsylvania, as well as the province of New Jersey, were similarly admonished for entertaining pirates, and were firmly advised to crack down on piracy. But instigating change in the colonies was not going to be easy, as evidenced by the plight of scrappy Robert Snead, a county justice in Philadelphia.

IT WAS IN APRIL 1697 that Snead first became acquainted with the proclamation ordering colonial governors to seize Avery and his men, and as a faithful subject of the king and a conscientious magistrate, he decided to act. Knowing that a few of Avery's men were in Philadelphia at that very moment, Snead marched over to Governor William Markham's house to tell him that it was his duty to apprehend the rogues. Snead, a former carpenter in Jamaica, had been in Pennsylvania for two years, and he was familiar enough with local politics to know that Markham would likely balk at his demand. It was common knowledge that Markham, a man of limited means and greedy disposition, had long welcomed pirates and their money to the colony. Rumors also abounded that Avery's men had made a "great present to him and his family," while more damning still was the fact that Markham's daughter had recently married James Brown, one of Avery's crew.

When Snead mentioned the proclamation, the governor coolly

claimed to have never seen it, which was clearly a lie; and when Snead offered to read it to him, the governor demurred. What about the pirates brazenly walking the streets of Philadelphia, and openly bragging about their exploits "over their cups," Snead asked—was the governor not aware of this? Markham again pleaded ignorance, adding that, anyway, "If people came here and brought money he was not obliged to ask them whence they came." Snead said that he could prove that Avery's men were in Philadelphia, and that Markham's failure to arrest them would be a black mark against him. The governor was not moved. Disgusted by this obstinacy, Snead leaned in close to Markham and said that he "saw plainly that there was an understanding between him [the governor] and the pirates, and that none were so blind as those that would not see." Such insolence enraged Markham; nevertheless, he did admit to knowing the whereabouts of some of Avery's men, adding that "the pirates had been civil to him," and that the money they brought with them "was an advantage to the country." Stymied, Snead walked away fuming.

As it turned out, the contentious meeting had not been private. Markham's wife and daughter had been listening from an adjoining room, and no sooner had Snead departed than they told Robert Clinton, one of Avery's men, what had transpired. Clinton immediately shared this information with two more of Avery's men, Edmund Lassall and Peter Claussen. On the street the very next day, the pirates accosted Snead and called him an "informer" for the Crown. This sent Snead back to the governor's house, where he told Markham about the harassment and his belief that the governor's family members had tipped off the pirates. Markham's emboldened wife and daughter, both of whom were in the room, admitted that they were to blame, adding that Snead "deserved to be called an informer." Furious, Snead said that Markham had left him no choice. He was going to arrest the pirates himself.

Snead asked two of his fellow justices, Edward Shippen and Anthony Maurice, to assist him, and they both consented. But unbeknownst to Snead, one of Maurice's relatives was married to Claussen, and after conferring with Markham, Maurice reversed his position, telling Snead he would not help. When Snead threatened to report Maurice to the king if he didn't change his mind, the recalcitrant justice came around.

Clinton, Lassall, and Claussen were arrested and brought before the three justices, who agreed that it was clear that the men had been on the *Fancy*. Snead wanted to lock them all up, but the other justices allowed them to post bail, and they walked out of the courthouse free. A few weeks later, Snead, hearing that the pirates planned to flee, arrested them again. This time he had a surprise witness. Markham's son-in-law and former pirate, James Brown, ratted out his old crewmates, confessing that they had indeed been on Avery's ship, and had shared in the plunder. Unfortunately, there is no record of how Brown's wife, the governor's daughter, reacted to his confession, but one imagines that she couldn't have been too happy with her "informer" husband. The justices ordered the attorney general to issue an arrest warrant, but the pirates spent only a few days in jail before being bailed out a second time.

Thwarted once more in his mission, the stubbornly determined Snead would not give up. He issued his own warrants, but that only raised Markham's ire. The governor said Snead had no right to issue warrants without first apprising him, and then he called Snead "a rascal" and "dared" him to issue his warrants again, threatening to "commit" him if he did. Snead said he should not have to endure such abuse for simply doing his job. This defiance only further enraged the governor, who now ordered the constables to ignore Snead's warrants and strip him of his weapons, thereby leaving him defenseless against the pirates who were repeatedly threatening him with harm.

Despite this obstruction of justice, Snead persisted, and managed to get the three pirates jailed yet again. However, he knew better than to trust the jail or the jailer. He offered to have an extra guard placed on duty, which the sheriff insisted was unnecessary. That evening, Clinton and Lassall escaped, supposedly through a hole in the wall where a fourteen-by-ten-inch plank had been dislodged. The following day, a mariner who visited the jail cast doubt on that theory. He knew Clinton, who, he said, "was a very fat gross man," and claimed that there was no way that such a corpulent fellow could have climbed through such a small hole. The inescapable conclusion was that the sheriff had let them walk out the front door on their own.

Markham grudgingly offered a £5 reward for their capture, after which a woman claimed she saw the heavily armed pirates hiding behind some bushes near the center of town. The complicit sheriff, however, dismissed her, saying she must have been mistaken. When Markham was told about the sighting, he, too, failed to take any action. "All people see," Snead acidly remarked, "how Arabian gold works with some consciences."

A few days later, Claussen was released. And not long after that, Lassall and Clinton came out of hiding, and were seen walking casually around Philadelphia, which was at the time more hamlet than city, with approximately four hundred houses and about 2,500 white residents, and a few hundred slaves. Snead pleaded with Markham to issue a warrant for the pirates' arrest, but was, not surprisingly, rebuffed. Spent and discouraged, Snead finally gave up.

THE LETTERS FROM THE Board of Trade urging governors to "repress piracy" were just the beginning of efforts to crack down on this scourge. Throughout the late 1690s and on into the beginning of the new century, the English government and colonial officials took a number of actions aimed at eliminating piracy and its support structure in America. They were aided in such efforts by an infusion of resources, freed up after the signing of the Treaty of Ryswick on September 20, 1697, which ended the Nine Years' War. And there was every expectation that those resources would be sorely needed, because privateering commissions were revoked at the end of the war, and if history was any guide, many of those unemployed privateers would soon turn to piracy.

The dynamic that typically led to a surge of piracy at war's end was eloquently described as early as 1629 by John Smith, who observed what happened after King James I of England ascended to the throne in 1604. In one of his first acts, James signed the Treaty of London, ending the Anglo-Spanish War. Almost simultaneously he outlawed privateering. "Those [privateers] that were rich rested with what they had," observed Smith, and "those that were poor and had nothing but from hand to mouth, turned pirates; some because they became slighted of those for whom they had got much wealth; some, for that they could not get their due; some, that had lived bravely, would not abase themselves to poverty; some vainly, only to get a name; others for revenge, covetousness, or as ill." With seemingly limited options to make their fortunes, these disgruntled former privateers became pirates.

Action to eliminate piracy in America occurred on a number of fronts. One of the most important was sacking governors who had coddled both pirates and the merchants who had traded with them. To that end, the pirate-loving pol, New York governor Benjamin Fletcher, was replaced by Richard Coote, the first Earl of Bellomont, who was not only made governor of New York, but also of Massachusetts and New Hampshire. Although he was appointed in 1697, Bellomont didn't arrive in New York until April 1698. Sixty-two years old, tall, portly, and gout-stricken, he was chosen by the king in large part because of his commitment to fighting piracy and his unquestioned integrity, as well as his reputation for hard work. An aristocrat of limited means, and quite desirous of becoming richer, Bellomont often complained that his salary failed to cover his expenses; however, there is no evidence that he stooped as low as many of his gubernatorial peers, who encouraged pirate payoffs to enhance their income.

Bellomont wasted no time going on the attack. A little more than a month after taking office, he harangued the provincial council about New York's dishonorable reputation as a place that supported and profited from piracy. When Bellomont brought up the fact that Fletcher and other colonial officials had protected pirates in return for money, customs collector Chidley Brooke responded rather candidly that such behavior "had not formerly been looked upon as so great a matter, and that all the neighboring Governments had done it commonly." This casual acceptance of illicit behavior launched Bellomont into a rage. "You might think it a peccadillo," Bellomont bellowed, "but the King and his ministers regarded it as a high offense." Brooke weakly responded that he did not "excuse it, but only stated what had been done." To show everyone in the colony that things were different now, Bellomont proposed a proclamation calling for all pirates to be arrested, and the council, cowed by the new governor's explosive anger and resolve, quickly assented.

The very next day, Bellomont met with the colonial assembly, and was equally combative. Declaring that piracy was an "odious practice detested by all civil nations," he promised to root it out because it was "not only injurious to the honor of his majesty, and the English nation, but also highly prejudicial to the trade of England, and particularly to the East India Company."

Bellomont backed up his words with action. He summarily fired a number of officials who shared Fletcher's proclivity for support-

Richard Coote, first Earl of Bellomont.

ing piracy, including Brooke and William Nicoll, the man who had helped the *Jacob*'s men come into the city unmolested, and who Bellomont called the "chief broker in the matter of protecting pirates." Bellomont also replaced many of the provincial councilors who were loyal to Fletcher, and a scattering of local sheriffs, labeling them "the scum of the people."

Bellomont now took aim at Fletcher, and his enmity toward his predecessor's cozy relationship with pirates bordered on mania. Bellomont deluged the Board of Trade with letters detailing, ad nauseam, Fletcher's voluminous misdeeds, with virtually every instance of Fletcher's support of piracy being noted, as well as other forms of corruption, including embezzling money from the troops and issuing corrupt land grants. The Board of Trade used Bellomont's dossier to hold hearings in London to determine whether Fletcher should be brought up on charges for his actions, and although it found him culpable for giving "great encouragement to pirates" and failing to prosecute them, Fletcher's case went no further, mainly due to his connections to men in high places. Still, Fletcher's government career came to an abrupt stop, and his reputation lay in tatters.

AFTER YEARS OF COMPLAINTS about his support of pirates, Governor Markham, too, got the boot. William Penn, the founder and proprietor of Pennsylvania, initially refused to believe reports detailing Markham's malfeasance. When Randolph told the House of Lords in early 1697 that Markham was "a favorer of the pirates," Penn took umbrage, responding that such a claim was "both foul and false." But continued scrutiny, especially by the Board of Trade, uncovered more examples of such "favor," and forced Penn to leave the comfortable surroundings of England and travel to the wilds of Pennsylvania to set things right, fearing that if he didn't, the king would revoke his charter.

Penn arrived at Philadelphia in December 1699 and soon discovered that his colony was firmly on the side of pirates. Robert Quarry, vice admiral of Pennsylvania, West Jersey, and Maryland, informed

*William Penn,
from an engraving
circa 1797.*

Penn that pirates "walk the streets with their pockets full of gold and are the constant companions of the chief in the government," and Penn could see for himself that such accusations were true. Quarry complained that he had encountered great difficulty in capturing pirates because the government of Pennsylvania had failed to give him "the least aid or assistance." Instead, both the people of Pennsylvania and their government representatives were too busy entertaining pirates and sheltering them from justice. Every person that Quarry had managed to send out to apprehend pirates had, in his words, been "abused and affronted and called enemies to the country, for disturbing and hindering honest men, as they are pleased to call the pirates, from bringing their money and settling amongst them."

Horrified by this state of affairs, Penn quickly issued a proclamation commanding all colonial officials "to use their utmost diligence vigorously to pursue, apprehend, and secure every" person suspected of piracy. He pushed a law through the provincial assembly called An Act Against Pirates and Sea-Robbers, which sought to give the proclamation some teeth. He also fired Markham, at the insistence of the Board of Trade, and assumed the role of governor himself.

Even though Penn readily admitted that pirates had been embraced by his beloved colony, he cast the blame for their presence on outside forces. He claimed that if "Jamaica had not been the seminary" where pirates learned their vile trade before heading to the Indian Ocean, and if some of Pennsylvania's neighboring colonies had not given pirates all manner of provisions, while at the same time eagerly taking their money, then the pirates would not have found their way to Pennsylvania, and the colony would "never [have] had a spot upon . . . [her] garment." In truth, there never would have been a spot, had not the people of Pennsylvania welcomed, aided, and abetted the pirates.

While Penn was curbing the collusion with piracy in his colony, another step in the fight against piracy came with the appointment of Jeremiah Basse as governor of East and West Jersey in 1697. He came by his hatred of pirates honestly, having been on a vessel off the coast of Puerto Rico when pirates captured it. According to Basse, his captors used him and his fellow prisoners "extremely hard, beat us, pinched us of victuals, [and] shut us down at night to take our lodging in the water-cask," before finally releasing them.

As governor, Basse sent a steady stream of correspondence to the home government, sounding the alarm about piracy, and, in particular, the role of the various colonies in promoting it. "You cannot be insensible," he wrote to the Board of Trade, "of the dishonor as well as damage suffered by this nation through the increase of piracies under the banner of England in any part of the world. . . . The Colonies in the Islands and Main of America have not a little contributed to this increase." He urged the king to take action to "suppress these sea-wolves and secure our East India trade," as he and other Jersey officials aggressively pursued pirates throughout the colony.

THE APPOINTMENT OF BELLOMONT and Basse, and the removal of Markham, contributed to the fight against piracy. Pirates and those who supported them were put on notice that the authorities were watching and waiting to catch them in the act. Some successes ensued. For example, Basse's efforts did manage to nab and jail a few pirates, and just three months into his administration, Bellomont was able to report to the Board of Trade that community leaders in New York raised a "clamor" around him, since his efforts "ruined" New York by preventing pirates—and £100,000 in treasure and goods*—from coming into the colony. In subsequent years, Bellomont, too, captured a number of pirates, who were later sent to England for trial.

But such successes were limited in scope. Colonial governors, no matter how motivated and aggressive, faced concerted opposition from a wide array of people with vested interests. Since Bellomont's reforms and pronouncements infuriated colonial officials, merchants, and citizens who had for years benefited mightily from piracy, he encountered fierce resistance at every turn. On more than one occasion, when the governor sent customs collectors to seize pirated goods, they were waylaid by area merchants defending their investment, forcing Bellomont to send additional forces to secure the contraband and, in one case, to free two collectors who had been locked in a room and threatened with murder. Another time, a "chief-searcher" from the customs office quit his job rather than carry out Bellomont's order to confiscate a suspect East Indian shipment, fearing for his life.

To avoid having Bellomont's men impound their goods, area merchants began instructing their ships returning from Madagascar to bypass New York harbor, and instead offload at other places

---

* This amount is equivalent to roughly 10 percent of the value of the average annual trade that England carried on with America *and* Africa at the time. See John J. McCusker and Russell R. Menard, *The Economy of British America, 1607–1789* (Chapel Hill: University of North Carolina Press, 1991), 40.

along the coast from which the goods could be more easily smuggled into the city undetected. Even when Bellomont laid out traps for pirates who were in the area visiting their wives, he often failed to capture them because, he observed, "they are too well befriended in this town to be given up to justice." Due to all this obstruction and chicanery, Bellomont called New York City "a nest of pirates," and asserted "unlawful trade and pirates' spoil from the Red Sea is what . . . [the people here] thirst after."

ANOTHER STEP IN THE FIGHT against piracy in the colonies involved firepower. Toward the end of the 1690s, pirate sightings along the coast of America were on the rise, as were attacks. Although a couple of English naval ships patrolled the coast of America, colonial governors begged the home government to offer greater protection. Such requests came at a propitious time. The English navy had bulked up during the recent war and was well on its way to becoming the vast fighting force that would eventually make the English the lords of the oceans. Finally, at the end of the decade, the admiralty, urged on by the Board of Trade, agreed to send more ships to New England, New York, and Virginia. As the experience in Virginia shows, one well-manned, capably commanded, and properly armed naval ship could make quite a difference.

In July 1699 the pirate vessel *Providence Galley*, with twenty-six guns and 130 men, approached the mouth of Chesapeake Bay. Its captain was Englishman John James, a sinewy man of average height, with broad shoulders, whose face was disfigured by smallpox. Around his neck hung gold chains, one with a golden toothpick dangling from it. Earlier in the year, James led a mutiny aboard the galley,* overthrowing the Dutch captain, and then marooning him, along with fifteen of the crew, on one of the Berry Islands in the Bahamas, with only three pistols and a bottle of gunpowder. Since the mutiny, the *Providence Galley* had been on a tear, capturing countless ves-

---

* A low, flat vessel with sails and banks of oars.

sels and, reportedly, accumulating silver and gold treasure worth an astonishing, although hardly believable, three million pounds. Now, low on supplies and with his galley in disrepair, James was heading to Virginia to commandeer provisions, sails, and rigging.

On July 23, the *Providence Galley* easily overpowered the *Hope*, a relatively small merchant vessel, just beyond the Virginia Capes (Cape Charles and Cape Henry). The pirates stripped their victims of a few useful items, but the real treasure was information onboard about the *Essex Prize*, a Royal Navy ship whose job was to guard area waters and protect merchant vessels heading in and out of Chesapeake Bay. The *Hope* was carrying back to London many months of records from the *Essex Prize*, and once James perused them, he instantly knew the strength of his potential foe. He decided, then and there, that he could, and would, take her in a fight.

Two days later the *Essex Prize* was anchored off Cape Henry when its captain, John Aldred, spied an unknown vessel in the distance chasing a trader, the *Maryland Merchant*. Aldred ordered a pursuit, and when the *Essex Prize* got within range, the mystery vessel raised a Union Jack up its mainmast, along with a bloody flag indicating that it would give no quarter. While Aldred was angling for a better position, his antagonist unleashed a furious broadside, firing all of its guns on one side of his ship, which was returned in kind. Although Aldred still didn't know the identity of his attacker, there could be no doubt that it was a pirate ship. James, on the other hand, knew exactly what ship he was firing on, and he fervently hoped that the *Essex Prize* would soon be his.

Aldred quickly realized that the *Essex Prize*, carrying only sixteen guns and about fifty men, didn't have a chance against the larger ship in an open-water fight. He decided that the best strategy was to lure the ship away from the *Maryland Merchant* and into shoal waters, hoping to ground or bilge it (break a hole in the hull), while at the same time giving the merchant vessel time to escape. Aldred tried to tempt James into taking the bait, but the pirate was too clever to fall for the ruse. Instead, he turned his attention to the *Maryland Merchant*, firing a shot across its bow to halt its flight.

After taking the captain and crew of the *Maryland Merchant* aboard, James continued his pursuit of the *Essex Prize* until he figured out that its captain was not willing to engage him. He then returned to the *Maryland Merchant* and picked it clean.

Aldred raced to shore and dispatched a messenger to deliver a letter to Francis Nicholson, now the governor of Virginia, informing him of the engagement. News of pirates along the coast infuriated Nicholson, not only on account of the damage they did to commerce, but also because he hated them with a passion. "I always abhorred such sort of profligate men and their barbarous actions," Nicholson had written a few years earlier, "for sure they are the disgrace of mankind in general, and of the noble, valiant, generous English in particular." But, lacking a military vessel that could take on James and his men, there was nothing Nicholson could do. Two days later, the governor's anger flared anew when he learned that the *Providence Galley* had taken the *Roanoke Merchant*, plundered it, and forced some of its men to join the pirate crew. Nicholson braced for more bad news, but it didn't come. After taking the *Roanoke Merchant*, James's men voted to leave the area for better hunting grounds, and with that, they were gone.

The *Providence Galley*'s attacks panicked the region. The governor and his council now had proof that the relatively diminutive *Essex Prize* was incapable of protecting the colony and its merchant vessels against a well-armed pirate ship. And the fear of more attacks was only heightened in the late summer and early fall of 1699 as news spread of pirates plundering dozens of ships along the American coast. Realizing that their only hope was a stronger naval presence, Nicholson wrote to the admiralty, imploring the aid of another, larger ship. On April 20, 1700, that ship arrived just in the nick of time.

THE HMS *SHOREHAM*, a mere six years old, mounted thirty-two guns and had a crew of 128 men. Its captain, William Passenger, was an able commander, and his orders were clear. The *Shoreham* was to relieve the *Essex Prize*, and Passenger was to cruise the Chesapeake and the area around the Virginia Capes to defend the colony from pirates. If he found any, he was to "take, sink, burn, or otherwise destroy" them. A little more than a week after arriving, Passenger began acting on those orders.

In the late afternoon of April 28, Passenger and Nicholson were chatting at the home of Colonel William Wilson in Kecoughtan (modern-day Hampton) when Aldred rushed in with alarming news. A merchant vessel had barely escaped an attack by a pirate ship just off Cape Henry. Although Nicholson urged Passenger to wait until morning to set out, the captain went directly to the *Shoreham* and got underway. Poor winds, and the pilot's unwillingness to brave the shoal-pocked waters in the dark, slowed their progress, and Passenger was forced to anchor about nine miles from the pirate ship, which was reported to be in Lynnhaven Bay.

This delay proved fortuitous for Nicholson. Immediately after Passenger departed for the *Shoreham*, Nicholson rallied the militia along the coast. But, as a man of action, he wanted to be a part of the attack, so when the *Shoreham* anchored just offshore, Nicholson took the opportunity to come aboard. Early the next morning, the *Shoreham* weighed anchor and sailed toward the bay. Soon the pirate ship *La Paix* came into view.

La Paix, or Peace, had been anything but peaceful for many months. Starting out from Tortuga in late 1699, under the leadership of Frenchman Lewis Guittar, the twenty-gun *La Paix* had an enviable streak of success, taking seven prizes and turning a couple of them into consorts. Captured seamen were asked to join the pirate company, and if they refused, they were made prisoners. One of Guittar's men tried to lure seamen into the fold by appealing to their greed. "You sail in a merchantman for twenty-five shillings a month," the pirate sneered, "and here you may have seven or eight hundred pounds if you can take it." *La Paix*'s most recent prize was the *Nicholson*, taken late in the day on April 28 in Lynnhaven Bay. It was transporting seven hundred hogsheads of tobacco to London, and Guittar happily added the vessel to his growing pirate fleet.

Soon after taking control of the *Nicholson*, Guittar made what turned out to be a critical mistake. Days earlier, one of his prisoners, unaware of the *Shoreham*'s arrival, had told him that the *Essex Prize* had already departed for London, leaving the coast undefended. When Guittar interrogated the *Nicholson*'s crew, however, its carpenter said that there was a naval ship on the coast at that very moment, although some of his crewmates claimed he was mistaken. Guittar accused the carpenter of lying, and as punishment, the pirates placed the poor man's thumb in a musket's flintlock and tightened the screw until it pierced his flesh. Then, they beat him with the flat sides of their swords. Later that evening, when another prisoner aboard told Guittar that he had seen a "great ship" in the distance, the cocky Frenchman dismissed him, saying "there is no man of war here, and if it be a merchantman I will have him by and by." Confident that there was no force in the vicinity capable of threatening him, Guittar allowed his men to drink themselves into oblivion.

Around dawn on April 29, the *Shoreham* came within a half mile of *La Paix*. Guittar could scarcely believe what he was seeing, realizing that he was face-to-face with one of her majesty's finest. Pandemonium broke out within the pirate fleet as seamen were roused from their drunken stupors. Fifty prisoners were hustled down into the hold, and *La Paix* was readied for battle. Passenger, in contrast, was relishing the coming engagement, boasting that "this is but a small fellow, we shall have him presently."

Though the battle raged until the late afternoon, the two ships pummeling each other with broadsides, and firing muskets and pistols when within range, *La Paix* was ultimately outgunned. With its sails shredded, its masts splintered, its hull "almost beaten to pieces," and its rudder shattered, the pirate ship ran aground. At three o'clock, Guittar surveyed the damage and raised the white flag, calling for a truce.

But the indefatigable Guittar had one more trick up his sleeve. He used the fifty prisoners as bargaining chips. He ordered his men to lay a trail of gunpowder leading to the ship's magazine, and then forced one of the prisoners to swim to the *Shoreham* to deliver the following ultimatum—"tell the commander in chief if he will not give me and my men quarter and pardon I will blow up the ship and we will all die together." To reinforce that message, the men of *La Paix* began chanting "broil, broil," signaling their willingness to immolate all aboard should their terms be denied. Nicholson, who had fought bravely during the fray, agreed to grant the pirates quarter, and refer them to the mercy of the king. The pirates then surrendered and were taken into custody. In the end, twenty-six pirates were killed during the battle, and about half that number was injured, eight of whom would later die of their injuries. Four lay dead on the *Shoreham*, with many more injured.

Three of Guittar's men had not been on *La Paix* during the fight, and hence they did not fall under the terms of the surrender (two of them were so drunk that they slept through the battle on one of the prize ships). Nicholson put the men on trial, and upon being found guilty of piracy, they were hanged. Guittar and the rest of his men were shipped to England, where the king, feeling unmerciful, put them on trial. Ultimately, Guittar and more than fifty of his crew were found guilty and executed.

AT THE SAME TIME that the Crown was fighting piracy by replacing corrupt politicians and sending warships to the colonies, it was also focusing on employing the law to effect change. A statute reaching back to the sixteenth century required pirates to be shipped back to England for trial. Even *if* a colony wanted to comply with the Crown, it was expensive to do so, creating a strong disincentive that effectively hobbled the law. As a result, by the late 1690s, a significant number of accused pirates had been thrown in jail in the colonies but hadn't been brought to trial. To fix this problem, in January 1700 the Board of Trade urged the king to order colonial governors to send the accused, along with witnesses and evidence implicating them, to London so that they could be prosecuted. The king complied, and dozens of men were shipped to England, ultimately found guilty of piracy, and hanged.

But even before the king ordered these pirates to be shipped to

England, efforts were under way to create a system that would make such transatlantic shipments of pirates unnecessary. In the mid- to late 1690s, at the Crown's urging, a number of colonies adopted laws to try pirates, but they were poorly crafted, and often intentionally toothless, rendering them largely ineffective. Finally, in April 1700 parliament, "having in view the refractoriness of New England and other plantations," passed the Act for the More Effectual Suppression of Piracy, which allowed pirates to be tried in the colonies in vice-admiralty courts by special commissioners of Oyer and Terminer (hear and determine). But it was to be trials with a critical difference. Since, in the relatively small number of piracy trials that had taken place in the colonies, sympathetic juries of their peers had often refused to find the pirates guilty, this new law eliminated juries altogether. Instead, the commissioners, pulled from the ranks of high-ranking colonial officials, military officers, and established merchants and planters, would decide each case. The assumption was that they were more likely than a jury to adhere to the letter of the law and not be swayed by local passions. As in England, the sentence that came with a conviction of piracy was death.

Furthermore, the law also aggressively expanded the definition of piracy. Mutineers, as well as those who failed to defend their ships against pirates, would now be treated as pirates, and anyone who aided, abetted, supplied, or encouraged pirates in any way, including those who received or concealed their goods, would be tried as accessories to piracy. If found guilty, they would be put to death (such accessories, however, were not to be tried in the colonies, but rather had to be sent back to England to face justice). To give mariners more incentive to resist, all mariners who were wounded fighting pirates were eligible for a financial reward, and if they died, their heirs could claim the same. Anyone who uncovered a plot to commit piracy was also compensated.

At the same time, parliament went one step further, passing a new law: An Act to Punish Governors of Plantations in this Kingdom, for Crimes By Them Committed in the Plantations. Under this, governors would be held to the same legal standards as everyone else, and harboring or financing pirates was now a crime for which they could be tried. Furthermore, according to England's attorney general, the new law provided that any governor found guilty of supporting piracy would also forfeit the colony's charter.

The king's order to ship pirates en masse to England for trial, along with the two comprehensive antipiracy statutes, was further proof that fighting piracy in the colonies was now a Crown priority.

THE BATTLE AGAINST PIRACY was furthered by the English government's reaction to the ill-fated voyage of Captain William Kidd, arguably the world's most famous pirate, who really wasn't much of a pirate at all. Kidd's story is full of many twists and turns and a cast of hundreds, if not thousands. Entire books have been written about his exploits, and no doubt there are others to come. But, for the purposes of our tale, only the outline of his story is necessary, just enough to understand how his actions in the Indian Ocean affected the course of piracy in America.

Born in Dundee, Scotland, in 1654, the son of a mariner, Kidd was a powerfully built and voluble man with a quick temper, and a streak of arrogance that was often on display. He served as a buccaneer and then privateer in the Caribbean before arriving in New York City in 1691, where his help in putting down a political rebellion made him a favorite of the incoming governor. His entrée into the upper reaches of local society was further cemented by his marriage to Sarah Bradley Cox Oort, a recent widow who brought with her a considerable estate. With his strong ties to the sea, Kidd, however, soon grew tired of his patrician life and, at the age of forty-one in 1695, desirous of adventure and a highly reputable position, he set sail for London to obtain an officer's commission in the Royal Navy.

Though unable to land the naval post he desired, Kidd received a much more unusual type of command. Through the influence of one of his New York associates, Robert Livingston, Kidd was introduced to Lord Bellomont, who was already angling for the governorship of New York. While it is not clear who came up with the idea—

Residence of Captain William Kidd in 1691, in New York City.
It is no longer standing, but would have been located at the corner
of modern-day Pearl and Hanover Streets.

whether it was Kidd, Livingston, Bellomont, or some combination
of the three—an ingenious scheme was hatched. Given the plague
of pirates infesting the Indian Ocean, why not give Kidd a ship
and send him there to hunt down the rogues? Such an expedition
would be especially timely and helpful, since the English navy was
stretched thin due to King William's War and could not spare any
ships to pursue this aim. If Kidd were successful, he would not only
bring back treasure that could enrich the sponsors of this enterprise,
but he would also help to reduce the scourge of pirates. A win-win
for everyone involved.

    With Bellomont taking the lead, a group of investors was assem-
bled. It included Bellomont, Livingston, Kidd, and a few high-ranking
government officials, as well as King William himself, who was a silent
partner with a ten percent stake. Kidd was ultimately granted two privateering commissions. One allowed him to capture pirate ships and,
in a break with tradition, he, his crew, and the investors would be
able to split the proceeds—the ship and any goods or treasure—rather
than have them go to the original owners. Furthermore, the percentage of the proceeds normally reserved for the admiralty was elimi-

nated. The second commission allowed him to attack French ships. After all, the Nine Years' War was still raging, and the French were despised just as much as pirates. Like all privateering commissions, they operated on a "no purchase, no pay" basis, meaning that if Kidd and his men didn't capture any prizes, they would earn nothing—a recipe that could bring great success, or abject failure.

Commissions meant nothing without a ship to command, and Kidd and his investors chose the brand-new 287-ton *Adventure Galley*, which boasted thirty-six guns. A versatile vessel, its sails and oars gave it the ability to travel and maneuver in all types of conditions. With a partial crew aboard, the *Adventure Galley* left England in late April 1696, heading for New York City to recruit more men to fill out the ship's roster.

A respected man about town already, and now with impressive royal commissions in hand, Kidd was warmly received by his fellow New Yorkers, and most especially by the two Sarahs in his life, his wife and daughter. Broadsides announcing the call for crewmen were posted, but nobody signed on. The problem, Kidd discovered, was the distribution of shares. The men were to be guaranteed 25 percent of the plunder, with the rest going to Kidd and the other investors. To prospective crewmen this was unacceptable. Typically, the crew on privateers got 60 percent of the haul. Realizing he had a serious problem, Kidd, without consulting his investors, went out with a new call for recruits, in which he promised them the usual 60 percent. As word of the new arrangement spread, men scrambled to sign on, for what could be better than government-backed licenses to plunder that offered such golden opportunities for profit? New York being a veritable "nest of pirates," as Bellomont would later point out, it is not surprising that many of Kidd's new crewmen were former pirates themselves.

With the full complement of 154 men now aboard, Kidd was ready to set sail for the Indian Ocean. Governor Fletcher, who observed Kidd's preparations, and who knew of the terms of his command, sensed the great potential for problems on the horizon. "One Captain Kidd lately arrived," Fletcher commented, "and produced a commission under the Great Seal of England for the suppression of piracy. . . . He sailed from hence . . . It is generally believed here that they will get money *per fas aut nefas* [by fair or unfair means], and that if he misses the design named in his commission he will not be able to govern such a herd of men under no pay."

The *Adventure Galley* departed from New York in September 1696, arriving at Tuléar on Madagascar in late January 1697. After heading north to the Comoro Islands at the end of February to careen and further victual the ship, roughly fifty of Kidd's crewmen contracted tropical illnesses and died. Kidd managed to recruit replacements, but there was no shaking the sense of gloom and restlessness that had settled on the ship. This was partly due to the deaths, but even more so from the fact that roughly eight months had passed since the trip began, and they had not captured a single prize, meaning that the men had earned nothing.

At the end of April, Kidd decided to remedy that situation by heading north to the Strait of Bab-el-Mandeb to capture one of the Mughal ships loaded with treasure as it returned from the annual pilgrimage to Mecca. Instead of hunting pirates, Kidd was ready to become a pirate himself. "Come, boys," Kidd told his men, "I will make money enough out of that fleet."

In mid-August seventeen Mughal ships sailed through the strait, escorted by three European guard ships, including the East India Company's *Sceptre*, boasting thirty-six guns and captained by Edward Barlow. The *Adventure Galley* fell in behind the fleet, and as it approached one of the lagging Mughal ships, the *Sceptre* fired a few shots at the intruder, correctly assuming it was a pirate ship. Winds were light, giving Kidd a slight advantage because his ship, being a galley, had oars to propel it. As he urged his men on, they rowed toward a large Mughal ship, hoping to take it before the guard ships could respond. When the *Adventure Galley* came within range, the Mughal ship fired a warning shot, and Kidd's men replied with multiple blasts of their own, scoring a few hits. But Barlow, determined to protect his charges, ordered his men to lower the boats and, using ropes, tow the *Sceptre* toward the engagement. As they

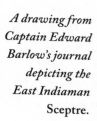

A drawing from Captain Edward Barlow's journal depicting the East Indiaman Sceptre.

came close, cannon fire boomed from the *Sceptre*, convincing Kidd to give up the chase.

Foiled, Kidd called his men together to vote on their next move, and they decided to head to India. At the end of August, off the Malabar Coast, the *Adventure Galley* stopped a small vessel flying English colors with a cannon shot across its bow. It was the *Mary*, owned by an Indian merchant, captained by Thomas Parker, and heading to Bombay. While Kidd spoke with Parker in the *Adventure Galley*'s cabin, a number of Kidd's men rowed over to the *Mary* with bad intent. To persuade the *Mary*'s crew to divulge the location of any valuables, Kidd's men grabbed a few of them, tied their hands behind their backs, and then lifted them off the deck by the ropes attached to their wrists. While the dangling men were writhing in agony, Kidd's men hit them about the body with the flat sides of their swords until they gave up what they knew. Having found a small amount of money, navigational instruments, guns, and a variety of goods, including bales of pepper and coffee, Kidd's men rowed back to the *Adventure Galley* with their plunder.

Before letting the *Mary* proceed on its way, Kidd ordered his men to return some, but not all, of the purloined items, and he forced Captain Parker to come aboard the *Adventure Galley* to act as pilot. A Portuguese man fluent in a number of languages was also taken to act as interpreter. Now that Kidd and his men had robbed a vessel flying English colors, and absconded with its captain and another man, they had crossed the line into the realm of piracy.

About a week later, Kidd pulled into the port of Karwar on the western coast of India, where the East India Company maintained a small factory. Kidd's goal was to obtain wood and water, but the stop proved more eventful than that. Nine of Kidd's men deserted, two of whom marched into the factory and told the company's agents there that they had left Kidd because "he was going upon an ill design of piracy," and they wanted no part of it. The deserters also informed the agents that Kidd had captured an English vessel (the *Mary*), and had forcibly taken aboard Captain Parker and an interpreter. Even more alarming, the deserters said that Kidd planned to attack Mughal ships.

The agents sent two emissaries to gather more information from Kidd, and to try to get him to release Parker and the interpreter. But Kidd forcefully "denied that he had any such persons onboard" (in fact, he had hidden them "in a hole" below decks). When the emissaries returned, their observations of Kidd and his unruly crew convinced the agents that Kidd had indeed turned pirate, and they shared their conclusion with their superiors in Bombay. The agents noted that both Kidd's unusual commission, and his great strength, "being a very lusty man," had early on "procured respect and awe" from the crew, but his penchant for "fighting with his men on any little occasion," and threatening to shoot anyone who dared contradict him, had caused his men to "dread him," and become "very desirous to put off their yoke." But by the time they had penned these words, Kidd had departed, hoping to quell the growing dissatisfaction among his crew with a capture of a valuable prize.

For the next few months, Kidd conducted a fruitless search for potential victims, and his men continued to simmer and stew over their lack of success. The *Adventure Galley*'s gunner, William Moore, was particularly upset that Kidd had not let the men take an East India Company ship they had encountered after ransacking the *Mary*. One day, Moore was grinding a chisel when Kidd, a strong man with a quick temper, walked over and accused the gunner of questioning his decision to leave the company ship alone. Moore said he had done no such thing, whereupon Kidd called Moore "a lousy dog," to which Moore responded, "If I am a lousy dog, you have made me so; you have brought me to ruin, and many more." Infuriated, Kidd bellowed, "Have I ruined you, ye dog?" Kidd paced back and forth a few times, and then grabbed a wooden bucket held together with iron bands, swinging it down on Moore's head and fracturing his skull. As the stricken gunner was brought below for the surgeon to tend to him, Kidd yelled after him, "You are a villain!" By the next morning, Moore was dead. A few months later, when talking to the surgeon about Moore's death, Kidd expressed little concern about repercussions, boastfully asserting, "I have good friends in England that will bring me off for that."

Three weeks later, one of Kidd's men spied a sail on the horizon, and the pirates began pursuit. When the *Adventure Galley* finally came up to the ship, some nine hours later, a warning shot brought it to a halt. The *Adventure Galley* was flying a French flag at the time, a common ruse used by mariners to flush out potential enemy ships, and Kidd was hoping that this display would get the other ship's captain to show his hand. As it turns out, the ship, the *Ruparell*, captained by Michael Dickers, was a Dutch-owned vessel. When Dickers boarded the *Adventure Galley* and went below to the captain's cabin, he was greeted by one of Kidd's French crewmen, who asked to see Dickers's papers. Like most merchantmen sailing in dangerous waters, Dickers kept many different types of passes on his ship to deal with different contingencies. Thinking that the *Adventure Galley* was, in fact, French, Dickers handed over his French pass, expecting that it would protect him. As soon as the papers changed hands, Kidd stepped forward and gleefully exclaimed, "By God, have I catched you? You are a free prize to England."

The *Ruparell* was rechristened the *November* by the pirates, and its relatively paltry cargo of foodstuffs and fabric was sold at a nearby Indian port, providing Kidd with a small amount of cash that he distributed to his weary and still grumbling crew. Over the next two months, the *Adventure Galley*, towing the *November* behind, attacked two more small merchant ships, adding little to their wealth.

Then, on January 30, 1698, Kidd used the French-flag ruse once again to ensnare the *Quedah Merchant*, a four-hundred-ton ship filled to the brim with fabrics, opium, sugar, iron, and saltpeter worth between 200,000 and 400,000 rupees, the equivalent of about £25,000 to £50,000. As soon as the *Quedah Merchant*'s captain, English-man John Wright, handed over his French pass, Kidd claimed the ship as a prize. When Kidd boarded his new acquisition, the *Quedah Merchant*'s supercargo, or representative of the owner, offered him 20,000 rupees to set the ship free, but Kidd, backed by the vote of his crew, turned him down, claiming that the cargo was worth far more than that. Kidd retained the *Quedah Merchant*, but sold part of its cargo at a nearby Indian port, netting roughly £8,000, which was shared with his men, while numerous bales of goods in the hold were kept for future sale.

In the following months, the *Adventure Galley* took three more small vessels, stripping them of their cargo. With the *Adventure Galley* now in sad shape, and in need of careening and repairs, Kidd and his men sailed it, along with the *Quedah Merchant* and the *November*, to Madagascar, arriving at St. Marie over a number of weeks in April and May 1698. There, Kidd encountered an old associate from their privateering days in the Caribbean, Robert Culliford, the captain of the *Resolution*, which was anchored in the harbor. Culliford and his crew were well-known pirates who had been operating in the Indian Ocean for some time. This made Culliford wary of Kidd, who he knew had a commission to hunt for pirates. Culliford feared that Kidd had come to take him and his men as prisoners. But Kidd put Culliford's mind at ease, telling him that he "was as bad as they," and that before Kidd would do him any harm, he "would have my soul fry in hell-fire." Then they drank rum punch to celebrate their reunion.

Kidd stayed at St. Marie for many months, and during that time divided the loot among his crew and decided to abandon the leaky and decrepit *Adventure Galley*. He turned the *Quedah Merchant* into his flagship, giving it a new name, the *Adventure Prize*. About one hundred of Kidd's men, hoping to net more treasure, switched allegiance and signed on to Culliford's crew, leaving with him in June for another pirate voyage.

Toward the end of 1698, accompanied by a meager crew of twenty, and a handful of slaves, Kidd headed to the Caribbean. A rude surprise awaited him on the island of Anguilla in early April 1699. About five months earlier, James Vernon, King William III's secretary of state, had issued a proclamation declaring Kidd and his men pirates, and demanded that they be apprehended at all costs.

The impetus for this dramatic action came from the East India Company, and for good reason. The company was still reeling from the Henry Avery affair, and the captures of the *Fath Mahmamadi* and the *Gang-i-Sawai*, when Kidd appeared, roiling the waters of the Indian Ocean yet again. The *Quedah Merchant*, far from being a French ship, was leased to a member of Emperor Aurangzeb's court, and other high-ranking court officials had taken out shares in the voyage. When news arrived that an English vessel, with a commission from the king no less, had plundered another Mughal ship, the wrath of the Aurangzeb came down once again on the East India Company. In a repeat of the Avery affair, company officials were imprisoned in their factories until reparations were paid, and further commitments made to provide protection for Mughal ships. The company, in turn, demanded that the English government act swiftly and resolutely against Kidd, resulting in the call to seize him and his men. And to emphasize the enormity of Kidd's plight, the king also issued a blanket pardon to all pirates who had committed acts of piracy in the Indian Ocean, if they surrendered themselves before April 30, 1699—the hope being that with a pardon in hand, the pirates would not return to their former ways. Two pirates, however, were exempted from the blanket pardon—Avery and Kidd.

The noose was tightening, and Kidd, a wanted man, feared that there was no safe place for him in the Caribbean, a view that was reinforced when the Dutch governor of St. Thomas refused to grant him protection. His only option, he thought, was to travel back to New York, where he hoped his supporter Bellomont, now governor, would save him. But first, he needed a new ship since the *Adventure Prize* was leaking badly.

Fortuitously, after leaving St. Thomas, Kidd ran across a local merchant named Henry Bolton, who not only sold him the sloop *Saint Antonio*, but also found buyers for some of the goods Kidd had accumulated. These transactions took place while the *Adventure Prize* was lashed to trees at the mouth of a river at the eastern end of Hispaniola. Kidd, and those of his men who wanted to continue on, transferred their treasure and belongings to the *Saint Antonio*, and then headed north. A significant amount of goods remained on the *Adventure Prize*, which was left in Bolton's care, with Kidd promising to return for the ship and the goods within three months.

By June, the *Saint Antonio* was moored off of Oyster Bay, Long Island, and over the next few weeks Kidd cruised between Long Island Sound and Narragansett Bay. In the meantime, he sent emissaries to Lord Bellomont, then in Boston, to negotiate on his behalf. Kidd's version of events, as presented to Bellomont, was decidedly self-serving and selective. Kidd claimed that he never acted contrary to his commissions. He admitted to taking only two ships—the ones with French passes—and said that was done by his men against his will, and that when he tried to return the ships to their rightful owners, his men imprisoned him in his cabin, threatening to murder him. He asserted that his men had mutinied on St. Marie and left him en masse to join Culliford. He had £10,000 with him, he said, and had left another £30,000 of goods on the *Adventure Prize* in a safe harbor in the West Indies. Such relatively paltry amounts must have come as quite a shock to Bellomont, given that the rumors preceding Kidd's return had excitedly claimed that he brought with him treasure worth as much as £400,000. To help prove his story, he sent the two French passes to Bellomont, and he pleaded with the governor to grant him a pardon, promising that if he did, Kidd

Map of Long Island, New York, circa 1679.
An arrow identifies Gardiners Island.

would bring the *Saint Antonio* and its treasure into Boston, and also retrieve the *Adventure Prize* from the Caribbean.

Bellomont wrote to Kidd, telling him that if all he said was true, the governor didn't doubt that he could obtain a royal pardon, and also receive help in fitting out his ship so that it could retrieve the *Adventure Prize*. This was enough of an assurance for Kidd, and at the end of June he headed for Boston. But before starting this journey, he and a few of his men deposited a significant amount of their treasure—gold bars, bags of silver, and bales of cotton and silk fabric—on Gardiners Island, off the tip of Long Island, asking John Gardiner, the island's owner, to keep the items safe until they returned. Still other valuables were lodged with a few of Kidd's friends who had connected with him while he hovered off the coast.

In Boston, Kidd met with Bellomont and the provincial council on a number of occasions, telling his story and defending his actions. When asked to write down a narrative of his voyage, he repeated in much greater detail the outlines of what he had earlier described to Bellomont through his emissaries, with a few new twists added. Instead of claiming that the two ships with French passes were taken against his will, Kidd simply presented those captures as legal prizes. He also added colorful detail to the events at St. Marie, averring that he had urged his men to capture Culliford and his crew of pirates, but they had refused, saying that "they would rather fire two guns into him [Kidd] than one into the other [Culliford]." After his men supposedly mutinied, Kidd maintained that they took a great many guns and supplies from the *Adventure Prize* and repeatedly threatened to murder him. So fearful was Kidd for his life, he averred, that he barricaded himself in his cabin each night, placing heavy bales of calico behind the door and distributing throughout the room some forty pistols, loaded and primed, and ready for shooting should anyone try to break in. Kidd also claimed that Culliford's men went to Edward Welch's house, which was four miles inland, where Kidd had placed his locked chest for safekeeping. The pirates broke open the chest and took from it "ten ounces of gold, forty pounds of plate [silver], [and] 370 pieces of eight," along with the daily journal Kidd had kept during the voyage. Predictably, Kidd's tale made no mention of the time he had spent pursuing the Mughal convoy leaving the Red Sea, or of the other ships he had captured or attacked during his trip.

Even if Bellomont believed Kidd's story—and it appears he didn't, later declaring that he "quickly found sufficient cause to suspect him very guilty, by the many lies and contradictions he told me"—the governor really didn't have any other option than to arrest him. After all, the Crown had labeled Kidd a pirate and ordered his arrest, and to disregard that would have been political suicide for Bellomont. His situation was made stickier still by the fact that he was one of the sponsors of Kidd's venture. That connection was already threatening Bellomont's reputation as a fierce adversary of piracy, which he had built up during his years as governor. Arresting Kidd could, he undoubtedly thought, help diminish that threat. Finally, there was the money to consider. As one of Kidd's sponsors, Bellomont had a stake in the £40,000 that Kidd claimed he had brought back. If Kidd were innocent of piracy or pardoned, Bellomont would get a relatively small share of the treasure, perhaps as little as £1,000 after paying off his debts. But if Kidd were arrested as a pirate, Bellomont, as vice admiral of the colony, would be eligible for one-third of the valuables, a calculus that most certainly factored into his decision to arrest Kidd on July 6 and have him thrown in jail.

The king was thrilled when he heard the news that Kidd was captured, and he sent a ship to Boston expressly to collect the infamous pirate. It wasn't until April 1700, however, that Kidd arrived in London, along with a few of his men, and scores of other prisoners and alleged pirates. Also on the transatlantic trip was all of Kidd's treasure that Bellomont could track down, including the items that Kidd left on Gardiners Island, which added up to about £14,000. As for the riches that were supposed to be on the *Adventure Prize* in the Caribbean, Bellomont sent a ship to find them, but it had no success. The *Adventure Prize* had been burned, and whatever wealth it contained had long since disappeared. Despite his most fervent hopes, Bellomont would never benefit from any of Kidd's treasure, since the governor died on March 5, 1701.

Even before Kidd arrived back in London, his case had become the focus of a battle royal between the Whig and the Tory factions of the government. Bellomont was a Whig, as were Kidd's other high-level backers, and when their scheme was launched, the Whigs were ascendant. But by the time of Kidd's capture and return to England, the Whigs were much weakened, and the Tories gleefully used Kidd's supposed turn toward piracy as a means of pummeling their political opponents, hoping to hang Kidd's purported transgressions around their necks. The animus made for some bruising rhetorical battles as well as a contentious failed vote to censure the Whigs. In the end the Whigs survived, bloodied, and only slightly bowed. Nevertheless, the Whigs knew that there would have to be an ultimate reckoning, and they hoped that placing Kidd on trial, and having him convicted, would put the controversy to rest. As staunch Whig Secretary of State James Vernon wrote a few years earlier, "Parliaments are grown into a habit of finding fault, and some Jonah or another must be thrown overboard, if the storm cannot otherwise be laid. . . . Little men are certainly the properest for these purposes." And Kidd was, in Ritchie's words, "a very little man."

The wheels of English justice ground slowly in Kidd's case, and it was more than a year before he finally came to trial. For most of that time he remained locked up in Newgate Prison, a particularly horrific place that one early eighteenth-century observer called "a habitation of misery . . . a bottomless pit of violence, a Tower of Babel where all are speakers and no hearers." In this hellhole, with only the barest of essentials, and in nearly continuous solitary confinement, Kidd's health rapidly deteriorated.

On May 8 and 9, 1701, Kidd was tried in the admiralty court for the murder of gunner Moore, and for multiple piracies, including the taking of the *Quedah Merchant* and the *Ruparell*. On the murder charge, Kidd claimed that his men were on the verge of mutiny, and that he was provoked into lashing out at Moore, the ringleader of the uprising. "It was not designedly done," Kidd said, "but in my passion, for which I am heartily sorry." And because he killed Moore in an unpremeditated manner, Kidd argued that at most he was guilty of manslaughter, not murder.

During the trial for piracy, with respect to the taking of the *Quedah Merchant* and the *Ruparell*, Kidd contended that although both ships had French passes, and were, therefore, legitimate prizes, he had tried to give them back after discovering their Mughal connections, but his men had voted him down. Kidd's ability to prove that the ships were legitimate prizes was severely compromised, however, since the passes, which Bellomont sent to London, had mysteriously vanished. Kidd had requested that they be delivered to him multiple times so that he could prepare his defense, but he was told they were nowhere to be found. As it turns out, the passes were rediscovered in the early twentieth century in the records of the Board of Trade, but why they had been hidden so long, and how they got there, remains a mystery. Some have claimed that the passes were deliberately withheld, perhaps by a Whig politician, to ensure Kidd's guilt. While that is certainly possible, even if Kidd had possessed the passes, it is unlikely that the outcome would have changed. Kidd was tried for other piracies as well, and for those the evidence provided by some of his crew, who had turned state's evidence, was powerful and damning.

In the end, Kidd was found guilty of both murder and piracy and sentenced to be hanged, along with six of his men who were also

Cover page for "The Trial of Captain William Kidd," a booklet that was eagerly read by the public, which was fascinated by his story.

THE
Arraignment, Tryal, and Condemnation
OF
Captain William Kidd,
FOR
MURTHER
AND
PIRACY,
Upon Six feveral Indictments,

At the Admiralty-Seffions, held by His Majefty's Com-
miffion at the *Old-Baily*, on *Thurfday* the 8th. and *Friday* the 9th.
of *May*, 1701. who, upon full Evidence, was found Guilty,
receiv'd Sentence, and was accordingly Executed at *Execution-
Dock*, *May* the 23d.

AS ALSO,
The TRYALS of *Nicholas Churchill*, *James Howe*, *Robert
Lamley*, *William Jenkins*, *Gabriel Loff*, *Hugh Parrot*, *Richard Barlicorn*,
Abel Owens, and *Darby Mullins*, at the fame Time and Place
for PIRACY.

Perufed by the Judges and Council.

To which are added,
Captain *KIDD*'s Two Commiffions:
One under the Great Seal of *ENGLAND*, and the Other under
the Great Seal of the Court of *Admiralty*.

LONDON:
Printed for *J. Nutt*, near *Stationers-Hall*. 1701.

found guilty of piracy.* After hearing the final verdicts, Kidd spoke to the court. "My lord," he said, "it is a very hard sentence for my part. I am the innocentest person of them all, only I have been sworn against by perjured persons."

On May 12, in a last-ditch effort to delay his date with death, or possibly gain a pardon, Kidd sent a petition to Robert Harley, the Tory Speaker of the House, offering a deal. He claimed that there was £100,000 worth of treasure and goods on the *Adventure Prize*, which was still at Hispaniola, just waiting to be retrieved—apparently, he hadn't been told that the ship had been burned, and that whatever treasure it might have held was long gone. Furthermore, Kidd, said

---

* Five of those men were later pardoned by the king.

that he wanted the Crown to "have the benefit of" that magnificent sum, which was a healthy increase from the £30,000 he had mentioned to Bellomont. All the government needed to do was outfit a ship and bring him along as a "prisoner" to provide directions. If he failed to produce the bounty, Kidd would ask for "no favor but to be forthwith executed according to" his sentence.

Kidd's gambit was ignored, and on May 23 he was taken in a horse-drawn cart from the prison to Execution Dock. Huge crowds lined the streets and followed the three-mile procession to get a glimpse of him. The gallows was set up between the high- and low-water mark, the traditional spot for pirates to be hanged because it highlighted that the crime had taken place within the admiralty's jurisdiction.

Kidd had been drinking rum earlier in the day, and when he reached the gallows in the late afternoon he was drunk. In his final speech he heaped blame on everyone except himself. His former crewmembers who had testified against him were liars, and much of their supposed evidence was merely hearsay. The supporters and initiators of the venture had turned on him, and had "been instrumental in his ruin!" The death of gunner Moore was unintentional. Having vented his spleen, Kidd shifted course, growing somber as he "expressed [an] abundance of sorrow for leaving his wife and children without having the opportunity of taking leave of them[.] . . . [T]he thoughts of his wife's sorrow at the sad tidings of his shameful death was more occasion of grief to him than that of his own sad misfortunes."

At six in the evening, with a noose around his neck, Kidd was sent to meet his maker, but instead he hit the ground. The rope had broken. According to Paul Lorraine, the priest at Newgate Prison, this unexpected reprieve and jarring fall shook Kidd back to his senses, and when the hangman grabbed him and placed another noose around his neck, Kidd experienced a last-minute conversion, "declaring openly that he repented with all his heart, and died in Christian love and charity with all the world."

This time the rope held. Kidd's limp body remained in place

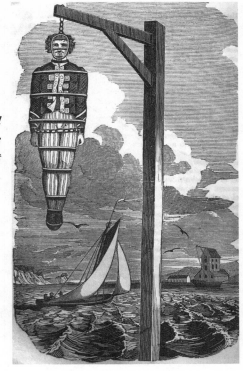

Captain William Kidd
hung in an iron cage
at Tilbury Point
(1837 engraving).

long enough for three tides to wash over him, a symbolic ablution to take away his sins. Afterward, the body was taken to Tilbury Point, twenty-five miles downriver, near where the Thames exits to the sea. Slathered in tar and encased in an iron cage so as to prolong the display of the body, Kidd was dangled from a gibbet.* There he remained, a ghoulish specter, slowly disintegrating for many years as a silent warning to all mariners who passed by.

Although Kidd most certainly committed piracy,† one can't help

---

* A wooden post or gallows-like structure from which the body of an executed criminal was hung for all to see.

† In many instances, determining whether someone was or was not a pirate is a creative exercise in perspective and judgment. In a Rashomon-like manner, different people can interpret the same event in a different manner. When it comes to piracy, this is even more of a problem since the "facts" are often in dispute, with different witnesses or observers claiming that things did or did not happen, or that one interpretation is more

but feel sorry for him, and think that he was, perhaps, treated worse than might otherwise have been the case had things played out differently. With access to the French passes, it is possible that he could have successfully defended himself against the most serious charges of piracy with respect to the *Quedah Merchant* and the *Ruparell*, leaving him with only a few other acts of piracy that were relatively minor in the scheme of things. As for the murder charges, if the court had accepted his contention that he had killed Moore in a fit of passion, and, thereby, was guilty only of manslaughter, that would have lightened the sentence. And had he not been caught up in such a heated political battle, and earned the enmity of the Aurangzeb, the powerful East India Company, and the English government, he might not have become the "Jonah" of this story.

Kidd's depredations in the Indian Ocean and his trial were widely covered and discussed in England and the American colonies, giving him a notorious celebrity. But it was the rumors of his magnificent stores of buried treasure that made Kidd one of the most mythic characters in the history of piracy. With some claiming—wildly inaccurately, of course—that Kidd had plundered treasure worth as much as £400,000, many people assumed that he must have hidden the bulk of it in some out-of-the-way place, since only a fraction of that amount was ever recovered. That belief has fueled a flood of fantasies of finding the treasure that began even before Kidd was hanged at Wapping, and which have persisted to the present day, transforming Kidd into a legend.

---

correct than another. This is certainly true with the Kidd case. Some historians believe that Kidd was not a pirate at all, and that if he did commit piratical acts it was because his men forced him into it, and, in fact, he had in some instances stood up to his men and kept them from committing even more piracies. I do not agree with that analysis, and instead believe the version that I have presented, a perspective that is also shared by other historians. But, even if Kidd were innocent, and the trial a travesty of justice, it would not change the course of the narrative for this book, because that is driven by how the Kidd case played out, and how Kidd's actions were perceived by the relevant actors—especially the English government—at the time. For an excellent analysis of Kidd's case that concludes that he was not a pirate, and that he was treated unfairly by the court, which relied on biased or one-sided testimony, please see Richard Zacks, *The Pirate Hunter: The True Story of Captain Kidd* (New York: Hyperion, 2002).

Although Gardiner family legend claims that Captain William Kidd buried some of his treasure on Gardiners Island, there is no evidence that he did so. Contemporary documents indicate that John Gardiner simply held the treasure, assuming that Kidd would return for it one day. Nevertheless, the legend has persisted, and it influenced Howard Pyle, who created this 1921 image of Kidd overseeing the burial of the treasure on the island.

THE KIDD AFFAIR AFFECTED the course of American piracy in a few ways. Kidd's attack on the *Quedah Merchant* and the *Ruparell* threatened the East India Company's very existence, making Kidd a potent symbol of the company's precarious position on the Indian subcontinent. The company used Kidd's symbolic power to lobby the English government to take steps to curtail piracy in the Indian Ocean, and, therefore, help to protect the company's position. But it wasn't only Kidd's actions that fueled the company's efforts. The Avery affair, along with all the attacks by other Red Sea Men, contributed to the company's desire to fight piracy.

One of the company's major concerns was Madagascar's critical role in supporting pirates and serving as a launching pad for their raids. The company realized that the pirate haunts on Madagascar, especially St. Marie, were supplied primarily by slave traders from the American colonies. If that trade could be curtailed, or eliminated, the pirates would suffer, and their numbers would most likely decline. To that end, the company was instrumental in the passage of the East India Act of 1698, a law that reinstated the company's recently lapsed monopoly on *all* trade east of the Cape of Good Hope. And unlike in the early 1690s, when the company and the English government paid scant attention to the Madagascar slave trade, now they focused on it with laser-like intensity. In short order, the pipeline of slaves from Madagascar to the colonies was shut off, and so too was one of the pirate's most valuable connections to the outside world. And if American merchants had any thoughts of violating the monopoly, a cluster of business failures erased them. In July 1698 four ships left New York heading to Madagascar, but only one returned. Pirates captured two, and an armed company vessel took the other. These major losses made New York merchants eager to seek other, less dangerous, trading opportunities. Thus, in late 1700 Bellomont noted that the illegal trade "from Madagascar seems to be at a stand at present."

Another East India Company priority was getting the government to send a naval squadron to the Indian Ocean to protect company and Mughal shipping from pirates. The company had first requested that such a force be sent after Avery's attacks, but nothing was done. Kidd's depredations convinced the government to take action, and the squadron was ultimately dispatched in the spring of 1699, with orders not only to offer pardons to those pirates who surrendered, but also to attack those who did not.

By the end of the year, the directors of the East India Company expressed cautious optimism, claiming, "We have great reason to believe piracy is now at an end in the East Indies." The directors' optimism, however, proved to be premature. Piracy in the Indian Ocean would continue well into the first few decades of the new century, as the pirate haunts on Madagascar slowly diminished to insignificance. But even though piracy in the Indian Ocean would continue for a number of years, by 1700 the American contribution to it was virtually nonexistent.

Finally, Kidd's exploits helped convince parliament to pass the Act for the More Effectual Suppression of Piracy because his actions provided further proof of the desperate need to clamp down on piracy in the American colonies. Many of Kidd's men had been recruited in New York, and many ultimately made their way back to the colonies, where they were often welcomed and protected by the locals.

THE CROWN'S AND PARLIAMENT'S multifaceted attack on piracy in America coincided with and was spurred on by shifts in England's economy. At the turn of the eighteenth century, England was coming into its own as a major world power with extensive colonial holdings that fed its rising economic might. As pirates became a growing threat to England's development and dominance, the government, with its powerful merchant class urging it on every step of the way, increasingly fought back to protect its position, implementing measures to defeat the pirates. And since the American colonies were the wellspring for so much piratical activity, it made sense that they would also be a primary target for remedial action.

No single element of the government's battle against piracy had a decisive impact, but in combination they achieved significant success. The aggressive antipiracy posture of the Board of Trade, the appointment of pirate-fighting governors, the stepped-up naval presence off the American coast and in the Indian Ocean, the passage of new laws to suppress piracy, the pardons, the mass shipment of pirates to London for trial, and the elimination of the Madagascar slave trade, all contributed to a decline in American piracy shortly after the dawn of the eighteenth century.

This decline was not yet apparent in June of 1700, when a government official from Virginia reported to the Board of Trade that "all the news of America is, the swarming of pirates not only on these coasts, but all the West Indies over, which doth ruin trade ten times worse than a war." At the same time, Governor Joseph Blake of South Carolina observed, "The sea [is] now so abounding with them [pirates] that a ship cannot stir for them in this part of the world." But by the end of the year, the situation had changed. In late 1700, Governor Bellomont observed that piracy "is in its wane." And George Larkin, the man that the Board of Trade sent to the colonies to teach them how to conduct a piracy trial under the new law, told the board in October 1701, "I don't hear of any pirates that have been lately upon these coasts."

While top-down government policies did diminish piracy, attitudes on the ground were less malleable. Many politicians, merchants, and colonists who had, in effect, been weaned on the fruits of piracy, and who had long welcomed pirates into their midst as respected members of the community, were not quite ready to share the central government's disdain for this class of men. As a result, pirates, especially those with money, could still find many safe havens in America. According to one observer, in 1700 a half-dozen pirates were hanged in South Carolina "because they were poor," while five other pirates who were in the colony at the same time were free to walk about in public, and "were not molested in the least," because they were wealthy, each having large quantities of gold and silver coins, as well as many precious jewels. Larkin told a similar tale. After seeing two of Kidd's men living freely in Pennsylvania, he wrote to the Board of Trade in December 1701, "These fellows have been hugged and caressed after a very strange manner by the Religious people of those parts, no money to be seen amongst them now but Arabian Gold." And as proof that "pirates are esteemed very honest men" in many of the colonies, he observed that "the President of the Council of New Hampshire, Secretary of the Province and Clerk of the inferior Court, is going to marry his daughter to one of these villains."

Around the same time that Larkin was making these comments, the general peace that had reigned since the signing of the Treaty of Ryswick, which ended the Nine Year's War in 1697, was about to be shattered. In 1702, England would be engulfed in another war that would, like the last one, greatly affect the course of piracy in America.

CHAPTER 5

War's Reprieve

*A Dutch painting, circa 1705, titled "Naval Battle of Vigo Bay,
23 October 1702. Episode from the War of the Spanish Succession."
In this battle, an Anglo-Dutch fleet destroyed or captured more
than thirty French and Spanish ships.*

THE WAR OF THE SPANISH SUCCESSION, CALLED QUEEN ANNE'S
War in the colonies, had many belligerents, but in the main it pitted
England (which would become Great Britain after the union with
Scotland in 1707), the Dutch Republic, and the Holy Roman Empire

against France and Spain. Between 1702 and 1713, when the war ended, American piracy simply was not a salient issue. The official correspondence between the colonies and the mother country, which in earlier years had been rife with alarming stories about piracy, was suddenly almost silent on the subject. The main reason for this was the war itself, and the fact that it provided potential pirates with legal and fairly well-paying forms of employ utilizing their nautical skills. Many former and would-be pirates were sucked into the Royal Navy, which ballooned from about twenty thousand men in 1701 to nearly fifty thousand by the war's end, and where a seaman's average salary was roughly double what he could earn during peacetime. Others found their niche on one of the more than 1,600 privateering vessels that were commissioned, and which held out the alluring possibility of great riches with a few impressive captures.

Although there were a few scattered reports during the war about pirates embarking from the colonies, or plundering along the American coast, only one noteworthy and well-documented case of piracy took place. It originated in the small Massachusetts fishing town of Marblehead.

IT WAS AN OMINOUS note that merchants John Colman and William Clarke read on Wednesday afternoon, August 1, 1703. Lieutenant John Quelch, the second in command on the brigantine *Charles*, had just ridden a hard twenty miles from Marblehead to Boston to deliver the missive, which came from the *Charles*'s commander, Daniel Plowman. In it, Plowman said that his physical condition was getting "worse and worse," and that he didn't think he could proceed. He implored Colman and Clarke—two of the *Charles*'s owners—to come to Marblehead early the next morning, so "that we may take some speedy care in saving what we can." How, Colman and Clarke wondered, could things have gone so terribly wrong?

The project seemed like such a good investment when it was launched months earlier. Hoping to capitalize on the war, which they viewed as a brilliant business opportunity, Colman and Clarke, along with three other prominent Boston merchants, pooled their resources and decided to outfit the *Charles* as a privateer. To that end, they asked Joseph Dudley, the governor of Massachusetts and New Hampshire, to issue a letter of marque, giving Plowman permission to attack enemy ships off Acadia and Newfoundland.

Dudley obliged on July 13, 1703. Plowman now had carte blanche to "fight, take, kill, suppress and destroy, any pirates, privateers, or other subjects and vassals of France, or Spain." If Plowman was successful, any vessels, money, or goods that he seized from the enemy were not to be distributed to his men or backers until after an admiralty court judged the enemy ship and its contents a lawful prize. Plowman also had to maintain a journal detailing his actions, which would help the court determine whether Plowman had acted in accord with his commission.

Little is known about the *Charles*, other than it was a newly built eighty-ton brigantine. Dudley called it "perfectly fitted for service," and it was likely seventy to eighty feet long, and had ten or so cannons onboard, along with a great variety of smaller arms.

With the commission in hand, Plowman sailed the *Charles* from Boston to Marblehead to provision for the voyage and fill out the ship's forty-five-man roster. Not long after, Plowman fell ill. His rapid decline is what prompted him to send Quelch to Boston on August 1 with that worrying note, which, in turn, spurred Colman and Clarke to ride to Marblehead with Quelch the very next day.

One of the leading fishing communities in America, Marblehead was a hard-drinking, rough-edged place full of profane, independent-minded, and irreligious people. Most of Marblehead's 1,200 residents made their modest living in the coastal waters of Massachusetts, or on the Grand Banks, fishing for cod. Evidence of their toil was displayed on the numerous wooden platforms called fish flakes near the water's edge, where the gutted, filleted, salted, and splayed cod baked under the sun until they were rock hard and ready to be shipped across the Atlantic to be sold in markets throughout Europe.

The *Charles* was too large to pull up to one of the town's wharves,

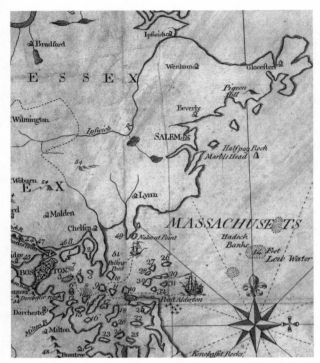

Detail from a 1775 map showing the town of Marblehead, located along the coast between Boston to the southwest and Gloucester to the northeast. The heavily indented shoreline of Marblehead can be seen just to the south of Salem.

so it rode just offshore, its men and materials ferried to and fro by smaller boats. After arriving in Marblehead, Colman and Clarke sent word to Plowman that they were eager to meet, but the stricken commander responded through one of his crew that he could not see them since he was "very weak." He urged them to immediately send the *Charles* to Boston, where, he said, everything must be offloaded "in order to prevent all manner of embezzlements. . . . [T]he sooner your things are landed on shore, the better." He beseeched them not to hire a new commander and let the ship sail, because he ominously warned "it will not do with these people," meaning the crew. Although canceling the trip would lose the merchants money, Plowman argued that that was better than having the trip proceed, a course that would, he was certain, "in three months" time result in "all [being] totally lost."

Unfortunately, there is no record of Colman and Clarke's reaction to Plowman's distressing and enigmatic communication, nor do we know what they said to the crewman who delivered the note, or if they sent further instructions to Plowman. And one wonders why Colman and Clarke didn't simply board the *Charles* to discuss the situation face-to-face with Plowman, who despite being ill could still presumably talk. Whatever was said or done, the merchants soon departed for Boston, likely to confer with their partners, while aboard the ship a majority of the crew decided to mutiny and become pirates.

Plowman was locked in his cabin, a marlinspike holding the door shut, and a sword-wielding crewman was placed on guard. Quelch wasn't aboard when the mutiny was launched, but when he returned to the brigantine, he did not object, and in fact willingly assumed command.

On August 4, the *Charles* sailed from Marblehead. Two days later, Plowman was either killed or died of natural causes—the record does not indicate which—and his body was unceremoniously pitched over the side. Crewmembers Mathew Pymer and John Clifford, not wanting to be part of the illicit venture, begged to be set ashore, but their pleas were ignored.

Soon after the *Charles* left, the owners began to worry, and then their worry quickly turned to alarm. Assuming that the *Charles* was heading to the West Indies, they sent an open letter to governors in that region on August 18, 1703, telling them that they believed that Captain Plowman was dead, and that the men of the *Charles* had mutinied, "which," they said, "makes us fear that their design is not to do justly by us." The owners enclosed a letter from Governor Dudley, which expressed the same concerns, and both letters asked local officials to secure the *Charles* and any prizes it might bring in, if the ship entered one of their ports. But the owners' assumption was wrong. The *Charles* was heading much farther south, to Brazil.

BRAZIL, THEN A PORTUGUESE colony, had been chosen as a destination because of its wealth and the sorry state of its coastal defenses. At the end of the 1600s, vast alluvial gold deposits were discovered in the state of Minas Gerais in southeastern Brazil, precipitating a gold rush of epic proportions. Word of these finds filtered back to the American colonies, and the men of the *Charles*, confident that they would meet with little resistance, hoped to get their share of the riches by pillaging ships transporting the precious metal from port to port, and back to Portugal.

The *Charles* arrived off the coast of Brazil in early November, and between the fifteenth of that month and February 17, 1704, Quelch and his men plundered nine Portuguese vessels ranging in size from small fishing boats to a two-hundred-ton ship. Goods seized included sugar, rice, rum, ceramic dishes, fish, salt, cloth, coins, cannons, gunpowder, and a 112-pound bag of gold dust—all told, estimated to be worth £10,000.

During this run, the *Charles* stopped at a couple of Brazilian ports for provisions, where Quelch told the locals that they were hunting for French and Spanish prizes, even though that was clearly not their intent. The men of the *Charles* had no doubt that they were looting Portuguese ships. Not only had they brought on an interpreter in Brazil who could speak both Portuguese and English, but they also found Portuguese flags, documents, and coins onboard the vessels they plundered.

The captures were fairly uneventful, with a couple of exceptions. For two days the *Charles* chased the largest ship, which fired off its cannons three times before striking its colors and allowing the pirates to board. An altercation ensued, and the ship's captain, a man named Bastian, was shot and killed by one of the *Charles*'s men. Bastian's black slave was then taken from the ship, as were a variety of goods. On one of the smaller prizes, a white man, originally from Jutland (now Denmark), decided to jump ship and join the *Charles*. But when he demanded that Quelch give him an equal share of the booty, the crew, not being in a sharing mood, voted to set him ashore with a gun and some powder and shot.

With the captures off the Brazilian coast, the men of the *Charles* officially became pirates. Nearly three months before the *Charles* left Marblehead, Portugal and England had signed a treaty, becoming allies in the fight against the French and the Spanish. Accordingly, the *Charles*'s attacks on Portuguese ships were in fact attacks on an English ally—an even riskier enterprise, given the tenuous relationship between European powers, and the punitive measures available to monarchs.

After the last capture, in mid-February, the *Charles* sailed home. Quelch was well aware of their predicament, and the illegality of their actions, which is why he decided to cover their tracks. In the vicinity of Bermuda, he gathered the crew on the main deck, telling them that if anyone in New England asked them where they got their treasure, especially their gold, they were to say that they had "met with some Indians [in the Caribbean] who had got a great treasure out of a wreck," and they took it from them. Quelch also ripped out six pages in the *Charles*'s journal, which covered its time off the coast of Brazil, and he ordered that all documents with Portuguese writing be thrown overboard.

THE FIRST NOTICE OF the *Charles*'s return was rather innocuous and optimistic. "Arrived in Marblehead," announced the *Boston News-Letter* in mid-May 1704, "Capt. Quelch in the brigantine that Capt. Plowman went out in, are said to come from New-Spain & have made a good voyage." Once ashore, Quelch immediately rode to Boston to meet with Colman and Clarke. He arrived bearing bags full of coins and gold dust, and with a fanciful story to tell. The coins and gold dust was the owners' share of the loot, and the story was the same Quelch had told his crew. Clearly, Quelch thought that by paying off the owners, they would not ask too many questions and be content with a good return on their investment. Colman and Clarke took the valuables but were very suspicious of the story, and soon after Quelch left, his account of events began to unravel.

Of course, the owners were predisposed not to trust anything Quelch said, given that he had left Marblehead nine months earlier without informing them, and that, contrary to the original privateering plan, he had gone south, not north. Further eroding their trust was Quelch's admission that much of the rest of the booty had been distributed to the crew, and those crewmembers had gone their separate ways. This ran counter to the normal procedure for a privateer, which was to have their prizes (vessels), as well as any plunder taken from them, adjudged by an admiralty court to determine the appropriate disposition of the captured property.

Once Colman and Clarke began investigating Quelch's improbable story, any trust they may have had in him completely evaporated, in large part because of his and his men's almost comical sloppiness in covering their tracks. Despite Quelch's admonition to his crew to dispose of any Portuguese documents, when Colman and Clarke searched the *Charles*, they found a number of them onboard. Not only that, but there was at least one Portuguese flag, as well as a bag of sugar with Portuguese instructions on it, stating that it should be delivered to a merchant in Lisbon. And most of the coins Quelch had given to Colman and Clarke were Portuguese. The merchants also discovered that during his initial trip to Boston, Quelch had visited the silversmith John Noyes, who melted down a significant quantity of Quelch's coins into ingots. What better way for a pirate to hide his money?

Now, quite certain that Quelch and company had engaged in piracy, and fearing that they would be judged accomplices if they didn't come forward, Colman and Clarke visited Isaac Addington, secretary of the Massachusetts Bay Colony, on May 23, and submitted a sworn statement that read in part: "By what we have observed of the management of the present commander and company; as also by what we find onboard the said vessel moves us to suspect that they have plundered and made spoil some of her majesty's friends and allies, contrary to her majesty's declaration of war, and the commission and instructions given them."

Governor Dudley was in New Hampshire at the time, but in his absence Lieutenant Governor Thomas Povey sprang into action. That same day, Quelch and six of the crew were arrested, and the following day Povey issued a proclamation published in the *Boston News-Letter*, which listed the names of thirty-four other crewmembers who, Povey said, were suspected of being pirates, and should be apprehended by any means possible.

On May 26 Povey received a report from Rhode Island stating that five of Quelch's men had purchased a small boat four days earlier with the intention of heading to Long Island. Povey asked Samuel Cranston, governor of Rhode Island, to apprehend them. Cranston issued warrants for their arrest, but only one of the men was taken, who was then sent "from constable to constable" to Boston. About the same time, a few other crewmembers were captured in Massachusetts.

On May 29, Governor Dudley, having returned from New Hampshire, issued his own proclamation, which reiterated much of what Povey's had said, but added that confessions elicited from some of the suspects had made it clear that piracy and murder had been committed against the subjects of Portugal. Dudley also warned that any person who harbored or in any way assisted the wanted men, or concealed any of the treasure, would be considered an accessory and punished to the full extent of the law.

On June 7 Dudley dispatched a three-man commission to hold a court of inquiry in Marblehead with the goal of tracking down additional crewmen and their treasure. The commission's most prominent member was fifty-two-year-old Harvard-educated Samuel Sewall, the acting chief justice of the Superior Court, who was among the wealthiest men in the colony. He had been one of the judges in the 1692–93 Salem witch trials, which had found more than thirty people guilty of witchcraft, nineteen of whom were subsequently hanged. One other person, Giles Corey, also lost his life as a result of the witch hysteria. After his wife, Martha, had been convicted for witchcraft and sentenced to hang, Giles refused to answer the judges' questions about his possible connection to witchcraft, choosing instead to remain silent in an attempt to maintain the integrity of his last will and testament, which he feared would be invalidated if he entered a plea and was found guilty. To force him to plead either guilty or not guilty, the judges—following the letter of the law in cases in which the accused refused to speak—ordered

*Judge Samuel
Sewall, circa 1728.*

Giles to be "pressed." To that end, he was placed in a shallow pit in a field, with a wooden door laid upon his chest, and then rocks were piled on the door. Slowly, the weight crushed the life out of him, but still he did not utter a word. Finally, after nearly two days of this agonizing torture, Giles Corey took his last breath.*

Over time, Sewall's central role in the witch trials became a great burden on his soul, and in a truly courageous act, he later apologized, taking the "blame and shame" for sending innocent people to their death. In yet another singularly honorable and historic act, Sewall penned *The Selling of Joseph, A Memorial*, in 1700, the "first pamphlet condemning African slavery and the slave trade in North America."

On their way to Marblehead, Sewall and the other commissioners stopped overnight in Salem, where they heard a rumor that a couple

---

* Many accounts claim that Giles Corey uttered the words "more weight" when the law enforcement officials implored him to speak and claim his guilt or innocence, but there is no evidence that he ever said that, or anything else, during his ordeal. It seems clear that the "more weight" story is just that, a story or legend with no basis in fact.

of Quelch's men were on Cape Ann planning to join well-known privateer Captain Thomas Larrimore on his *Larrimore Galley*, and by that means make their escape. Acting on this information, at around midnight the commissioners issued a warrant to search for the men.

Early on June 8 the commissioners rode the last few miles to Marblehead in driving rain. They set up their court of inquiry by the fireside at Captain John Brown's house, where they proceeded to take testimony from the locals. At six the next morning the commissioners were awoken by the breathless arrival of an express rider from Cape Ann, who told them that the previous night between nine and eleven "pirates, double-armed" had been "seen in a lone house there."

This news set off a call to arms across the region. The commissioners issued warrants instructing militias throughout the county to head to the Cape Ann town of Gloucester to capture the pirates. To that end, Justice Sewall's brother, Major Stephen Sewall, departed Salem on the fishing shallop* *Trial*, accompanied by a smaller pinnace and about twenty militiamen, while another group of militia sailed from Marblehead with Paul Dudley, the governor's son and the colony's attorney general, aboard.

Meanwhile, Justice Sewall and one of the other commissioners rode to Salem, where they took an affidavit from Francis Gahtman, the former surgeon on the *Larrimore Galley*. Gahtman said that he had strenuously warned Larrimore against harboring Quelch's men, telling him that if he did so, it would be in violation of the governor's proclamation, thereby making him as "guilty of piracy" as the men he was protecting. Larrimore didn't care, and according to Gahtman, told him to "mind [his] own business and be gone." When Gahtman tried to get help in bringing Quelch's men to the local authorities, one of Larrimore's men pummeled him with "five blows," and then dragged the surgeon onto the *Galley*, telling him to stay put. But Gahtman was able to sneak ashore, and he rode to Salem to alert the authorities.

After finishing the affidavit, Sewall, accompanied by the Essex

---

* A workboat designed to navigate shallow waters.

County sheriff and local militiamen, began the seventeen-mile ride from Salem to Gloucester. Their numbers swelled along the way with the addition of militia from Beverly and Manchester (now Manchester-by-the-Sea). As this impressive force approached Gloucester, a messenger rode up with disquieting news. The *Larrimore Galley* had sailed that morning, and many of the men aboard were pirates.

Discouraged, Justice Sewall and company pushed on to Gloucester, and after his brother arrived, they all repaired to Captain Davis's house to dine while considering their next move. They ultimately resolved to go after the *Larrimore Galley*, but there was a major problem with the plan—nobody was willing to take the lead in this admittedly risky and dangerous expedition, and without a leader, nobody wanted to follow. Finally, Major Sewall offered to captain the fishing shallop *Trial*, and then forty-two men quickly signed on.

Shortly after sunset on June 9, the men aboard the *Trial* gave the commissioners on shore "three very handsome cheers," before departing Gloucester Harbor, towing the pinnace behind. Local intelligence indicated that the *Larrimore Galley* was sailing for the Isle of Shoals, about twenty-five miles to the north, and that is where the *Trial* headed.

Justice Sewall remained in Gloucester for the night, and the next morning visited his sister-in-law—Major Sewall's wife, Margaret—in Salem before his return trip to Boston. She was quite unnerved by her husband's mission. According to the justice, "the wickedness and despair of the company they pursued, their great guns and other warlike preparations, were a terror to her," and she concluded that these vile men, the pirates, "would not be taken without blood."

JUST A FEW HOURS before Justice Sewall called upon his sister-in-law, Major Sewall was laying a trap off the Isle of Shoals. Even before he saw the *Larrimore Galley* in the distance, Sewall ordered all of his men to lay down on the main deck with their muskets and swords by their sides. Therefore, the only men visible as the *Trial* came within sight of the *Larrimore Galley* were the four fishermen who worked on the shallop. Sewall's plan was to get right next to the *Larrimore Galley* before Larrimore could discover what was happening.

But there would be no surprise. As the *Trial* approached his ship, Larrimore sensed trouble. He quickly ordered his men to prepare for action, whereupon they took the lead aprons off the touchholes of the galley's guns, and pulled the tompions* out of their muzzles.

Seeing this, Sewall ordered his men to stand, guns at the ready, while at the same time he yelled to Larrimore to come aboard. The privateer refused, so Sewall got into the pinnace and boldly rowed over to the *Larrimore Galley* with a few of his men to parley. What transpired is not known, but Sewall must have been sufficiently persuasive, because Larrimore, his men, and the suspected pirates gave up "without [Sewall's men] striking a stroke, or firing a gun." Sewall also recovered forty-five ounces of gold dust from Quelch's men. The next day, Sewall brought the *Larrimore Galley* back to Salem, where seven of Quelch's men, along with Larrimore and his lieutenant, were hauled to jail.

On the way back to Salem, Sewall dropped off a contingent of Gloucester militiamen, who informed the local populace that two of the suspected pirates were in the vicinity, and should be apprehended. The citizenry went on the alert, and according to the *Boston News-Letter*, "being strangers and destitute of all succors, . . . [the men] surrendered themselves" on June 12, and were sent to the Salem jail. Five days later, Major Sewall, "attended with a strong guard," brought all nine suspected pirates to Boston's jail. To show their gratitude, Massachusetts's officials awarded Sewall and his fellow officers £132 for their valiant service.

In the end, only about half of the *Charles*'s crew was captured— the rest simply disappeared, along with their cut of the loot. Shortly after Sewall brought in his prisoners, the trial of Quelch and company began.

---

* Wooden plugs placed in the muzzle of a cannon or mortar to keep out dust and moisture.

GOVERNOR DUDLEY CONVENED the nineteen-person High Court of the Admiralty on June 13 at Boston's Town House, which served as the city's town hall and the colony's seat of government. This was a momentous occasion, being the first such trial to take place in the colonies under the recently passed Act for the More Effectual Suppression of Piracy. At their arraignment, three men who had been aboard the *Charles*—Mathew Pymer, John Clifford, and James Parrot—pleaded guilty to "piracy, robbery, and murder," and were then "received into the Queen's mercy" so that they could be witnesses on behalf of her majesty. Next, Quelch and twenty of his men were accused of the same crimes, to which they all pleaded not guilty.

The trial began on June 19, and by the 21st it had ended. Attorney General Dudley led the prosecution, while James Menzies, an equally distinguished jurist, represented the accused. The damning particulars of the *Charles*'s voyage were laid out in great detail, and Quelch, along with eighteen others, was found guilty and sentenced

Conjectural drawing of Boston's First Town House, which served as the seat of government between 1657 and 1711, when a fire destroyed it. Quelch and company were tried here.

Cover of
The Arraignment, Tryal,
and Condemnation of
Capt. John Quelch,
And Others
of His Company,
*published in London
in 1705.*

THE
Arraignment, Tryal, and Condemnation,
OF
Capt. John Quelch,
And Others of his Company, &c.
FOR
Sundry *Piracies, Robberies,* and *Murder,* Committed upon the Subjects of the King of *Portugal,* Her Majefty's Allie, on the Coaft of *Brafil,* &c.

WHO

Upon full Evidence, were found Guilty, at the *Court-Houfe* in *Bofton,* on the Thirteenth of *June,* 1704. By Virtue of a Commiſſion, grounded upon the Act of the Eleventh and Twelfth Years of King *William, For the more effectual Suppreffion of Piracy.* With the Arguments of the QUEEN's Council, and Council for the Prifoners upon the faid Act.

PERUSED

By his Excellency *JOSEPH DUDLEY,* Efq; Captain-General and Commander in Chief in and over Her Majefty's Province of the *Maffachufetts-Bay,* in *New-England,* in *America,* &c.

To which are alfo added, fome PAPERS that were produc'd at the Tryal abovefaid.

WITH

An Account of the Ages of the feveral Prifoners, and the Places where they were Born.

LONDON:
Printed for *Ben. Bragg* in *Avemary-Lane,* 1705.
(Price One Shilling.)

to be hanged. Two of the individuals originally charged, a young cabin boy, and Plowman's clerk, who had been deathly ill most of the voyage, were deemed not guilty. Larrimore and his lieutenant, who were not part of the trial, were later shipped to England as accessories to the piracy, but what became of them is not known.

During the trial, Menzies pointed out a number of potential problems with the case, including the claim that Pymer, Clifford, and Parrot should not have been allowed to testify because they hadn't in fact officially received the queen's pardon, and were, therefore, accomplices, and not competent to serve as witnesses. Menzies also argued that it was against the law to find all the defendants guilty of murder when only a single individual committed the act (the identity of that individual was not 100 percent clear, since there was disagreement among the crew, but the weight of the evidence implicated the brigantine's cooper, Christopher Scudamore). While there might have been irregularities in the trial—a point with which even some of the members of the court of admiralty seemed to agree—there is no doubt that Quelch and the others were in fact guilty of piracy.

THE EXECUTIONS WERE SET for June 30. In the meantime, the condemned men languished in Boston's dank and gloomy jail, but were hardly left alone with their thoughts. Daily visits by Cotton Mather, as well as other ministers, punctuated the monotony, as they acted on their fervent belief that their holy duty compelled them to pray with the men, and cajole or persuade them through their religiously fueled pronouncements to repent for their sins, and thereby gain entry into the Kingdom of God.

Mather was a highly learned and somewhat pompous man who sought fame and rarely missed an opportunity to capitalize on the

Mid-nineteenth century engraving of Cotton Mather, after painting by Peter Pelham, 1728.

notoriety of dramatic public events. And he sincerely believed what fellow theologian George Bull had said—that "the minister's tongue is a chief tool and instrument of his profession." So, Mather not only shared his message of repentance with the condemned pirates, but also with his 1,500-person congregation, the largest in New England. On the Sunday after the trial concluded, he delivered a sermon full of fire and brimstone—a type of address that would come to be known as an execution sermon, which used the story of those doomed to hang to convince the living to mend their evil ways. "Will our merciful God at last sanctify these displays of his vengeance [pirate executions]," Mather pleaded, "that never any more of them that see or hear these things, may after this, go to *get Riches & not by Right*. Let all people *hear & fear*, and never do thus *wickedly any more!*" He also landed a blow against privateering, and in the process, gave a rationale for why Quelch and his men might have veered into wickedness. The "privateering stroke," Mather argued, "so easily degenerates into the piratical," in large part because privateering is "carried on with so unchristian a temper, and proves an inlet unto so much debauchery, and iniquity, and confusion." To ensure that his message reached the widest audience, Mather published the sermon. Its sale not only earned Mather money but also gave his words a touch of immortality. "Sermons preached," Mather dryly observed, "are like showers of rain, that water for an instant; but sermons printed, are like snow that lies longer on the earth." By that measure, Mather produced a veritable blizzard, publishing 388 works during his lifetime, many of which were transcribed sermons.

Governor Dudley ultimately decided that only seven men would be executed, while the rest, whom the governor called "young and ignorant fellows," were referred to the queen for clemency, and were later pardoned. Dudley failed to state the reason for his leniency, but there seems little doubt that his decision was politically motivated, and was designed to allay the anger of those who believed either that Quelch and his men were in fact privateers, and should never have been prosecuted, or that, even if they had committed piracy, their crimes should have been overlooked on account of the treasure they brought back to the colony, which at the time was suffering through another currency crisis. As Dudley noted in a letter to the Board of Trade, there were many "rude people, who were greatly surprised that any body should be put to death that brought in gold into the province, and [they] did at the time speak rudely of the proceeding against [the pirates] . . . and assisted to hide and cover those ill persons."

The attitude of Dudley's "rude people" illustrated that when it came to balancing the needs of the colony against the dictates and laws of the Crown, for many, the colony's needs were paramount. And this episode, like so many others recounted in this book, shows how the immediate reality of life in America meant more to some colonists than the abstract notion of an overseas monarch ruling over a government that didn't give the colonies a voice in determining their own future. It could even be argued that colonists' support of piratical behavior was another sign of the burgeoning of a distinct American community, finding its voice and coalescing around economic factors.

On Friday, June 30, the seven condemned men, their hands bound behind their backs, marched the three-quarters of a mile from the jail to Scarlet's Wharf, on the edge of Boston Harbor. They were accompanied by Mather and fellow minister Benjamin Colman, and guarded by forty armed musketeers, as well as town constables and the provost marshal—an impressive force that Dudley felt was necessary given the passions aroused by the trial. At the head of the procession, the marshal of the admiralty court proudly held aloft a two-foot mace made of silver and in the shape of an oar, the august symbol of the court and British naval authority. Throngs of spectators lined the streets and ran after the marchers, jeering and cheering, and lending a circus-like atmosphere to the otherwise grim proceedings.

At the wharf, the condemned, along with many officials, boarded boats that took them to the gallows at Hudson's Point, near where the Charles River flowed into the harbor, and just below Broughton's Hill (modern-day Copp's Hill, the location of the Copp's Hill Burying Ground). Justice Sewall was "amazed" to see that there were as many as 150 boats and canoes on the river, packed with passengers, and even more people lining the hill.

Executions had been taking place in New England since 1623, and typically generated intense public interest. They were often seen as a time for the community to come together, and for friends and relatives to travel from near and far to witness the spectacle, reconnect, and share news with one another. They always brought out large crowds, but the multitude that showed up on this warm June day was a record breaker, and for good reason. On April 24, 1704, less than a month before the *Charles* returned to Marblehead, Boston postmaster John Campbell launched the *Boston News-Letter*, the "first continuously published newspaper in America."* Consisting of only one sheet of paper, printed on both sides and issued once a week, the *News-Letter* spread information more effectively and rapidly than word of mouth did, creating a much broader shared sense of community than had previously existed. But to succeed, the paper needed copy that people wanted to read, and what could be better than a story involving piracy? From the announcement of the *Charles*'s return, up until the day of the executions, the *Boston News-Letter* covered the events as they unfolded. The gubernatorial proclamations, the pursuit of Quelch's men, and the results of the trial, were all there, providing a dramatic saga that generated excitement and anticipation. Although most of the observers were Bostonians, plenty of out-of-towners were also in attendance, including Sewall's cousin Moody who had come down all the way from York, Maine.

It was low tide when the boats with the prisoners arrived at the place of execution. A pungent aroma scented the air, a mixture of human sewage—delicately called night soil—which was daily dumped at the harbor's edge, and decaying fish left behind

---

* The very first newspaper in the American colonies, and the only one to precede the *Boston News-Letter*, was called *Publick Occurences, Both Foreign and Domestick*, which was also published in Boston, but there was only one issue, appearing on September 25, 1690.

by fishermen who had offloaded their catch at nearby wharves. The seven men were helped up the ladder to stand on the gallows' narrow wooden stage, nooses dangling by their side from the crossbeam above. Just before making his ascent, Quelch told minister Colman, "I am not afraid of death; I am not afraid of the gallows, but I am afraid of what follows. I am afraid of a great God, and a judgment to come." Upon reaching the stage, Quelch showed a jauntier side, doffing his hat and bowing to the audience.

Silence was called for, and then Mather stood up and steadied himself in a boat just offshore to begin his sermon, his final shot at redeeming the pirates' souls. "We [the ministers] have told you often, yea we have told you weeping, that you have by sin undone yourselves . . . we have shown you how to commit yourself into his saving and healing hands," and how to express repentance. "We can do no more, but leave you in his merciful hands!" Mather also had a message for those watching, since execution sermons were not only aimed at the condemned, but also, and even more importantly, at the public, who were in Mather's eyes sinners as well. "Great GOD," he intoned, "grant that all the spectators may get good by the horrible spectacle that is now before them!" And to the "seafaring tribe," in particular, he hoped that the execution would cause them to be "saved from the temptations, which do so threaten them! So ruin them!"

On the heels of Mather's sermon word came down that the governor had dramatically reprieved one of the condemned at the last moment, Francis King, who now, most thankful and penitent, was escorted from the gallows and returned to jail. Dudley was undoubtedly moved to take this step by the same calculation he had made in referring many of the convicted pirates to the queen for clemency. And like the others, King, too, was later pardoned by her majesty.

The remaining six men were each given a chance to address the crowd. A few were remorseful, and asked for forgiveness, with one exclaiming, "Lord, what shall I do to be saved?" Another bitterly commented, "It is very hard for so many men's lives to be taken away for a little gold." Quelch questioned whether justice was done.

John Bonner's 1722 map of "The Town of Boston in New England."
Hudson's Point, where pirates were hanged, is located at the far right of
the map, just to the right of the words "Ferry to Charles-Town."

"Gentlemen," he said, "I desire to be informed for what I am here, I am condemned only upon circumstances." And when another of the men warned the crowd to "beware of bad company," Quelch yelled, "They should also take care how they brought money into New England, to be hanged for it."

Speeches over, the nooses were put in place. "When the scaffold was let to sink," Sewall wrote in his diary, "there was such a screech of the women that my wife [Hannah] heard it sitting in our entry next [to] the orchard, and was much surprised by it." The noise must have been loud indeed, since Sewall's house was a mile away.

Nobody recorded what happened to the men after the ropes went taut. It is unlikely that they fell far enough, fast enough to have their necks broken, leading to a relatively quick death. Instead, like most people who were hanged, they probably died of asphyxiation, as the tightening of the rope around the neck cut off the airway and blood flow from the carotid arteries, depriving the brain and body of oxygen. In that situation, the person remained conscious for a short time, during which the legs would spasmodically kick, a characteristic movement that was variously called "the marshal's dance," "dancing to the four winds," or "dancing the Tyburn jig"— Tyburn being a village just outside of London where for centuries local criminals had been hanged. Witnessing such gyrations was often too painful for the friends or relatives of the person being hanged, and they would rush forward and "pull the dying person by the legs, and beat his breast, to dispatch him as soon as possible." If the person was not assisted in his journey out of this world, and instead left dangling, he might last for quite a few torturous minutes before expiring.

In the aftermath of the hangings, a budding poet from Salem composed light verse to commemorate the event.

> *Ye pirates who against God's laws did fight,*
> *Have all been taken which is very right.*
> *Some of them were old and others young*
> *And on the flats of Boston they were hung.*

Massachusetts's officials were quite pleased with the trial and its outcome, especially since it gave them an opportunity to erase some of the lingering doubts harbored by the Crown about the colony's commitment to fighting piracy. "We crave leave," the Massachusetts Provincial Council wrote to her majesty Queen Anne, "also humbly to express our just resentment and detestation of the piracies and robberies lately committed by Capt. Quelch and company, and we hope the speedy justice that has been done upon those vile criminals will vindicate the government from the imputation of giving any countenance to, or favoring of such wicked actions."

As for the treasure, the governor confiscated quite a bit from the captured pirates, a few citizens voluntarily turned in illicit money they had received, and the owners of the *Charles* were forced to relinquish their shares. But much of the treasure was never recovered. A considerable amount was taken by the crewmembers who escaped justice, and even those who didn't likely offloaded some of their loot before being captured.

About £750 of the reclaimed treasure was used to cover the costs of imprisoning, trying, and hanging the pirates, and rewarding those, like Major Sewall, who had gone after the *Larrimore Galley*. Governor Dudley sent the remaining treasure, roughly 788 ounces of gold, to London. There, it was brought to the famed mathematician, physicist, and astronomer Sir Isaac Newton, who was serving as the Master of the Royal Mint, a position he had eagerly sought after a long and distinguished scientific career. Newton assayed the gold, finding it to be much contaminated with iron, yet still worth an impressive £3,164, the bulk of which ultimately went to paying off war debts.

THE TRIAL OF QUELCH and his men signaled an important change in the fight against piracy. Armed with the newly minted Act for the More Effectual Suppression of Piracy, and bolstered by a renewed Crown determination to bring pirates to justice, Massachusetts had launched a blistering salvo in the war against pirates. But that war still had a long way to go. A few years after the Treaty of Utrecht was signed on April 11, 1713, bringing the long and bloody War of the Spanish Succession to an end, piracy came roaring back, unleashing a wave of panic upon the American coast and forcing the colonies and the Crown to battle back on multiple fronts. The pirates who instigated this explosion of marauding were quite different from their predecessors, the Red Sea Men, both in the targets they chose and their impact on the colonies.

CHAPTER 6

Interlude, or a
Pirate Classification

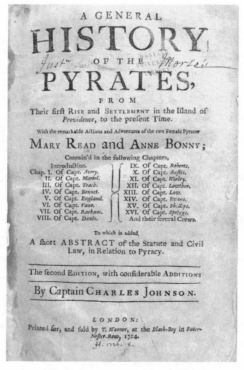

Title page for the second edition of Johnson's A General History of
the Pyrates, *1724 (the full title of the first edition, published earlier the
same year, was* A General History of the Robberies and Murders of
the Most Notorious Pyrates). *This book, more than any other,
created the popular image of pirates.*

EVERYONE KNEW IT WAS COMING. WELL BEFORE THE CON-
clusion of the War of the Spanish Succession, British government
officials, merchants, and citizens feared that the ensuing peace would
result in an outbreak of piracy, and that privateering would be the
main culprit. While privateering gave England greater firepower,
it also raised the prospect of increased piracy at war's end, when
it was expected that many of the suddenly unemployed privateers,
unwilling to abandon a life of relative freedom and the potential for
great profits, would become pirates—a troubling transition that had
occurred in so many previous conflicts that it seemed to be an immu-
table law. As William Bignall, deputy postmaster of Jamaica, noted
in January 1708, "It is the opinion of every one [that] this cursed
trade will breed so many pirates, that when peace comes we shall be
in more danger from them than we are now from the enemy."

This fear was amplified with the passage of the Prize Act of 1708,
which was designed to increase the number of privateers by altering
the economic benefits of pursuing that line of work. In the early
years of the war, the Crown took 10 percent of whatever a privateer
captured. The Prize Act made privateering even more alluring by
eliminating the Crown's cut, leaving all the profits to be distributed between the officers, crew, and the backers of the venture. As
an added emolument, in those instances where a privateer captured
a man-of-war, a £5 bounty was awarded for every man aboard the
enemy ship.

The Act worked brilliantly, and the number of privateers grew, as
did the concerns of those who looked to the future. In 1709, Edmund
Dummer, the surveyor general of the British Navy, raised the alarm.
He informed the Board of Trade that he had received "great complaints" from officials and merchants in the Caribbean "against" the
Prize Act. They argued that it was "ruining all trade with the Spanish West Indies" because the crew of merchantmen and men-of-war
were jumping ship to sign on as privateers, drawn to that service
by the prospect of a big payday. More ominously, the complainants

worried that when peace came, the Act would have served only to "leave to the world a brood of pirates to infest it."

Additional concerns centered on what would happen to the navy men put out of work by the peace. During the war, the British Royal Navy had bulked up to a muscular fifty thousand–strong fighting force, yet within two years of signing the Treaty of Utrecht, the navy shed more than thirty-six thousand men, raising the specter that some of those idled mariners, lacking alternative job prospects, would turn to piracy.

Such worries about unemployed privateers and navy men were well founded. After the war, many did become pirates, but not immediately. For a couple of years there was only a minor increase in piracy because commerce, especially in the Caribbean, boomed once hostilities ceased, thereby creating employment opportunities for unemployed mariners who were absorbed into the crews of the expanding merchant fleet.

This peaceful and prosperous situation, however, soon changed. Despite the peace treaty, the Spanish *Guarda Costa* (Coast Guard) and Spanish privateers launched an aggressive campaign that harassed and seized numerous British merchant ships operating out of Jamaica, often falsely accusing them of transporting contraband. Many British seamen were put out of work, and more than a few of them were briefly dumped in Spanish jails, where they were terribly abused. With the British Crown unable or unwilling to intervene, this produced a growing body of furious, dispossessed, impoverished mariners with bleak prospects for the future. Even on the remote chance that they could find another job on a merchant ship, with so many out-of-work mariners prowling Port Royal's wharves, it was a buyer's market. Therefore, those few merchants who were hiring could get away with offering paltry wages that were less than half what navy seamen got during the war, adding to the anger on the waterfront, and making it a breeding ground for would-be pirates.

Small-scale insurrection was another reason that piracy surged a few years after the peace treaty was signed. Samuel Johnson, famed British essayist, biographer, and literary critic, observed, "No man will be a sailor who has contrivance enough to get himself into jail; for being in a ship is being in a jail, with the chance of being drowned. . . . [And] a man in a jail has more room, better food, and commonly better company." Johnson wasn't being tongue-in-cheek, and in fact there is plenty of evidence that the sailor's life could be quite miserable even under the best of circumstances, with a stern yet fair captain. But when a tyrannical captain—who led by fear, intimidation, and the liberal use of corporal punishment—was in charge, being a crewmember was truly a living hell. Many sailors in this position chose not to endure, but to rebel. By one estimate, "at least thirty-one mutinies erupted on merchant ships during the 1710s and 1720s," and about half of those mutinous crews became pirates. As an early eighteenth-century antipiracy tract asserted, one of the main reasons seamen gave for mutinying and turning pirate was "the too great severity their commanders have used both as to their backs and bellies." This corrosive dynamic is what the pirate William Fly, whose story opened this book, claimed had led him and his men to mutiny, pointing to the captain's "barbarous usage" as the proximate cause. And that is why Cotton Mather, in lecturing his congregation on the eve of Fly's execution, specifically addressed the masters of vessels, urging them to "not be too like the *Devil*" in treating their crew, so as not to "lay them under *temptations* to do *desperate things*." As a pirate captain from the late 1710s told a gathering of his peers, "Their reasons for going pirating were to revenge themselves on base merchants, and cruel commanders of ships."

A devastating disaster also fueled the upturn in piracy. During the final years of the war, the traditional Spanish treasure fleets had been unable to make their annual journeys across the Atlantic, resulting in the accumulation of a vast backlog of money and goods sitting in warehouses at Spanish American ports. This led to a corresponding economic crisis in Spain, a country on the verge of bankruptcy. Further delays after the war meant that it wasn't until May 1715 that the long-awaited fleet of eleven ships, commanded by Captain-General Don Juan Esteban de Ubilla, finally sailed from Havana bound for Cádiz. Onboard these ships were jewels, coins, ingots, and exotic goods from the Orient worth an estimated seven million pieces of eight. Accompanying the fleet was a lone French ship, *Le Grifon*, carrying cargo for Havana's governor.

Early on July 30 the fleet was hugging Florida's east coast, not far from modern-day Vero Beach, when the sun disappeared behind billowing black clouds, the wind started howling, and mounting waves began pitching the ships about like corks. As the hurricane intensified, according to one of the sailors who survived the tempest, "It was so violent that the water flew in the air like arrows, doing injury to all those it hit, and seamen who had ventured much said they had never seen the like before." By the following morning, the entire fleet had been destroyed, the ships' backs broken as they were dashed against the jagged reefs or run ashore. Only *Le Grifon*, which had sailed farther out to sea, survived the tempest. More than one thousand men, roughly half of the entire complement, lost their lives, with the battered survivors struggling to swim ashore and haul themselves onto the beach. Wreckage from the fleet was strewn over thirty miles of ocean and sand.

News of the disaster quickly spread in ever-widening circles throughout the Atlantic. The image of gold, silver, and jewels carpeting the ocean floor fed thousands of fantasies, and led to a rush of mariners sailing to the Florida coast to recover some of the booty. Alexander Spotswood, the lieutenant governor of Virginia, excitedly wrote to the king in October 1715, alerting him to the opportunity and urging him to encourage his subjects to capitalize on the situation by "attempt[ing] the recovery of that immense treasure." The mania that took hold was particularly acute in Jamaica, where the captain of a British Navy frigate complained that many of his men were "mad to go wrecking," and as many as five sailors a day were deserting the ship, thinking that "they have [the] right to fish upon the wreck[s], although the Spaniards have not quitted them." The hemorrhaging of his crew was so great that the captain feared that soon he would not have enough men to sail the ship home. Despite Spain's herculean salvage efforts, some interlopers succeeded in extracting riches from the seafloor, or violently wrestling them from Spanish salvors.

Whether successful or not, many erstwhile treasure hunters decided to continue their search for loot by becoming pirates.

Another, less obvious, factor contributing to the postwar rise of piracy was the concerted attack on logwood cutters. For decades Englishmen, and a smattering of Frenchmen and Dutchmen, had lived on the Yucatán Peninsula, along the edge of Campeche Bay and the Bay of Honduras, where they harvested logwood, also known as bloodwood (*Haematoxylum campechianum*). A rather scraggly, leguminous tree that thrives in coastal forests, logwood has dark red heartwood that produces a dye capable of coloring fabrics a deep black or purple. Demand for these rich hues was so great among the European aristocracies that a ton of logwood commanded as much as £100 in the early 1700s.

The loggers, called Baymen, were former seamen, more than a few of whom were drawn from the ranks of pirates and buccaneers. Baymen were a constant irritant to the Spanish who claimed this entire region as their own. The *Guarda Costa* staged periodic raids to disperse the trespassers, with limited success. But after many Baymen descended on the wrecked treasure fleet off the Florida coast, the infuriated Spanish retaliated with an all-out assault that effectively drove the loggers from their jungle lairs. Cut off from their livelihood, many Baymen reverted to their old ways, while others became pirates for the first time: according to one contemporary estimate, an astonishing 90 percent of the dispossessed Baymen turned to piracy.

Piracy also grew by a combination of invitation and coercion. Pirates typically asked the men aboard their victim ships to sign on to the pirate crew, especially when additional hands were needed to operate and maintain the vessel or create a more menacing and effective fighting force. Coopers and doctors were in particularly high demand because of their unique skills, as were so-called "artists," or men proficient in the art and science of navigation. Many of these potential recruits, motivated by poor treatment on the ships from which they came, and dreams of great wealth, willingly volunteered to join the pirates. Others were reluctant or horrified by the thought of turning pirate, and so they were forced to sign on, often with the threat of severe punishment if they refused. Of course, pirates greatly preferred volunteers to forced men, since the former were more likely to be loyal and less inclined to cause trouble. By the same token, many pirates would not force married men to join their crew, fearing that strong attachments to home would increase the chances that the men would be unruly or try to escape.

An exceptionally frightful example of a man being strong-armed to join a pirate ship took place in 1725, when the pirate captain Philip Lyne chose Ebenezer Mower, the cooper aboard the Boston-based *Fancy*, to join his crew on the *Sea Nymph*. After Mower declined the invitation, one of Lyne's men hit Mower over the head with an axe handle. When the bloodied and dazed cooper still didn't consent, the same pirate shoved Mower's head down against the lip of the hatch, raised his axe, and "swore that if he did not sign their articles immediately, he would cut his head off." Rather than carry through on his threat, the pirate dragged the still-reluctant Mower, who was now fervently begging for his life, to the captain's cabin, where additional leverage was applied, the nature of which is not known (although it is hard to imagine anything more terrifying than the threat of having your head chopped off). A short while later, Mower exited the cabin and announced "that he was ruined and undone, for they forced him to sign their articles."

In many instances, forced men asked their former crewmates to place an ad in local newspapers stating that they had been coerced to join the pirates, the hope being that such an affirmation would help with their defense should they ever be brought to trial for piracy. John Daw, a mariner from Newport, Rhode Island, did just this in January 1721. He was a mate on a brigantine anchored off the Caribbean island of St. Lucia when pirates captured his ship and asked him to sign their articles. Daw refused, whereupon the pirates slashed his scalp multiple times with a sword, tied him up in the rigging, and then "whipped him almost to death," while holding a loaded pistol to his head. Asked if he was now ready to sign, Daw again said no, but after another round of abuse, he finally relented. The pirates released the brigantine after plundering it for three days, and when it returned to Newport late that summer, its captain and two of the crew, at Daw's urging, placed an ad in the *Boston News-Letter* that laid out the gruesome details of his ordeal.

No matter what they did before they became pirates, all pirates, with the exception of those who were forced, had to make a conscious decision to pursue this "career" path. For those who chose piracy, the perceived advantages were compelling. As one pirate reportedly said, "In an honest service there is thin commons, low wages, and hard labor; in this [piracy], plenty and satiety, pleasure and ease, liberty and power; and who would not balance creditor on this side, when all the hazard that is run for it, at worst, is only a sour look or two at choking [hanging]? No, a merry life and a short one, shall be my motto." While this man's perspective is a bit too rosy, given the often-harsh realities of the pirate life, there is no doubt that both the actual and imagined benefits of piracy were quite alluring.

With the average pirate ship having roughly eighty men, pirates had far less work to perform, and much more time to relax, than their peers on more thinly manned merchant vessels. And the frequent availability of copious quantities of liquor certainly contributed to the merriment aboard. For some, these two features were more than enough reason to become a pirate, or "go on the account," which was the common terminology for taking up piracy. Consider Joseph Mansfield, who claimed at his piracy trial in 1722 that "the love of drink and a lazy life" were "stronger motives . . . than gold" in drawing him into the pirate life.

But the most tempting benefit of all, and the one that drew most pirates into the fold, was the possibility of riches. Stories of Morgan's and Avery's successes, and the big hauls of a few other pirates, not to mention treasure-laden tales of the old English sea dogs such as Sir Francis Drake, were well known to mariners, and those stories sparked the imaginations and propelled the actions of those who chose to become pirates. But like gamblers who enter a casino full of hope, only to be crushed by the reality of the odds stacked against them, many who began with great expectations quickly discovered that a life of ease and wealth was beyond their reach.

FOR ALL OF THESE reasons, the number of pirates in the Atlantic exploded a few years after the end of the war in 1713, and remained relatively high until the late teens or early 1720s, when the numbers quickly dwindled. By 1726, the traditional marker for the end of the Golden Age of Piracy, there were few pirates to be found. According to the historian Marcus Rediker, "It appears that 1,500 to 2,000 pirates sailed the sea between 1716 and 1718, 1,800 to 2,400 between 1719 and 1722, and 1,000 in 1723, declining rapidly to 500 in 1724, to fewer than 200 by 1725 and 1726." Over this span, Rediker estimates that roughly 4,000 pirates were active. And by pursuing such an ignominious course, they contributed to the most dramatic, intense, and deadly era in the history of American piracy.

These pirates had an enormous impact. One early eighteenth-century chronicler claims that the merchants of Great Britain "suffered more by" the "depredations" of pirates between 1716 to 1726 than they suffered at the hands of France and Spain during the War of the Spanish Succession. And the numbers seem to bear this out. According to the historian Ralph Davis, the total loss of British merchant ships during the war was about 2,000, "and may well have been far greater." Determining the number of ships taken by pirates during this same time span is a little more difficult to assess, but Rediker has produced some reasonable estimates. Based on his review of the historical record, and adding to that an educated guess where data are lacking, he claims that pirates captured and plundered more than 2,400 merchantmen. Of course, Davis's and Rediker's numbers are not directly comparable, since the ships lost during the war were actually lost to Britain, while most of those taken by pirates were only plundered and released. Be that as it may, given that pirates did burn, sink, or commandeer quite a few ships they plundered, and that having one's ships plundered is also a very tangible form of loss, the claim that pirates did more damage to merchant ships than did enemy combatants appears reasonable, or at least plausible. Even if the loss of British merchant ships during the war was as high as seven thousand, as one source claims, the number of ships captured, plundered, and destroyed by pirates is nevertheless quite impressive by comparison.

UNFORTUNATELY, WE KNOW PRECIOUS little about the early lives of the pirates who operated between 1716 and 1726. This is hardly surprising. Only the lives of the wealthy, the wellborn, and the famous were documented at this time, and even in those cases the written trail could be frustratingly brief. For the tradesmen, the small-time merchants and artisans, and even more so the poor, only faint whispers hint at where they came from. And since it is from these lower classes that the vast majority of pirates sprang, their lives before they burst onto the scene because of their crimes are largely terra incognita.

Nevertheless, there are a few markers. Most pirates, having been drawn from the ranks of privateers, and merchant or naval ships, were former seamen. Given the rigors of life afloat, and the wide range of specialized skills necessary to operate a ship of any kind, it makes sense that pirate crews comprised mainly men of the sea, rather than landlubbers who would be out of their element, and wouldn't know a mizzen topgallant sail from a flying jib, or a cat-head from a hawsehole. As to their national origins, more than half of the pirates came from Britain or the American colonies, while various Caribbean countries were also well represented, along with a few other European and African nations.

While little is known about these early biographical details, much more can be said about the men as soon as they became pirates—their adventures memorably imprinting themselves onto history. Although the record is not as rich as one would hope, since pirates of this period hardly left any written accounts in which they revealed themselves, or reflected on the life they led, their motivations, or the nature of their felonious colleagues. Plenty was written *about* pirates, however. What is known has to be pulled from the accounts provided by those who were captured by pirates, trial records, letters to and from government officials in America and Great Britain, and other contemporary sources, such as newspaper articles, jailhouse interviews, and a few pamphlets and books. Of the latter, none is more important than a massive tome titled *A General History of the Robberies and Murders of the Most Notorious Pyrates*, written by Captain Charles Johnson. First published in 1724, and expanded in subsequent years, *A General History* focuses mainly on those pirates who sailed the seas between the late 1710s and the mid-1720s, but also reaches as far back as the late 1600s to the exploits of Thomas Tew and Henry Avery.

For many years it was thought that Daniel Defoe, of *Robinson Crusoe* fame, was the actual author of *A General History*, and that Charles Johnson was just a pen name, but subsequent scholarship strongly points to the mysterious Johnson as being the true scribe. Unfortunately, not much more than his name is known, yet by his command of the language of the sea, and intimate knowledge of pirate customs and activities, he likely was either a seafaring man, or someone who had extensively studied the subjects. It is undeniable, however, that Johnson entirely made up a number of things, added literary embellishments, and took liberties with many of the quotes he ascribed to pirates, especially the ones that are too flowery or filled with unconvincing politically motivated ramblings that seem more like editorials than something a relatively uneducated pirate would say. And, in some instances, he is the only source for certain stories, raising questions about their authenticity. Nevertheless, much of his history is corroborated by the contemporary documents that he clearly used to construct his mini-biographies of the most famous pirates of the day. Johnson has been widely relied on by pirate historians for centuries, and, judiciously used, he is an indispensable source. As historian David Cordingly observed, "It could be argued that Johnson created the idea of a Golden Age [of piracy] by his detailed and vivid account of the lives of those western pirates who were operating" between the end of the 1600s and 1726.

What becomes clear upon evaluating the known sources of information on the pirates of this period (1716–26) is that any analysis of these "banditti of all nations" is data-constrained. In other words, although estimates place the number of pirates in the multiple thousands, most of them are ghosts of history, in that we know virtually nothing about them. This doesn't mean that it is impossible to offer a portrait of them, but rather that one must understand that such a portrait has its limitations. It is also important to point out that despite these limitations, we know much more, on average, about the pirates who operated during this period than we do about those who preceded them. Indeed, it is this former group of pirates who have fueled most of the subsequent literature on piracy, and it is they who are most responsible for the popular image of pirates that exists today.

In light of all these caveats, then, what generalizations are warranted about the pirates who roamed the Atlantic from 1716 to 1726? Most of the known pirates were in their twenties, reflecting an age profile similar to that seen in the merchant service and the Royal Navy. Virtually all pirates were men. The only known exceptions are Anne Bonny and Mary Read, who were part of "Calico" Jack Rackham's pirate crew. There is so little documentation about these two that it is almost impossible to say much about them. From the available fragments, it appears that they typically dressed as men, especially during battle, but their sexual inclinations were more traditional, with Bonny being Rackham's lover, and Read having another suitor aboard. One of the people plundered by Rackham offered an image of the two women in action. They "wore men's jackets, and long trousers, and handkerchiefs tied about their heads; and that each of them had a machete and pistol in their hands, and [they] cursed and swore." The only reason this witness knew that they were women is "by the largeness of their breasts."

Rackham and his crew had a short and relatively unsuccessful run of marauding in 1720 before being captured and brought to justice later that year. Their trials in Jamaica are memorable not only for the multiple hangings that ensued (Rackham included), but even more so for the legal gambit—unique among pirates—used by Bonny and Read. During the proceedings, both women were deemed to have

Anne Bonny (left) and Mary Read (right) in the 1724 second edition of Johnson's A General History of the Pyrates.

eagerly participated in the piratical attacks, often fighting with more relish and resolve than their male counterparts. The court found them guilty of piracy, and they were condemned to hang. Immediately after that sentence was handed down, however, the two women "pleaded their bellies," informing the court that they were pregnant. Upon confirming that this was indeed the case, the court gave both of them a temporary stay of execution.

On the day that Rackham went to the gallows, Bonny made it clear that she was extremely disappointed in her erstwhile lover. By Johnson's telling, "She was sorry to see him there, but if he had fought like a man, he need not have been hanged like a dog." As for the ladies, Reed died in jail from an unspecified illness soon thereafter, and Bonny simply disappeared from the historical record, her fate unknown. However remarkable this case is, it is beyond the scope of this book, since Rackham's piracies took place exclusively in the Caribbean, and had little effect on the American colonies. As far as is known, there were no female pirates during the Golden Age who operated along the shores of the American colonies, or on pirate ships leaving from those shores.

The incomplete records have nevertheless made room for some to speculate on pirates' social lives aboard their ships, often extrapolat-

HISTORIE DER ZEE-ROOVERS.

The title page from the 1725 Dutch edition of Johnson's A General History of the Pyrates. *The bare-chested woman wielding a sword is no doubt a loose representation of either Anne Bonny of Mary Read, whose stories appear in the book. Beneath her feet are images of treasure, wrecked ships, chains, a scale for weighing silver and gold, and Mercury, the god of commerce. Behind her is a pirate flag and pirates hanging from the gallows.*

ing from what we know about the period more broadly. For instance, the existence of an all-male environment aboard pirate ships, and the lengthy periods of time during which these men shared close quarters, has led some to claim that homosexuality was rife among pirates. Indeed, assuming that pirates engaged in sex with other male pirates is certainly reasonable. After all, even though "sodomy," or "buggery" as it was then called, was a hanging offense in the Royal Navy, there were more than a few cases of such relations on naval ships, and those were only the ones where people were caught in the act and reported. Same sex relationships were, of course, not uncommon in the broader society as well. Nevertheless, as historian Hans Turley argued, "The evidence for piratical sodomy is so sparse as to be almost nonexistent." If anything, the record, limited though it is, points to pirates as being testosterone-fueled womanizers who made liberal use of female prostitutes when ashore. This does not mean that pirates didn't engage in sex with other men, but rather that there is no clear evidence that they did—a reflection more on what makes it into the historical record, than historical reality. As Cordingly concludes, "It seems likely that the percentage of pirates who were actively homosexual was similar to that in the Royal Navy, and reflected the proportion of homosexuals in the population at large."

The racial makeup of pirate ships is also subject to the whims of the historical record, though more can be said on this subject, arguably, than the sex lives of pirates at sea. A significant number of black men sailed on most, if not all, pirate ships. But determining their exact roles, and what white pirates thought of them, is very difficult, in large part because when pirate ships were captured, even if there were black crewmembers, they were usually not tried as pirates along with their white peers. Instead, government officials and the broader public viewed them as property and sold them off as slaves, thereby leaving little or no trace of their activities in the trial transcripts or local media coverage.

Profile of a black pirate in Charles Ellms, The Pirates Own Book, or Authentic Narratives of the Lives, Exploits, and Executions of the Most Celebrated Sea Robbers *(Boston: S. N. Dickinson, 1837).*

From the available evidence, however, it seems that many blacks on pirate ships were African slaves taken from captures, who remained slaves and either labored for their new pirate masters, performing low-level tasks such as cooking, or were resold, being viewed as nothing more than human chattel. Such treatment suggests, unsurprisingly, that white pirates, for the most part, harbored the same prejudices as their peers in the broader society, and viewed racial distinctions and divisions in a similar light. As historian Jeffrey Bolster observed, "To many white pirates the majority of blacks were pawns, workers, objects of lust [when pirates had sex with female slaves], or a source of ready cash."

Yet this is only part of the story. Evidence shows that many black pirates—likely a combination of former slaves, escaped slaves, and freedmen—became valued crewmembers who fought alongside their white pirate brethren and shared in the spoils. One analysis of the pirate crews operating between 1715 and 1726 "suggest[s] that perhaps 25 to 30 percent of them were black," but their specific positions onboard, and how they were treated by their white crewmates, is for the most part unknown. Whether white pirates who accepted blacks as crewmembers had a more enlightened and equitable view of their fellow man than their peers, or simply welcomed blacks as readily available and competent force multipliers, is not clear. Either way, "it would seem," as historian Kenneth Kinkor argued, that "the deck of a pirate ship was the most empowering place for blacks within the eighteenth-century white man's world"—although not all the time, and certainly not for all blacks.

Not surprisingly, we don't know a great deal about what pirates looked like, since such details were often left out of the historical record by the pirates themselves, as well as their victims. Still, it seems clear from what is known, that the average pirate dressed in a similar fashion to other sailors of the day. According to historian James L. Nelson, "This would mean loose 'slop trousers' or breeches to the knee, a standard work shirt made out of canvas or calico, a belt, from which a knife could be hung, a neckerchief or bandana draped around the neck or head, a waistcoat or short blue jacket, wool stockings, and a Monmouth cap knitted from wool or a tricorn hat [one that has the brim turned up on three sides, giving it a triangular shape with three points]." In times of battle, pirates would add pistols and swords to their outfit, either hung from their belts or attached to a sash thrown over their shoulder. With respect to footwear, in warmer climes pirates often went shoeless, but when leather shoes were donned, they were typically of the slip-on variety and not laced, for laces were apt to catch on things and add an unnecessary element of maintenance and danger. For added protection from the elements, especially water, pirates frequently coated their outerwear with tar. And whatever pirates wore, their clothes and shoes would become increasingly tattered over time because pirates, like sailors, usually had only one or two outfits, which they used roughly, wearing them around the clock, and washing them infrequently in salt water, since fresh water was such a scarce resource.

Of course, there were many exceptions to the characteristic pirate uniform. All pirates, crewmen and captain alike, could become regular fashion plates when the situation allowed. If plundered vessels happened to be transporting passengers of the upper crust of society, or merely carrying cargo for that class, pirates would eagerly help themselves to the finest garments and jewelry for their own use, either by looting the cargo, or literally stealing the shirts off their wealthy victims' backs. Like Captain Tew, who paraded through the streets of New York in sumptuous clothes and gold necklaces, pirates of this period were happy to dress in a way that signified their success, and as a means of disrespecting the class-based norms of the society of which they were no longer a part.

As for pirates' physical appearance, most of them certainly would have looked quite similar to other mariners of the day. If the pirates were white, long exposure to the sun would result in a deep tan, and for those with darker complexions, they, too, would tan to a deeper hue. Whether the pirates were white, brown, or black, the wind, sun, and salt water would give their skin a leathery, weathered aspect. Facial hair was common, and the hair on the top of their head could be short or long, and, if the latter, it was often tied off in the back. Pirates tended to be on the slimmer side and sinewy, because of both the often-limited quantity of food onboard and the demands of the job. Like other mariners, pirates faced many dangers and suffered many injuries, which is why some had wooden legs, wore eye patches, or were disfigured in other ways (although wooden legs were quite rare, since maneuvering on a ship is difficult enough with two good legs). This being an era of almost nonexistent oral hygiene, pirates, like most everyone else in Western society, probably had crooked, discolored, and often missing teeth—and some might, indeed, have been made of gold. It almost goes without saying, that beyond their physical appearance, pirates undoubtedly smelled quite ripe, another feature they shared with their contemporaries.

AT SEA FOR MOST of their relatively short careers, unmoored from the rigid centuries-old legal codes that structured mainstream society, the pirates who sailed the Atlantic between 1716 and 1726, like the pirates and buccaneers of the seventeenth century, adopted many democratic procedures to guide their actions. Most importantly, the entire crew comprised an informal body, called the common council, which selected the captain by a majority vote. In the same manner it determined when and where they would go to search for prizes, which ships they would attack, and how they would resolve particularly thorny issues not covered by the pirate articles (see below).

Although the captain was unquestionably in charge during the chase and the fighting, his power was not unconditional. He served at the pleasure of the crew, who, if they found him wanting, could vote him out. While captains varied widely, most of them shared certain characteristics, among them being respected by the crew, exhibiting bravery in the heat of battle, and being a skilled mariner. Though the captain typically resided in the captain's cabin, which was the most spacious and comfortable accommodation onboard, he ate the same food as the rest of the men, and if any of them wanted to enter his cabin, swear at him, or dine at his table, they had every

right to do so, since they did not think of themselves as being inferior in any way to the man they chose as their leader.

The crew also elected the quartermaster. Second in command,
he served as both a "trustee" for the crew, and a "civil magistrate" of
sorts. He, not the captain, was the first man to board a prize, decid-
ing how much treasure and goods to take for the company, and how
much to leave behind, if any at all. The quartermaster also managed
the storage and distribution of the loot, determined the fair alloca-
tion of food and liquor, and resolved minor disputes among fellow
pirates. Because of the respect and deference he was accorded, the
quartermaster often was elevated to captain if the sitting one was
killed or voted out. Beyond the captain and the quartermaster, there
were instances in which other officers, gunners, coopers, and boat-
swains were elected to their position as well.

Pirates consented to abide by the articles of agreement, also called
the pirate's code, which was a contract that governed their behavior,
the distribution of treasure, and the compensation provided in case
of injury, the last of which one historian calls their "social security system." To signify allegiance to the code, the pirates signed
their names to the document. The articles of the notorious pirate
Edward Low, who will come into focus later in this narrative, were
as follows:

> 1. The captain shall have two full shares, the [quarter]-
> master a share and a half, the doctor, mate, gunner, carpenter,
> and boatswain, one share and a quarter. [The rest of the crew-
> members got one share.]
>
> 2. He that shall be found guilty of striking or taking up
> any unlawful weapon either onboard of a prize, or aboard the
> privateer [the pirates here referring to themselves as privateers],
> shall suffer what punishment the captain and the majority of
> the company shall think fit.
>
> 3. He that shall be found guilty of cowardice in the time
> of engagement shall suffer what punishment the captain and
> majority of the company shall think fit.

4.   If any jewels, gold or silver, is found onboard of a prize to the value of a piece of eight, and the finder do not deliver it to the quartermaster in twenty-four hours time, [he] shall suffer what punishment the captain and the majority of the company shall think fit.

5.   He that shall be found guilty of gaming, or playing at cards, or defrauding or cheating one another to the value of a royal of plate [one silver reale], shall suffer what punishment the captain and majority of the company shall think fit.

6.   He that shall be guilty of drunkenness in time of engagement shall suffer what punishment the captain and company shall think fit.

7.   He that hath the misfortune to lose any of his limbs in the time of engagement and in the companies' service, shall have the sum of six hundred pieces of eight, and kept in the company as long as he pleases.

8.   Good quarters to be given when craved.

9.   He that sees a sail first shall have the best pistol, or small arm aboard of her.

10.   And lastly, no snapping [firing] of arms in the hold.

All pirate articles contained many of these same elements, but they were not identical. Variations on the theme, as well as unique additions, were common. For example, one set of articles included a provision that attested to the pirates' sense of honor and chivalry. "If at any time we meet with a prudent woman," it said, "that man that offers to meddle with her, without her consent, shall suffer present death." Another pirate code illustrated the lighter side of shipboard life, stating that "the musicians" would "rest on the Sabbath Day, but the other six days and nights, none without special favor." That same code also established a curfew of sorts: "The lights and candles to be put out at eight o-clock at night; if any of the crew, after that hour, still remained inclined for drinking, they were to do it on the open deck." No matter how detailed the articles, they didn't cover every eventuality. When novel situations arose, it was typically up to the quartermaster to decide the appropriate action, such as meting out punishment for offenses not mentioned in the articles.

Much has been made of the pirates' use of democratic decision making, especially since democracy was hardly in vogue in the society at large, this being many decades before the American and French Revolutions ushered in broadly, though certainly not completely, democratic forms of government in the United States and France. European governments in the early 1700s, with their monarchs and parliaments, were far from democratic. Merchant and naval ships were essentially dictatorships, with the captain and other officers clearly in charge, and no opportunity for the crews to vote on anything, short of "voting" to mutiny. As for privateers, while they too had articles of agreement that embraced many of the same elements as pirate articles, such as identifying the shares to be distributed, and providing for compensation should any limbs or other body parts be lost, the captain of a privateer was clearly in charge, and could not be voted out of office, nor were the other officers elected to their positions.

Needless to say, pirates were not political theorists who valued democratic ideals because they thought they made for the best form of government. They had other reasons for governing themselves in the manner that they did. Many pirates were formerly employed on merchant or naval ships, and a significant number of them chose to become pirates in large part because they wanted to escape autocratic and abusive captains. It would be very surprising, therefore, if upon becoming pirates, those very same men would seek to re-create the power structure they had just left behind. Pirates were so infuriated by cruel captains that when boarding a merchant prize, one of their first actions was to perform what has been called the "Distribution of Justice." To that end, they would ask the crew whether their captain had treated them well. If the crewmembers sang the praises of their captain, he was spared any punishment, and typically released with or without his ship after it had been plundered; but if the captain was found to be a brutal leader, he was beaten, or in extreme cases, killed. In this manner, pirates were able to exact revenge for the miserable treatment so many of them had endured in their former lives as sailors.

Given this dynamic, it is no wonder that pirate captains served at the pleasure of the crew, and that the pirates also elected a quarter-master who looked out for their interests. As a British pirate in 1721 observed, "Most of them [pirates] having suffered formerly from the ill-treatment of their officers, provided carefully against any such evil, now [that] they had a choice in themselves." He added that the election of the quartermaster was yet another indication that pirates wanted "to avoid putting too much power in the hands of one man."

With respect to the articles themselves, which typically called for a vote before doling out punishments, and provided for a very equi-table distribution of the spoils, this was not done to comport with some abstract democratic ideal or political philosophy, but rather because it was an efficient way to get things done, create support for actions taken, avoid disputes, and develop cohesion among the crew. In other words, since a pirate ship was, in effect, a floating society, pirates simply set up practical, sensible, and easily enforced rules to ensure that their society functioned as smoothly as possible. And sharing the spoils in a relatively fair and even manner was cer-tainly not original to the pirates of this era. Not only did the bucca-neers operate in a similar manner, but also common fishermen since time immemorial often divided what they caught into largely equal shares, with the captains and specialized crewmen getting more than the rest. Furthermore, the willingness of many pirates to force men to sign on when they needed extra manpower or special skills, and the fact that more than a few pirates treated blacks as slaves and sold them as such, belies the notion that true democracy was the pirates' guiding principle.

THE PIRATES' SINGLE MOST important asset, other than their will and determination, was their ship, which they came by in many ways. Mutineers-turned-pirates obtained it by virtue of violent take-over. Other pirates started with very small boats and traded their way up to larger, more impressive vessels through capture. In one case, as we shall see, a man built a vessel specifically to fulfill his pirate ambitions.

However pirates came by a ship, they were always on the lookout for a better one, with the definition of "better" being circumscribed by certain broad specifications. The ship had to be especially seaworthy, of course, since pirates roamed throughout the Atlantic in good weather and bad, facing every condition imaginable, from calm seas to raging hurricanes with immense waves. The ship had to be fast and highly maneuverable—able to hit-and-run—for if the pirates couldn't catch their intended victims, and quickly retreat in times of danger, they would have exceedingly short careers. It had to be relatively large, and carry a commanding array of guns, or cannons, since pirates overpowered merchantmen by intimidation or force; either way, the pirate ship needed to be big and threatening enough, or capable of applying sufficient strength, to get its victim to surrender. Although pirates wanted nothing more than to have a large and powerful flagship, there were limits to their zeal to move up the hierarchy of vessel impressiveness, for they didn't want to sacrifice seaworthiness and maneuverability for size.

Pirate vessels ranged from sloops and schooners to snows, brigantines, and, in rare instances, frigates. But the most common vessel was a sloop sporting between ten and twenty guns, able to comfortably accommodate up to seventy-five men. Sloops were the "main small workhorse vessels of the 17th and 18th centuries." With their shallow draught and sharp lines, they were exceptionally fast, easy to handle, and capable of sailing on the high seas as well as in the more constricted waters along the coast—all features that made them a favorite with pirates.

The most important armament on pirate ships was their cannons, which fired iron balls of three, six, nine, or twelve pounds and more, and which could shatter hulls, topple masts, and kill any unfortunate seaman who got in the way. Cannons also fired canisters filled with iron pellets, called partridge or swan shot, which exploded beyond the end of the muzzle, creating a lethal spray of

A brigantine, circa 1742.

*Late nineteenth-century reproduction of a 1729 mezzotint
by William Burgis, depicting an armed British sloop in front of
Boston Light. This eight-gun sloop is similar to the
sloops used by pirates of the day.*

Frontispiece from The Sea-Gunner *by John Seller, a how-to book about using cannons at sea, printed by H. Clark, in London, 1691.*

metal. Bar shot—a bar of iron with thickened ends, similar in form to a modern dumbbell—was another devastating projectile, which spun on its axis, shredding any rigging or sails it smashed into.

Multiple men were required to operate each cannon, a major part of the reason that pirate ships had such large crews. Firing a cannon weighing thousands of pounds, and mounted on a rolling wooden carriage, was a specialized and highly choreographed skill, a ballet of sorts. It involved swabbing the bore and muzzle to remove dirt and sparks, then adding in succession the gunpowder, a wad of paper or hay, and the projectile, and then ramming it all down, setting the primer, and rolling the cannon through the gun port into place before finally igniting the charge. And, of course, firing a cannon was one thing, hitting a target another. In anything other than completely calm conditions, the gunners had to time the shot just right, in between the waves' troughs and crests, so that the projectile's trajectory hit its mark.

For additional firepower, pirates relied on pistols, muskets, and small cannons mounted on the bow or stern of a vessel, called chase guns. Spherical iron grenades filled with gunpowder, and corked with a wood plug through which a cloth fuse was strung, were also used. The favored type of sword in close battle was the cutlass. Usually no longer than twenty or thirty inches, which made them easier to carry and wield in the tight confines of a crowded deck, cutlasses typically had slightly curved, thick blades that were particularly effective at slashing and stabbing one's enemies, as well as cutting through rigging lines and sails.

PIRATES WENT AFTER THEIR prey in a fairly predictable fashion. Given the ocean's immensity they typically frequented traditional shipping lanes and trade routes, or hovered near busy ports to increase the chance of encountering potential prizes. As Johnson pithily observed, "Where the game is, there will the vermin be." The search for "game" usually had a seasonal component, with most pirates' peregrinations being dictated by the weather. In the winter, when freezing temperatures and stormy seas made northern waters inhospitable, pirates migrated south to the Caribbean, or to the east and the equatorial coast of Africa. Then, when the temperatures climbed back up in the spring, pirates often headed north to search for their quarry.

To keep their potential victims from fleeing, and to gain the element of surprise, pirates often employed deception, trickery being a common and generally very effective game on the high seas. Typically, national flags or ensigns raised aloft identified whether a ship was a friend or foe, but pirates, as well as merchantmen and naval ships, usually carried an array of flags from which to choose, should they want to present themselves as something other than what they actually were. Hence, a pirate spying a French merchant ship in the offing might raise a French flag, hoping to put the ship's captain at ease, and keep him from sailing away. If all worked according to plan, the French ship would allow the pirate ship to come in close, not thinking anything amiss. Once within range, the pirates could announce their true identity with a well-placed shot across the bow, by sending a boarding party, or by raising a black flag, that most iconic of pirate symbols.

Many pirates didn't use deception to lull potential victims into a false sense of security, but instead raised a black flag as soon as they began the chase. The black flag was intended to strike fear into the hearts of sailors who spied it fluttering atop the pirate ship's mast by sending the unmistakable message—surrender immediately, or else we'll attack. Being risk averse, pirates always hoped for surrender. They never wanted to fight if they could avoid it, because there was no upside to battle. Fighting not only placed the pirates and their ship in jeopardy, but it also could result in grave damage to the vessel they were trying to capture, as well as its potentially valuable cargo. Fortunately for the pirates, they rarely had to resort to force, since intimidation, courtesy of the black flag, worked so well.

The oldest known pirate flag that has survived. According to the Åland Maritime Museum in Finland, which owns the flag, it "was acquired by an unknown Ålandic sailor from a North African Mediterranean port, probably in the late 1800s or early 1900s. The flag is made of cotton, bleached and tattered by age. The skull and bones are sewn on and the details are painted. The flag [background] originally would probably have been black. It has been dated to the late 1700s or early 1800s."

While not every pirate during this period used a black flag, most did. Each pirate's flag was unique, but virtually all of them contained imagery symbolizing death, typically white in color and arrayed on a stark black background, which itself was the traditional color for death. Among the most common images were an entire skeleton, or a skull and crossbones, also called the "death's head," which was a long-established motif for adorning headstones. Cutlasses were also used, as were hourglasses, the presence of which underscored that time to make a decision was quickly running out.

Although a few pirates' flags are described in contemporary documents, giving the reader a good sense of how they looked, no actual pirate flags from the Golden Age have survived, and there are scarcely any contemporary illustrations to point to, other than a couple that can be seen in Johnson's *A General History*. Most drawings of pirate flags that one often sees in pirate books, or on pendants, were created long after the Golden Age was over, with many making their first appearance in the twentieth century. As such, they are simply an artist's best guess, based on the limited historical record, as to what those flags actually looked like. And there is no doubt that in some cases, modern depictions of pirate flags have little in common with the historical banners they are attempting to depict.

The first known use of the black pirate flag was in 1700, when a French pirate off the Cape Verdean island of Santiago fought under "a sable ensign with . . . a death's head and an hour glass." By the 1710s and 1720s, the black flag was routinely employed by pirates, and was sometimes referred to as the Jolly Roger for reasons that are not entirely clear. Some claim that it derives from *Jolie Rouge*, or pretty red, the term used to describe the red flag that pirates and other mariners employed to indicate that no quarter would be offered. Or, perhaps, it is a variation on "Old Roger," a colloquial term for the devil that was commonly used at the time. Some have even surmised that it is a reference to the smiling, or "jolly," visage that some people see when they gaze upon a skeletal head. Whatever the etymology of Jolly Roger, it proved to be a very effective calling card that produced dramatic results.

When merchant ships saw the black flag, they would typically strike their colors, heave to, and wait for the pirates to board. By virtue of a relatively small number of cases in which pirates mercilessly attacked merchant ships that opposed them, they had a well-earned reputation of being ruthless killers when provoked. As the *Boston News-Letter* reported in 1718, merchant crews "that have made resistance [to pirates] have been most barbarously butchered, without any quarter given to them, which so intimidates our sailors that they refuse to fight when the pirates attack them." Facing such a potentially vengeful and deadly foe, it is not surprising that most merchant crews would rather surrender than risk their lives defending their ship, especially since they were just hired hands who had no personal investment, beyond their wages, in the vessel or its cargo.

FOLLOWING A SURRENDER, the plundering, sorting, and decision making quickly commenced. First, the pirates, with the quartermaster in the lead, boarded the captured ship and began the search for loot, torturing the crew and passengers if necessary to find out where it was hidden. This was truly a moment of discovery, because pirates didn't know in advance what the ship might contain, and whether the prize was worth the time, or the ammunition and blood, spent to capture it.

In addition to valuable cargo and treasure, the pirates were also on the hunt for more mundane and practical items that were absolutely necessary to their survival. Voyaging for many months on end, and almost universally unwelcome at ports throughout the Atlantic, pirates were forced to supply many of their ship-related and dietary needs at sea. This often meant stripping their prizes of everything from cordage, sails, and tools to casks of dried fish, flour, and water. In fact, when looking across the range of pirates that operated between 1716 and 1726, one is struck by the ordinary nature of much of their plunder. Although there were some notable exceptions, it was the relatively rare pirate during this period who amassed a fortune, or even a respectable nest egg.

Illustration by Howard Pyle (1921) of pirates forcing a man to his doom
by walking the plank. No pirates during the Golden Age are known to have
done this. This was a common literary embellishment added to fictional
pirate stories in an effort to enliven them. If the pirates wanted to kill a man,
they were much more straightforward about it, using a gun or sword,
or simply pitching the victim over the rail and into the sea.
There are, however, a few cases in the nineteenth century of
pirates making their victims walk the plank.

Eventually, pirates had to decide what to do with their prize. If
it was a good ship, the pirates might take it as a consort, splitting
the crew to man the new acquisition. In this way, over time and

with multiple captures, pirate captains could end up commanding a small squadron of ships, the ultimate goal of any leader who harbored grand ambitions. Or, if the prize were an exceptional ship, the pirates might transfer to it entirely, leaving their old ship behind. When a ship was abandoned, any of the captured crew not absorbed by the pirates would usually be allowed to sail away on the unwanted vessel. But if the prize were to become a pirate ship, or be burned or scuttled, as often happened, the remainder of the prize crew would typically be set ashore, or kept prisoner until another ship was captured and let go with the prisoners aboard.

Another decision made at this time was whether structural modifications were needed. This was especially important when the prize was to be transformed into a pirate ship. To get the ship battle-ready, the pirates might eliminate structures on the main deck for ease of movement, remove bulkheads below decks to make more room for artillery, pierce new gun ports in the hull to increase the ship's firepower, and change the rigging to increase speed and improve handling.

OF THE THOUSANDS OF PIRATES who operated in the Atlantic between 1716 and 1726, and plagued the American colonies, most were relatively minor characters who were neither particularly memorable nor interesting. They flashed across history's stage like shooting stars, leaving hardly a trace behind and disappearing quickly from view. But, a few pirates of this era burned brighter than all the rest, by virtue of their personalities and exploits, and their stories command attention.

CHAPTER 7

Treasure and the Tempest

A Spanish periagua, circa 1744. This is the type of vessel that Samuel Bellamy and Paulsgrave Williams used to launch their piratical career.

IN THE EARLY FALL OF 1715, SAMUEL BELLAMY AND PAULSGRAVE Williams embarked with a small crew from New England, heading to Florida, hoping to salvage treasure from the corpses of the Spanish fleet that had a few months earlier been demolished by the hurricane off the Florida coast. They were an odd couple. Bellamy's early history is obscure, but it appears that he originally hailed from Hittisleigh, Devon, in western England, where his family were

One of a series of "Pirates of the Spanish Main" cards that the Allen
& Ginter Company produced circa 1888 and inserted into its
cigarette packs. This one shows Samuel Bellamy and a scene of the
wreck of the Whydah, *both imagined by the illustrator.*

farmers. During the War of the Spanish Succession, he crewed on either a merchant or a navy ship. In the turbulent aftermath of the war, Bellamy lost his job, and according to legend, he ended up in Eastham, a small fishing and agricultural town located on the outer reaches of Cape Cod, just beyond its sandy elbow jutting into the Atlantic. There, he pursued a local girl named Mary, or Maria, Hallett, who returned his affections, but her parents, prosperous farmers, frowned on the budding relationship and would not let their daughter marry a lowly sailor. Angered by this rejection, Bellamy set off to find his fortune, promising to return as a man of means worthy enough to make Mary his bride.

Although there was indeed a young woman named Mary Hallett in Eastham at the time who came from a well-to-do family, there is no evidence that Bellamy wooed her, or that he ever settled anywhere on the Cape. But, whether or not the story that Cape Codders tell to this day is true, there is little doubt that Bellamy landed in New England after the war and, in 1715, decided to seek his fortune. And the man he teamed up with to help him achieve his dream was Williams, who brought to the partnership an entirely different background.

A married and successful silversmith from Newport, Rhode Island, with two children, the thirty-nine-year-old Williams came from an illustrious family. His grandfather, Nathaniel Williams, was a lieutenant in the colonial militia, and constable and selectman in Boston, who built a large estate in the city, including a sizable chunk of what later became Beacon Hill. His father, John Williams, was a successful merchant who split his time between Boston and Block Island, and also served in the Massachusetts General Assembly, and as Rhode Island's attorney general. Paulsgrave's mother, Ann, was closely related to the principal founders of Charlestown, Massachusetts, and Block Island.

How and when Williams and Bellamy connected is not known, but by the fall of 1715, they had purchased a vessel and were heading for Florida, with Bellamy serving as captain of the fledgling venture. It would be nearly two years before they returned to New England's waters with a considerable fortune, and what happened next would rank as one of the worst disasters in the history of America's pirates.

ARRIVING AT THE SITE of the Florida wrecks in January 1716, Bellamy and Williams encountered a maritime traffic jam. Multiple British ships were busy combing the ocean floor looking for silver and gold, but they were having little luck. The Spanish and interlopers from other countries had already salvaged much of the treasure, and what remained proved maddeningly difficult to find. Bellamy and Williams didn't fare any better, and when they were forced from the area by Spanish military ships in late January, they had little to show for their efforts.

Discouraged, but still eager to find their fortune, Bellamy and Williams decided to become pirates.* They headed to the Bay of Honduras, and by March had recruited more men, trading their

---

* Many books written in recent years about Bellamy's piratical career refer to him as "Black Sam Bellamy," an appellation he supposedly earned because either he had jet-black hair or a swarthy complexion. However, this author could not find a single contemporary source that referred to him as "Black Sam," nor could I find any reference to his hair or complexion. Hence, my decision not to refer to him as "Black Sam," despite the intriguing nature of the moniker.

original ship for two large, highly maneuverable, and fast-sailing canoes called periaguas. Over the next few weeks, they plundered a few small ships, and in early April had a major score when they double-crossed another pirate, Captain Henry Jennings.

Initially, Bellamy and Williams joined forces with Jennings's small pirate fleet to capture a French merchant ship, the *St. Marie*, in the sheltered bay of Bahia Honda on the northwestern coast of Cuba. During the attack, Bellamy and Williams took the lead, using a most unusual tactic. They and their men stripped off all of their clothes and approached the *St. Marie* in their periaguas wearing only their pistols, swords, and ammunition boxes. If the mere sight of these heavily armed, naked, and fierce-looking men wasn't enough to cause the *St. Marie*'s captain to surrender, then a few bursts of gunfire from one of Jennings's ships, plus Bellamy's threat that if the French resisted, they would be given no quarter, did the trick.

Jennings tortured the Frenchmen to get them to divulge where they had hidden nearly 30,000 pieces of eight on shore, which was retrieved in short order and placed onboard the *St. Marie*. While the pirates were relishing their good fortune, they learned that the French merchant ship *Marianne* was just twenty miles up the coast. Hoping to gain another prize, Jennings dispatched a few of his ships, but they were too late. Pirate captain Benjamin Hornigold, on the sloop *Benjamin*, had already captured the *Marianne* and left the area.

Livid at being bested, Jennings led the *Barsheba* and the *Mary* out of the harbor to chase Hornigold, leaving the rest of his fleet behind. Soon after Jennings departed, Bellamy and Williams saw their chance, and with incredible swiftness they launched a surprise attack, which resulted in them taking control of the *St. Marie*. It wasn't the ship, however, that they wanted, but rather the money onboard. So, they quickly transferred the coins to one of their periaguas and made their escape. When Jennings returned after a fruitless search for Hornigold and was told of the betrayal, he took his anger out on Bellamy and Williams's abandoned periagua, having it "cut to pieces."

NOT LONG AFTER TAKING flight from Bahia Honda, Bellamy and Williams encountered the man Jennings had sought—Benjamin Hornigold, who was already a legend among the pirates of the Caribbean. A British privateer in the War of the Spanish Succession, Hornigold switched to piracy at the war's end, and since then had been terrorizing merchant ships in the tropics, leading a group of pirates who called themselves the "Flying Gang." Their primary base of operations was Nassau, a small town on the British island of New Providence, one of more than seven hundred islands that make up the Bahamas. New Providence had been pillaged multiple times by the French and Spanish during the war, leaving behind a frightened and bedraggled population of perhaps one hundred or so British colonists, who had no real government to speak of and were struggling just to survive.

Detail of a 1715 map of the West Indies showing the Bahama Islands to the north of Cuba and east of the tip of Florida. The Bahamian island of New Providence is very small and located roughly in the middle of this image.

Hornigold and a few of his fellow pirates landed in Nassau in 1713 and essentially took over the town, establishing it as the base for what historian Colin Woodard has called "The Republic of Pirates." It was a perfect location, sitting astride the major shipping routes between the Caribbean and the American colonies, as well as those leading to Europe. The sheltered anchorage at Nassau was another plus, as was the availability of water, wood, and food on New Providence and the surrounding islands. The numerous inlets, harbors, and bays throughout the Bahamas not only offered the pirates excellent places to hide before launching attacks, or retreat if being chased, but they also provided convenient locations to careen their ships.

As word of the pirate republic spread, other pirates flocked to Nassau, using it as their base of operations as well, with some boasting that they would make New Providence "a second Madagascar." And like Madagascar, New Providence became a magnet for traders who were more than willing to sell supplies to pirates and purchase goods stolen from plundered vessels at cut-rate prices. Many of those traders came from the American colonies, and they proved crucial to the pirates' survival and strength. As one colonial merchant observed, "The pirates themselves have often told me that if they had not been supported by the traders from" Rhode Island, New York, Pennsylvania, and other colonies, "with ammunition and provisions according to their directions, they could never have become so formidable."

The dramatic influx of pirates led a British official to claim in 1715 that the Bahamas had "been almost reduced to a nest of pirates." It wasn't only merchant ships that these pirates attacked. According to one contemporary who fled New Providence, the pirates "commit great disorders on the island, plundering the inhabitants, burning their houses, and ravishing their wives." Thus, many of Nassau's residents had left the island "for fear of being murdered."

Bellamy and Williams eagerly signed on to Hornigold's gang, and shortly thereafter Hornigold made Bellamy captain of the *Marianne*, which mounted eight cannons. About a week later, Hornigold's gang crossed paths with the French pirate ship *Postillion*, captained by Olivier Levasseur, a former privateer nicknamed La Buse, meaning the Buzzard or Hawk. Hornigold and La Buse decided to join forces. Over the next few months, this pirate flotilla made a number of captures, some without Hornigold, who for a short interval was busy in Nassau selling the *Benjamin* and acquiring a new ship called the *Adventure*. They were all together again along the coast of Hispaniola by mid-summer of 1716, but not for long.

Hornigold, unwilling to let go of the war despite the peace, and still loyal to his mother country, vowed to attack only the French and the Spanish, leaving British ships alone. Although he had broken his rule at least once, for the most part he did not waver in his determination. The problem was, neither Bellamy nor La Buse agreed with Hornigold's stance, and had in fact attacked a couple of British vessels in Hornigold's absence. Any merchant ship, regardless of nationality, was, they argued, fair game. So, when Hornigold balked at attacking yet another British ship in August, the majority of the men under his command voted to sack him as commander of the pirate fleet, and place Bellamy in charge. In a sign of how much they still respected their former leader, the pirates agreed to give Hornigold and the twenty-six men who stuck by his side their share of the plunder, as well as the use of the sloop *Adventure*. The rest of the *Adventure*'s crew, who had voted to oust Hornigold, transferred to Bellamy and La Buse's ships. Deflated but still proud, Hornigold sailed for Nassau, while Bellamy and La Buse, with nearly two hundred men between them, set out on their own.

Ranging from Cuba to the Leeward Islands and down nearly to the coast of Venezuela, Bellamy and La Buse plundered a variety of ships over the next five months, Bellamy adding to his crew by welcoming those who elected to become pirates, and forcing those who resisted to join against their will. Bellamy's most unusual recruit was John King, a ten-year-old who had been traveling as a passenger with his mother on the British sloop *Bonetta* from Jamaica to Antigua. When Bellamy asked if any of the *Bonetta*'s crew wanted to become a pirate, King eagerly said yes. His mother begged him not to go, and implored Bellamy not to take him, but the headstrong boy was resolute. The *Bonetta*'s captain later recalled that the lad said he would "kill himself if he was restrained, and even threatened his mother" with harm if she should stand in his way. So, a pirate he became.

Bellamy's and La Buse's greatest success came in November off the Dutch island of Saba not far from St. Kitts, where they captured the *Sultana*, a British merchant ship with twenty-six guns. It was considerably larger and more powerful than the *Marianne*, so Bellamy, with the pirate crew having voted to approve the shift, took command of the *Sultana*, while Williams was voted in as the new captain of the *Marianne*. Weeks later, after a few more captures, La Buse and his men took their share of the plunder, and left to pursue their own course.

Bellamy and Williams had done quite well as pirates. According to one estimate, they had plundered at least fifty-two ships since their partnership began. But their most impressive capture was yet to come.

AT THE BEGINNING OF April 1717, Bellamy and Williams were cruising near the Windward Passage, a strait connecting the Caribbean Sea to the Atlantic Ocean, when they spotted a large ship on the horizon. Thinking it a potential prize, the pirates piled on the sails and made chase flying British flags, but try as they might they couldn't catch up.

The elusive vessel was the *Whydah*, a three-hundred-ton British slave ship with eighteen guns, only two years old, and captained by Lawrence Prince. A few days earlier, the *Whydah* had left Port Royal, Jamaica, after it had delivered its human cargo of five hundred slaves. The name of the ship hinted at the nature of its ghastly trade. The kingdom of Whydah (or Ouidah, as it is sometimes called), located on Africa's west coast on the edge of the Gulf of Guinea, was actively involved in slave brokering, exporting up to twenty thousand slaves per year. It was far and away the region's largest slaving port, and British slavers were some of the kingdom's best customers.

Captain Prince was a veteran of the slave trade, having made multiple trips between Africa and the Caribbean. He was well aware of the threat pirates posed and remained continually on guard. He knew the two ships following him were suspicious, despite their ensigns, and he chose to flee rather than find out if his suspicions were correct.

It took Bellamy and Williams three days, covering some three hundred miles, to get within cannon-range of the *Whydah*. By now, Prince had no doubt they were pirates, because Bellamy and Williams had replaced the British ensign with a pirate's flag showing "a death's head and bones across." With the ships closing in, Prince ordered two of the stern-mounted guns to fire, the balls from which fell harmlessly into the water. Despite this show of bravado, Prince didn't have the heart to fight what would certainly be a lopsided battle. The *Whydah* appeared to be outmatched in firepower, and by what he could see, the pirate ships had far more men than his fifty-man crew. After weighing the possibilities, he ordered the *Whydah* to heave to, and surrendered.

The pirates boarded the *Whydah*, and quickly realized their good fortune. Not only was the *Whydah* a much newer and better vessel than the *Sultana* or the *Marianne*, with ample room for additional armaments, but it was also chock-full of treasure. In exchange for the slaves at Port Royal, Captain Prince had received sugar, indigo, and Jesuit's bark,* as well as a large quantity of silver and gold. To fully explore their prize, the pirates took the *Whydah* to nearby Long Island, in the Bahamas, and anchored it in a sheltered cove alongside the *Sultana* and the *Marianne*.

Upon inspection, the pirates decided to make the *Whydah* their flagship and give the *Sultana* to Prince. Over the next few days, ten cannons were transferred from the *Sultana* to the *Whydah*, raising its complement to twenty-eight guns, while additional cannons from the *Sultana* were placed in the *Marianne*'s hold. The silver and gold, deemed to be worth between £20,000 and £30,000, was packed in

---

* Also called "sacred bark," it comes from the cinchona tree, and was used to make the malaria drug quinine.

bags weighing fifty pounds each and stowed in the *Whydah*'s main cabin. With such a huge haul of cash, the rest of the cargo held little allure, and the pirates transferred as "much of the best and finest goods" as it could carry to the *Sultana*. There was also a one-way exchange of personnel. Three of Prince's men were forced to join the pirates, while either five or seven men came aboard voluntarily. Finally, Bellamy gave Prince a little more than £20 worth of silver and gold "to bear his charges."

WITH SPRING FAST APPROACHING, Bellamy and Williams turned their ships north. Their plan was to head straight for the Virginia Capes, at the mouth of Chesapeake Bay, spend ten days searching for prizes, and then slowly work their way up the coast until they reached the coastal islands of mid-Maine, where they would careen their ships. Williams also wanted to stop at Block Island to reconnect with his relatives, and likely share some of his wealth.

At the beginning of April, about 120 miles off the coast of South Carolina, Bellamy and Williams captured a merchantman bound for Charleston from Newport. The master, Captain Beer, was taken aboard the *Whydah* while the pirates plundered his sloop. The pirates then voted to sink the sloop, even though Williams, and possibly Bellamy, was in favor of letting Beer and his sloop go. According to Johnson, after the vote, Bellamy broke the news to Beer in this fashion:

I am sorry they won't let you have your sloop again, for I scorn to do any one a mischief, when it is not to my advantage; damn the sloop, we must sink her, and she might be of use to you. Though you are a sneaking puppy, and so are all those who will submit to be governed by laws which rich men have made for their own security; for the cowardly whelps have not the courage otherwise to defend what they get by knavery; but damn ye altogether: damn them for a pack of crafty rascals, and you, who serve them, for a parcel of hen-hearted numbskulls. They vilify us, the scoundrels do, when there is only this difference, they rob the poor under the cover of law, forsooth, and we plunder the rich under the protection of our own courage. Had you not better make then one of us, than sneak after the arses of those villains for employment?

Beer responded by telling Bellamy that "his conscience would not allow him to break through the laws of God and man," which only set off a further harangue by Bellamy.

You are a devilish conscience [conscientious] rascal! Damn ye, I am a free prince, and I have as much authority to make war on the whole world as he who has a hundred sail of ships at sea and an army of 100,000 men in the field; and this my conscience tells me! But there is no arguing with such sniveling puppies, who allow superiors to kick them about deck at pleasure.

It is an impressive speech, which is widely quoted in the pirate literature, but it is virtually certain that it never transpired. First, there is no contemporary record of it (Johnson reported it years after the fact). When Beer got to port after being plundered, there is no evidence that he wrote this speech down, or shared it with the local press. Second, the wording seems much too flowery and fraught with political philosophy for it to have come from the mouth of a relatively uneducated pirate captain, a former common seaman. Third, the latter part of Bellamy's diatribe sounds suspiciously like a conversation that Alexander the Great, the king of Macedonia in the fourth century BCE, supposedly had with a pirate he had captured. When the king asked the pirate how dare he claim the right to take control of the sea by force, the pirate responded, "What thou meanest by seizing the whole earth; but because I do it with a petty ship, I am called a robber, whilst thou dost it with a great fleet [and] art styled emperor." Like a number of incidents included in Johnson's book, it appears that Bellamy's speech was made up.

Johnson probably got the idea for this speech from the fact that one of the sailors captured by Bellamy in the Caribbean later claimed that the pirates "pretended to be Robin Hood's men." In Johnson's rendition, Bellamy seems to view himself, and his men, as having a similar rebellious streak aimed at fighting the rich and powerful by plundering them. However, the fact that Bellamy's men said they "pretended to be Robin Hood's men" seems to imply that it might have been said in jest, or in a sarcastic manner. Furthermore, this claim of affinity with Robin Hood appears to be unique in the annals of piracy. No other pirate is known to have made a similar declaration. But even if Bellamy's, or any other pirate captain's, men did think of themselves as Robin Hood–like characters, then their selfish goal was to take money from the rich, or from anyone for that matter, and give it to the poor people whom they cared about most—themselves! Pirates had no broader or altruistic political agenda, and gravitated to this lifestyle for monetary gain, not to enact social change.

After sinking Beer's sloop, Bellamy and Williams sailed toward Virginia. A couple of days later, a thick fog rolled over the ocean, and the two ships lost sight of each other. When the fog lifted, Bellamy and Williams each found themselves alone at sea. Rather than rue their predicament, or let sentiment get in the way, they continued pirating with the expectation that they would meet up again off the Maine coast, if not before.

Over the next few weeks, Williams captured only two small vessels of little value. In between cruising for prizes, he headed to Block Island, where he released Captain Beer, visited family members, and gathered food and other supplies. He also added three men to his crew, though whether they joined voluntarily or were essentially kidnapped is not clear.

Bellamy didn't fare much better. In the days immediately following the separation he captured three small merchant ships in quick succession off the coast of Virginia. One was scuttled and another released, but Bellamy decided to keep the third one—a one-hundred-ton snow called the *Ann Galley*—as a consort, and to provide manpower to help careen the *Whydah*. He placed eighteen of his trusted men aboard, bringing its total complement to twenty-eight, including the *Ann Galley*'s original crew, who were woven into the pirate ranks. Richard Noland, erstwhile quartermaster on the *Whydah*, was elected the *Ann Galley*'s new captain.

News of the five vessels Williams and Bellamy took sent the region's merchants into a panic. "Our coast is now infested with pirates," a Virginia merchant informed the Board of Trade on April 15. "God knows what damage they'll do to trade. Ships are daily going out and coming in," for fear of getting captured. Traffic from Chesapeake Bay came to a virtual standstill. The merchant pleaded with the government to send more naval ships, and said that if they didn't arrive, he was "afraid twill not be long before we have more fatal news of these pirates. Certainly this trade deserves more care from the Crown than to be left in this naked condition."

Shortly after penning this letter, the agitated merchant and his peers were given a reprieve when both pirates left the area. Bellamy set his sights on Maine, and by the early morning of April 26, his small flotilla was between Nantucket Shoals and George's Bank, just to the east of the Cape's elbow. At the same time, Williams was about 150 miles away, near the tip of Long Island. Although neither knew it, this day would tragically alter their fortunes.

AROUND NINE IN THE MORNING on April 26, one of the crewmembers aboard the *Mary Anne* saw two ships in the distance, closing in. The Irish trading vessel, captained by Andrew Crumpsley, had left Nantasket a few days earlier bound for New York. The *Whydah*, flying the king's ensign, soon came alongside the *Mary Anne*, and Bellamy demanded that it strike its colors. The *Whydah* lowered its boat, and seven pirates rowed over to the *Mary Anne* and climbed aboard, all but two of them "armed with muskets, pistols, and cutlasses." Thomas Baker, the leader of this threatening contingent, strode up to Crumpsley with his sword drawn and ordered him to gather up the ship's papers, along with five of his crew, and row back to the *Whydah*. The seven pirates, and three of the *Mary Anne's* crew, stayed behind.

Bellamy perused the ship's manifest, and was delighted to see that in its hold were seven thousand gallons of Madeira wine, a wildly popular libation imported from the verdant Portuguese island of the same name off the northwestern coast of Africa. He immediately dispatched four of his men to bring some of it back, but they ran into an obstacle. Coils of the *Mary Anne's* anchor cable blocked the hatchway to the hold where the pipes of wine were stored. Rather than move the heavy cables, the pirates grabbed five bottles of "green wine" from the main cabin, along with some cloths, and returned to the *Whydah*.

With the *Whydah* leading the way, sailing northwest by north, Bellamy ordered the *Mary Anne* to follow, and behind them trailed the *Ann Galley*. Visibility slowly deteriorated, and by four in the afternoon the fog had become so thick that Bellamy decided to lay to, or bring the vessel into the wind to cause it to stop, while he considered how best to proceed. As the *Ann Galley* came up under the *Whydah's* stern, Noland told him that they had spotted land just a few hours earlier. This news greatly concerned Bellamy because he didn't know these waters well, and with fog so dense, the chances of foundering on the coast were vastly increased. Bellamy thought about forcing Captain Crumpsley to pilot them, but he was not confident of his local knowledge either. Less than half an hour later, out of the mist appeared a potential solution to Bellamy's dilemma.

When the sloop *Fisher* hove into view, about seven miles to the east of the cape, Bellamy hailed it and demanded to know from where it had come. The *Fisher's* captain, Robert Ingols, responded that they left Virginia and were bound to Boston with a cargo of tobacco and hides. Bellamy wasn't looking for another prize; however, he was looking for help, so his next question was whether Ingols was familiar with this coast. When Ingols replied in the affirmative, Bellamy ordered him to lower his boat, and row over to the *Whydah* along with his mate. Ingols's new job was piloting the pirates beyond the cape and quite likely all the way to the coast of Maine. To make sure that the *Fisher* followed, Bellamy sent four armed pirates to board it.

As the sun disappeared and darkness settled over the water, Bellamy put out a lantern on the stern of the *Whydah* and ordered the rest of the vessels to put lights out as well, to help them stay together in the deepening gloom. At one point, Bellamy shouted to the men on the *Mary Anne* to "make more haste," whereupon pirate John Brown "swore that he would carry sail till she carried her masts away."

If Bellamy had been aboard the *Mary Anne*, he would have known why it was lagging behind. For one thing, it was leaking badly, forcing the men to continually man the pump, and leading a few of the pirates to "damn" the vessel, and "wish they had never seen her." The other equally serious impediment was alcohol. Earlier in the day, one of Bellamy's men, Simon Van Vorst, warned Alexander Mackconachy, the *Mary Anne*'s cook, that if Mackconachy didn't "find liquor" onboard, he "would break" his neck. With that mortal incentive in mind, Mackconachy and a few of the other men muscled the heavy cable away from the lower hatch and retrieved a couple of the pipes of wine. From then on, the pirates had been drinking liberally, and come nightfall they were more than a bit drunk, which was a particular problem since the inebriated pirates had been switching off at the helm with their more sober prisoners in shifts.

The pirates' impaired condition didn't stop them from complaining about their prisoners' sailing skills, and once again Mackconachy was the target, with Thomas Baker threatening to shoot him "through the head because he steered to the windward of his course." To drive the point home, Baker said that "he would make no more to shoot him, than he would a dog, and that he should never go on shore to tell his story." The liquid courage also made the pirates boastful. At one point Baker lied, telling one of the prisoners "that the king had given them a commission to make their fortune, and they were sworn to do it." Another pirate added that they would "stretch" that commission "to the world's end."

Before they made it "to the world's end," however, they needed to get past the outstretched arm of the Cape, and that was looking increasingly dicey. In the early evening the wind and waves started picking up, and by ten it was a full-blown gale, with gusts approaching hurricane force, lightning dancing across the sky, rain coming down almost horizontally in sheets, and waves growing to monstrous heights. Thomas Fitzgerald, the *Mary Anne*'s mate, was at the helm when he lost sight of the lights from the other vessels. At around eleven, he heard the dreaded sound of breakers dead ahead, and realized that the wind from the east was driving the *Mary Anne* onto the shore. The men rushed to trim the sails and turn the vessel in an effort to claw their way clear of the land, but before they could do so the *Mary Anne* plowed into Pochet Island, in Orleans, just to the south of Eastham.

The crash knocked the men off their feet, but the ship was still intact. To reduce the strain on the hull, Baker took an axe and cut down the foremast and the mizzenmast. As Fitzgerald later recalled, a few of the pirates "cried out saying, for God's sake let us go down into the hold and die together." And there, by the quavering light of a candle, as waves violently pounded the hull and the wind screeched outside, Fitzgerald complied with the pirates' request, and read for an hour from the common-prayer book, giving some measure of solace to men convinced they were doomed.

Meantime, the *Ann Galley* and the *Fisher*, farther up the coast, had lost sight of the two other vessels, but not each other. Hearing the breakers in the distance, captain Noland ordered the *Ann Galley* and the *Fisher* to come to anchor. The iron flukes dug into the sand and, despite the surging seas, both vessels held their positions. The *Whydah*, however, was not so lucky.

AT ABOUT THE SAME time that the men aboard the other three vessels were fighting to keep from being wrecked, Bellamy and his men were waging the same battle, somewhere off the coast of modern-day Wellfleet, which at the time was part of Eastham.* Bellamy ordered the half-ton anchors lowered, but the storm was too

---

* Wellfleet was part of neighboring Eastham until 1763, achieving town status after forty years of petitioning.

powerful to resist. The *Whydah*, its anchors dragging behind, plowed into sandbars about one thousand feet from the shore, and roughly ten miles north of where the *Mary Anne* had struck. The crash sent the pirates flying, and transformed cannons and cargo into missiles that shot across the decks, crushing or maiming any who were in the way. The impact and the subsequent pounding of the waves broke the *Whydah* into pieces that, along with the vessel's contents, were strewn over four miles of coastline. Men who weren't pitched overboard by the initial collision or the waves sweeping over the decks were flung into the bone-chilling waters of the Atlantic as the ship's skeleton was torn apart.*

It is not clear exactly how many men were aboard the *Whydah* at the moment of impact, with reported numbers ranging from 130 to 163. However many there were, only two survived and were able to swim to shore—John Julian and Thomas Davis—while Bellamy, the primary author of this piratical tale, met his ignominious end in the churning waters of the violent sea.

Julian was either an Indian from Cape Cod, or a Moskito Indian from Central America, while Davis was an unmarried twenty-two-year-old Welshman who had been carpenter on the *St. Michael*, one of the merchant vessels that Bellamy and La Buse had captured in December 1716. Davis had been unwilling to go with the pirates, and when Bellamy forced him to join the *Whydah*, Davis made Bellamy promise that he would release him as soon as the next vessel was taken. When that time came, Bellamy forgot about his promise, and instead put Davis's fate up to a vote of the crew, which came down hard against the carpenter, damning him and saying that rather

---

*   Some have used the fact that the *Whydah* crashed off of Eastham as proof that Bellamy was, in fact, heading to Eastham in order to visit the love of his life, Mary Hallett. There is, however, no evidence that such an assignation was on Bellamy's mind, or, as was discussed earlier, that Bellamy and Hallett even knew each other. Instead, all of the available evidence, including the few clues left by some of Williams's crew who were later examined by authorities, indicates that both Bellamy and Williams were heading to Maine, not the Cape. But conjecture about a romance between Bellamy and Hallett does make for a good story.

than let him go, "they would first shoot him or whip him to death at the mast."

Swimming to shore was only the beginning of Davis and Julian's ordeal. With the storm raging, there was no gently sloping beach that they could drag themselves onto. Instead, still being battered by the breaking waves, and with their body temperature falling fast, they were confronted with steep sand cliffs, sections of which were nearly eighty feet high. Using their fast-waning strength, they were able to claw their way up the cliff face, struggling to gain purchase on the crumbling wall of sand, cascades of which gave way each time they planted their hands or feet. Once they made it to the top in the early morning hours of April 27, nearly spent, the two men split up. Julian's whereabouts for the next day or so are unknown, but Davis began walking inland, and at 5 a.m., about two miles from the edge of the cliff, he banged on the door of local farmer Samuel Harding.

Initially annoyed to be bothered by a stranger so early in the morning, Harding became almost giddy with excitement when Davis told him who he was, and how he got there. The residents of the Cape viewed a shipwreck as a great opportunity. In coastal communities throughout the world, for as long as ships sailed the seas, residents took advantage of wrecks, scavenging them for anything of value—the owner of the ship, or the government, which might have a claim to the wreck and its contents, be damned. To these so-called wreckers, what they could salvage on the beach or in the water was like manna from heaven. Wreckers were often called, in high American slang, "mooncussers" because they supposedly prayed for dark and cloudy nights, when wrecks were more likely, and were thought to curse the brightly shining moon, since it helped mariners find their way. In the late eighteenth century, the Reverend John Troutbeck, from Isles of Scilly in Great Britain, is credited with giving voice to the dreams of wreckers everywhere, by uttering the following invocation—"we pray to thee, O Lord, not that wrecks should happen, but that if any wrecks should happen, Thou wilt guide them into the Scilly Isles for the benefit of the poor inhabitants." This

*1. Illustration by Howard Pyle (1921) titled
"The Buccaneer Was a Picturesque Fellow."*

2. *The front and back of a two-escudos coin, or doubloon, minted in Seville, Spain between 1556 and 1598. Sold at auction in 2010 for $1,770.*

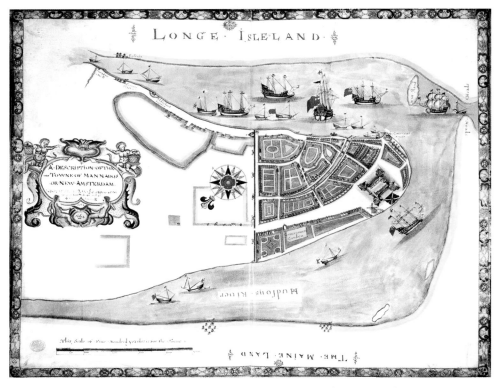

3. *A view of New Amsterdam in 1664. Notice the wall (fortification) extending across the entire top of Manhattan Island, shown near the middle of the image.*

4. *A 1697 map of Madagascar. The island of St. Marie (Nosy Boraha) is very small. Its border, which is shown in green, can be seen directly north of the ship illustration, and to the left of the words "Ocean Oriental."*

*5. Early eighteenth-century
portrait of William Kidd by
Sir James Thornhill.*

6. Captain William Kidd welcoming a woman aboard the Adventure Galley *in New York harbor. Print of a 1920 painting by Jean Leon Gerome Ferris.*

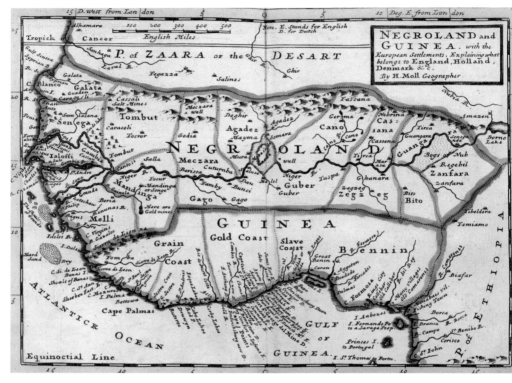

7. *This 1736 map shows "Negroland" and the Guinea coast,
which encompasses the main locations for the slave trade out of Africa.
The kingdom of Whydah (or Ouidah) is located in the vicinity
of the words "Slave Coast" on the map.*

8. Illustration by Howard Pyle (1921) titled
"Then the Real Fight Began."

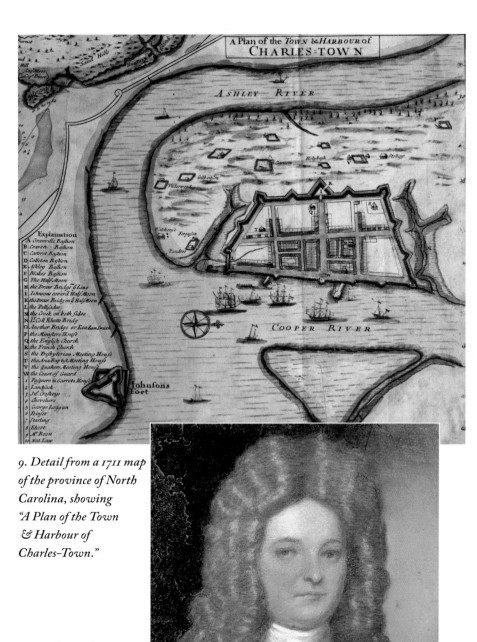

Explanation
A Granville Baſtion
B Craven Baſtion
C Carteret Baſtion
D Colleton Baſtion
E Aſhley Baſtion
F Blakes Baſtion
G The Half-Moon
H the Draw Bridge & Line
I Johnſons covered Half-Moon
K the Draw Bridge in y Half-Moon
L the Palliſadoe
M the Creek on both ſides
N 1ſt: old Rhets Bridg
O Another Bridge or Rat Zan Smith
P the Miniſters Houſe
Q the Engliſh Church
R the French Church
S the Presbyterian Meeting Houſe
T the AnaBaptyſt Meeting Houſe
V the Quakers Meeting Houſe
W the Court of Guard
1 Faſquero & Garrets Houſe
2 Landſack
3 Iuo Croſkeys
4 Chevaliers
5 George Loggan
6 Poinſet
7 Starling
8 Elicot
9 Mr Boon
10 Nat Law

Johnſons Fort

9. *Detail from a 1711 map of the province of North Carolina, showing "A Plan of the Town & Harbour of Charles-Town."*

10. *A pastel on paper portrait of Colonel William Rhett, circa 1710, by Henrietta De Beaulieu Dering Johnston.*

11. Painting by William Hogarth of Woodes Rogers on the right, along with his son and daughter, and at the far left, a female servant, circa 1729.

12. Pirate flag design attributed to Edward Low, as confirmed by contemporary newspaper accounts. The skeleton is holding an hourglass in one hand, and a dart in the other, which has punctured the heart, causing blood to drip from it. This same design has also been attributed to Blackbeard, although the author has not seen any contemporary accounts that corroborate that.

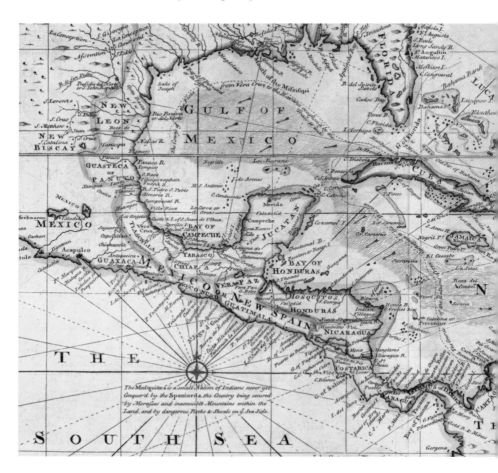

13. *Cover of* American Boy *magazine, March 1922, featuring the artwork of Frank Schoonover, which shows Blackbeard leading a charge.*

14. *Detail of a 1720 map showing the Caribbean and the adjacent coasts of North and South America.*

15. Since obtaining rights to an actual image of Johnny Depp as Captain Jack Sparrow was too difficult, here is a picture of a man posing as Depp/Sparrow in Hollywood, California. It's not the real thing, but a very good impersonation.

16. The Whydah's *bell, suspended in preservative solution within a tank on display at the* Whydah *Pirate Museum in West Yarmouth, Massachusetts.*

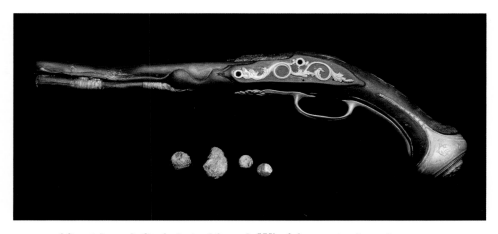

17. A Scottish-made flintlock pistol from the Whydah, *sporting brass dragons on its side plates and handle, along with the lead shot, wadding, and part of cartridge that were found inside the pistol's barrel.*

18. Some of the treasure recovered from the Whydah, *including pieces of eight, doubloons, jewelry, and silver and gold ingots.*

19. Cover of 1911 edition of Robert Louis Stevenson's Treasure Island, *illustrated by Nathaniel C. Wyeth.*

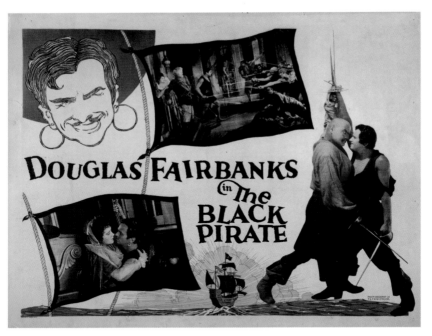

20. This 1926 silent film starred Douglas Fairbanks, one of the most famous actors of the silent era, often referred to as "The King of Hollywood." His son, Douglas Fairbanks Jr., was also a very famous actor.

21. In honor of my finishing this book, my daughter, Lily, did this small painting of a pirate ship looking for its next victim.

same philosophy animated Harding and his fellow Cape Codders, the only difference being that they would substitute their towns for the Scilly Isles.

As Harding well knew, this was not just any wreck, but a pirate shipwreck, meaning that scavenging might provide an exceptionally valuable return. Rather than let the exhausted carpenter rest beside the hearth, Harding gave Davis a blanket for warmth, readied his horse and wagon, and then asked Davis to climb in and lead him back to the wreck site. Harding made two round trips before word spread, and by ten in the morning there were nearly a dozen more wreckers searching the beach, a number that swelled greatly before the end of the day, when it wasn't only the beach, but also the visible remains of the *Whydah* offshore, that were being picked over. The wreckers searched for human debris as well. With each passing hour, more corpses washed ashore and were checked for valuables—jewelry, coins, and silver buckles—in a grisly postmortem. As one observer noted, the good people of Eastham and other nearby towns who went a-wrecking that day "got a great deal of riches."

MEANWHILE, THE *MARY ANNE* had mostly withstood the punishing storm, and at dawn the following day the ten survivors hopped out onto Pochet Island, where they passed the next few hours eating sweetmeats and drinking wine taken from the vessel. Bellamy's men also hastily concocted a cover story, telling the three crewmembers of the *Mary Anne* to refer to Brown as their captain, and to say that they, along with the rest of the pirates, were his crew.

Around ten, two local men, John Cole and William Smith, spying the *Mary Anne* and the people nearby, paddled their canoe to the island to investigate. Apparently they didn't suspect anything was amiss because they ferried the ten crewmen to the mainland and then took them to Cole's house. Cole offered them refreshments and noted that the men "looked very much dejected and cast down," and were eager to know the quickest way to Rhode Island (where, most likely, they hoped to find Bellamy's partner in crime,

Williams, or possibly seek refuge with his extended family). Suddenly emboldened, Mackconachy went off script and revealed to his host that seven of the men sitting around his fire were pirates, and that he and the others had been taken captive by them just the day before. Their cover now blown, the pirates rushed from the house, forcibly taking their prisoners with them.

As soon as the pirates left, Cole alerted Joseph Doane, the justice of the peace and a representative to the General Court who, in turn, assembled a small posse and went in pursuit. The pirates had made a beeline for the nearby Eastham Tavern, possibly to obtain horses to make their escape, and that was where Doane caught up with them. His questioning elicited confessions, whereupon he marched the pirates and the crewmen of the *Mary Anne* to the Barnstable jail. Not long after that, Doane also had Davis and Julian in custody. A few days later, all of the prisoners were taken on horseback and transferred to Boston's jail, where they were shackled in heavy iron chains while they awaited their fate.

AT THE SAME TIME that the pirates were escorted to the Barnstable jail, the *Ann Galley* and the *Fisher* were already sailing away. They had survived the storm anchored in place, and, having no idea what had happened to the other vessels, cut their cables and headed east, away from the Cape, as soon as the wind shifted direction and began blowing offshore. About ten miles out, captain Noland ordered the men on the *Fisher* to grab anything of value and board the *Ann Galley*. The *Fisher*'s mast was cut and pitched overboard, and its hatches left open so that the abandoned vessel would soon sink in the still choppy seas. The *Ann Galley* then headed north for the coast of Maine, where Noland still expected to reconnect with Bellamy and Williams.

DOANE DIDN'T ARRIVE AT the *Whydah* crash site until Sunday morning, April 28. The beach was alive with activity. Like vultures descending on a carcass, more than two hundred Cape Codders from as far as twenty miles away had swarmed the wreck site, taking all the valuable items they discovered in the water, along the beach, and on the 102 corpses that lay scattered about. Doane warned the ravenous wreckers that any salvaged items belonged to the king, and ordered them to turn over what they had found. Not surprisingly, only trifling things were offered up.

Massachusetts governor Samuel Shute, alerted within days of the crash, ordered Captain Cyprian Southack to head to the site of the wreck and reclaim what valuables he could. A well-known cartographer and privateer who lived in Boston, Southack showed up on May 3, and was greeted with a unified wall of resistance. Upon learning what the local residents had done, he demanded in the name of the governor that they hand over what they had scavenged, threatening to search their houses and places of business if need be to find anything they might be hiding. But "these people are very stiff," he later recalled, and they would give up "nothing of what they got on the wreck." Even when the governor's proclamation arrived a few days later, ordering all citizens to deliver any "money, bullion, treasure, goods, and merchandise" taken from the wreck, and threatening residents with punitive action should they hold anything back, the reticent Cape Codders held their ground. They had clearly decided that the treasure they sifted from the sand, pulled from the shallows, or stripped from the corpses that washed ashore, would enrich them and their descendants, rather than the colony or the Crown.

Southack's own recovery efforts fared little better. He scoured the beach and sent men in whaleboats to search the waters around the wreck, but their work was hobbled by continued bad weather. Ultimately, Southack was only able to reclaim a few things, including cut-up cables, sails, two cannons, two anchors, and some furniture. Those items were subsequently sold at two public auctions in Boston over the next few months, netting £265, which was remitted to Southack to reimburse him for expenses he accrued while conducting his disappointing search on the Cape.

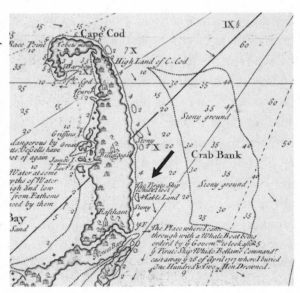

Detail of Cyprian Southack's map of Massachusetts, circa 1734. A thick arrow (not original to the map) points to where Southack wrote "The Pirate Ship Whidah *Lost." Below that to the right is more text in which Southack informs the reader that he buried 102 men from the wreck who had drowned.*

ACCORDING TO ONE OF their crew, both Williams and Bellamy had agreed before they left the Caribbean to meet up at Richmond Island, off the coast of Cape Elizabeth, Maine. But for reasons that are unknown, after leaving the Cape behind, the *Ann Galley* sailed to Monhegan Island, which is nearly fifty miles from Richmond Island. There the pirates waited a little more than a week for the *Whydah* to arrive, in the meantime sending out the galley's longboat on a few successful piratical forays in the area. On May 9, the dispirited men on the *Ann Galley* gave up waiting and began sailing back to the Caribbean.

After riding out the storm near the tip of Long Island, Williams took the *Marianne* north toward Maine, capturing four small trading vessels along the way, one of which he kept to help with careening. On May 18, he arrived at Richmond Island, but only stayed there for a day or two before sailing another thirty miles northeast to Damariscove Island, where he and his men cleaned their ship. Still wondering what had happened to the *Whydah* and its consorts, Williams weighed anchor at Damariscove Island on May 23 and headed south. Two days later, near Provincetown, he stopped the *Swallow,* a schooner from Salem, Massachusetts, whose master relayed horrible news. He told Williams that the *Whydah* was gone, and that the remnants of Bellamy's crew were being held in Boston's jail. The personal as well as financial loss that Williams and his men felt must have been almost unbearable. Not only were many of their friends and partners dead or in jail, but the massive treasure they had stolen from scores of ships in the Caribbean was gone for good. No doubt very depressed, and cursing their bad luck, Williams and his men, like the men of the *Ann Galley*, sailed for the Caribbean.

IN THE AFTERMATH OF the *Whydah*'s crash, Governor Shute's emotions ran the gamut from elation to anger to fear. He was overjoyed that the pirates had foundered on the coast, and that the survivors were safely ensconced in jail, awaiting trial. At one point, he even thanked God for "guarding our sea coast, by taking into his own hands a great number of wicked pirates, that came with designs to rob and spoil us." He was also furious with the wreckers and their fellow citizens on the Cape who chose to hoard the riches they found rather than turn them over. And he was fearful of what the pirates who got away might do next.

Shute's fears were realized when, just a few days after Bellamy's men were locked up in Boston, news arrived that the *Marianne* had plundered two merchant ships off Martha's Vineyard and forced one man to join their crew. Shute was in New Hampshire at the time, attending to gubernatorial business, but in his absence, Lieutenant Governor William Dummer sprang into action. He ordered the frigate HMS *Rose* and a colonial sloop armed with ninety men to track down the *Marianne*, as well as the *Ann Galley*, which, it was feared, might also go on the hunt. At the same time, Dummer placed a one-week embargo on all shipping leaving the colony, to reduce the chances that the pirates would capture more vessels.

The entire region was on alert. Rhode Island's governor, Samuel Cranston, equally alarmed by the *Marianne*'s recent attacks, ordered "two good sloops, well armed and manned" to go "in quest of the pirates." He wrote a note to his fellow governor, stating his most fervent hope that God would bless Shute's efforts to "surprise and capture those inhuman monsters of prey so as our navigation may be made more safe and secure."

The search efforts failed, and by the time the HMS *Rose* gave up in late May, both the *Ann Galley* and the *Marianne* had already left New England waters. On his way down the coast, Williams and the *Marianne* threw the more southerly colonies into a panic, plundering ships off the coasts of New Jersey, Delaware, Virginia, and the Carolinas. After one of the vessels he had been pursuing made a futile attempt to escape, Williams "barbarously beat" the captain for being so bold. Among the items that Williams and his men stole from their unlucky victims were clothes, sails, rigging, flour, wine, cannons, and 350 ounces of silver that were buried in a ship's ballast for safekeeping, but were reluctantly retrieved by the captain when Williams threatened to burn the ship unless all of the money onboard was turned over.

Recalcitrant captains weren't the only problem Williams faced on his cruise down the coast. Off Sandy Hook, New Jersey, the forced men aboard the *Marianne* attempted a mutiny but were viciously beat back by Williams and his loyal supporters. In the melee, five or six of the mutineers were wounded, and although none died of their injuries, three of them lost their lives when Williams hanged them from a yardarm.* Finally, after weeks of terrorizing the American coast, the *Marianne* took leave of the colonies and sailed south.

From this point forward, Williams largely fades from the historical record, and the last known sighting of him is off Africa in 1720, where he was quartermaster on a pirate brigantine captained by La Buse, the same pirate whom he and Bellamy had sailed with in 1716. It appears that Williams was not altogether happy with his demotion, for it was common knowledge among La Buse's prisoners that Williams liked to be addressed as "captain," and that such flattery

---

*   The outer extremity of a ship's yard—the yard being a horizontal spar on a mast from which the sails are set.

was the best way to stay on his good side, what little of it might have remained.

BELLAMY'S MEN LANGUISHED IN jail until October 1717, when their trial began. But they were not left entirely alone. Toward the end of their incarceration, Cotton Mather visited them many times, strenuously encouraging them to repent. Mather also repeated a story that had been ricocheting throughout the colonies. He claimed that after the *Whydah* had wrecked, the pirates had "horribly *murdered all their prisoners* . . . lest they should appear as *witnesses* against them. The doleful *cries* heard upon the shore, a little before she sank; and the bloody *wounds* found in the bodies afterwards thrown ashore; were two great confirmations of this report." This made for wonderful reading, but it was pure fabrication. The pirates were too busy trying (unsuccessfully) to save themselves to have any time to murder anyone; the only "prisoners" aboard the *Whydah* at the time, not including forced men, were Captain Crumpsley and five of his crew; and there was no evidence that they, or anyone else who was washed ashore, had been murdered. As for people hearing "doleful cries," or other utterances coming from the doomed ship, the intense violence of the storm guaranteed that nobody on shore heard anything but the shrieking of the wind and crashing of the waves.

Although nine pirates were captured, only eight of them went before the Court of Admiralty in Boston, since Julian, the Indian, apparently was sold into slavery. Two trials ensued. The first, which began on October 18, was for the seven pirates who survived the wreck of the *Mary Anne*, while the second trial began on October 28 and focused on Thomas Davis, the only survivor, along with Julian, of the wreck of the *Whydah*. At the outset of both proceedings, James Smith, the king's advocate, painted a damning portrait of the pirate as the "Enemy of Mankind," who has earned, through foul deeds, his lowly and utterly disreputable status. "He can claim the protection of no prince," Smith intoned, "the privilege of no country, the benefit of no law; He is denied common humanity, and the very rights of nature, with whom no faith, promise nor oath is to be observed, nor is he to be otherwise dealt with, than as a wild & savage beast, which every man may lawfully destroy."

In the first trial, the charges against the seven men pertained to the seizing and plundering of the *Mary Anne*, and not to any earlier acts of piracy. All of them pleaded innocent, claiming that they had been forced by Bellamy to join his pirate crew. Smith attempted to destroy this defense by arguing that the men had not been forced, and even if they had been, that could "never excuse their guilt, since no case of necessity can justify a direct violation of the divine and moral law, and give one the liberty of *sinning*." And guilty they were, Smith asserted, because they had clearly committed piratical acts, and when they had the chance to escape and, thereby, renounce piracy, by sailing off with the *Mary Anne*, they instead blindly followed Bellamy to their doom.

The court found six of the men guilty, and sentenced them to hang. The seventh man, however, Thomas South, was found not guilty. In so doing, the court pointed to testimony from multiple witnesses that proved that South had indeed been forced, and had not participated in piratical acts. Instead, he had come aboard the *Mary Anne* unarmed, had been "civil and kind" to its crew, and had revealed to one of them his plan to escape from the pirates as soon as possible.

In the second trial, Davis faced charges that he was part of Bellamy's crew, and as such, had been involved in the taking of the *Whydah* and one other vessel off the Virginia Capes. The testimony of South, as well as some of Davis's former crewmates, proved to the satisfaction of the courts that Davis had been forced and had not taken an active part in the piracy, resulting in a not-guilty verdict. Upon hearing this, Davis dropped to his knees and profusely thanked the judges, who then admonished him to stay out of trouble.

ON FRIDAY, NOVEMBER 15, the six condemned men were paraded from the prison to the place of execution at Hudson's Point. Mather accompanied them on what he called this "long and sad walk," finally arriving at "the Tree of Death," where he said he "prayed with them, and with the vast assembly of spectators, as pertinently and as profitably as I could." Mather later published a pamphlet in which he recorded his conversations with the pirates that, in his telling, were full of many heartfelt admissions of sin and hopes for salvation. After recounting the grim scene of the pirates' hanging, Mather concluded the pamphlet with a final and stunningly bold claim—"Behold, Reader, The End of *Piracy!*" He couldn't have been more wrong.

CHAPTER 8

The Gentleman Pirate and Blackbeard

Blackbeard as portrayed in the 1726 edition of Johnson's A General History of the Pyrates.

Between the crash of the *WHYDAH* at the end of April 1717, and the executions of Bellamy's men the following November, pirates continued to plague the American colonies. In addition to Williams's depredations, La Buse struck a few nasty blows, including one in which his men slashed and brutally beat the captain of a New Hampshire merchant ship captured off the coast of North Carolina and then threatened to skin and burn him alive before letting him go. The litany of attacks prompted one of Philadelphia's most successful merchants and future mayor of the city, James Logan, to write to a friend near the end of the year, complaining, "We have been extremely pestered w[i]th pirates who now swarm in America and increase their numbers by almost every vessel they take." Of all those pirates, there were two who would go down in history as among the most notorious and fascinating, less so for their attacks in 1717 than for their bold captures the following year, and the dramatic manner in which their pirating careers intertwined and came to a violent end. They were Stede Bonnet, the "gentleman pirate," and Edward Thatch, better known as Blackbeard.

BORN INTO A PROSPEROUS sugar plantation–owning family on Barbados in 1688, Bonnet's early life was one of wealth and privilege. Waited on by servants and slaves, given a liberal education, taught to enjoy the finer things in life, and quite familiar with the job of running the plantation, in 1708 he was fully prepared to take over his family's estate, which had been held in guardianship for him in the wake of his parents' death. A year later, at the age of twenty-one, he married Mary Allamby, the daughter of another plantation owner, and they settled in Bridgetown, Barbados's capital and the location of its principal harbor. By 1717, the couple had four children, one of whom died before reaching his first birthday, and Bonnet had gained the title of "Major"—an indication of his status on the island

A view of Bridgetown, Barbados, circa 1695.

where he was "generally esteemed and honored," and considered a "Gentleman of good reputation."

At this time, and perhaps earlier, Bonnet's friends and associates began to notice that he suffered from "a disorder in his mind, which had been too visible" to ignore, and he began to act uncharacteristically for a man of his social standing. Some have speculated that Bonnet's sudden change in behavior was due to depression, or even insanity, while others have traced its origins to some "discomforts" he found in his married life.

Either in late 1716 or early 1717, he commissioned the building of a sixty-ton pirate sloop fitted with ten guns, and christened it *Revenge*. Inexplicably, Bonnet had decided to abandon his plantation and his family, and become a pirate. Of course, he couldn't share his intentions with the shipwrights, his fellow planters, or any local officials. For years, pirates had profited mightily at the island's expense, attacking merchantmen sailing to and from Barbados. The island's upstanding citizens would look none too kindly upon one of their own going on the account, and would certainly put a stop to his plan had they known its design. Instead, Bonnet probably claimed that he was going to be a privateer, and would soon obtain a commission to hunt pirates from the governor at Jamaica or some other British outpost in the Caribbean. It is quite possible that this is also the story he told his wife, Mary, assuming they were still on speaking terms.

When recruiting crewmembers for his expedition, Bonnet most likely approached men in Bridgetown's bars and wharves and told them, in hushed tones, that he wanted them to sign on as pirates, not privateers. That he was offering them a salary, instead of a share of the plunder, as was customary for both pirates and privateers, was unusual to say the least, and undoubtedly bewildered some of his potential recruits. Despite this odd financial arrangement, and the fact that Bonnet lacked any seafaring experience, his pitch was per-suasive, because in the spring of 1717 the *Revenge* set sail, with a complement of 126 men.

In addition to the typical supplies one would expect, includ-ing food, water, rum, ammunition, powder, rigging, and sails, the *Revenge* had some very unusual items onboard, at least for a pirate ship. Not wanting to divorce entirely from the life he was leaving behind, Bonnet had his captain's cabin stocked with books from

Stede Bonnet as depicted in the 1725 edition of Johnson's **General History of Pyrates.**

his personal library. But that is the only connection he wanted to maintain. Hoping to shield his identity and not besmirch his family name, Bonnet asked his men to address him as Captain Edwards during the trip.

Being a novice at sea, Bonnet had to rely completely on his crew to sail the ship, and he ordered them to head for the Virginia Capes. Despite Bonnet's inexperience as a pirate leader, the *Revenge* enjoyed considerable success throughout the late spring and early summer, sailing near the capes and as far north as the east end of Long Island, plundering five merchant vessels and burning one to its waterline. By late August, Bonnet and his men were off the coast of Charleston, South Carolina (at the time called Charles Town, in honor of King Charles II of England—its name changed to Charleston in 1783).

CHARLESTON WAS THE CAPITAL of South Carolina and its largest city, with a population hovering around three thousand, most of whom lived on sixty-two acres of high and relatively dry ground located near the tip of a marsh-pocked peninsula at the confluence of the Ashley and Cooper Rivers. On any given day, a diverse mix of individuals could be found on the town's broad and straight dirt streets, including wealthy planters, farmers, merchants, traders, sailors, Indians, prostitutes, indentured servants, and an ever-increasing number of slaves. "It was," said one chronicler of the town, "a potpourri of nationalities and racial groups and a corresponding Babel of languages and sounds."

The only fortified city in the American colonies, Charleston was surrounded by earthen and brick walls intended to protect it from attack. South Carolina's plantation economy, fueled by rice cultivation and the production of naval stores from longleaf pines (tar, pitch, and turpentine), was almost entirely dependent upon slave labor. South Carolina imported more slaves than any other colony, and all of them were brought into Charleston, where they were auctioned off to the highest bidder. Given this veritable flood of shackled humanity, it is not surprising that blacks outnumbered whites in the colony by a margin of nearly two to one.

Maritime traffic to and from the busy port of Charleston had to navigate the treacherous Charleston Bar, a series of submerged shoals about eight miles southeast of the city. The *Revenge* positioned itself just beyond the bar, waiting for victims to sail by, and on August 26 two vessels fell into the trap. The first was a brigantine captained by Thomas Porter, heading in from Boston, followed by Captain Joseph Palmer's sloop from Barbados. Rather than plunder them so close to Charleston, and likely raise an alarm in the city, Bonnet took the vessels to a secluded inlet on the North Carolina coast. After relieving Palmer's vessel of its cargo of rum and sugar, Bonnet's men used his sloop to careen the *Revenge*, and then they torched it. They then turned their attention to the brigantine, stripping it of its cargo, anchors, cables, and nearly all of its rigging and sails. Palmer, his crew, and the slaves he had been transporting were subsequently loaded back onto the brigantine, as the *Revenge* sailed away.

Bonnet had left the brigantine in a perilous situation. With barely any sails and rigging, Porter made slow progress down the coast, and he was soon "forced to let" most of those aboard, including the slaves, to "have his boat to go on shore, else they would have all been starved for want of provisions." The brigantine finally arrived in Charleston in mid-September, at which point Bonnet and his men were already back in Nassau. When Palmer reported his encounter with the *Revenge* to the local authorities, he relayed an interesting piece of information. Although the crew of the *Revenge* had referred to their captain as Mr. Edwards, Palmer knew that was not his real name: being from Barbados, he recognized Major Bonnet, and told the authorities the true identity of the guilty pirate.

ON THE WAY TO the Bahamas, the *Revenge* came across a Spanish man-of-war. A prudent pirate, especially one in a sloop mounting a mere ten guns, would not dare tangle with so formidable a foe, and instead would steer clear with all deliberate speed. But Bonnet

Blackbeard as depicted in the 1736 edition of Johnson's General History of Pyrates, *with lit matches burning at the end of his braided hair, emitting wisps of smoke.*

was no such pirate. Emboldened by his success along the American coast, he chose to attack the man-of-war, but quickly regretted this foolhardy decision. The Spanish ship unleashed a barrage of fire that killed or wounded thirty or forty of Bonnet's men, with Bonnet among the severely injured. Amazingly, the *Revenge* itself, though heavily damaged, had not been completely disabled, and the remaining crew were able to sail away, avoiding a coup de grâce. When the crew of *Revenge* arrived at Nassau Harbor a short while later, Bonnet, for the first time, came face-to-face with Edward Thatch.

MORE INK HAS PROBABLY been spilled writing about Thatch, or the legendary Blackbeard, than any other pirate of the Golden Age, yet we know precious little about him, and so much of what has been written is based on nothing more than imagination or educated guesses. Although his contemporaries most commonly used *Thatch* as the spelling for his last name, he was also referred to as *Teach*, *Tach*, *Tack*, *Thatche*, and *Thache*. His birthplace is hotly contested, with claims made for Bristol (England), Jamaica, North Carolina, Virginia, and Philadelphia; the first two tend to garner the most support. Of course, since his birthplace is uncertain, so too is his birth year. And while it is often claimed that he served as a privateer in the War of the Spanish Succession, there is no clear evidence to that effect.

Another controversial part of Blackbeard's personal biography is his appearance. The only firsthand accounts of what he looked like are frustratingly terse. A crewman on one of the ships Blackbeard captured in late 1717 said that he "was a tall spare man with a very black beard which he wore very long." A naval officer who battled Blackbeard a year later commented that he went by the "name of Blackbeard, because he let his beard grow, and tied it up in black ribbons."

No one built up the mythology of Blackbeard more enthusiastically than Johnson, who took these short eyewitness descriptions and whipped them into one of the most celebrated passages in the history of piracy. Johnson said of Thatch that he had "assumed the cognomen of black-beard, from that large quantity of hair, which like a frightful meteor, covered his whole face, and frightened America more than any comet that has appeared there a long time." Blackbeard grew his beard, Johnson continued, to "an extravagant length; as to breadth, it came up to his eyes. He was accustomed to twist it with ribbons, in small tails, after the manner of our ramillies wigs,* and turn them about his ears." During battle, he "wore a sling over his shoulders, with three brace of pistols, hanging in holsters, like bandoliers; and stuck lighted matches under his hat, which, appearing on each side of his face, his eyes naturally looking fierce and

---

* A Ramillies wig is one with a length of braided or unbraided hair hanging down the back that is tied off with ribbons or bows at the top and the bottom, sort of like a fancy pigtail.

wild, made him altogether such a figure that imagination cannot form an idea of a Fury from Hell to look more frightful."

Of course, Johnson, who was writing a few years after Blackbeard had died, might actually have received these details from mariners who had come into contact with the pirate. But there is reason to believe that he used some literary license in painting this dramatic portrait. This is especially the case when it comes to the "lighted matches," since not a single contemporary account penned while Blackbeard was alive mentions them. One would think that sailors who were captured by or who fought Blackbeard might have, at the very least, noted flames shooting out from under his hat, quite apart from the fact that this seems to be a particularly dangerous way of going into battle, even for a pirate who was intent on instilling fear in his victims.

Another area in which fiction seems to have slayed fact concerns Blackbeard's purported brutal behavior. He is often portrayed as a ruthless, even murderous character who terrorized his foes. But with the exception of the battle that would take his life, and one other instance in which his men viciously whipped the captain of a merchant ship who refused to divulge where he had hidden valuables, there is no evidence of Blackbeard harming anyone to get what he wanted. "In fact," as historian Arne Bialuschewski observes, "the image of Blackbeard as a fearsome and ruthless villain was created by the media of the day." In reality, Blackbeard's success was achieved in the manner preferred by pirates the world over—through intimidation and the threat of overwhelming force.

What can be said with considerable assurance is that Blackbeard did, indeed, sport a black beard, and he was a strong leader who inspired confidence in his men during his relatively short piratical career. That famed career was less than a year old when the *Revenge* sailed into Nassau in the late summer of 1717.

BONNET AND HIS CREW entered Nassau's harbor knowing that this was the most formidable pirate stronghold in the Atlantic, and likely the world, and they were awed by the scope of the pirate army arrayed before them. A thirty-two-gun ship stood guard in the harbor, and many other pirate vessels, including Hornigold's ten-gun sloop and Blackbeard's six-gun sloop, were anchored nearby. Beyond, on the shore, there were many hundreds, and perhaps more than one thousand, pirates going about their business, relaxing, drinking, dividing their booty, and planning their next expedition.

As the Nassau pirates listened to the men of the *Revenge* tell the tale of their successes, and their near-death experience with the Spanish man-of-war, they were no doubt alternately impressed and amused. The *Revenge*'s inexperienced captain with the upper-class, gentlemanly pedigree must have elicited intense curiosity, if not some sympathy, for his trial by fire and grievous wounds.

Blackbeard, who had earned his pirating skills as part of the Flying Gang, where he appeared to be one of Hornigold's protégés, viewed the *Revenge* as an opportunity. The damage inflicted by the Spanish man-of-war could be repaired, and the *Revenge* was a better, more powerful vessel than Blackbeard's sloop. So Blackbeard, perhaps with Hornigold's help, convinced the still-injured Bonnet that it would be best for all if he stepped down as the captain of the *Revenge*, and let Blackbeard take his place. Bonnet would remain aboard and continue to use the captain's quarters while he recuperated, but he would no longer be the master of his own ship.

The *Revenge* was repaired, reprovisioned, and fitted with two more guns, giving it a total of twelve. With the addition of Blackbeard's crew to the survivors of Bonnet's, the *Revenge* now had an impressive 150 men, making the sloop very crowded indeed. Looking for game, Blackbeard headed to the American coast in late September. Over the next month, never staying in one place for more than forty-eight hours, he and his men plundered at least ten vessels from North Carolina to New York, sinking one, dismasting a few others, and keeping one sloop with six guns as a consort. Although the pirates found some goods to their liking, especially the rum, they recklessly threw tons of unwanted items overboard, either for sport or out of spite. A passenger who had shipped more than one thousand pounds of cargo pleaded with the pirates to leave him enough cloth to make just one suit of clothes, but they ignored him, pitching everything he owned into the sea.

When Blackbeard's victims reported their ordeals back on shore, a few of them made special mention of Bonnet's unusual presence. As one paper noted, on "the pirate sloop is Major Bennet [Bonnet], but [he] has no command; he walks about in his morning gown, and then to his books, of which he has a good library onboard." The same account added that Bonnet was still suffering mightily from his wounds.

During this spree, Blackbeard evinced a particular hatred for New Englanders. Either back in Nassau, or from one of the vessels he captured, Blackbeard learned of Bellamy's fate, and that members of his crew were awaiting trial in Boston. Blackbeard knew Bellamy from when he was part of Hornigold's Flying Gang, and like many pirates, he felt a sense of comradeship with all of those who went on the account. To express his anger at the imprisonment of his fellow pirates, and hopefully instill enough fear in the hearts of Bostonians to get them to carefully consider how they treated their prisoners, Blackbeard threatened all New Englanders he encountered, telling them that if Bellamy's crew suffered, he would "revenge it on them."

A FEW WEEKS LATER, the *Revenge* and its consort were back in the Caribbean. On November 28, while they prowled the waters about one hundred miles east of Martinique, an unusually large vessel came into view. It was the frigate *La Concorde*, a 250-ton French slaver, with sixteen guns (and ports for up to forty). It had left the African kingdom of Whydah at the beginning of October with 516 slaves crammed below decks. Under normal conditions, the *Concorde* would have had an excellent chance of defending herself against two pirate ships of the size and power that Blackbeard commanded. Not only was it well armed, but when *La Concorde* left Nantes, France, in March, it also had a crew of seventy-five, many of whom had been on other slave voyages and were thus well prepared for any threats posed by pirates. The conditions on the vessel, however, were far from normal.

Sailing from France to Whydah, *La Concorde* was battered by severe storms that ripped away its figurehead and drowned a crewman who was swept overboard. The misery worsened on the transit across the Atlantic. According to *La Concorde's* captain, Pierre Dosset, sixteen crewmen perished and another thirty-six were laid low with "scurvy and the bloody flux [dysentery]." With so few men capable of action, Dosset couldn't have fought back even if he had wanted to. So, when Blackbeard moved in with his pirate flag waving from the mast, the French captain promptly surrendered.

Blackbeard took *La Concorde* to the nearby island of Bequia, where the sorting commenced. *La Concorde* became Blackbeard's new flagship and was christened *Queen Anne's Revenge.* To make it more powerful, six cannons were brought aboard from a small sloop that Blackbeard had taken the month before off the American coast. Most of the pirates joined Blackbeard on the *Queen Anne's Revenge,* and the rest went with Bonnet who, having recovered sufficiently from his injuries, reassumed command of the *Revenge.*

This French merchantman, circa 1714, is thought to be quite similar to La Concorde, *which Blackbeard transformed into* Queen Anne's Revenge.

Blackbeard bulked up his crew by forcing ten of *La Concorde*'s men into his ranks. One was a common sailor, but the other nine were strategic additions chosen for their specialized skills—three doctors, two carpenters, a caulker, a cook, a navigator, and a gunsmith. Four other men joined voluntarily, with one proving his value immediately by turning informant. Louis Arot, a fifteen-year-old cabin boy, told Blackbeard that Dosset and his officers were hiding bags of gold dust. This prompted the pirates to threaten to "cut the throats" of the crew unless the bags were quickly retrieved, and in short order they were handed over.

Sixty-one slaves from *La Concorde* were also transferred to the *Queen Anne's Revenge*, many of whom were later released when one of Blackbeard's consorts accidentally grounded on Grenada, forcing it to lighten its load to free itself. Some of those slaves were ultimately returned to Dosset after being identified by the unique brands burned into their skin, showing them to be the "property" of *La Concorde*, and reflecting the often-brutal methods slavers used to retain their slaves. As for Dosset, and what remained of his crew and human cargo, they were left on Bequia, but they weren't marooned. Blackbeard gave them the small sloop he had stripped of its guns, as well as a few tons of beans to keep them from starving. In two trips, Dosset was able to ferry his charges to Martinique, a little more than one hundred miles away. No doubt as a nod to their recent travails, and with a touch of morbid humor, the French named the sloop *Mauvaise Rencontre*, or Bad Encounter.

FOR MONTHS, BLACKBEARD AND BONNET sailed together throughout the Lesser Antilles, capturing numerous ships and greatly increasing the firepower of the *Queen Anne's Revenge*, bringing its complement up to forty guns and swelling the size of its crew to an astounding three hundred. Then, toward the end of March 1718, the two pirate captains split up for unknown reasons, but quite possibly because Blackbeard might have tired of his less than well-seasoned consort. A short while later, in the early evening of March 28, Bonnet saw a merchantman in the distance, not far from the island of Roatán in the Gulf of Honduras. Despite the fact that this four-hundred-ton ship dwarfed the *Revenge* and had twenty-six guns onboard, Bonnet, displaying the same recklessness he displayed when attempting to take on the Spanish man-of-war, decided to take the vessel.

Captain William Wyer, of the *Protestant Caesar* out of Boston, saw the *Revenge* sailing toward him. Convinced that it was a pirate, Wyer prepared for battle. At about nine o'clock, the *Revenge* came under the *Protestant Caesar*'s stern and fired several shots. Wyer's men countered with the *Protestant Caesar*'s stern chase guns and a volley of small arms. Bonnet then hailed the *Protestant Caesar* with a speaking trumpet, identifying himself as a pirate, and telling them that if they fired again, he would give them no quarter.

Wyer wasn't afraid of this puny pirate, and for his answer he let his guns do the talking. The *Revenge* and the *Protestant Caesar* fought at close range for three hours, both the ships and the crews sustaining significant injuries. At midnight, the *Revenge* gave up its attack and sailed away, while the *Protestant Caesar* continued on to the coast of Honduras to get a load of logwood.

A few days later, the *Revenge* sailed to Turneffe Atoll, about twenty-five miles off the coast of modern-day Belize City. Bonnet and his men were surprised to find the *Queen Anne's Revenge* anchored in one of the lagoons, along with another small sloop Blackbeard had added as a consort. The reunion was not a sweet one for Bonnet. His men were infuriated with his lack of skill and leadership, which had already twice placed many of them in grave danger, and they wanted nothing more to do with the man. With the consent of Bonnet's crew, Blackbeard took control of the *Revenge* and installed one of his men, named Richards, as captain. According to Johnson, Blackbeard tried to make Bonnet feel better about his denouement, "telling him, that as he had not been used to the fatigues and care" of running a pirate ship, "it would be better for him to" leave it behind, and instead, "live easy, at his pleasure," on the *Queen Anne's Revenge*, "where he would not be obliged to perform the necessary duties of a sea voyage." Whether Bonnet was let down easy by Blackbeard, or summarily dumped by his men, the end result was the same— Bonnet was now just a passenger on a pirate cruise, and no doubt a very depressed one at that.

While the pirates were still at anchor, the merchantman *Adventure*, captained by David Herriot, sailed into the lagoon. Thinking that the *Queen Anne's Revenge* was the *Protestant Caesar*, Herriot came in closer but then, realizing his mistake, and believing that the strange ships were Spanish, he suddenly tacked about, trying to escape. While the *Adventure* was turning, the pirates fired on it, and the *Revenge* slipped its cable, raised its black flag, and pursued the fleeing ship. Upon coming alongside the *Adventure*, Captain Richards ordered Herriot to let down his boat and come aboard. Herriot complied, and Richards sent five of his men to the *Adventure*, who brought it to anchor nearby. Blackbeard liked the *Adventure* so much that he decided to add it, as well as its crew, to his growing pirate armada. Herriot was transferred to the *Queen Anne's Revenge*, and Blackbeard's quartermaster, Israel Hands, was made captain of the *Adventure*.

Turneffe continued to be a productive hunting ground for the pirates, and in short order they plundered a few more sloops that had the misfortune of sailing into the lagoon, including the *Land of Promise*, captained by Thomas Newton, which the pirates took on as a third consort. On April 6, Blackbeard and his entourage left Turneffe with a very specific goal in mind. Bonnet's men had told him of the *Revenge*'s embarrassing encounter with the *Protestant Caesar*, and Blackbeard decided that he needed to teach Captain Wyer a lesson. Blackbeard shared his plan with Newton, telling him that he was going to burn the *Protestant Caesar* so that "he might not brag when he went to New England that he had beat a pirate."

On the morning of April 8, Blackbeard found his target off the coast of Honduras. Captain Wyer had fifty tons of logwood onboard, and was planning to load more that day, when he saw a chilling sight. The *Queen Anne's Revenge* and the *Revenge*, their black flags waving in the wind, were bearing down on the *Protestant Caesar*.

Flanking them were three other pirate sloops with red flags aloft. Wyer called his officers and men to the main deck, and asked "if they would stand by him and defend the ship." If the ships were Spanish, Wyer's men said they "would stand by him as long as they had life, but if they were pirates, they would not fight." Although it should have been clear by virtue of the flags that they were pirates, Wyer decided to find out for sure, and sent his second mate on the ship's boat to determine who they were. When word came back that it was the notorious Blackbeard, as well as the pirate sloop he and his crew had humiliated just a few weeks before, Wyer's men panicked. They all went ashore immediately, fearing that if they stayed they would be "murdered by the sloop's company." Wyer, being no fool, left with them.

For three days Blackbeard's flotilla anchored near the *Protestant Caesar*, plundering it of its valuables. Finally, on April 11, Blackbeard, in a forgiving mood, sent word to Wyer that if he came aboard the *Queen Anne's Revenge*, he would not be harmed. When Wyer arrived, Blackbeard said he was "glad" that he and his men had left their ship, for if they hadn't, the *Revenge*'s crew "would have done . . . [them] damage for fighting" back. Still, Blackbeard told Wyer that he wouldn't be returning to his ship. Because the *Protestant Caesar* "belonged to Boston," and Boston had executed six of Bellamy's men, Blackbeard said that to avenge his fellow pirates he must set the ship ablaze. The following day, Blackbeard's men burned the *Protestant Caesar* to the waterline. Wyer and his men were placed on the *Land of Promise*, along with Captain Newton and his men, and they were let go.

For more than a month, Blackbeard and his three consorts slowly made their way north, passing by the Cayman Islands, Cuba, and the site where the Spanish treasure fleet was wrecked in the summer of 1715. Along the way they captured at least twenty ships, added more crew, and kept a Spanish sloop, mounted with eight guns, that was taken near Havana. By May 22, 1718, Blackbeard was just off the coast of Charleston preparing to execute his boldest venture yet—blockading the entire city.

———

BLACKBEARD'S FOUR VESSELS—*Queen Anne's Revenge, Adventure, Revenge*, and the Spanish sloop—with a combined total of almost four hundred men, spread out in an arc just beyond the Charleston Bar, in short order capturing a pilot boat and five other vessels—two leaving the city for London, two heading in the opposite direction, and one coasting sloop. As word of the massive pirate force lurking nearby spread throughout the city and beyond, panic spread among the people, and none of the vessels in the harbor dared to leave.

Blackbeard ordered the prisoners, roughly eighty in number, to be brought aboard the *Queen Anne's Revenge*, where he examined their papers and interrogated them to find out what valuables they had, which the pirates then collected. It was not a particularly impressive haul, amounting to about £1,500 worth of gold and pieces of eight, as well as various provisions and miscellaneous cargo. Having fleeced the prisoners, Blackbeard sent them back to their respective vessels in such a precipitous rush that "it struck great terror in the unfortunate people, verily believing they were then going to their destruction; and what seemed to confirm them in this notion was" the fact that all prisoners, young and old, of high station and low, were locked below decks, not a pirate among them.

Huddled in the dark, the prisoners feared that at any moment their vessel might be torched or scuttled, but before they had too long to dwell on their possible demise, they were suddenly brought back into the light, and taken once again to the *Queen Anne's Revenge*. While they remained in a fearful state on the main deck, Blackbeard convened his men in council to decide their next step. With so many prisoners aboard, the pirates could potentially use them as bargaining chips to get a great ransom from the city in the form of gold or silver. One prisoner was a particularly valuable hostage—Samuel Wragg, a member of the South Carolina Provincial Council, who was heading to London with his four-year-old son. In the end, however, the pirates set their sights on a more practical type of treasure. Back in the Caribbean or on the journey up the American coast, a number of the pirates had become sick, possibly with syphilis or some tropical disease. They were in desperate need of treatment, so the doctors aboard Blackbeard's ship drew up a list of medicines that were required, and the pirates agreed that a fully stocked medicine chest would be their only demand.

Blackbeard shared his plan with his prisoners and told them that he would be sending a couple of his men into Charleston to deliver an ultimatum to the governor—turn over the medicine chest, or we will kill the prisoners, deliver up their severed heads, and set their ships ablaze. If that were not enough, according to one Charlestonian, the pirates also "threatened to come over the bar . . . to burn the ships that lay before the town and to beat it about our ears." If the demand were met, however, the pirates would set the prisoners free.

Mr. Wragg protested. He believed that the chances of success would be greatly increased if the pirate envoys were accompanied by one of the prisoners, who could "truly represent the danger they were in, and induce" the officials "readily to submit." Blackbeard gathered his men once again, who agreed with Wragg's advice. When Blackbeard asked who might be sent with his men, Wragg volunteered, but Blackbeard felt he was too valuable to let go, so a Mr. Marks was chosen instead.

Marks, along with Richards, the captain of the *Revenge*, and a few other pirates, departed in a boat on their mission, which they were given twenty-four hours to accomplish. Upon arriving in Charleston, Marks approached Governor Robert Johnson with the pirates' demands. Johnson called for a meeting of the provincial council, and together they immediately decided to provide the requisite medicine chest. They didn't really have a viable alternative. The colony was in terrible shape, just having come off years of brutal fighting and deprivation due to various Indian wars, and the officials were worried about the city's ability to mount a satisfactory defense should the pirates make good on their threat and attack. Turning over the medicine seemed the safest and easiest way to appease the pirates, get them to release the prisoners, and leave.

While the medicines were being collected, Blackbeard's men

made quite the scene in Charleston, parading themselves "to and fro in the face of all the people," as men and women looked on in horror, viewing the pirates as "robbers and murderers." When the medicine chest was delivered to Blackbeard within the allotted time, he made good on his side of the bargain. The captured vessels were released, along with the nearly naked prisoners, the pirates having stripped them of their clothes and valuables.

Still thirsting for retribution, Blackbeard shared an ominous piece of information with his prisoners before their release, letting them know that he planned to go "to the northward and swear revenge upon New England men and vessels." A day later, Blackbeard and his consorts sailed away, having kept Charleston bottled up and on edge for the better part of a week. As news of this audacious attack and his plans for revenge radiated out from Charleston, Blackbeard's reputation as a pirate soared, and he finally lived up to the billing that scribe Johnson later gave him—America was now truly "frightened" of Blackbeard, "more than any comet that" had streaked across the sky in "a long time."

Although the medicine chest was not an inconsiderable ransom— its value at the time being about £300 to £400—many people have wondered why the pirates didn't ask for more than just the medicine, or, taking it one step further, why they didn't attack Charleston and help themselves to whatever loot they could find. The prisoners certainly gave the pirates considerable leverage to demand more, but they chose not to use it. As for launching an all-out attack on the city, there are good reasons why Blackbeard and his men would have viewed that as a very dangerous proposition. While the pirates had substantial firepower at their disposal, and a menacing army of hundreds of men, Charleston was hardly defenseless, despite cautious colonial officials' doubts about their ability to repel invaders. The one hundred cannons that lined the city's fortifications would have posed a serious obstacle to any waterborne assault, as would a number of small, armed vessels in the harbor, which, as we will soon see, had the ability to be an effective fighting force. Even if the pirates managed to land relatively unscathed—a very big if—they would have had to confront the local militia, and a few thousand scared and angry residents. If the pirates ever contemplated such an attack, they almost certainly would have concluded that the very real risks, including the potential loss of many men, and some or all of their vessels, outweighed the potential rewards. Had Blackbeard and his men managed to subdue and plunder the city, such a momentous assault on one of the colony's most important ports would have elicited the wrath of the British Navy, resulting in a massive manhunt that Blackbeard would have wanted to avoid at all costs.

INSTEAD, FOR SIX DAYS Blackbeard's pirate armada sailed along the coast toward North Carolina, their ultimate destination being Topsail (now Beaufort) Inlet, a narrow channel through the Outer Banks about ten miles west of Cape Lookout. After leaving Charleston, they plundered the *Princess*, a brigantine carrying eighty-six African slaves. Blackbeard took fourteen of them aboard, casually commenting to the *Princess*'s captain that "he had got a baker's dozen,"*—a phrase that indicates that Blackbeard viewed these men as slaves, not prospective crewmen. A few days later, Captain Richards and the *Revenge* lost sight of the other pirate ships. On his own, Richards captured a merchantman out of Boston, which he plundered and then let go. When he caught up to the *Queen Anne's Revenge* and told Blackbeard about the encounter, instead of complimenting his underling, Blackbeard tongue-lashed Richards for not torching the New England vessel when he had the chance.

On June 3, the pirates headed into Topsail Inlet. The three smaller vessels made it through the channel to the sound beyond without any difficulty, but the *Queen Anne's Revenge* shuddered to a stop after plowing into a submerged sandbar. Blackbeard ordered the *Adventure* to come to his assistance, but it too grounded about a gunshot distant from Blackbeard's ship. Both vessels were wrecked,

---

* Since a baker's dozen is thirteen, not fourteen, Blackbeard appeared to be using the term rather broadly.

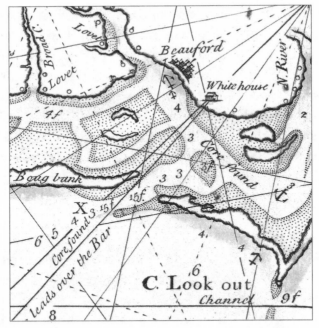

*Detail from a 1738 map of North Carolina, showing Topsail (Beaufort)
Inlet. Clearly evident is the shallow water and many shoals that
have bedeviled mariners for centuries.*

their hulls now breached, with seawater rushing in. All the men and treasure on the two crippled hulks were then transferred to the *Revenge* and the Spanish sloop.

According to one of the men who had been on the *Queen Anne's Revenge*, "It was generally believed that Thatch run his vessel aground on purpose to break up the companies, and to secure what moneys and effects he had for himself and such other of them as he had most value for." Some have argued that the *Adventure*, too, was intentionally grounded as part of the same plot. It is also quite possible that the groundings were unintentional, as others have speculated. The waters off North Carolina's Outer Banks, including its myriad inlets and bays, have been dubbed the graveyard of the Atlantic on account of the innumerable wrecks that have occurred there because of its shifting shoals and tempestuous seas—the most famous example being the USS *Monitor*, the Union ironclad that foundered during a storm about sixteen miles southeast of Cape Hatteras on December 31, 1862. Even today, ships with fancy navigational equipment and modern charts occasionally ground while attempting to negotiate Beaufort Inlet. No evidence suggests that Blackbeard or any of his men were familiar with the underwater topography of the area, so it is certainly plausible that the crashes were not by design. Why would Blackbeard intentionally destroy his prize ship, and possibly a second vessel, when they helped to make him the most powerful pirate afloat? Whether the groundings were intentional or not, Blackbeard did take advantage of the situation to cheat his fellow pirates.

Right after the two ships were lost, Blackbeard gave the captaincy of the *Revenge* back to Bonnet, who immediately left with a few of his men on a small boat for Bath, located about one hundred miles away on Bath Creek, a tributary to the Pamlico River. Incorporated in 1705, Bath was the capital of the colony, but despite its illustrious designation, it was a very small town. In 1708, Bath had only twelve houses and a population of around fifty or sixty. By the time Bonnet arrived ten years later in June 1718, Bath had certainly grown, but not all that much. It boasted a respectable library, with nearly two hundred titles, a small common, a courthouse, and the governor's townhouse, from which Governor Charles Eden conducted the colony's business.

Tired of the lifestyle, and hoping to reclaim his honor, Bonnet wanted to leave piracy behind, and his goal was to induce Eden to grant him a pardon under the Act of Grace announced by King George on September 5, 1717. As originally issued, this Act allowed a pirate who surrendered before September 5, 1718, to be granted a pardon for any piracies committed prior to January 5, 1718. It was generally understood that colonial governors had the discretion to extend that January date to cover later piracies, and in fact in a few months the king would officially extend the date to August 18, 1718. Bonnet no doubt had confidence that Eden would be compliant, thus giving him an opportunity to have his nefarious record expunged.

Blackbeard, too, had decided to obtain a pardon from Governor Eden, but rather than accompany Bonnet, he waited until he left.

With the help of his most trusted men, Blackbeard then transferred all of the treasure and most of the provisions to the Spanish sloop, which he christened the *Adventure*. Observing this activity, David Herriot—whose vessel, also called the *Adventure*, Blackbeard had commandeered months earlier at Turneffe Atoll—spoke up. Herriot asked Blackbeard for a boat so that he and a few others could escape to someplace in North Carolina or Virginia. Instead of offering a boat, however, Blackbeard and his coconspirators trained their guns on Herriot and sixteen other men and marooned them with no food or water on an uninhabited island more than three miles from the mainland. After that, Blackbeard, along with one hundred men— forty white, and sixty black—sailed to Bath on the *Adventure*, leaving behind many pirates, who constituted the rest of his former crew.

It is not known whether Blackbeard shared any of the loot with the men he abandoned, or took all the treasure, although one can imagine that it might have been difficult for Blackbeard to simply sail away from more than two hundred fellow pirates who had been so wronged without, in effect, paying them off. Whether paid off or not, those pirates slowly spread out through the countryside, making their way to towns and cities in North Carolina and beyond, perhaps accepting royal pardons, some melting into the local population, others returning to piracy.

Blackbeard and Bonnet never saw each other again, and what remained of their lives followed very different paths, yet in the end they shared a similar fate. To tell their stories, we will now leave Blackbeard and his associates aside for the time being, and focus on what became of Bonnet.

GOVERNOR EDEN GRANTED BONNET a pardon in early June 1718, and the former pirate told the governor that he planned to head to St. Thomas to obtain a privateering commission from the Danish governor to fight the Spanish. Bonnet then sailed back to Topsail Inlet to pick up the *Revenge* and begin his new life, but upon learning of Blackbeard's treachery he became furious. Still eager to head out, he gathered a crew from the ranks of the pirates Blackbeard had abandoned, and Bonnet also rescued the men who had been marooned. Famished after having spent one day and two nights on the island without food or water, they were understandably ecstatic when the *Revenge* showed up, and were easily convinced to sign on, rounding out the crew of thirty-one. To put more distance between his pirate past and his privateering future, Bonnet rechristened the *Revenge* the *Royal James* and ordered the men to refer to him from now on as Captain Thomas Richards.

Before leaving the area, a bumboat* selling cider and apples pulled up alongside the *Royal James*, and the peddler told Bonnet that he had heard that Blackbeard was off North Carolina's Ocracoke Island. His fury unabated, Bonnet immediately set out in pursuit of his erstwhile partner in crime, but after searching for four days, failed to find him. With supplies running low, and no other leads as to Blackbeard's whereabouts, Bonnet reluctantly headed to the coast of Virginia to stock up before sailing to St. Thomas.

Off Cape Henry, the *Royal James* stripped a vessel of ten barrels of pork and about four hundred pounds of bread. Not wanting to violate his pardon and be labeled a pirate, Bonnet attempted to give this transfer of goods the veneer of legality by giving the vessel's captain ten casks of rice and an old cable, trying to make it appear to the world that what had occurred was simple barter, and a fair trade. Relieved that he wasn't physically harmed, the captain was nevertheless angered by this unwelcome transaction.

Bonnet and his men continued to plunder vessels between Cape Henry and Delaware Bay, trying to maintain the fiction that they were not pirates by continuing to give those they ransacked something of value in return for what they took. But by mid-July both Bonnet and his men tired of their charade, and gave in to their true nature, embracing what they already were. From now on, instead of "trading" for the goods, they simply took them, along with a few men who volunteered to join their venture.

---

* A small boat that sells provisions to vessels in port or moored offshore.

On July 29, not far from Cape Henlopen, at the mouth of Delaware Bay, the *Royal James* captured the sloop *Fortune*, captained by Thomas Read, and decided to keep it as a consort. Up until this point, Bonnet's men had avoided violence, but upon boarding the *Fortune*, Bonnet's quartermaster, Robert Tucker, "fell to beating and cutting people with his cutlass."

Two days later, off Whorekill (now Lewes, Delaware), in the dark of night, the *Royal James* overtook the sloop *Francis*, coming from Antigua. Bonnet's men boarded the sloop, cutlasses at the ready, whereupon Captain Peter Manwaring begged them to "be merciful, for you see we have nothing to defend ourselves." The pirates promised they would, as long as Manwaring and his crew were "civil." In the main cabin the pirates gorged themselves on fresh pineapple, drank rum punch, and sang songs. Feeling festive, they implored the *Francis*'s mate to join in the revelry, but he demurred, saying that he "had but little stomach to eat."

The next morning, after the pirates took food and money, and numerous hogsheads of rum from the *Francis*, Bonnet released Captain Read's son and a woman passenger, who were ferried to Whorekill by five armed pirates. Before sending them off, Bonnet told the boy to share a message with the local residents—namely, "that if any of the inhabitants offered to hurt the hair of the head of any person belonging to his" crew, Bonnet "would put to death and destroy all the prisoners he had onboard, and would also go ashore and burn the whole town." Clearly, Bonnet was getting into the swing of being a pirate captain once again.

Since leaving Topsail Inlet, Bonnet and his men had plundered thirteen vessels. Having now accumulated plenty of food and alcohol, it was time to halt this crime spree and repair the *Royal James*, which was leaking like a sieve. Bonnet put a few of his men on the *Fortune* and the *Francis*, and took both sloops and their crews to North Carolina's Cape Fear River, about four hundred miles to the south. Along the way, he shared the money they had robbed, which came to a relatively paltry £10 to £11 per man, the equivalent of about two months' wages for a skilled carpenter at the time.

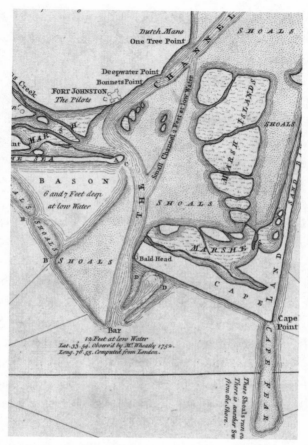

Map showing Cape Fear and the Cape Fear River in 1753.
Note "Bonnets Point" to the left of the "C" in "Channel."

On August 12, the *Royal James* and its consorts reached their destination, anchoring in one of the creeks on the river's lower reaches. Bonnet planned to wait there until mid-October, after the worst of the hurricane season had passed. The calmer seas, he hoped, would ease his voyage to St. Thomas, his dream of applying for a privateering license still alive despite recent lapses. Fortunately for Bonnet and his men, on the same day that they arrived on the river, they captured a shallop, the wooden planks of which were used to mend the *Royal James*. But their luck would not last. Within a matter of weeks, word spread that there were pirates at Cape Fear, careening and refitting. When news of their hideout reached Charleston, Colonel William Rhett, the fifty-two-year-old treasurer of South Carolina, surged into action.

RHETT HAD EARNED HIS military bona fides leading the colony's naval forces when they repulsed a French fleet threatening Charleston during the War of the Spanish Succession. A famously courageous man, with a volatile temper, he hated pirates, more so because of the anguish that they had recently unleashed on his beloved city. He vowed to do everything in his power to avoid a repeat performance. Arguing that the pirates at Cape Fear must be stopped before they beset Charleston, Rhett told Governor Johnson that he would gladly lead a preemptive attack. Johnson needed no convincing. Shortly after Blackbeard's blockade of Charleston, Johnson had written to the Board of Trade, complaining that the city was "continually alarmed" by pirates, "and our ships taken to the utter ruin of our trade." Johnson wanted nothing more than to rid South Carolina's waters of these nasty brigands, so he promptly issued Rhett a commission to proceed, and supplied the necessary funds for the expedition even though the colony's coffers were severely depleted on account of the recent Indian wars. Rhett quickly outfitted two sloops, Captain John Masters's *Henry*, and Captain Fayrer Hall's *Sea Nymph*, each mounting eight guns, with a combined force of 130 men.

On September 10 Rhett boarded the *Henry* as overall commander of the expedition, and the two sloops sailed to nearby Sullivan's Island to make final preparations. That same day, a merchantman sailed into Charleston with alarming news. The captain, a Mr. Cook, reported that a twelve-gun brigantine with ninety men, captained by the pirate Charles Vane, was lurking just off the coast and had plundered three vessels, including his. Vane was not alone. He had a consort, a sloop with eight guns and twenty men, captained by Charles Yeats. Furthermore, Cook said that while he was Vane's prisoner, he had overheard the pirates say that they intended to head south to the nearest inlet to careen their ships.

Vane was a ruthless pirate, already notorious in the colonies for torturing his victims. After capturing a merchant sloop in the Bahamas earlier in the year, Vane's men tied the hands and feet of one of the crew, and lashed him to the bowsprit, the spar projecting from the prow of the ship. To compel the poor man to confess where money was hidden onboard, the pirates shoved lit matches under his eyelids, while placing the muzzle of a loaded gun in his mouth. Given Vane's brutal reputation, it is not surprising that the news that he was close to Charleston sent the city's inhabitants into a panic.

This development changed the goal of Rhett's expedition. Instead of heading to Cape Fear, he vowed to go after Vane and Yeats. Once preparations had been completed on September 15, the *Henry* and the *Sea Nymph* sailed from Sullivan's Island over the bar, heading south. For nearly a week, they searched every inlet and bay along the coast, but came up empty. Unbeknownst to Rhett, Vane had already fled the area, while Yeats had gone in a dramatically different direction.

For months Yeats had been chafing under the leadership of Vane, who had been treating Yeats and his men more like lackeys than respected fellow pirates. Consequently, Yeats and his crew vowed to escape, and take advantage of the king's pardon. Their opportunity came a day or two before Rhett left on his expedition. In the middle of the night, Yeats slipped his sloop's cable and sailed into the mouth of the North Edisto River, about thirty miles south of Charleston. From there, he dispatched a boat to the city carrying a message for the governor. Yeats and his men would surrender themselves in return for a pardon and, to sweeten the deal, they would also hand over the ninety-odd Africans that Vane had stolen from one of the captured vessels and placed on Yeats's sloop for safekeeping. Governor Johnson responded favorably, and soon thereafter the pirates sailed into Charleston to receive their pardons, while the Africans were returned to their owners, continuing their tragic journey onto plantations and farms in South Carolina and beyond.

Meantime, having failed to find Vane or Yeats, Rhett called off that search on September 20, and pursued his original goal of surprising the pirates holed up on the Cape Fear River. The *Henry* and the *Sea Nymph* arrived there in the early evening of the 26th, and slowly made their way up the river. They soon spotted the masts of the *Royal James*, the *Fortune*, and the *Francis* in the distance, just behind a point of land. Before the sloops got much closer, however, they grounded on a bar, and it was very late before the incoming tide refloated them. By then it was too dark to launch an attack, so Rhett's men settled in for the night, on guard, preparing for the battle to come.

But the element of surprise had been lost. A pirate lookout spied the sloops, whereupon Bonnet sent three canoes to investigate, hoping to add two more prizes to his collection. When the pirates saw that the sloops were filled with armed men, however, they returned with the troubling news. Roused to action, throughout the night the pirates readied themselves, realizing that the next day they would be fighting for their lives.

A few hours before dawn, Bonnet summoned Manwaring, captain of the *Francis*. In a boastful and defiant mood, Bonnet told the captain that if the sloops had been sent from South Carolina to apprehend the *Royal James*, and if the pirates escaped, he was going to send Governor Johnson a letter that he had just penned, the gist of which was that he would utterly destroy all shipping coming into or leaving the colony.

Early the next morning, as dawn illuminated the scene and the opposing forces came into sharp relief, the *Royal James* swooped down the river. Bonnet hoped to fight his way past the sloops, keeping up a constant barrage of fire, and make it to the open ocean, where he had confidence that he could outdistance his pursuers. Rhett expected that, and ordered the *Henry* and the *Sea Nymph* to cut off Bonnet's escape route. The sound of gunfire filled the air as the *Royal James* attempted to outflank its attackers, but this only forced the vessel closer to the shore and into shoal water. Suddenly, the *Royal James* ran aground, coming to a shuddering halt, as did the two sloops. The *Henry* was within pistol-shot of the pirates, with the *Sea Nymph* a bit further away.

The positioning couldn't have been worse for Rhett and his men. The *Royal James*, which was closer to the shore, was tilting away from the two sloops, but they were tilting toward the *Royal James*. Consequently, the pirates were somewhat shielded by their exposed hull, while Rhett's men had little concealment on their decks. For five hours, as the tide slowly rose, the antagonists savaged each other with blistering volleys of musket and small arms fire. At one point, the pirates "beckoned with their hats in derision" to the South Carolinians, daring them to come aboard, an invitation that Rhett's men answered with "cheerful huzzahs," telling the pirates that "it would soon be their turn."

Bonnet paced the deck, urging his men on, and declaring, "If anyone refused to fight, he would blow their brains out." One man who had signed on as a privateer, but balked when Bonnet returned to piracy, did refuse, insisting that he "would die before he would fight." Bonnet was about to grant his wish, but before pulling the trigger, he was distracted when a man whom he "loved very well" was shot and killed.

As Bonnet mourned the death of his friend, the swelling tide lifted the *Henry* first. Rhett sailed it out to deeper water where his men fixed its rigging, which had been "much shattered in the engagement." With the *Royal James* still grounded, Rhett took advantage of the situation, and sailed the *Henry* straight for the pirate sloop, preparing to deliver the "finishing stroke."

Although Bonnet had been willing to kill any of his men who refused to fight, when it came to sacrificing his own life, he drew the line. Believing that he could not defeat the force arrayed against him, and not willing to die trying, Bonnet raised the white flag of surrender. Rhett's men took possession of the *Royal James*, and the South Carolinians were thrilled to discover that their anonymous foe was none other than Major Stede Bonnet.

All three vessels were awash in blood. Twelve of Rhett's men had been killed, and eighteen wounded, while the pirates' tally was seven dead and five wounded, two of whom later succumbed to their injuries. After heading upriver to collect Bonnet's two prizes and repair

Illustration by Howard Pyle (1921) titled "Colonel Rhett
and the Pirate," depicting Bonnet's surrender.

damage to their vessels, the victors brought the vanquished back to
Charleston, arriving there on October 3, 1718.

CHARLESTON HAD NO PUBLIC JAIL, so most of the pirates were
put in the watch house,* surrounded by the militia. Bonnet, in a
nod to his higher social status and background, was afforded better

---

* A building in which a watchman stood guard to warn the townspeople of any suspicious or threatening vessels entering the harbor.

treatment, being placed under guard at the marshal's house. He was soon joined by David Herriot and Ignatius Pell, the *Royal James*'s boatswain, both of whom had agreed to testify against the pirates.

The vice-admiralty trial didn't begin until the end of October. During that interval, Charleston was the scene of significant unrest that, unfortunately, is only hinted at in the historical record. While the majority of Charleston's citizenry, especially the merchants and government officials, were quite pleased and relieved that the pirates had been apprehended, there was a vocal minority that viewed the pirates in a much more favorable light. This group was likely a combination of those who had benefited in the past from pirate largesse, recently pardoned pirates (of which there were many in the city), and friends or supporters of Bonnet who felt that his gentlemanly lineage somehow counterbalanced his crimes. According to Thomas Hepworth, the province's assistant attorney general, these people engaged in violent protest in an effort to free the pirates, and at one point they threatened to burn down the city if their demand wasn't met.

On October 24, in the midst of these disturbances, Bonnet and Herriot made their escape, leaving behind Pell, who refused to flee.* The escape may have been due to the incompetence of the two sentinels guarding the marshal's house, but local officials believed that bribery was involved, courtesy of Bonnet's supporters—a contention that gains credence in light of the fact that some person provided Bonnet and Herriot with arms and a canoe that they used to abscond up the coast, hoping to reach North Carolina.

Upon learning of the escape, Governor Johnson "sent hue and cries and expresses by land and water, throughout the province," to alert the citizenry and publicize a substantial £700 reward for the capture of the fugitives. This elicited a number of search efforts, all of which failed. But when Johnson received information that Bonnet and Herriot were at Sullivan's Island, the governor once again summoned Rhett, who agreed to investigate.

---

* Herriot's decision is odd, since by turning evidence for the king he was surely promised immunity from prosecution.

Having been forced from their design due to bad weather, Bonnet and Herriot had indeed backtracked to Sullivan's Island, where Rhett found them on November 5. In the brief firefight that ensued, Rhett's men killed Herriot and wounded a black man and Indian who had apparently been assisting the escapees. The next morning, Bonnet was back in Charleston, now placed under tighter guard.

WHILE CHARLESTON WAS DEALING with civil unrest and the escape of Bonnet and Herriot, another wave of panic gripped the city. Just before the escape, Governor Johnson was informed that a large pirate ship with fifty guns and two hundred men was lurking beyond the bar and had already captured a few vessels. It was thought that the pirate Christopher Moody, who, like Vane, had a particularly bad reputation, captained the ship. Fearing another blockade, Johnson called the city council together to discuss their strategy, and they decided to go on the offensive. Four vessels anchored in the harbor were chosen to lead the attack and impressed into action, including the *Sea Nymph*, Bonnet's *Royal James*, and the merchantmen *Mediterranean* and *King William*. It was a powerful force, boasting about seventy guns total, to which were added three hundred men who had answered the governor's call for volunteers. But the expedition was delayed when the vessel owners—placing their economic concerns over their loyalty to the colony—demanded that they first be given assurance that their costs would be covered, and that they would be indemnified against losses incurred. After heated debate, Johnson and the council acquiesced.

With Johnson in overall command on the *Mediterranean*, the flotilla sailed down the harbor the evening of November 4, anchoring well inside the bar. Early the next morning the fleet headed out. All of the ships' guns, and most of the men aboard, were hidden so as to appear as nothing more than merchantmen to avoid alarming the pirates and, instead, lure them to attack. Beyond the bar, Johnson spied a ship thought to be Moody's, and a sloop, assumed to be his consort.

The pirates fell for the ploy. Black flags flying, they sailed in between the governor's ships and the harbor, hoping to keep them from retreating back into port. Reaching the *King William* first, the pirate sloop demanded its surrender. Hearing this, Johnson gave the prearranged signal. Raising their Union Jacks aloft and uncovering their guns, the South Carolinians unleashed a deafening broadside, accompanied by musket and small arms fire from the hundreds of men who had suddenly appeared from below decks.

Severely damaged from the gunfire, the pirate ship nevertheless managed to break through to the open ocean, with the *Mediterranean* and the *King William* in hot pursuit. As for the pirate sloop, which had only six guns and forty men, the overwhelming firepower of the *Sea Nymph* and the *Royal James* quickly beat it into submission. Taking place within sight of the city, this battle was viewed with enthusiasm by the many Charlestonians who witnessed the action from the tops of their houses, and from the masts of ships in the harbor, where they had positioned themselves for the purpose of viewing the skirmish.

Further out to sea, it took the *Mediterranean* and the *King William* many hours to chase down the pirate ship, which had lowered its black flag in a feeble attempt to disguise its identity, and, in an effort to lighten its load and hasten its flight, had pitched its boat and various pieces of cargo over the side. When the *King William* finally caught up, it fired its chase guns, killing a few of the men aboard the pirate ship. With hardly any options left, the ship promptly surrendered.

The two pirate vessels harbored many surprises. For one, it wasn't Moody who had been defeated, but a rather minor pirate named Richard Worley, whose erstwhile career had begun just a few months earlier. Starting out in New York with only a small boat and a handful of men under his command, Worley swept down the coast to the Bahamas, plundering vessels, trading up, and adding to his crew as he went along. Worley had been on the sloop, and he, along with many of his men, was killed during the fight.

The other pirate ship turned out to be the *Eagle*, bound from London to Virginia, which Worley had captured off the Virginia

Pirate flag design attributed to pirate Richard Worley.

Capes. Still aboard were 106 convicts, including 36 women, who were being delivered to Virginia and Maryland to serve as laborers and indentured servants—this being a practice implemented by parliament to rid the mother country of its most dangerous subjects by sending them across the ocean, and one that Benjamin Franklin later claimed was the equivalent of the American colonies gathering all of their rattlesnakes and shipping them off to England. Apparently, the pirates had planned to escort the women to an uninhabited Bahamian island, their intentions almost certainly carnal in nature.

As for Moody, he had indeed been off the coast of Charleston plundering ships, as originally reported. But some locals who were sympathetic to him had learned of the governor's plan, and took a boat from the city to warn him of the impending attack, giving Moody enough time to depart before the governor could mobilize his forces. Thus, Worley had blundered into a trap set for someone else. The twenty-four surviving pirates were put on trial on November 19, and in less than a week, five were acquitted, while nineteen were found guilty and hanged.

IN THE MEANTIME, the trial of Bonnet's men had commenced on October 28, judge Nicholas Trott presiding. One of the most learned jurists in British America, Trott was also a Hebrew scholar with a tremendous fondness for sprinkling his statements from the bench

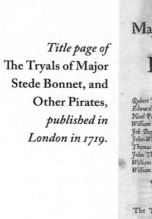

Title page of
The Tryals of Major
Stede Bonnet, and
Other Pirates,
published in
London in 1719.

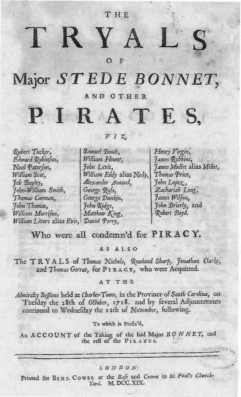

THE

TRYALS

OF

Major STEDE BONNET,

AND OTHER

PIRATES,

VIZ

Robert Tucker,	*Samuel Booth,*	*Henry Virgin,*
Edward Robinson,	*William Hewet,*	*James Robbins,*
Neal Paterson,	*John Levit,*	*James Mullet alias Millet,*
William Scot,	*William Eddy alias Nedy,*	*Thomas Price,*
Job Bayley,	*Alexander Annand,*	*John Lopez,*
John-William Smith,	*George Rofs,*	*Zachariah Long,*
Thomas Carman,	*George Dunkin,*	*James Wilfon,*
John Thomas,	*John Ridge,*	*John Brierly,* and
William Morrifon,	*Matthew King,*	*Robert Boyd.*
William Livers alias Evis,	*Daniel Perry,*	

Who were all condemn'd for **PIRACY**.

AS ALSO

The TRYALS of *Thomas Nichols, Rowland Sharp, Jonathan Clarke,*
and *Thomas Gerrat,* for PIRACY, who were Acquitted.

AT THE

Admiralty Seffions held at *Charles-Town,* in the Province of *South Carolina,* on
Tuefday the 28th of *October,* 1718. and by feveral Adjournments
continued to Wednefday the 12th of *November,* following.

To which is Prefix'd,

An ACCOUNT of the Taking of the faid Major *BONNET,* and
the reft of the PIRATES.

LONDON:
Printed for BENJ. COWSE at the *Rofe* and *Crown* in *St. Paul's Church-*
Yard. M. DCC. XIX.

with proverbs and quotes from the Bible, which he did during this particular trial with astonishing frequency. Trott's uncle, who went by the same name, was the governor of the Bahamas who offered pirate Henry Avery protection for a price in April 1696, a quid pro quo for which he had been ultimately censured by the home government and booted from his position. It is quite possible that the shame brought upon the family by his uncle could have spurred Judge Trott to develop his especially damning view of pirates, singling them out from among the larger class of thieves for the "heinousness" and "wickedness" of their crimes against humanity.

Over the span of eight days, thirty-three men were tried for acts of piracy relating to the plundering of the *Fortune* and the *Francis*. All pleaded not guilty; most offered no defense, while a few claimed that they had been forced, or had not participated at all in the piracies.

Four were acquitted, and twenty-nine found guilty and sentenced to hang. In his concluding statement on November 5, Trott, sounding the same theme so often invoked by Cotton Mather, implored the convicted men to repent and find forgiveness in God's eyes, quoting Isaiah 1:18, "for though your sins be as scarlet (even dyed in blood), yet He can make them white as snow." Three days later, the pirates were executed at White Point, along the edge of the harbor.

Bonnet came to trial on November 10. Attorney General Richard Allein, referring to Bonnet as the "Archpirata," alluded to the sympathies aroused by his unusual background, stating that he was pained to hear that some people in the city say that they favored Bonnet because "he was a gentleman, a man of honor, a man of fortune, and one that has a liberal education." In Allein's view, such qualifications only amplified the gravity of his crimes. "How can a man be said to be a man of honor," Allein posited, "that has lost all sense of honor and humanity, that is become an Enemy of Mankind, and given himself up to plunder and destroy his fellow creatures, a common robber, a pirate?" To Allein, Bonnet was clearly a fallen man.

Bonnet pleaded not guilty to taking the *Francis*, asserting that he had planned to be a privateer, had not consented to or participated in the piracy, and had repeatedly asked to be put ashore. The testimony against him, however, was overwhelming. In one exchange, Bonnet, acting in his own defense, asked Captain Manwaring whether he had actually heard Bonnet order his men to take goods from the *Francis*. "I am sorry you should ask me that question," Manwaring replied, "for you know you did." The irate captain yelled at Bonnet that he had been stripped of all he had in the world, and because of that, Manwaring said, he suspected that his "wife and children are now perishing for want of bread in New England." Had he been single, Manwaring continued, his abduction would not have mattered, but, he added, "my poor family grieves me."

When Bonnet was found guilty for the taking of the *Francis*, he changed his plea with respect to the taking of the *Fortune* from not guilty to guilty, forlornly realizing that a second trial on that count would end the same as the first. On November 12, Trott sentenced

Bonnet to be hanged. The sympathetic citizens whom Attorney General Allein had disparagingly referred to during the trial now stepped forward to ask the governor to grant Bonnet a reprieve so that the king could ultimately decide whether or not to issue a royal pardon. Bonnet added to the chorus by writing a letter begging the governor, as "a Christian," to look upon him "with tender bowels of pity and compassion." Bonnet also wrote a letter to Rhett, imploring him to intervene with the governor on his behalf. But all was for naught. On December 10, the city turned out to watch Bonnet, his hands bound and holding a nosegay, be carted to White Point, where he was hanged.

Bonnet's hanging provided a fitting coda to the most explosive and consequential passage in the history of piracy in South Carolina. "The execution of forty-nine outlaws in a month," historian David Duncan Wallace cogently observed, "stands unparalleled in American his-

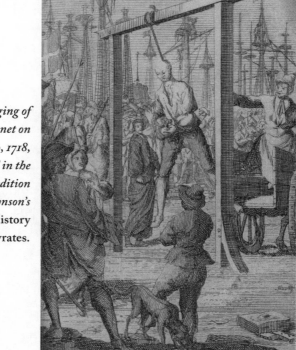

The hanging of Stede Bonnet on December 10, 1718, as portrayed in the 1725 Dutch edition of Johnson's **A General History of the Pyrates.**

tory as an attack of an aroused community on crime." But Bonnet and Worley were not the only pirate captains taken down during this time. Blackbeard's reign, too, would soon come to a dramatic end.

WHEN BLACKBEARD ARRIVED IN Bath in mid-June 1718, Bonnet had already left and was about to discover Blackbeard's treachery at Topsail Inlet. Like Bonnet, Blackbeard and his men were granted royal pardons. Governor Eden also convened a vice-admiralty court and declared the *Adventure* a legal prize, giving Blackbeard owner-ship of it free and clear. While many of Blackbeard's men left Bath at this juncture, history offers few clues as to where they went, or what they did with their lives. For his part, Blackbeard settled in the area, along with about twenty to thirty of his men, appearing to all the world to have given up piracy for good. Eden, of course, knew of their notorious past, but if he had any qualms about granting pardons, declaring the sloop a prize, or having former pirates in his midst, he never expressed them. Even if Eden had been convinced that Blackbeard and his men didn't deserve pardons, and should be arrested instead, he couldn't have mustered a force capable of doing so. If anything, the pirates could have taken over the diminutive town with ease.

Blackbeard's life in Bath is shrouded in mystery, and there is pre-cious little evidence to draw upon to paint a portrait of his activities there. Notwithstanding later claims that he had a house in town, there is no proof of this, and it is quite possible that he spent most or all of his time on the *Adventure*, while it was moored on the creek or the river, or off Ocracoke Island, located about fifty miles from Bath across Pamlico Sound, and which served as one of his favor-ite retreats. According to Johnson, Blackbeard often "reveled night and day" with Bath's farmers, by whom "he was well received, but whether out of love or fear, I cannot say." While Governor Eden does mention having to quell "some disorders committed" by the pirates during their drunken parties, there are no other known men-tions of such festivities or other public disturbances.

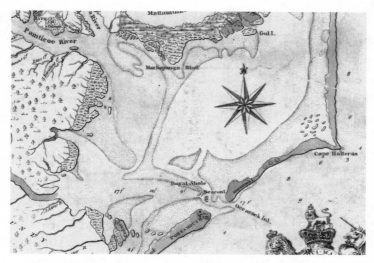

Detail from a 1770 map of North Carolina, showing Ocracoke
("Occacock") Inlet, Ocracoke Island, and the Pamlico ("Pamticoe") River.
On the north side of the Pamlico River, at the top left corner
of the image, is the town of Bath.

Johnson also claims that Blackbeard "married a young creature of about sixteen years of age," in a ceremony performed by the governor himself. This was supposedly Blackbeard's fourteenth wife, and after he had "lain" with her "all night, it was his custom to invite five or six of his brutal companions to come ashore [from the *Adventure*], and he would force her to prostitute herself to them all, one after another, before his face." While there are a couple of very brief contemporary, secondhand accounts referring to Blackbeard's marital status, a recent in-depth genealogical study found that "there is no direct evidence that Blackbeard had a legal wife." It is possible that his marriage(s) were never officially recognized, but it strains credulity to believe that he had as many as fourteen wives.* As for Blackbeard's villainy in prostituting his wife, assuming he even had one, this story is almost certainly made up by Johnson to reinforce

---

* In the course of writing this book, the author met two people who claim to be the descendants of Blackbeard, based on their family lore.

the depraved image of pirates so prevalent in the press of the day, and also to add a colorful, salacious story that would help sell more copies of the book.

As with Bonnet and many other pirates who received a royal pardon, Blackbeard and his men, "like dogs to their vomits," ultimately reverted back to their old ways, unable to resist the lure of unearned profit. By the end of August, Blackbeard was once again on the hunt for prizes, using the *Adventure* as his strike force. On the morning of August 24, not far from Bermuda, Blackbeard's men spotted two potential targets, and chased them for three hours before catching up. They were the *Rose Emelye* and the *Toison d'Or* ("Golden Fleece"), heading from Martinique back to Nantes, France. Although they were much larger than the *Adventure*, Blackbeard captured both of them, first taking the unarmed *Toison d'Or*, and then using it and the *Adventure* in a pincer-like movement to force the *Rose Emelye* to surrender. A search of the latter yielded hundreds of bags of cocoa and nearly two hundred barrels of refined sugar. Placing such a large quantity of goods onboard the *Adventure* was impractical, so Blackbeard decided to use the *Rose Emelye* as a transport, and take it back to Ocracoke Island. As for the *Rose Emelye*'s crew, Blackbeard transferred them to the *Toison d'Or*, and ordered its captain to continue on his way to France, threatening to burn his ship if he didn't. The encounter could have turned out much worse for the Frenchmen, given that Blackbeard told them that if there hadn't been a second ship, he would have "thrown them into the sea."

About the middle of September, Blackbeard anchored the *Adventure* and the *Rose Emelye* near the southern tip of Ocracoke, where the sugar and cocoa was unloaded from the latter and stored under a tent on land. Soon thereafter, Blackbeard and a few of his men journeyed back to Bath. They met with Governor Eden, and four of Blackbeard's men signed affidavits claiming that they had discovered the French ship abandoned at sea. The vice-admiralty court that Eden convened accepted the men's sworn accounts and condemned the ship, declaring it a wreck, and effectively giving Blackbeard the salvage rights to the contents of the *Rose Emelye*. A short while later,

An 1880 engraving of Alexander Spotswood, lieutenant governor of Virginia.

under the pretense that the *Rose Emelye* was leaky and would pose a threat to navigation if it sank, Blackbeard got permission from Eden to haul it into the shallows and burn it, which he did, thereby eliminating the main evidence of the pirates' capture.

While Eden saw nothing suspicious with respect to Blackbeard's story about the *Rose Emelye,* and accepted it at face value, his peer to the north was not so naive. Alexander Spotswood, the lieutenant governor of Virginia, was convinced that Blackbeard had gone back to piracy, and he vowed to end his marauding once and for all.

BORN IN THE ENGLISH possession of Tangier, the forty-two-year-old Spotswood served in the military prior to coming to America, achieving the rank of lieutenant colonel by the time of his appointment as lieutenant governor in 1710. His title notwithstanding, Spotswood was the top political official in the colony, for although George Hamilton, the Earl of Orkney, was the actual designated governor, he never visited the colony and left its operations largely in the lieutenant governor's hands. Spotswood, who resided in Williamsburg, the colony's capital, harbored a deep hatred for pirates. In July 1716, he urged the Lords of the Admiralty to take heed of "the dangerous consequences of suffering such a nest of rogues to settle" on New Providence, and warned that the "whole trade of this continent may be endangered if timely measures be not taken to suppress this growing evil." Two years later, the "rogues" that Spotswood was most concerned about were Blackbeard and his men.

Not long after being pardoned, some of Blackbeard's men made their way to Virginia, alarming Spotswood. He had no confidence that they were reformed, and he believed that if they weren't restrained from carrying arms and gathering in large groups, they would "seize upon some vessel and betake themselves again to their old trade as soon as their money was spent." To keep this from happening, Spotswood issued a proclamation on July 10, 1718, that required any former pirates entering Virginia to hand over their arms to a justice of the peace or a military official, and forbade them from traveling or associating together in numbers greater than three. If former pirates didn't comply, and engaged in any "unlawful and riotous concourse," they could be forcibly stripped of their weapons and thrown into jail.

Proclamations are simply words if not supported by action, and Spotswood soon found out that the will to act was lacking. A short while after the proclamation was issued, a large number of Blackbeard's men, heavily armed, traveled across Virginia on their way to Pennsylvania. Along the way they attempted to lure sailors from merchant ships to join them, their plan apparently being to return to piracy. Local government officials sought to take action but could not find any men willing to put their own lives on the line by assisting in "disarming and suppressing that gang."

In the ensuing months, Spotswood's concern about Blackbeard and his men only deepened as the evidence mounted that they had gone back to "their old trade." Spotswood received letters from North Carolina merchants complaining about the unruly behavior of Blackbeard and his men, and when Captain Ellis Brand of the HMS *Lyme*, which was then stationed in Virginia, sent a man to North Carolina to find out what Blackbeard had been up to, the information he brought back painted a troubling picture. Ellis's informant reported that multiple sources had told him that Blackbeard had been busy "insulting and abusing the masters of all trading sloops and taking from them whatever goods or liquors he pleased." In an attempt to avoid being labeled a pirate, Blackbeard had paid "such prices" as he thought fit for the goods he took.

But the event that truly enraged Spotswood, and convinced him that Blackbeard had surely returned to piracy, was the taking of the *Rose Emelye*. Unlike Eden, Spotswood did not accept Blackbeard's story, and in the end, it was the capture of the French ship, along with Blackbeard's other purported transgressions, that compelled Spotswood to take action. His justification was neatly laid out in a letter he sent to the Board of Trade, in which he told them that Blackbeard and his men were once again pirating along the coast, and that they had recently brought in a ship loaded with sugar and cocoa that they pretended was found as an abandoned wreck at sea, and which they had burned to hide its true identity. Having at the same time received many complaints from North Carolina merchants about "the insolence of that gang of pirates, and the weakness of that government to restrain them," Spotswood judged it high time to destroy "that crew of villains." What Spotswood most wanted to avoid was a future in which Blackbeard became emboldened enough to fortify Ocracoke Island, transforming it into "a general rendezvous" of pirates who might focus their sights on attacking Virginia's merchant vessels, thereby threatening the colony's extremely lucrative tobacco trade. Spotswood's fear was only heightened when it was discovered that Charles Vane had visited the island in October, and he and his crew of pirates spent a week carousing with their old friend Blackbeard.

Spotswood devised his plan to "extirpate this nest of pirates"— with the help of Captain Brand and George Gordon, the captain of the HMS *Pearl*, another naval ship stationed in Virginia—before it

Blackbeard's and Charles Vane's men carousing on Ocracoke Island in late October 1718 (1837 engraving). Whether there were actually any women in attendance, as the picture indicates, is unknown.

could serve as a launching point from which the pirates could terrorize the Virginia coast. They agreed on a two-pronged land and sea attack, since it was not known whether Blackbeard and his men would be in Bath or at Ocracoke. Brand would lead the overland forces, comprising two hundred sailors and Virginia militiamen, while thirty-four-year-old Lieutenant Robert Maynard of the *Pearl*, the oldest naval officer then serving in America, would head up the maritime offensive.

Organizing that offensive, however, posed a serious logistical problem. Because of the shallowness of the waters off Ocracoke, neither the *Lyme* nor the *Pearl*, both of which had deep drafts, could be used as transport or attack vessels. Although smaller vessels could be hired, that meant someone would have to pay for them. Brand and Gordon were happy to provide the men, but they balked at spending money on vessels, so Spotswood volunteered to hire them at his own expense.

The services of two small sloops, the *Ranger* and the slightly larger *Jane*, were engaged, with twenty-five men placed on the former, and thirty-five on the latter, which would be the vessel on which Maynard sailed. While these sloops could easily navigate the shallow and twisting channels around Ocracoke, they had no cannons, which meant that Maynard's men would have to rely on their personal weapons in going up against a foe with nine guns at his disposal. Had the forty-gun *Pearl* and the twenty-four-gun *Lyme* been able to confront the pirates, it would have been no contest, but with the unarmed sloops, the outcome of any battle was much less predictable.

To help ensure that the maritime invasion benefited from good intelligence, Spotswood sent a messenger to one of the merchants in Bath who had originally alerted him to Blackbeard's illicit activities, asking him for information about the condition of the *Adventure*, the size of its crew, and the location where it typically moored. That same merchant was also asked to send two pilots familiar with the waters off Ocracoke to Williamsburg, where Spotswood picked up the cost of their employ.

The plan was devised in extreme secrecy. Spotswood didn't tell the colony's assembly or the council about his plot, because he feared that if it were shared with them, word of the invasion would get back to Blackbeard, on account of there being many in Virginia who favored pirates. Nor did Spotswood inform Governor Eden of his plan to invade his colony, which, of course, was an entirely illegal act. Spotswood had a less-than-charitable view of North Carolina, which he considered an unsophisticated backwater run by incompetent leaders who were incapable of defending their colony. Not only did Spotswood lack confidence that North Carolina could deal with the pirate menace within its own borders, but he also believed the rumors he had heard that Eden, as well as Tobias Knight, the colony's secretary chief justice and collector of customs, were in league with Blackbeard, having been bought off with purloined goods and money.

To create a financial incentive for the naval forces he was sending to North Carolina, in mid-November Spotswood urged Virginia's General Assembly to pass a law that would provide rewards for the capture of the pirates. Since Spotswood didn't want to expose his secret mission, he launched a different argument to get the legislators to act. Spotswood had recently placed William Howard, Blackbeard's former quartermaster, on trial for piracy after he had entered the colony. Spotswood told the legislators that during the trial, information had come to light that Blackbeard and his men had threatened to wreak havoc on Virginia's shipping for the taking of Howard and, therefore, it was "absolutely necessary that some speedy and effectual measures be taken for breaking that knot of robbers." Whether that information was true or not, the argument worked, and on November 24, the assembly passed the Act to Encourage the Apprehending and Destroying of Pirates. It contained a list of rewards that would be offered for capturing or, if resistance was encountered, killing pirates found in Virginia or North Carolina, and adjacent coastal waters between November 14, 1718, and the same day the following year. Blackbeard was the only pirate that the Act mentioned by name, and the reward for him was set at £100. Other rewards included £40 for any other pirate captain, £20 for any boatswain or carpenter, and £10 for any other crewmembers. By the time this Act was passed, Spotswood's invasion of North Carolina had already begun.*

AT THREE IN THE AFTERNOON on November 17, the *Ranger* and the *Jane* sailed down the James River, while Brand's overland force departed later that evening. By the afternoon of November 21, Brand's men were still about fifty miles from Bath, but Maynard's sloops had reached the southern tip of Ocracoke Island. They soon spied two sloops at anchor in an inlet facing Pamlico Sound, which to this day is known as Teach's (or Thatch's) Hole. With evening coming on, Maynard anchored the *Jane* and the *Ranger* for the night.†

---

* Apparently, Spotswood told Captains Brand and Gordon that he would be introducing this bill soon after the invasion began, and that it would most assuredly pass. The captains were, therefore, willing to allow the invasion to proceed on the promise that the financial incentives Spotswood promised would actually be in place once their forces returned victorious, as they expected them to be.

† This next section covers the battle between Blackbeard and Maynard. Contemporary accounts of this event, including the only one written by an eyewitness, are very

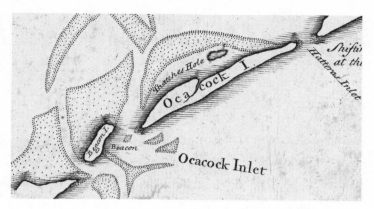

Detail from a 1733 map of North Carolina, showing Ocracoke—
here spelled "Ocacok"—Island, and just above it "Thatches Hole."

Unaware of the force amassed nearby, Blackbeard, along with about twenty of his men, spent that evening drinking and carousing with local trader Samuel Odell, who had arrived earlier on his own sloop. The following morning, the sea was calm and the winds very light, and the only sounds to be heard were birds greeting the break of day. At nine, Maynard ordered the *Ranger* to make way for the sloops, still not certain that one of them was Blackbeard's. The *Jane* followed close behind. Not long after setting out, the *Jane* grounded, and then the *Ranger* did the same. Men on the *Jane* began furiously throwing heavy materials overboard to lighten its load, while the *Ranger*'s crew staved their water casks to the same end. Both sloops were soon afloat again, but that precious element of surprise had been lost.

Even if they had been in drunken stupors, Blackbeard's men would have been alerted by all the nearby commotion. Realizing that he was under attack, Blackbeard ordered his men to cut the *Adventure*'s cable and get underway. To intimidate their attackers,

short, very different, and sometimes contradictory. As a result, they leave a lot to the imagination. Many authors have taken these bare bones accounts and added numerous details to create extremely dramatic and long narratives of the battle. I have tried to stick to the contemporary accounts as closely as I can, making judgment calls where necessary.

the pirates began shooting at the approaching sloops. It appeared that Blackbeard's plan was to head out of the channel that the sloops had just entered by engaging them in a running battle. As Blackbeard tried to reach the channel's mouth, the *Ranger* headed straight for the *Adventure*, with the *Jane* right behind, its men straining at their oars to close in.

When the *Jane* pulled to within about half a pistol shot of the *Adventure*, there was a brief conversation between Maynard and Blackbeard. According to a second-hand account in the *Boston News-Letter*, the exchange was as follows:

> Teach called to Lieutenant Maynard and told him he was for King George, desiring him to hoist out his boat and come aboard. Maynard replied that he designed to come aboard with his sloop as soon as he could, and Teach, understanding his design, told him that if he would let him alone, he would not meddle with him; Maynard answered that it was him he wanted, and that he would have him dead or alive, else it would cost him his life; whereupon Teach called for a glass of wine, and swore damnation to himself if he either took or gave quarter.

Maynard's own account of the conversation is similar, but briefer, and makes one wish that the naval officer had not been so laconic. "At our first salutation," Maynard wrote, Blackbeard "drank damnation to me and my men, whom he styled sniveling puppies, saying, he would neither give nor take quarter."

As soon as the talking was over, Blackbeard took full advantage of his superior firepower and unleashed a booming broadside of partridge and swan shot that killed the commander of the *Ranger* and severely wounded five of his men, including the second and third in command. Shorn of its officers, the *Ranger* fell behind and was not a factor until the very end of the battle.

The broadside also wounded many men on the *Jane*, but they continued to fight. In an amazing display of marksmanship, or, more likely, a lucky shot, they severed the *Adventure*'s jib halyard, the line holding the jib—a triangular sail—up, which caused the sail to collapse and thus slowed the vessel down. Not wanting to expose any more of his men to blasts from Blackbeard's cannons, Maynard ordered all of them below decks, while he went into the cabin at the stern of the ship. Maynard was not only retreating to get out of harm's way, but he was also setting a trap. Before going to the cabin, Maynard ordered the pilot and a midshipman to stay on deck and alert him as to what Blackbeard was doing. If it worked out as Maynard hoped, the pirates would soon come to him.

Seeing that the *Jane*'s decks were clear, Blackbeard thought that his cannons had done their deadly work, and the battle was all but won. To deliver the coup de grâce, Blackbeard brought the *Adventure* alongside the *Jane* and led his men over the rails, with a rope in his hand to lash the vessels together. As soon as Blackbeard was aboard, the pilot signaled Maynard, who, along with twelve of his men, rushed to the main deck, catching the pirates off guard. During the six-minute melee that ensued, the combatants slashed, thrust, and shot at one another at close range, their grunts, screams, and groans intermingled with the sounds of clashing steel and exploding gunpowder.

When the smoke finally cleared, the great Blackbeard lay dead, and the rest of his men who had followed him onto the *Jane* were either killed or severely wounded. At about the same time, the *Ranger* arrived, and its men boarded the *Adventure* and beat the remaining pirates into submission. While doing so, one of the navy sailors was killed by friendly fire. Pirates who lost their nerve and jumped overboard, rather than fight to the end, were shot in the water as they tried to escape. None of them survived, and one corpse was found in the reeds days later, with buzzards circling overhead.

According to Maynard, none of his men on the *Jane*, whom he said "fought like heroes," were killed during the fight, but many of them were "miserably cut and mangled." Although various accounts disagree on the numbers, overall, approximately ten navy sailors and ten pirates died, and more than twenty sailors were wounded. May-

Maynard and Blackbeard battle to the death (1837 engraving).

nard took nine pirates prisoner, three of whom were white, and the rest black.

One of the men wounded on the *Adventure* was trader Odell, who had visited Blackbeard to celebrate but was caught up in the battle. Although Odell fought with the pirates, Maynard and his men owed him a debt of gratitude, for if it had not been for his quick thinking, the death toll off Ocracoke that day would have been much higher. Before the fighting started, Blackbeard instructed one of his crew, a black man named Caesar, to blow up the ship in the event that the pirates were defeated. Caesar was in the hold, ready to light the ammunitions magazine, when Odell and one of his crewmen wrestled the flame out of his hand.

THE DEATH OF BLACKBEARD is arguably the most famous or, at least, iconic event in the history of piracy. Not surprisingly, the exact way in which he was killed is the subject of debate. The *Boston News-Letter* offered a colorful secondhand account of Blackbeard's final moments for an enraptured public:

> Maynard and Teach themselves two begun the fight with their swords, Maynard making a thrust, the point of his sword against Teach's cartridge box, and bended it to the hilt. Teach broke the guard of it, and wounded Maynard's fingers but did not disable him, whereupon he jumped back and threw away his sword and fired his pistol, which wounded Teach. Demelt struck in between them with his sword and cut Teach's face pretty much; . . . one of Maynard's men being a [Scottish] highlander engaged Teach with his broad sword, who gave Teach a cut on the neck, Teach saying, well done lad, the highlander replied, if it be not well done, I'll do it better, [and] with that he gave him a second stroke, which cut off his head, laying it flat on his shoulder.

Johnson, and many subsequent authors, embellished this description, transforming Blackbeard's death into a scene worthy of a Hollywood epic. But the accuracy of the *News-Letter*'s blow-by-blow is highly questionable, considering that all Maynard had to say about Blackbeard's demise is that "he fell with five shot in him, and twenty dismal cuts in several parts of his body." Maynard added, "I have cut Blackbeard's head off, which I have put on my bowsprit, in order to carry it to Virginia." Blackbeard's headless body was pitched into the murky water of Pamlico Sound, where, according to legend, it took a few laps around the *Jane* before sinking out of sight.

Maynard hung Blackbeard's severed head from the bowsprit
of the Jane *for all to see (1837 engraving).*

NEWS OF BLACKBEARD'S DEATH slowly radiated outwards throughout the colonies and across the Atlantic to England, generating intense interest, as well as great relief that another notorious pirate had met his just end. The story fascinated twelve-year-old Benjamin Franklin, who was then an apprentice to his older brother James, a printer in Boston. Benjamin had recently taken a keen interest in poetry, and James encouraged his younger brother to try his hand at writing ballads about unusual events or occurrences, which could then be printed and hawked on the street. Blackbeard's death struck Benjamin as a good choice for such an endeavor, especially since the event had generated particular interest in Boston, the home of Lieutenant Maynard's sister, Margaret. So, he composed what he called "a sailor's song, on the taking of *Teach* (or Blackbeard), the pirate."

Writing in his autobiography many years later, Benjamin labeled the song "wretched stuff, in the Grub-street-ballad style"—*Grub Street* being defined by Samuel Johnson, in his famed 1755 work, *A Dictionary of the English Language*, as "Originally the name of a street in Moorfields in London, much inhabited by writers of small histories, dictionaries, and temporary poems; whence any mean production is called *grubstreet*." Apparently, the song didn't sell well either, perhaps explaining why a verified copy of it has never been found. Nevertheless, there have been a few candidates put forward in the ensuing centuries that some have claimed to be either snippets from the song, or the song in its entirety. For one candidate that is often quoted, only the final stanza survives.

> *Then each man to his gun,*
>   *For the work must be done,*
> *With cutlass, sword, or pistol;*
>   *And when we can no longer strike a blow,*
> *Then fire the magazine boys, and up we go.*
>   *It is better to swim in the sea below*
> *Than to hang in the air, and to feed the crow,*
>   *Said jolly Ned Teach of Bristol.*

Another more plausible candidate is a ballad called "The Downfall of Piracy," which first appeared in print in a 1765 songbook, and quite possibly could be a direct descendant, if not a reproduction, of Franklin's original song. Its final stanza is as follows:

> *When the bloody fight was over, we're informed by a letter writ,*
>   *Teach's head was made a cover, to the jack staff of the ship:*
> *Thus they sailed to Virginia, and when they the story told,*
>   *How they kill'd the pirates many, they'd applause from*
>   *young and old.*

However the actual song went, it didn't impress Benjamin's father, Josiah, who, as Benjamin later recalled, "discouraged me by ridiculing my performances, and telling me verse-makers were generally beggars. So I escaped being a poet, most probably a very bad one"— and America gained a great statesman.

IN THE AFTERMATH OF the battle at Ocracoke, much work was left to be done. Maynard collected all of Blackbeard's papers, the 140 bags of cocoa, and ten casks of sugar he had stored on land, and brought them to Bath. There, he reunited with Brand and his overland forces, who had arrived in the capital a day after the battle. Brand also captured six of Blackbeard's men who were in Bath at the time, and he confiscated a large quantity of sugar and cocoa that was hidden in Knight's barn under some hay.

On January 3, 1719, under sunny skies, the victorious Maynard sailed up the James River aboard the *Adventure*, with Blackbeard's decomposing and no doubt pungent head hung from the bowsprit. As Maynard passed by the *Lyme* and the *Pearl*, he saluted the ships with nine cannon blasts, which the naval ships returned in kind. As a warning to those who might consider piracy a profitable career, Spotswood had Blackbeard's head mounted on a pike along the edge of the river—a location later christened Blackbeard's Point. According to legend, Blackbeard's head was eventually taken down, and the top half of his skull was turned into a punch bowl that was "enlarged with silver, or silver plated," and used for a time at one of the taverns in Williamsburg. If this in fact is true, the grisly artifact is lost, for it has not turned up since.

Although Maynard brought back clear proof that he had killed or captured many pirates, the reward money that Virginia owed him and his men was not paid for four years, with political and bureaucratic hangups to blame for the delay. All of the goods that Maynard and Brand had seized, including the *Adventure* itself, were sold at public auction, generating £2,238, which was shared among the crews of the *Lyme* and *Pearl*. This was a decent, though not an especially impressive, amount of money, being enough to purchase roughly eleven thousand gallons of Madeira wine, or nearly three hundred barrels of gunpowder. It seems that, after a much-storied career as a pirate, Blackbeard, and his small coterie of men, did not actually have all that much in the way of treasure.

Spotswood's invasion of North Carolina spawned a series of dramas that played over many years, the complicated details of which go well beyond the scope of this book. Suffice it to say that the invasion strained an already rocky relationship between Virginia and North Carolina, with claims and counterclaims of illegal or, at least, objectionable behavior flying back and forth. They included accusations of collusion between North Carolinian officials and Blackbeard and his men, with Knight facing the most intense scrutiny. The sugar and cocoa found hidden in his barn, and his apparent reluctance at handing it over to Brand, was held up as proof that Knight had been bought off by the pirates. Also, a rather guarded letter from Knight to Blackbeard found onboard the *Adventure*, and penned just a couple of days before Maynard's arrival in Ocracoke, was viewed by some as being an attempt on Knight's part to warn Blackbeard of the coming attack. So serious were these charges that Governor Eden's council placed Knight on trial to determine whether he had, in fact, been an accomplice to piracy. Knight put up a spirited defense, claiming that he was merely storing the sugar and cocoa as a favor to Blackbeard, and that the letter was nothing more than a conversation between friends, and that it neither said, nor implied anything about Virginia's expedition—which was, in fact, true. After weighing the evidence, the council found Knight not guilty.

Eden, too, came under suspicion for having colluded with Blackbeard, but no formal charges were brought against him. Nevertheless, history has not been kind to his reputation. Many historians look to his granting Blackbeard a pardon, and to his giving Blackbeard salvage rights to the *Rose Emelye*, as circumstantial proof that Eden had an agreement with Blackbeard to allow him to continue pirating in exchange for some form of kickback. In his first edition of *A General History of the Pirates*, Johnson had clearly stated that such an agreement had been struck, but in a later edition, he revised his opinion of the governor, stating that "it does not seem, by any matters of fact candidly considered . . . [that Eden] held any private or criminal correspondence" with Blackbeard, and furthermore, that Eden appeared to be "a good governor, and an honest man." With respect to the case of the *Rose Emelye*, Johnson pointed out that Eden had followed the correct procedure for condemning the ship and disposing of its cargo, and that any other court of vice admiralty, given four affidavits attesting to the ship's wrecked state, and no counterclaims, would likely have come to the same conclusion. Although Blackbeard's story that the *Rose Emelye* had been found floating at sea with no crew or papers onboard seems laughable in light of common sense and Blackbeard's notorious background—a perspective that Spotswood certainly shared—there is no clear evidence that Eden or the court did anything illegal, or took bribes from any of the pirates.

The trial of the pirates took place on March 12, 1719, in Williamsburg. Unfortunately, the trial records have been lost, but the result is known. Of the fifteen defendants, thirteen were found guilty and hanged. Odell, the trader with bad timing, was acquitted, because even though he had fought alongside Blackbeard and his crew, he proved that he was not in fact a pirate. Israel Hands, Blackbeard's former quartermaster and, for a time, captain of the *Adventure*, was found guilty but he was saved from execution at the last moment, when a ship from London arrived with a new royal proclamation that extended the date for granting pardons to pirates who surrendered. Embracing this opportunity, he walked away a free man. According to Johnson, Hands returned to England, where a few years later he was seen "in London, begging for bread."

CHAPTER 9

Fading Away

*Pirate captain Edward Low in the 1736 edition of
Johnson's* A General History of the Pyrates. *The winds
are a reference to the hurricanes he and his men encountered
on their approach to Brazil late in 1722.*

BLACK FLAGS, BLUE WATERS

THE TWO YEARS BETWEEN APRIL 1717 AND MARCH 1719 were the most dramatic period in the history of piracy in America. At various times, crews led by Captains Bellamy, Williams, La Buse, Bonnet, Blackbeard, Worley, Vane, Moody, and other men whose piratical deeds were of lesser consequence, terrorized the coast from Maine to South Carolina, sending tremors of fear throughout the colonies. A few of the colonies fought back, achieving great success. Their brave efforts led directly to the downfall of some of history's most infamous pirates, like Bonnet and Blackbeard, and even though Bellamy and many of his men were destroyed by natural forces, the survivors were rounded up by Massachusetts officials who were determined to see that justice was done. At well-publicized trials in Boston, Williamsburg, and Charleston, colonial officials added to the already significant death toll of pirates by condemning sixty-eight men to the gallows, sending out an unmistakable message that the colonies had declared war on them.

This period also marked the high point for piracy along America's coast. Between 1719 and 1726, the number of pirates plaguing the colonies would plummet to an insignificant level. Of the many factors contributing to this decline, one was, of course, colonial resolve to fight piracy at sea and in the courts. Another critical determinant was Britain's increased efforts to eliminate pirates throughout the Atlantic, using a combination of pardons, stricter laws, naval force, executions, and the eradication of the pirate stronghold at New Providence.

The Act of Grace issued by King George on September 5, 1717, was followed by another pardon opportunity in 1719. The results were mixed, and generally disappointing. While many pirates accepted the pardons, most of them, like Bonnet and Blackbeard, returned to their old ways. But these Acts of Grace were combined with an incentive plan for capturing or turning in pirates who failed to accept the pardon by a certain date. After that time, any person who apprehended a pirate, or provided information that led to a capture, would receive a reward from the Crown—£100 for a pirate captain, £40 for every lieutenant, master, boatswain, carpenter, and gunner, £30 for every lower-ranked officer, and £20 for other crewmembers. And if a bold pirate turned on his captain and helped bring him to justice, he would be eligible for a £200 reward. Although it is hard to measure the impact of such bounties, there is evidence that in some cases they led to arrests and convictions.

In 1721, the 1700 Act for the More Effectual Suppression of Piracy was supplemented by another similarly named statute, which added to the Crown's armamentarium in the battle against pirates. In addition to reiterating the penalty of death for anyone found guilty of piracy or being an accessory to piracy, and continuing financial awards for injuries sustained while engaging pirates, the new law *required* the officers and crew of all armed merchant ships to fight back in order to keep their ship from falling into the hands of pirates. Those individuals who failed to do their duty would be stripped of their wages and thrown into jail for six months.

The 1721 law also changed the calculus for officers aboard British naval ships. Over the years there had been many complaints from colonial officials that some of those officers, contrary to their instructions from the admiralty, spent more time trading with pirates than hunting them down, in order to supplement their naval pay. Under the new law, any officer caught trading with pirates would be brought before a court-martial and, if convicted, would lose his position and any wages due him and never again be allowed to serve in the navy. The 1721 law placed merchants, their captains and crews, and naval officers on notice that the cost of associating with pirates, or failing to fight against them, would be enormous.

Despite the existence of a number of naval officers who viewed pirates as profit centers, naval ships, for the most part, were still effective tools for fighting piracy. That is why colonial officials from America and the Caribbean had long been begging the mother country to send more naval forces to colonial ports, and in September 1717, the king finally consented. On the fifteenth of that month he issued a proclamation in which he noted, "unless some effectual means be

The HMS Alarm, *a fifth-rate British warship, circa 1781.*
The fifth rates that were cruising America's coast in the 1710s and
1720s would have looked quite similar.

used" to reduce the number of pirates infesting the seas near Jamaica and the American colonies, "the whole trade from Great Britain to those parts will not only be obstructed, but in imminent danger of being lost." The means he chose was to send additional ships across the Atlantic, and give them direct orders to focus their energy on eradicating the pirates.

In subsequent years, the number of naval ships cruising the American colonies rose to five—one more than had been on station in 1715—and a few more ships were sent to Jamaica, Barbados, and the Leeward Islands, as well as to Newfoundland to protect the fishing fleets. They weren't the navy's largest ships, most being fifth- or sixth-raters according to the navy's classification system, with between twenty and forty guns, but they were quite capable of confronting and beating almost any pirate ship they encountered. While the American colonies had certainly hoped for more firepower, especially since a handful of ships and a few hundred sailors could not possibly police the entire American coast, those five ships and their men did act as a deterrent, and in a couple of cases they

Pirate captain
Bartholomew Roberts
in the 1736 edition
of Johnson's
A General History of
the Pyrates.

Cap.ᵗ BARTHOLOMEW ROBERTS.

fought pirates and won—including the instance of the *Lyme* and the *Pearl*, which were instrumental in vanquishing Blackbeard. The additional naval ships in the Caribbean and off Newfoundland had some successes as well.

The navy's most impressive victory came not in the western Atlantic, but rather off the coast of Africa, where it defeated Bartholomew Roberts, or Black Bart as he came to be known after his death, the most successful pirate of the Golden Age. Although this success was not achieved in American waters, it nevertheless had a significant impact on piracy on both sides of the Atlantic.

ROBERTS WAS SECOND MATE on a British slaver sailing to the Gulf of Guinea when the pirate Howell Davis captured his ship in early 1720. Roberts quickly warmed up to the pirate life, and when Howell was killed less than two months later, Roberts, already a favorite among the crew, was elected captain. Over the next two years, he and his small but powerful squadron of pirate ships reportedly plundered more than four hundred ships along the coasts of Africa, Brazil, and Newfoundland, as well as in the Caribbean, though none off the American colonies.

Captain Samuel Cary, whose ship *Samuel* was attacked in July 1720 by Roberts off the coast of Newfoundland, provides a fascinating glimpse of the pirates' marauding behavior. Upon boarding, they stripped the passengers and crewmen of all their money and clothes, with the exception of what they were wearing, while aiming guns at their breasts, threatening to shoot anyone "who did not immediately give an account of both, and resign them up." Then, "with madness and rage," the pirates ripped open the hatches and entered the hold "like a parcel of furies," blasting the locks off trunks, slashing their way into boxes of goods, taking what they wanted, and throwing what they didn't over the side. All the while, the pirates were "cursing, swearing, damning, and blaspheming to the greatest degree imaginable," proclaiming that they would never be hung up along the Thames like Captain Kidd because if they were ever beaten by a superior force, they would "fire one of their pistols to their powder, and all go merrily to hell together!" The pirates ridiculed the king's Act of Grace, saying that they didn't have enough money yet, but when they did, they would certainly take the king up on his offer, and "thank him for it." Despite the fact that Roberts had onboard his own ship a reported twenty tons of brandy, he and his men were more than happy to break into the cargo of fine wine that Captain Cary was carrying to Boston, cutting off the necks of the bottles with their cutlasses and chugging their contents. Just as the pirates were debating whether to burn Cary's ship, they saw another merchant vessel in the distance, and set Cary free in order to capture a new prize.

Roberts's pillaging alarmed British authorities, and in February 1722, the fifty-gun HMS *Swallow* finally caught up with him on the

Detail of engraving in the 1724 second edition of Johnson's A General History of the Pyrates, *showing in the foreground two of Bartholomew Roberts's ships off the coast of Guinea just as they are about to capture the many merchant ships in the distance. Roberts's flagship, the* Royal Fortune, *is shown with two pirate flags raised aloft.*

Guinea coast. In two separate and fierce battles, Captain Chaloner Ogle of the *Swallow* captured the three vessels under Roberts's command, including his flagship, the *Royal Fortune*. According to Johnson, Roberts, standing on the main deck of the *Royal Fortune* at the outset of the fight, "made a gallant figure . . . dressed in a rich crimson damask waistcoat and breeches, with a diamond cross hanging to it, a sword in his hand, and two pair of pistols hanging at the end of a silk sling, hung over his shoulders." His gallantry and sartorial splendor notwithstanding, Roberts was mortally struck during one of the *Swallow*'s initial broadsides, a round of grapeshot piercing his neck. The death of their leader disheartened the pirates and they soon surrendered, but not before dumping Roberts's body overboard, with all his arms and finery on, as had been his long-standing request should he expire.

More than a score of Roberts's men were killed or wounded during these engagements. Ogle* brought 262 captives to Cape Coast Castle, the capital of British possessions on the Gold Coast of Africa (modern-day Ghana). Nineteen of the wounded pirates died of their injuries soon thereafter, and the seventy-five black men Ogle had captured were sold into slavery. The rest of the pirates were put on trial, and while most were acquitted, imprisoned, reprieved, or sent into indentured servitude, fifty-two of them were executed. This singular event—the largest group hanging during the Golden Age of Piracy—was a major blow to piracy throughout the Atlantic. But it was only a part of a much larger whole. Between 1716 and 1726, more than four hundred pirates were reportedly hanged for their crimes, though it is likely that the true number was considerably higher. And for every pirate hanged, there was one or, possibly, two more who were killed by those who were sent to hunt them down. All of these grisly executions and battle deaths were a further sign to pirates that theirs was a losing game, and that an era was coming to an end.

YET ANOTHER CRITICAL SETBACK was the extirpation of the pirates in New Providence, the Bahamas. For years, government officials and merchants alike had been vigorously complaining about the "nest of rogues" operating out of this island and the serious threat they posed to trade. A contemporary government report on the situation in New Providence painted a troubling picture. "Here they [pirates] now reign, and being, as we hear, about four thousand men, and twenty or thirty vessels of all sorts, they rove about the sea, scouring the coasts of our colonies of Carolina, Virginia, nay, up as high as New-England, to the inconceivable prejudice of commerce, and ruin of our people." The mounting complaints finally compelled the king to take action, and when a private group of investors approached the government with a plan

---

* Ogle was later knighted for his role in vanquishing Roberts.

to get rid of the pirates and reclaim New Providence, the Crown gave its enthusiastic support.

The investors were granted a lease to govern the Bahamas for twenty-one years, during which time they were entitled to any income derived from trade and agriculture on the islands. In exchange, the investors agreed to send a sizable force of soldiers and colonists, along with armed ships and supplies, to colonize and fortify New Providence. The pardon issued by the king on September 5, 1717, was one of the key elements of the investors' plan, the hope being that it would induce the pirates in Nassau (as well as other places) to renounce piracy, thereby making the job of implementing civil rule on the islands much easier.

Woodes Rogers, a major booster of the plan, and one of its investors, was chosen to be the new governor of the Bahamas. He was already famous for his privateering voyage around the world during the War of the Spanish Succession, in which he not only captured a treasure-laden Spanish galleon, but also rescued Scotsman Alexander Selkirk from Más a Tierra, one of the Juan Fernández Islands located about 350 miles off the coast of Chile. Selkirk was a sailing master on an English privateer, the *Cinque Ports*, in 1704 when his rising animosity toward the captain, Thomas Stradling, combined with his fear that the ship was so leaky as to be unseaworthy, led him to ask to be set ashore on Más a Tierra. Stradling consented, and when Selkirk had a change of heart, the captain refused to let him back onto the ship, no doubt happy to be rid of this troublesome fellow. By the time Rogers found him in early 1709, Selkirk had spent four years and four months without any human contact, a trial of endurance and solitude that made him a minor celebrity upon his return to London. Many think that Selkirk's amazing tale of survival, recounted in Rogers's subsequent book, *A Cruising Voyage Round the World*, was the basis for Daniel Defoe's 1719 classic, *Robinson Crusoe*, although there are those who argue that Defoe's inspiration was gleaned from multiple sources. In 1966, the Chilean government renamed Más a Tierra as Robinson Crusoe Island, in honor of its most legendary resident. As for the seaworthiness of

Robinson Crusoe, from the 1720 French version of Daniel Defoe's book by the same name.

ROBINSON CRUSOE.

the *Cinque Ports*, Selkirk was prescient. It later sank, and half the men aboard drowned, while the rest survived on rafts that deposited them on the South American mainland.

Rogers arrived at Nassau at the end of July 1718 at the head of a convoy of four ships, carrying roughly three hundred colonists and soldiers supplied by the partnership. Accompanying them were three British naval ships, ordered by the king to protect them on their journey and offer support during the first few weeks of Rogers's mission. Word of the pardon had arrived at the Bahamas months earlier, and many pirates had already taken advantage of the Act of Grace, most notably Benjamin Hornigold, erstwhile leader of the Flying Gang, who was among the crowd that enthusiastically greeted Rogers when he stepped ashore. "I landed and took possession of the fort," Rogers would later write, "where I read out his majesty's commission in the presence of my officers, soldiers and about three hundred of the people found here, who received me under arms, and readily surrendered showing then many tokens of joy for the reintroduction of government."

Two hundred more pirates quickly accepted the pardon, but as Rogers ruefully noted a few months later, about one hundred of them had by then returned to piracy. Still, many didn't, and the changes that Rogers had instituted, including establishing a working government and strengthening the fort, were already having a positive effect. But what truly transformed the island was a trial, and subsequent executions, at the end of 1718.

In the fall of that year, Rogers commissioned Hornigold and another reformed pirate, John Cockram, to become pirate hunters. Soon thereafter, they captured a pirate sloop off the Bahamian island of Exuma. Three of the pirates were killed during the brief battle, and ten were brought back to Nassau. Nine of them were subsequently found guilty of mutiny and piracy during the two-day trial, but in the end only eight were hanged on December 12. The ninth pirate was very lucky indeed. Just before he was to be sent to eternity, Rogers announced that the young man was "the son of loyal and good parents in Dorsetshire," and, therefore, deserved a reprieve. No sooner had the beneficiary of Rogers's mercy stepped down from the stage beneath the gallows, than the wooden barrels holding up the stage were yanked away, causing it to drop, leaving the eight pirates dangling in midair, each doing his own version of the Tyburn jig. All the while, the black flag that had once united them fluttered in the breeze overhead.

On the way to the gallows, one of the condemned men "looked cheerfully" upon the assembled crowd and shouted "he knew a time when there were many brave fellows on the island, who would not have suffered him to die like a dog." But those days were gone, and nobody came to his aid. As historian David Cordingly notes, the

When Woodes Rogers became governor of the Bahamas for a second time (1728–1732), the colony officially adopted the following motto honoring Rogers's great success in the fight against piracy in 1718—"Explusis Piratis, Restituta Commercia"—which translates to "Pirates Expelled, Commerce Restored." In 1806, Great Britain minted a copper penny for use in the Bahamas, the front and back of which is shown here. On the front is the laureated head of King George III (reign 1760–1820), and on the back is a large ship under full sail, flying the Union Jack, with two smaller ships and mountains in the background. Beneath this tableau is the Bahamian motto, which remained such until 1973, when the Bahamas achieved its independence. Sold at auction in 2011 for $1,003.

hangings "marked the end of Nassau and the island of New Providence as a base for the pirates, and it was a clear signal to the hundreds of pirates still operating in the Caribbean that the Bahamas were no longer a free zone for piracy." This turn of events greatly weakened the Atlantic pirate community and was another step on the road to its ultimate dissolution. From this point forward, pirates would have no place of refuge, no "republic of pirates," but instead would be increasingly isolated and on the run.

ONE ADDITIONAL FACTOR CONTRIBUTED to the decline in piracy: a change in the American colonists' attitude toward pirates. In the late 1600s, pirates were usually welcomed by the colonies because they brought things of great value that colonists desired and needed; and, better yet, they got them by ransacking Mughal ships sailed by "infidels" in a faraway ocean, or by plundering the hated Spanish in the Caribbean. This meant that, from the colonists' perspective, piracy was typically seen as a beneficial activity that had little or no downside. While it is true that colonists viewed piracy in a harshly negative light when pirates attacked colonial ships in American waters, those attacks were not very numerous for most of this period.

The years after the end of the War of the Spanish Succession, however, were an entirely different situation. From 1716 through 1726, there were very few pirates bringing valuable commodities or money to the colonies from far away. The days of plundering Mughal ships in the Indian Ocean, and returning to American ports flush with treasure, were long over. Instead, the vast majority of the pirates were attacking American vessels off the coast, or in foreign waters, and placing colonial merchants, officials, and the broader citizenry on edge. Rather than supplementing the local economy, pirates were now damaging it. No longer were pirates the much-beloved fathers, brothers, and friends of colonists who enriched their communities, but rather they were outsiders who, for the most part, brought nothing but strife. Formerly embraced by the colonies, pirates were now seen primarily as a threat. Adding to the colonies' strong desire to eliminate, rather than encourage, piracy was the fact that the colonies themselves were more prosperous than they had been in the late 1600s, and, as a result, they had more to protect.

Of course, there were exceptions. When Stede Bonnet was placed on trial, and when Governor Spotswood was dealing with Blackbeard, it became apparent that quite a few citizens in those colonies were sympathetic to these pirates. But in the broader scheme of things, throughout the colonies as a whole, they were a distinct minority. To most American colonists, pirates had become personae non gratae. Just as the elimination of New Providence as a pirate enclave was a blow to piracy, so, too, was the colonists' changing attitude toward these maritime outlaws. Without any safe harbors to visit in the American colonies, and with an ever-shrinking number of locals to rely on, pirates over time became even more alone, more vulnerable, and more desperate.

With the dramatic decline in piracy that took place along the American coast between 1719 and 1726, only a few pirates were bold and successful enough to leave a significant mark on history. One of the most fascinating was the notorious, despicable, and arguably mentally deranged Edward Low.

BORN IN LONDON, Low went to sea at an early age, and had made his way to Boston sometime around 1710. He became a rigger in a local shipyard, performing the often-perilous high-wire work of equipping sailing vessels with the ropes, chains, and blocks and tackles necessary to make them seaworthy. In 1714, Low married Eliza Marble, joined the Second Church, and was on his way to becoming a family man. But tragedy soon upended his life. His son died in infancy, and not long after his daughter Elizabeth was born in 1719, his wife, too, died, leaving Low bereft and heartbroken. His melancholy state affected his work, and he was either fired or left on his own account. Abandoning Elizabeth sometime in 1721, Low signed on to a ship heading to Honduras to gather logwood.

According to one account, after Low's twelve-man crew returned to the ship with a partial load of logwood late one afternoon, Low

Allen & Ginter cigarette card insert, circa 1888, showing Edward Low and a scene of him "torturing a Yankee," both imagined by the illustrator. Other than one contemporary source that said Low was a small man, we know nothing about how he looked.

asked the captain for permission to come aboard so that he and his men could eat. Eager to fill the hold as soon as possible and sail from this dangerous place, so as to avoid being attacked by the ever-vigilant Spanish *Guarda Costa*, the captain refused the request, and instead sent a bottle of rum to the men, ordering them to go back to shore and continue working. Enraged, Low fired a musket at the captain, missing him, but fatally wounding another man. Before the captain could respond, Low and his crew fled down the coast.

It is likely that these men, with Low as ringleader, had been preparing for some time to either mutiny or go off on their own, and they took advantage of the captain's rebuff to take action. But whether their action had been premeditated or spontaneous, the result was the same. They became pirates, and the day following their escape, they commandeered another vessel and headed for the Cayman Islands, arriving at the end of 1721.

There, they joined forces with another recently minted pirate named George Lowther, who had led a mutiny aboard a British Royal African Company ship off the Gambian coast, and then proceeded to the Caribbean, where he and his crew aboard the *Happy Delivery* plundered a number of vessels. The newly arrived crew piled onto Lowther's sloop, with Lowther serving as captain, and Low as his lieutenant. Over the next five months in the Bay of Honduras, they captured numerous vessels from Boston, burning most of them, along with their logwood, and often subjecting their crews to cruel treatment. Come spring, they headed north.

Off the coast of Virginia on May 28, 1722, the pirates captured the *Rebecca*, a brigantine out of Charlestown, Massachusetts, which had been heading home from the Caribbean island of St. Christopher (modern-day St. Kitts). This acquisition allowed the pirates to split up. Lowther remained on the sloop, while Low became captain of the *Rebecca*, which was equipped with two cannons and four swivel guns. The pirate crew of about one hundred was divided down the middle. As for the *Rebecca*'s original crew and passengers, all but three of them, who were forcibly detained, were sent off on another

Pirate captain George Lowther in Amatique Bay, Guatemala.
In the background you can see his ship being careened.

vessel, ultimately returning to Charlestown. Lowther and Low then sailed off in different directions.

On June 3, Low and his men plundered three vessels in the vicinity of Block Island, relieving them of food, water, clothes, sails, masts, and gunpowder. The pirates viciously stabbed Captain James Cahoon of Newport, and greatly damaged his vessel and the two others, making them nearly inoperable—an apparent attempt on Low's part to buy more time to leave the area before his victims could alert local authorities. That night, Cahoon's vessel limped into Block Island Harbor, and the following morning, a whaleboat dispatched from the island was able to warn officials in Newport about the attacks, prompting the governor to immediately order "drums . . . to be beat about the town for volunteers to go in quest of the pirates." Before the day was done, 130 men had volunteered to man two heavily armed sloops that went looking for Low. Soon after Rhode Island's maritime posse sailed, word of the attacks reached Boston, and the Massachusetts government ordered Captain Peter Papillion to fit out an armed sloop and join in the search.

James Franklin, an older brother of Benjamin Franklin and publisher of the often-satirical and antiestablishment *New-England Courant*, one of the first newspapers in the American colonies, noted Papillion's preparations, writing, "'Tis thought he will sail sometime this month, if wind and weather permit." The government, already stung by many of the *Courant*'s earlier irreverent attacks on its actions on a variety of issues, took umbrage at Franklin's words, seeing them as, at best, making fun of the government's supposed sloth in chasing the pirates, and, at worst, implying that the government was somehow in league with the pirates, allowing them plenty of time to escape. Such purported aspersions angered the General Court, which immediately hauled Franklin in for questioning and found that his comments were "a high affront to this government." To punish Franklin, the court incarcerated him for nearly a month. In his enforced absence from the paper, his younger brother Benjamin assumed the mantle of publisher.*

Despite Franklin's tart observation, the Massachusetts government did take the pirate threat quite seriously. On June 12, Governor Samuel Shute issued a proclamation for a general fast, which included a great array of prayers for the Almighty's consideration, including one that implored God to make it so "that the pirates, those sons of violence may be prevented from doing any further

---

* The young Benjamin Franklin's participation in this publication, under James's tutelage, informed how he would later use the American press in the mid- to late eighteenth century to agitate against British rule.

A map from 1755 showing Cape Sable at the southern tip of Nova Scotia.
If you look closely, you can see Port Roseway (modern-day Shelburne)
just a little to the northeast of Cape Sable. It is located on
the northernmost edge of the deeply indented, two-fingered
bay below the "b" and "l" in "C. Sable Indians."

mischief on our sea-coasts." At about the same time, Papillion
set sail with more than one hundred men, but neither he, nor the
Rhode Island sloops, caught up with Low, and they returned to port
before long.

Knowing nothing of the search under way, Low proceeded up the
coast. He gathered water and stole sheep on Nomans Land, a small
island off Martha's Vineyard, and then plundered a couple of fishing
vessels in the vicinity. One of those was a Vineyard whaling sloop,
from which Low forced six or seven men to join his crew, two of
whom were white, and the rest members of the Wampanoag tribe.
A few days later, Low beat and then hanged and decapitated two of
the Indians. Why he did this is not known, but grisly evidence of

his murderous action soon came to light. According to a diary entry of the Vineyard's Reverend William Homes, a sea captain "sailing from the Eastward, found the dead body of a man floating upon the water with his head cut off and his hands and feet bound."

By Friday, June 15, Low had sailed all the way to Port Roseway (modern-day Shelburne), located at the southwest corner of Nova Scotia. When the *Rebecca* entered the port in the early afternoon, Low saw a great variety of vessels arrayed before him. They had come in from the fishing grounds offshore to use the safe, deep, and relatively capacious harbor as a place to rest until the Sabbath was over. Low anchored the *Rebecca*, and over the next few hours, more fishing vessels arrived. To remain inconspicuous and avoid setting off alarms, Low must have had most of his men hide below decks to make it appear that the *Rebecca* was nothing more than a merchant brig seeking shelter. For Low, this gathering of fishing vessels was an auspicious sight.

ONE OF THE FISHERMEN entering the harbor late that afternoon was Philip Ashton, captain of the schooner *Milton* out of Marblehead. He and his small crew had spent much of the week catching cod in the waters to the south of Cape Sable. Ashton saw the *Rebecca* in the distance and assumed it was a trader from the West Indies. At about six, Ashton noticed the *Rebecca*'s boat with four men aboard, rowing toward the *Milton*, and thought they were coming to pay a social call. But when the boat came alongside, its occupants jumped onto the *Milton*'s deck. Before the Marbleheaders knew what was happening, the pirates, according to Ashton's later telling, drew their pistols and cutlasses "from under their clothes, and cocked the one, and brandished the other, and began to curse and swear at us, and demanded a surrender of ourselves and vessel to them."

Low's men continued their spree, surprising about a dozen other fishing vessels in this same manner, bringing a few people from each back to the *Rebecca* for questioning, after which they were confined under armed guard on one of the fishing schooners that Low had

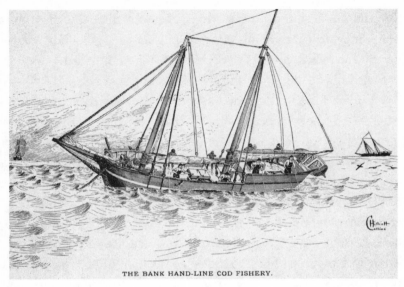

THE BANK HAND-LINE COD FISHERY.

A fishing boat similar to the type that Philip Ashton and his crew were on when Edward Low captured them.

transformed into a floating prison. The next day, Ashton and six of the other Marblehead fishermen were hauled before Low who, with a cocked pistol in his hand, demanded to know if any of them were married. So unexpected was the question, and so fearful were they of the menacing pirate standing before them, that the men were struck mute. This only enraged Low further, who placed the muzzle of his pistol against Ashton's head, and "cried out, 'you dog! why don't you Answer me?'" Low's threat that he would shoot Ashton and the others if they did not respond elicited hurried affirmations from the fishermen that they were not married, which curiously had an immediate calming effect on the pirate captain.

Low, like many other pirates of the time, preferred not to take on married men because of their strong attachments to home and family, and he had asked the Marblehead men their marital status in order to determine which fishermen he would ask to sign the pirate articles and join the crew. As Ashton would later learn, Low's motivation was even more personal. In subsequent months, as a forced man on the *Rebecca*, Ashton observed in Low "an uneasiness in the sentiments of his mind, and the workings of his passions towards a young child he had at Boston . . . which upon every lucid interval from reveling and drink he would express a great tenderness for, insomuch that I have seen him sit down and weep plentifully upon the mentioning of it." With the bittersweet memories of his daughter Elizabeth, and most likely his departed wife, Low knew firsthand how strong the pull of home could be.

Low asked the six Marblehead men before him to sign the articles. When they refused, he threatened them, but they held fast. Ashton was also subjected to another form of persuasion. After declining Low's invitation, he was sent below decks, where the pirates tried to win him over by offering him rum, treating him with "respect and kindness," telling him "what mighty men they designed to be," and asking him to "join with them, and share in their spoils." Neither this, nor Low's threat to shoot him if he didn't acquiesce, persuaded Ashton to sign the articles. His fellow Marbleheaders were equally resolute. In the end, it didn't matter to Low, for he added the men's names to articles nonetheless—they were going with him whether they wanted to or not.

On June 19, Low transferred the armaments and his crew to one of the fishing schooners—"new, clean, and a good sailer"—which he named the *Fancy*. All of his prisoners were placed on the *Rebecca*. Then, he ordered the *Rebecca* to sail to Boston, let the remaining fishing vessels go, and left Port Roseway behind in his wake.

Over the next eight months, Low sailed east across the Atlantic to the Azores and Cape Verde Islands, then crossed the Atlantic again, reaching Brazil, from there traveling north to St. Croix in the Caribbean, back down to Curaçao, and finally arriving at the Bay of Honduras in the late winter of 1723. Along the way, Low plundered more than ten vessels, adding a couple to his fleet. He also forced a few men to join, and welcomed others to his crew, which now stood at about one hundred strong.

Over the course of this journey, Low's trademark cruelty and maniacal rage began making more frequent appearances, setting him apart from most of the pirates during the Golden Age who,

The Portuguese captain who cut the rope holding the bag of gold coins, letting them plunge into the depths below.

typically, used violence and extreme brutality rarely, and only as a last resort. When Low overtook a Portuguese ship heading to Brazil, he tortured its crew to find where they had hidden their valuables. One of these unfortunate men, intimidated by Low, blurted out that the captain had hung a bag full of gold coins over the side of the ship, attached to a rope, and when the pirates boarded, he had severed the rope, letting the bag drop into the sea, rather than have it fall into the hands of the pirates. Furious, Low cut off the captain's lips and roasted them in front of his face, and then murdered the captain and the entire crew of thirty-two.

Low also lost two ships during this eight-month period—one when a prize crew simply sailed away, and another when a ship they were careening tipped so far over that water rushed in through the open ports, swamping the vessel and causing it to overturn and sink. The pirates themselves had some close calls, as well. They were nearly captured by a British man-of-war, but it grounded on a submerged reef after the pirates intentionally drew it into shallow waters. And when the pirates approached Brazil, they were pummeled by a hurricane that batted their ships about and threatened to send them to the bottom, causing many of the men to desperately cry out "Oh! I wish I were at home."

Throughout this time, Ashton, who spent much of the time in the hold trying his best to avoid his captors, was subject to frequent verbal and physical abuse, especially when he repeatedly refused to sign the ship's articles, which invariably resulted in being "thrashed with sword or cane." Close contact with the pirates, and with Low's cruelty, did nothing to lessen Ashton's intense hatred of them. "I soon found," he later recalled, "that any death was preferable to being linked with such a vile crew of miscreants, to whom it was a sport to do mischief; where prodigious drinking, monstrous cursing and swearing, hideous blasphemies, and open defiance of heaven, and contempt of hell itself, was the constant employment, unless when sleep . . . abated the noise and reveling." Tortured and miserable, Ashton dreamt of escape, and on March 9, 1723, he got his chance.

ON THAT LATE WINTER DAY, Low's mini pirate armada was off Roatán, an uninhabited lozenge of an island ringed by lush coral reefs, thirty miles long, a few miles wide, and located about forty miles from the Honduran mainland.* When Ashton saw the long-boat from one of Low's other ships heading for the island to fill water casks, he asked to be taken along. The men were reluctant at first, but Ashton pleaded with them, noting that he had not been on land since his capture in Port Roseway, while other men had gone ashore multiple times. The cooper, who was leading the watering party, relented, and Ashton jumped in.

Surprised by this opportunity, yet unwilling to let it pass, Ashton was not particularly well prepared for escape. All he wore was a pair of pants and a hat—no shoes, no shirt, no stockings, and no knife. Had he asked the cooper to wait while he gathered other useful items, suspicions surely would have been raised, given the simple

---

* Roatán is now one of the Bay Islands of Honduras.

nature of refilling the water supply. Whatever the consequences of his flight, Ashton was resolved never again to set foot on one of Low's ships.

After landing on shore, Ashton eagerly helped the men fill the first few casks, but then slowly ambled down the beach, picking up shells and stones, trying to appear as nonchalant as possible. When he was a few hundred feet away from the rest of the company, the tense captive edged toward the woods, but just as he was about to plunge in, the cooper—suddenly alert to Ashton's distance from the rest of the men—demanded to know where he was going. Ashton professed he wanted to gather coconuts, an excuse that seemed to satisfy the cooper, who returned to his task. Sensing that the window for his escape was just about to close, Ashton ran into the woods, moving as fast as he could in his bare feet and exposed skin through the sharp underbrush, ultimately hunkering down in a dense thicket that was far enough away so as to be well concealed, but close enough to the beach so that he could still hear what the pirates might say.

The casks full, the cooper yelled for Ashton to come down to the boat. Hearing nothing, the men began calling to Ashton, who stayed still and silent. Ashton heard one of them say, "The dog is lost in the woods, and can't find the way out again." The calls then became more insistent, and another comment made its way to Ashton's ears, "He is run-away and won't come again." In a final gambit, the cooper bellowed, "If you don't come away presently, I'll go off and leave you alone." That was exactly what Ashton wanted, so he said nothing. Finally, the boat departed. Ashton could see Low's ships offshore, and he worried that a search party would be sent to find him, but it never came—he wasn't valuable enough to Low as a prisoner to warrant one. A day after he stepped ashore, Ashton watched the pirates sail away. Standing at the edge of the beach, he was truly and utterly alone.

THUS BEGAN ASHTON'S GRUELING trial of survival on this uninhabited island. For the next nine months he spoke to no one and

*Roatán Island, where Philip Ashton spent two years before being
rescued by a brigantine from Salem, Massachusetts. The place where
Ashton first went ashore and spent most of his time is located
near the eastern end of the island, on the southern side.*

subsisted primarily on fruit and, for a short time, raw turtle eggs,
the result being a slow physical decline, compounded by severe bouts
of loneliness and depression. Then, as if out of a dream, a canoe
appeared coming toward the beach. In it was a grizzled Scotsman
who had lived with the Spaniards on the mainland for more than
twenty years, but upon being threatened with immolation for some
unknown crime, he had escaped to Roatán, where he planned to
stay. He was quite friendly, and Ashton enjoyed the company.

Three days later, the Scotsman left for a short hunting expedition on a nearby island, hoping to bring back wild hogs and deer.
Soon after he set off, a squall rolled in, which likely overturned his
canoe, for the Scotsman never returned. But his brief stay on Roatán
greatly benefited Ashton, since he left behind "five pound[s] of pork,
a knife, a bottle of [gun]powder, tobacco tongs, and flint." Now able
to kill, carve, and cook local game, Ashton's health and disposition
greatly improved, but he was still in desperate straits.

Ashton spent the next seven months alone again, but then was
joined by a group of eighteen British Baymen, or logwood cutters,
who came to the island in June 1724. When the first of the Baymen
stepped ashore and got a good look at Ashton, he "started back,"
Ashton later recalled, "frighted to see such a poor, ragged, lean, wan,
forlorn, wild, miserable object so near to him: But upon recovering
himself, he came and took me by the hand, and we fell to embracing

one another, he with surprise and wonder, I with a sort of ecstasy of joy." The Baymen welcomed Ashton into their group, gave him clothes, and shared their provisions. For six months this company lived unmolested, but in the fall of 1724, British pirates descended on Roatán, killing one Bayman and beating others before departing. Ashton and a few of the Baymen who had been hunting on another island avoided the attack. When they returned to Roatán, all of the Baymen left for the mainland, except for one who remained behind with his slave. Ashton, fearful of how he might be treated by the Spanish, and still hopeful that a British vessel would eventually sail by and rescue him, stayed put.

For a few more months, Ashton and his two companions remained together, and in March 1725, while they were hunting turtles on a nearby island, he saw two ships anchored offshore. As a boat from one of the ships rowed toward the beach, Ashton, who was hiding behind some brush, realized that the three men aboard were Englishmen "by their garb and air." Overjoyed, he rushed down to the water's edge, at which point the startled men stopped rowing and asked who he was. Ashton told them, and then asked them the same question. "Honest men, about their lawful business," came the reply, and with that Ashton invited them to come ashore, promising that there was nobody on the island who would harm them.

The larger ship was the HMS *Diamond*, but it was the smaller brigantine that proved to be Ashton's salvation. Not only was it from Salem, Massachusetts, the town adjacent to Marblehead, but Ashton also knew its captain, a Mr. Dove, who gladly welcomed Ashton aboard and even put him on the payroll. At the end of March, the brig began its voyage back to New England, and on May 1, 1725, nearly three years after he was captured by Low, and a little more than two years since running into the woods on Roatán, Ashton arrived in Salem. He thanked Captain Dove, and rushed straight to his father's house where he "was received, as one coming to them from the dead, with all imaginable surprise of joy."

Ashton's saga of suffering and endurance became the talk of New England, especially after the Reverend John Barnard of Marblehead

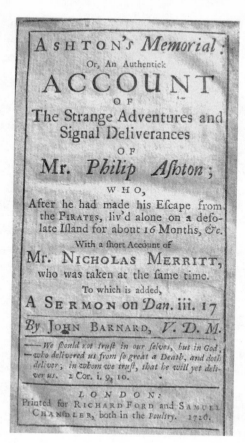

ASHTON'S *Memorial*:

Or, An Authentick

ACCOUNT

OF

The Strange Adventures and
Signal Deliverances

OF

Mr. *Philip Afhton*;

WHO,

After he had made his Efcape from
the PIRATES, liv'd alone on a defo-
late Ifland for about 16 Months, &c.

With a fhort Account of

Mr. NICHOLAS MERRITT,
who was taken at the fame time.

To which is added,

A SERMON on *Dan.* iii. 17

By JOHN BARNARD, *V. D. M.*

*— We fhould not truft in our felves, but in God;
— who delivered us from fo great a Death, and doth
deliver; in whom we truft, that he will yet deliver us.* 2 Cor. i. 9, 10.

LONDON:

Printed for RICHARD FORD and SAMUEL
CHANDLER, both in the *Poultry.* 1726.

*Title page of
Ashton's Memorial
by John Barnard.*

penned the book *Ashton's Memorial: Or An* [sic] *History of the Strange Adventures, and Signal Deliverances, of Mr. Philip Ashton*, which was published in October 1725. Barnard's main goal in telling Ashton's story was to illustrate God's great power, and show how, through his divine goodness, He protected those "whose hearts are perfect towards Him," and delivered them from danger. While many readers of Barnard's tract no doubt appreciated and absorbed this message, it is quite likely that its widespread popularity had less to do with its religious trappings than to the fact that it was a riveting tale of survival. Another reason why Ashton's story struck such a chord was that it came out in the wake of the wildly popular *Robinson Crusoe*, which appeared in 1719. In the era of shipwrecks and lost explorers, narratives of survival captured the reading public's attention, and Ashton was, to the delight of both the colonies and the mother country, "a real-life Robinson Crusoe."

BEFORE ASHTON'S CELEBRITY, IN the intermittent years of his life on Roatán, Low continued to blaze a path of destruction, becoming, according to one contemporary account, "the most noted pirate in America." Low's reign of terror continued the day after he left Ashton behind. On March 10, 1723, four New England vessels gathering logwood were anchored in a bay on the coast of modern-day Belize, when a Spanish ship manned by sixty men came into view. Part of the *Guarda Costa*, the Spaniards were on a mission to rid the coast of interloping logwood cutters. The Spaniards promptly captured three of the New England vessels, but the fourth cut its cables and escaped.

Less than four hours later, while the Spaniards were still celebrating their captures, three vessels sailed into the bay. Two were part of Low's fleet, while Lowther, Low's former partner in crime, captained the third. With well over one hundred men in all, the pirates easily took the New England vessels as well as the Spanish ship, as an orgy of bloodlust ensued.

Low and his men boarded the Spanish ship and put "all the Spaniards to the sword," except for seven who saved themselves by jumping into the water and swimming to shore. This massacre, along with Low's earlier murders of the Portuguese sailors, led John Hart, the governor of the Leeward Islands, to say of Low, "a greater monster never infested the seas." What happened to the three New England vessels is unclear, but the captain of the sloop that had eluded the Spaniards told a newspaper that, although one crewman from Newport was killed, the pirates "were more civil than was expected to the rest of the English."

Over the next three months, Low made his way north to Virginia, plundering nearly twenty merchant vessels. Along the way, he shed Lowther's company, and acquired a new flagship, the sloop *Fortune*, carrying ten guns and seventy men. Low's consort, the sloop *Ranger*, had eight guns, and about fifty men, and was captained by his former quartermaster, Charles Harris.

One of the ships Low attacked during this period was the merchant ship *Amsterdam*, captained by John Welland of Boston. The encounter took place on May 8, off the western tip of Cuba. Welland handed over £150 worth of silver and gold, and then was viciously abused aboard the *Fortune*, where he was repeatedly slashed and stabbed with a cutlass and had his right ear cut off. Bloodied and dazed, Welland was thrown below decks, where he lay bleeding for two or three hours.

His life literally slipping away, Welland begged one of Low's men for some aid, and soon the man returned with water and a doctor that Low had forced many months earlier to join his crew. The doctor dressed Welland's wounds, likely saving his life. But there was no saving his ship. After looting the *Amsterdam* of its money, three barrels of beef, and a black slave, Low sunk it. As for Welland, he was allowed to leave on another vessel with all of his crew, except for one man Low forcibly retained.

ON JUNE 7, a merchantmen recently plundered by Low was sailing back to its homeport when it encountered the HMS *Greyhound* off the southern tip of New Jersey. A sixth-rate frigate with twenty guns and 130 men, the *Greyhound* was stationed in New York, its mission to protect colonial commerce and capture pirates. Thus, when the merchant captain told the *Greyhound*'s commander, Peter Solgard, that Low was heading to Block Island, Solgard immediately went in pursuit. With Low's recent attacks causing alarm up and down the coast, Solgard relished the opportunity to capture or kill America's public enemy number one.

Three days later, about fifty miles south of the eastern tip of Long Island, at half past four in the morning, Solgard spied two ships roughly seven miles away. Thinking they must be Low and his consort, Solgard set a trap. At five, he tacked and stood southward "to encourage them to give chase." At the same time he ordered his men to prepare for battle.

The pirates took the bait. But getting to their potential prize posed a bit of a problem, since the winds were barely strong enough to fill their sails. So the pirates deployed their oars and began rowing. Two-and-a-half hours later, Solgard decided that this slow-motion chase had gone on long enough. The *Greyhound* turned to confront its antagonists.

By eight, the pirates were less than three-quarters of a mile off. To frighten their prey, the *Fortune* and the *Ranger* each fired a gun and raised their black flags, which exhibited "an anatomy [skeleton] with an hourglass in one hand, and a dart in the heart with 3 drops of blood proceeding from it, in the other." Rather than surrender, the *Greyhound* maintained its defiance, provoking the pirates to haul down their black flags and replace them with red or bloody ones, indicating that no quarter would be given. But in an instant, the pirates' confidence was shaken, as the *Greyhound* raised his majesty's colors aloft and began firing.

For an hour the sound of cannon blasts and small arms fire rent the air, with balls and grapeshot flying in both directions. One report claimed that Low could be seen on the deck of the *Fortune*, sword in hand, urging his men on. But no amount of motivation could change the fact that the *Fortune* and the *Ranger* were out-matched, so Low ordered his men to retreat. What followed was a long and laborious chase. The pirates left their guns and put all their energy into rowing, while eighty-six sailors on the *Greyhound* did the same.

Nearly six hours later, at three in the afternoon, the *Greyhound* finally closed in, and the battle commenced anew. Solgard maneu-vered the *Greyhound* in between the pirate sloops, but focused the bulk of his fire on the *Ranger*, mistakenly thinking that it must be Low's ship because it was the much more effective and aggressive fighter. After the *Greyhound* shot away the *Ranger*'s mainsail, Harris surrendered. Believing that he had captured Low, Solgard focused his attention on securing the *Ranger*. While he did so, Low, more concerned about saving his own skin than coming to the aid of his fellow pirates, took advantage of the lull in the fighting to abandon his consort, and the *Fortune* fled the scene.

As Solgard's men boarded the *Ranger*, one pirate refused to surrender. He "went forward with a pistol and flask in his hand, and having drank, uttered several imprecations, clapped the pistol to his head, and shot out his own brains." This brought the death toll on the *Ranger* to four, with eight wounded. The *Greyhound*, in contrast, suffered no deaths, and had seven wounded. Solgard, expecting to have Low in custody, was bitterly disappointed upon discovering that he had gone after the wrong ship.

Even though it took nearly an hour to transfer all of the prisoners to the *Greyhound* and lock them in chains, the *Fortune* was still enticingly visible in the distance. At five o'clock, Solgard, not wanting to let the real prize escape, began his pursuit. The chase continued into the night, when Solgard finally lost sight of the *Fortune* in the vicinity of Block Island. Giving up the chase, the *Greyhound* pulled into Newport Harbor, where the prisoners were marched under heavy guard to the town jail. A few days later, still intent on taking down the notorious pirate captain, Solgard left on a follow-up mission to capture Low, but again he returned empty-handed.

THE TRIAL OF THE *Ranger*'s crew at the Town House in Newport ran from July 10 to 12, 1723. Thirty-six men stood accused of "piratically and feloniously" plundering and sinking the *Amsterdam*, cutting off Welland's ear, and attacking the *Greyhound* and wounding seven of its sailors. In the end, eight men were acquitted, and twenty-eight were sentenced to death, two of whom were later reprieved and ultimately pardoned. In the aftermath of the trial, one of the condemned men took the time to provide a list of all the ships that Low and Harris had taken since the early part of 1723. The astounding number was forty-five.

The hangings took place on July 19 between noon and one o'clock, at Gravelly Point on the edge of Newport Harbor, before a jubi-

*An 1884 lithograph depicting Newport in 1730. If you look carefully, just
beyond the top of the mast of the second sailboat from the left you will see a
narrow spit of land extending into the water. That is Gravelly Point, where
Harris and twenty-five fellow pirates were hanged on July 19, 1723.
Goat Island, where the pirates were buried, is in the foreground,
where you can also see the fort, bristling with cannons.*

lant throng of onlookers. The twenty-six condemned men ranged
in age from twenty-one to forty, with most having been born in
Great Britain. A local minister, Nathaniel Clap, delivered a brief
sermon, and then the men were led to the gallows, from which hung
their black flag. "This flag they called 'Old Roger,'" observed Franklin's *New-England Courant*, "and often [the pirates] used to say they
would live and die under it." One witness noted, "Never was there
a more doleful sight in all this land, than while they were standing
on the stage, waiting for the stopping of their breath and the flying
of their souls into the eternal world." The pirates did not go quietly
into the hereafter. "Oh!" said another witness, "how awful the noise
of their dying moans." The bodies were then taken down and buried
"within the flux and reflux of the sea" on Goat Island.

According to an account published some years later, one of the condemned, Irishman John Fitz-Gerald, used his final days on earth to compose a poem that he gave to a visitor the day before he was hanged, hoping that it would serve as a warning to those who might follow his pitiful example. An excerpt of his effort ran thus:

> *In youthful blooming years was I,*
> *   when I this practice took;*
> *Of perpetrating piracy,*
> *   for filthy gain did look.*
> *To Wickedness we all were bent,*
> *   our Lusts for to fulfill;*
> *To rob at sea was our intent,*
> *   and perpetrate all ill. . . .*
> *I pray the Lord preserve you all*
> *   and keep you from this end;*
> *O let Fitz-Gerald's great downfall*
> *   unto your welfare tend.*

In the aftermath of the hangings, Solgard became something of a celebrity in the colonies, and to thank him for his heroics, the City of New York awarded him the "Freedom of the City." This formal document made him an honored citizen of the municipality. It was presented with a gold box engraved on one side with a scene of the battle, and on the other side with an inscription, *Quaesitos Humani Generis Hostes Debellare Superbum*, which translates, "The enemies of mankind having been sought out, to subdue the proud."

THE LOSS OF THE *RANGER* and half of his pirate force incensed Low and only fueled his brutal and sadistic tendencies. Two days after eluding the *Greyhound*, Low happened upon a Nantucket whaling sloop about eighty miles from land, captained by Nathan Skiff. The pirates boarded the sloop, whipped Skiff "about the deck," and, in what was becoming Low's signature move, cut off both his ears. "After they had wearied themselves with making a game and sport of the poor man, they told him that because he was a good master, he should have an easy death, and then shot him through the head." Sated, Low took a boy and two Indians with him, and ordered the three other men aboard to sink the sloop, and then told them to take the whaleboat and "go about their business." The weather being calm, they were able to row back to Nantucket in a little less than fifty hours, nourished only by water and biscuits. The sloop's other whaleboat had been off hunting when Low arrived, and its men, perceiving what was happening, rowed to a nearby sloop to warn them of the danger, and in that manner they were saved.

Next, Low captured two vessels out of Plymouth, Massachusetts, barbarously killing both of the captains. One was scalped, and had his chest cut open to get at his heart, which the pirates roasted and then forced one of his crewmen to eat. The pirates next set upon the other captain, "slashing and mauling him," and then cut off his ears and roasted them before making him consume his own flesh. So horrific were these injuries that the man soon died. Ominously, Low told one of the survivors, "He would do the like to all he meets."

Low's rampage continued a few weeks later off the coast of Nova Scotia, where he reportedly plundered upwards of forty French fishing vessels and slashed the faces, slit the nostrils, and cut off the ears and noses of his victims. When Low seized casks of wine and brandy from one of the vessels, its captain asked if he would be so kind as to write a sentence or two stating that he had taken the liquor, so that the owners wouldn't think that the captain had dishonestly sold it and pocketed the profits. Low cheerily agreed, and said that he would be right back with what the man requested. A few minutes later, Low returned with two loaded pistols, and "presenting one at . . . [the captain's] bowels," he told the petrified man that this "was one for his wine, and discharged it," and then he pointed the other pistol at the captain's head, saying this one is "for your brandy," and fired.

At the end of July, Low commandeered a larger ship called the *Merry Christmas*, to which he added a number of guns, bringing its complement to thirty-four, and made it his flagship. By this time he was sailing once again in the company of Lowther. They headed to the Azores, and then down the African coast as far as Sierra Leone, before recrossing the Atlantic to the Caribbean, plundering ships all along the way and engaging in all manner of cruelty.

And then Low suddenly disappeared from the historical record. What exactly happened is unclear. In one telling, sometime in the spring of 1724, Low, who had since split with Lowther, got into a quarrel with his quartermaster, and after killing him in his sleep, was forced by the rest of the crew into a small boat with a couple of other men. A day later, he supposedly was captured by a French vessel, brought to trial in Santo Domingo, and hanged. Another story claims that Low's barbarity had finally become too much for his men to bear, so they banished him and a few of his loyal supporters, giving them a sloop, and leaving them to an unknown fate. Yet another account has a pirate brigantine taking Low, burning his sloop, and marooning him and his men on a desolate island. Whether one or some combination of these stories is true, Low's notorious career as one of history's most brutal pirates mysteriously came to an end.

A LITTLE MORE THAN a month after the mass hanging at Gravelly Point in Newport, another pirate created an uproar in the colonies, and his story is fascinating less so for his captures than for his most unusual and violent end. John Phillips's piracy was launched in the summer of 1723 in Newfoundland, where he had been working in Petty Harbor as a fish splitter, the man in the codfish assembly line who receives the fish shorn of its head and entrails, and then with equal measures of dexterity and celerity cuts out the fish's backbone before handing the fleshy shell to the salter. Tiring of this monotonous work, and dreaming of riches, Phillips and four other men stole a schooner and went on the account. They christened it the *Revenge* and drew up articles, which were duly signed.

The small band proceeded to plunder three fishing vessels on the Grand Banks, forcing a few men to join, and taking on volunteers. One of the latter was twenty-seven-year-old John Rose Archer, who claimed to have sailed with Blackbeard, and who, because of his purported knowledge of things piratical, was elected quartermaster. Among the forced men was twenty-one-year-old John Fillmore, who would become the great-grandfather of Millard Fillmore, the thirteenth president of the United States. The young Fillmore's abduction was particularly sad in light of the obstacles he had to overcome to become a mariner.

As a boy in Ipswich, Massachusetts, a small fishing community just to the northwest of Gloucester, Fillmore dreamed of going to sea. His mother, however, stood in his way. Her deceased husband had been a sailor who was captured by a French frigate, imprisoned for years, and treated poorly before being released. She feared that her son might suffer a similar fate, so when he asked her permission to sign on to a voyage to the West Indies, she refused. Fillmore's persistence finally swayed his mother, but not in the manner he had hoped. While she wouldn't allow him to go on his original design, she did let him join a local fishing crew heading to the Grand Banks. Thus it was a cruel irony that in trying to protect her son, his mother had unintentionally sent him into harm's way.

Over the next five months, Phillips ranged from Newfoundland to the West Indies to the American coast, plundering many vessels. None of the goods taken was particularly impressive, mainly consisting of food, liquor, cloth, gunpowder, and cannon balls. One other thing Phillips gained was the enmity of many of his men. They had grown to hate him due to his mercurial nature and volcanic temper. He often berated and threatened them for even minor transgressions. "Phillips was completely despotic," Fillmore said, "and there was no such thing as evading his commands." Much of the crew, Fillmore claimed, "stood in such dread of him that they durst no more contradict his orders than they durst die." Obviously, the general rule onboard pirate ships, that the captain serves at the pleasure of the crew, either wasn't enforced in this situation, or Phillips's erratic and abusive behavior was willingly or grudgingly accepted by the majority of the men.

On February 4, 1724, off the Maryland coast, Phillips spotted a snow and gave chase, overtaking it three days later. Impressed by the snow's sailing abilities, Phillips added it as a consort and sent four of his men over to navigate it and keep an eye on its captain and crew, who were being held as prisoners below decks. Two of the men whom Phillips chose, Samuel Ferne and James Wood, were among the group of pirates angered by Phillips's unpredictable and abusive behavior. So, they hatched an escape plan.

Since the two ships kept lanterns burning at night to stay in company, Ferne and Wood decided to simply put out the snow's lights and slip away under the cover of darkness. But when Phillips saw the snow's lights extinguished, he divined their plan, put out his own lights, and followed them until the next morning, at which point the snow was still within sight. This game of cat and mouse continued for two more days before the *Revenge* finally caught up. Firing briskly at the snow, Phillips's men arrested its flight.

Phillips ordered Ferne to come aboard, but he refused and fired his pistol at Phillips, missing his target. Ferne and Wood then rushed below deck, and Ferne forced William Phillips (no relation to the captain) up onto the main deck. When he emerged from the hatch, one of the pirates on the *Revenge* shot him, leaving a wound so severe that his leg was later amputated.

As the standoff continued, the captain of the snow and all but one of his crewmen decided that they were on the losing end of this dispute, so they boarded the snow's longboat and rowed over to the *Revenge* to surrender to Phillips. They brought with them a message from Ferne and Wood. The two repentant runaways said that they, too, would surrender if the captain pardoned them and welcomed them back into the crew; otherwise, they would fight to the death. Phillips granted the pardon and sent the longboat to collect the two men.

That Ferne and Wood trusted Phillips to be a man of his word, given his recent track record, is astonishing. As soon as they stepped onto the *Revenge*'s deck, they discovered, all too late, that their trust was misplaced. Phillips thrust his sword clean through Ferne's body and then Wood's, finishing off each of them with a shot to the head. His fury dissipated, Phillips gave the snow back to its captain and crew, sending them on their way.

Phillips continued up the coast, capturing a few more vessels, including two ships leaving Virginia, which were stopped on March 27. John Mortimer, the captain of one of the vessels, refused to hand over his valuable geese and hogs. This infuriated Phillips, leading to a yelling match between the two, which quickly escalated when Mortimer, apparently a brave but reckless man, grabbed a hand-spike and struck Phillips. Not one to shy from a fight, Phillips drew his sword and ran Mortimer through, killing him. And that wasn't the only person he killed that day. While Phillips was on Mortimer's ship, one of the forced men on the *Revenge* tried to run off with the schooner, but was subdued, and Phillips cut him down with his sword.

Despite the many abject lessons in the ruinous consequences of trying to fight or escape from Phillips, a few of the forced men began to quietly conspire to rise up when the time was right. These included Fillmore, a carpenter named Edward Cheesman, and an Indian named Isaac Lassen. They continued to bide their time, waiting for their opportunity. It finally came just a few weeks later. On April 14, about forty miles southeast of Cape Sable, Nova Scotia, Phillips spied the *Squirrel*, a beautiful new fishing sloop from Gloucester on its maiden voyage, captained by Andrew Harradine. After capturing the *Squirrel*, Phillips decided to trade up. The following day, he transferred his men to the new vessel, placed the *Squirrel*'s crew on the *Revenge*, and sent them off. Harradine, however, became a forced man.

Whether Phillips was stupid, or simply believed in his own invincibility, is not clear, but he placed himself in a very precarious position. The loyal pirates aboard only slightly outnumbered the forced men and prisoners. Furthermore, unbeknownst to Phillips, while he sailed further up the coast of Nova Scotia, the ground was being laid for his undoing. As stealthily as possible, Fillmore and his fellow plotters brought Harradine and a few others in on their plan, which they executed on April 18.

Since the *Squirrel* was so new, there was still a bit of carpentry yet to be finished, and Phillips ordered some of the forced men to do it. Late in the morning on the designated day, Cheesman "brought up his tools under the pretence of working with them," spreading them out. Phillips was busy molding lead bullets, and some of the other pirates were walking the deck. Lassen was at the helm, and Fillmore, Harradine, and three or four other men in on the scheme were positioned in strategic locations. A few minutes later, at twelve, it was time for action.

Cheesman jumped up and grabbed the nearest pirate, pitching him overboard. A split second later, Lassen grabbed Phillips's arm, while Harradine reached for an adze and brought it down on the captain's head, instantly killing him. In the meantime, Fillmore dispatched another pirate with a broadax, and the other coconspirators lunged at the gunner and flung him over the rails. The remaining pirates, seeing the force arrayed against them, gave up.

Harradine piloted the *Squirrel* first to Gloucester, and then to Boston, where the pirates were jailed. According to contemporary accounts, the severed heads of Phillips and his boatswain were brought back in a barrel full of salt. A few days later, the *Boston News-Letter* reflected on Phillips's short and bloody dance across the stage of history. "It is almost incredible," the editors observed, "to think what dreadful havoc, mischief, and wickedness" Phillips and his accomplices "have acted and done in eight months time," having plundered "34 vessels, robbing and taking whatever they pleased, forcing, killing, beating, and abusing them, and often killing some of their own crew."

THE SUBSEQUENT ADMIRALTY COURT trials were held on May 12 and 13. They were well attended, with one group of observers causing quite a stir. A sizable number of fashionable and genteel women descended on the trials, much to the chagrin of the men in the audience. It was quite unusual for women to come to court, and for one man it was simply too much. Under the pseudonym of "Kitchen Stuff," he wrote a letter to *The New-England Courant* to vent his spleen, adding a little levity along the way. "His Maj-

esty's good subjects the male auditors," he wrote, "were unmercifully squeezed together upon that unusual cry in a court of justice,
make way for the ladies." A few of them "who made up the rear in
their march into the court chamber, by eagerly pressing forward, did
(contrary to the Law of Arms), mount their petticoats behind them,
and fired upon several of his Majesty's subjects unawares, who were
mortally wounded." Kitchen Stuff's greatest fear was that this invasion would set a dangerous precedent, because "we know that every
custom taken up by *ladies of quality* is presently followed by the trulls
and gossips of the vulgar herd." And if that were to happen, and the
courts were inundated by a feminine horde, he feared that it might
be impossible to obtain justice, for there would be such a tumult,
such a cacophony of conversation and commentary, that it would be
impossible to proceed with a trial. Although most modern readers
would certainly express disdain for Kitchen Stuff's condescending
and belittling attitude toward women, at the time it was published,
it reflected an all too common male perspective on the need to bar
women from such public, traditionally masculine events.

Despite Kitchen Stuff's concerns, the trials went off without a
hitch. Four of the pirates were found guilty, but two were given a
reprieve. The other two, John Rose Archer and twenty-two-year-old
William White, were sentenced to hang. Of course, the irrepressible
Cotton Mather, nearing the end of his life, was on hand to minister
to the condemned and offer a sermon to them and to his flock, which
he quickly rushed into print. After decades of writing and preaching
about the sins of such "sea-monsters," as he termed pirates, Mather
had grown rather cocky about his influence upon these men, and
their desire in their waning hours to have him tend to their suddenly
discovered religious needs. In a diary entry penned weeks after the
trial, Mather noted, "One of the first things which the pirates, who
are now so much *the terror of them that haunt the sea*, impose on their
poor captives is, 'to curse Dr. Mather.'" He added that the pirates
from Phillips's crew made him "*the first man*, whose visits and coun-
sels and prayers they beg[ged] for," and, in a final flourish, he added
that "some of them under sentence of death, choose to hear from me,

the last sermon they hear in the world." Mather had many qualities, but humility was not one of them.

Archer and White were hanged on June 2, 1724, at Hudson's Point. Just before being sent off, they offered a few dying declarations. Both placed a considerable amount of blame on drink for their denouement. White admitted that he "was drunk" when he "was enticed aboard the pirate." For his part, Archer said, "But one wickedness that has led me as much as any, to all the rest, has been my brutish drunkenness. By strong drink I have been heated and hardened into the crimes that are now more bitter than death unto me." Archer also added a plea for humane treatment. "I could wish that masters of vessels would not use their men with so much severity, as many of them do, which exposes us to great temptations."

Their corpses were taken to Bird Island* in Boston Harbor, where White was buried. Archer was hung up in chains for all to see. The following fall, Governor Dummer issued a Proclamation for a General Thanksgiving in which he thanked God for having "so far protected our sea coasts from the merciless pirates." And, giving a nod to the most unusual denouement of Phillips and his crew, the governor added that he was delighted that "it hath pleased God in a remarkable manner to deliver" the pirates "into our hands."

TWO WEEKS AFTER ARCHER and White were executed, in mid-June 1724, Alexander Spotswood wrote a letter to the Board of Trade from his house along the Rapidan River in Spotsylvania County, Virginia. He had been removed as Virginia's governor two years earlier, for reasons that are debated to this day, but were probably a combination of his having tangled once too often with the colony's powerful planter aristocracy, and having amassed more land than the Crown felt justified for one individual. Now, he wanted to return to London to resolve legal issues pertaining to his massive property holdings in America. But, as he made clear in the letter, he

---

* This island disappeared when Logan Airport was built.

was deathly afraid of voyaging across the Atlantic, for fear of what might happen if he were captured by pirates.

> Your Lordships will easily conceive my meaning [he wrote], when you reflect on the vigorous part I've acted to suppress pirates: and if those barbarous wretches can be moved to cut off the nose and ears of a master for but correcting his own sailors, what inhuman treatment must I expect, should I fall within their power, who have been marked as the principal object of their vengeance, for cutting off their arch-pirate Thatch [Blackbeard], with all his grand designs, and making so many of their fraternity to swing in the open air of Virginia.

Spotswood's record fighting pirates was, indeed, truly impressive. In addition to launching the bloody expedition against Blackbeard, and hanging thirteen of his men, Spotswood had also hanged other pirates, including a few who had the temerity to land in Virginia and proceed to make spectacles of themselves. This latter group included eight former crewmembers of the dreaded pirate Bartholomew Roberts, who had landed in Virginia in 1720 and, pretending to be visitors from London, proceeded to lavishly spend their "golden luggage" at taverns and on prostitutes. The men's free-spending ways and peculiar manners aroused suspicions, and Spotswood, believing them to be pirates, had the men thrown in jail. Six of the men were ultimately hanged, while the other two, who "showed just abhorrence of their past crimes," were pardoned and sentenced to serve on the navy ship stationed in Virginia.

When Roberts learned of the hangings, he vowed revenge on the entire state of Virginia, stating that he "would not spare man, woman, or child found in the country." This message was delivered to Spotswood by a Captain Turner, whose ship *Jeremiah* was captured by Roberts in the spring of 1721 on its way to Virginia. Fearing for their safety, Spotswood and Virginia's Executive Council increased the number of lookouts along the coast and beefed up defenses by mounting sixty or so cannons at the mouths of the colony's main rivers.

Despite his admirable record fighting pirates, and Roberts's very specific and pointed threat, Spotswood needn't have been so worried about sailing to London. By the summer of 1724, Roberts was dead, and the pirate menace throughout the Atlantic, especially along the American coast, had greatly diminished. In the end, no pirates bothered Spotswood during his journey. Over the next two years, the number of pirates continued to dwindle, to the point that when William Fly was hanged in Boston in July 1726, there were hardly any pirates left. The Golden Age of Piracy in the Atlantic had come to an end.

"Yo-ho-ho, and a Bottle of Rum!"

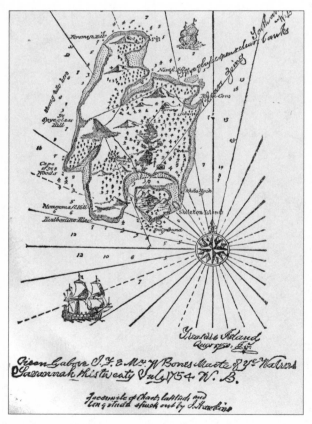

The treasure map of Skeleton Island included in Robert Louis Stevenson's *Treasure Island. In the lower left hand part of the map there is some writing that says "Bulk of Treasure Here," accompanied by a red X to mark the spot.*

A LTHOUGH ONLY RELATIVELY FEW PIRATES FROM THE GOLDEN Age became rich, their deeds, both real and imagined, have spawned a gold rush in the form of books, movies, plays, television shows, and video games that have created, and also cashed in on, people's intense fascination with these brigands of the sea. As a result, Golden Age pirates have become much more famous in death than they ever were in life. This process began while such pirates were still practicing their ghastly trade, most notably with the 1724 publication of Johnson's bestseller, *A General History of the Robberies and Murders of the Most Notorious Pyrates*, the granddaddy of pirate prose, which has served as the wellspring for so many of the tales of piracy that have followed.

Since that time, there have been many hundreds, perhaps thousands, of books on piracy and pirates of the Golden Age, ranging from factual to fantastical, and every combination in between. The reason for this literary explosion is clear. As one early-twentieth-century chronicler of pirates observed, "There is no theme in the gamut of the literature of travel and adventure that has a more absorbing interest to the ordinary reader, young or old, man or woman, than tales of piracy on the high seas."

The number of nonfiction book titles is impressive. They range from broad overviews, such as David Cordingly's *Under the Black Flag* and Marcus Rediker's *Villains of All Nations*, to more specific treatments of individual pirates or groups of pirates, including Colin Woodard's *The Republic of Pirates*, Stephen Talty's *Empire of Blue Water*, Angus Konstam's *Blackbeard*, and two books on Captain Kidd, Robert Ritchie's *Captain Kidd*, and Richard Zacks's *The Pirate Hunter*.* The level of scholarship exhibited by these, as well as other worthy titles, is impressive, and goes a long way toward dispelling many of the myths surrounding piracy in the Golden Age.

In terms of generating interest in pirates, however, fictional

---

* Full citations for these books are in the select bibliography.

BLACK FLAGS, BLUE WATERS

books, plays, and movies deserve the lion's share of the credit. Arguably the most famous work of fiction is Robert Louis Stevenson's *Treasure Island*, first published in 1883. Although it is set in the 1750s, it draws almost entirely on the themes and imagery generated by the Golden Age. With such memorable characters as pirates Long John Silver and Billy Bones, and the impressionable and brave young Jim Hawkins, Stevenson weaves a wonderfully dramatic story of the search for pirate treasure, replete with a map of Skeleton Island, on which X—actually "three crosses of red ink"—marks the spot where the loot is to be found (the familiar phrase "X marks the spot" to signify the location of treasure on a map was not one that Stevenson ever used). Punctuated by exciting battles between ruthless pirates and fearless Englishmen, *Treasure Island* has launched many children and adults alike into their own flights of fantasy, dreaming of what it would be like to find a pirate's hidden hoard.

And who could forget the catchy snippet of a pirate song spawned by Stevenson's fertile imagination, which Billy Bones drunkenly sings to the alarmed customers at the Admiral Benbow Inn?

> *Fifteen men on the dead man's chest—*
> *. . . Yo-ho-ho, and a bottle of rum!*
> *Drink and the devil had done for the rest—*
> *. . . Yo-ho-ho, and a bottle of rum!*

Less than a decade after *Treasure Island* was published, newspaper and magazine editor Young Ewing Allison used Stevenson's lone verse as the first stanza of a much longer poem he composed, called "Onboard the Derelict." When this poem was later paired with a pleasing tune, it was transformed into a sea shanty that has become a pirate anthem of sorts. To test its universality, simply sing out the first line of the verse above, and, odds are, you will hear in return a booming, "Yo-ho-ho, and a bottle of rum!"

Scottish novelist J. M. Barrie's early-twentieth-century books and play about Peter Pan—"the boy who wouldn't grow up"—also greatly boosted pirates' image in the popular culture. Peter's ongoing battle with the dreaded Captain Hook and his pirate band in mythical Neverland gives the story much of its emotional punch, and its almost mythological quality. Another entrant in this genre is W. S. Gilbert and Arthur Sullivan's comic opera, *The Pirates of Penzance*, which premiered in New York in 1879. Similar to *Treasure Island*, this work is not set in the Golden Age, but rather during Queen Victoria's reign (1837–1901). Nevertheless, it still harkens back to that age in many ways, and certainly has contributed to the appeal of pirates generally.

At one point in the opera, the Pirate King [or leader] is speaking with his apprentice, Frederic, who has decided to leave pirating behind and return to civilization to pursue his new calling as a pirate hunter. When Frederic begs the Pirate King to leave with him, the latter demurs, telling Frederic that although he doesn't "think much of" the "profession" of piracy, he believes that, "contrasted with respectability, it is comparatively honest." To reinforce this point, he then sings a song, the first verse and refrain of which goes:

> *Oh, better far to live and die*
> *Under the brave black flag I fly,*
> *Than play a sanctimonious part,*
> *With a pirate head and a pirate heart.*
> *Away to the cheating world go you,*
> *Where pirates all are well-to-do;*
> *But I'll be true to the song I sing,*
> *And live and die a Pirate King.*

> *For I am a Pirate King!*
> *And it is, it is a glorious thing*
> *To be a Pirate King!*
> *For I am a Pirate King!*

Movies have had an even larger impact than books and plays in creating the pirate craze, which shows no sign of diminishing, and, if anything, has intensified in recent years. Here again, *Trea-*

sure Island plays a major role, there having been at least a score of major motion pictures using Stevenson's gem as the basis for the plot and characters, including the most unusual and fun adaptation, the *Muppet's Treasure Island* (1996). Peter Pan, too, has been adapted to the silver screen nearly ten times. Other classic pirate movies include *The Black Pirate* (1926), *The Black Swan* (1942), *Captain Kidd* (1945), and much further afield, *The Goonies* (1985), an adventure/comedy in which a group of preteens intent on saving their neighborhood from demolition go on a danger-filled quest to find the lost riches of "One-Eyed Willy," a pirate whose treasure map they have stumbled upon. Even the movie *The Princess Bride* (1987), which is based on an equally popular book of the same name by William Goldman, has added to the pirate motif, with its repeated references to "the Dread Pirate Roberts," the name adopted by a series of pirates, each of whom builds on the reputation of those who went before them until they earn enough to retire, and hand off the much-feared name to the next in line.

Far and away, however, the most popular pirate movies of all time are the ones produced by Disney's *Pirates of the Caribbean* franchise. Begun in 2003, there are thus far five films in this series, which have earned billions of dollars at the box office worldwide. Johnny Depp's Jack Sparrow, the legendary captain of the pirate ship *Black Pearl*, serves as the franchise's anchor and is surrounded by an evolving cast of heroes and villains, including Will Turner, Elizabeth Swann, Blackbeard, Davy Jones, the ghostly Captain Salazar, Jack Sparrow's father (played by the peerless rocker Keith Richards), and the ferocious pirate captain Hector Barbossa, who serves, at various times, as Sparrow's nemesis and his brother in arms.

Television, too, has contributed to the prominence of pirates in the popular culture. *Black Sails*, a series that aired on the Starz network from 2014–2017, is one of the best examples. Centered on the Bahamian island of New Providence, just after the end of the War of the Spanish Succession, *Black Sails* has many characters whose names, if not their actions, are ripped from the pages of history, including Benjamin Hornigold, Ned [Edward] Low, Charles Vane,

Blackbeard, Woodes Rogers, and Anne Bonny. Complementing the fictional television series are a few pirate documentaries made for the same medium, which, through the use of expert narrative, recreations, and historical objects, attempt to give viewers a sense of what it meant to go on the account.

Finally, a number of video games have traded on the allure of pirates, with *Assassin's Creed IV: Black Flag* (2013) being one of the most popular. Like *Black Sails*, it is set in the Caribbean after the war, and it features some of the same pirates, including Blackbeard and Vane. After detailing a few of the game's main features, a *New York Times* video-game reviewer observed, "It's fun to be a pirate."

IT IS LARGELY BECAUSE of dramatic fictional representations that pirates have grabbed hold of our collective imagination. Many have daydreamed about leaving traditional society behind, boarding a ship, and throwing in their lot with hearty men—and women— intent on taking what they want and getting rich while enjoying the luxurious freedom of sailing the world's oceans with a hold full of rum, going where the wind will take them. Mark Twain captured this longing in his memoir, *Life on the Mississippi* (1883), when he admitted that even though he and his friends had one "permanent ambition," to be steamboatmen, "now and then we had a hope that, if we lived and were good, God would permit us to be pirates."

Historians can certainly poke holes in the fictional representations of pirates, especially those that depict them as unusually attractive, rakish yet good-natured rapscallions, having a grand old time looking for love, adventure, and treasure on the waves. Although it is true that greed and lucre is the main motivation for both fictional and real pirates, the supposed romance and glamour of piracy is imaginary. The reality of piracy is nothing like the breathless musings of a *New York Times* reporter in 1892, who complained: "It cannot but be a source of regret to every true lover of the picturesque that pirates are no more and piracy has lost its popularity. What tremendous fellows they must have been! What heroes, dandies, wits, were to be found among them! They were immensely superior to land brigands, . . . [who] are mere milk compared with Blackbeard and Capt. Kidd." While real pirates were incredibly intriguing and compelling characters, they were most definitely not "tremendous fellows"; instead, they were sea-borne criminals who were neither endearing nor heroic.

By the same token, fictional representations of pirates often get basic historical facts wrong. For example, in the 1952 film *Blackbeard the Pirate*, Blackbeard is placed in the seventeenth century, alongside buccaneer Henry Morgan. While that is a particularly arresting pairing with fascinating possibilities, the two men never crossed paths.

A number of historians who have been advisors on pirate movies and television shows have seen firsthand the difficulty of marrying history with Hollywood. Robert C. Ritchie was one of the first. After coming out with his seminal book on Captain Kidd in 1986, he became *the* historian consultant who many television and movie producers turned to in crafting their pirate projects, with an eye toward injecting them with some degree of verisimilitude. Although Ritchie would attempt to correct numerous misperceptions about pirates, he found himself, for the most part, fighting a losing battle. As it turned out, the producers, as well as the directors and scriptwriters, were more interested in creating a compelling drama than ensuring its accuracy. Reflecting on his brushes with the big and little screen, Ritchie understandably concluded, "I have become quite cynical about the role of the advisor."

Nevertheless, as a historian I am not particularly interested in dissecting or criticizing fictional accounts of piracy. They are often quite fun and entertaining, as they are meant to be. Rather than analyze them, I prefer to enjoy them.

A RECURRING THEME IN pirate fiction, and sometimes nonfiction, is buried treasure, and no pirate is more associated in the public mind with hidden riches than Captain Kidd. Ever since he left his silver and gold with John Gardiner on Gardiners Island off the tip of Long Island, there have been rumors and legends, passed down through the generations, that Kidd buried some of his treasure there as well. Not just there, but other places along the Atlantic coast, including spots in Delaware, New Jersey, Rhode Island, Maine, and Oak Island, Nova Scotia.* As a book on buried treasure published in the early twentieth century noted, "The hoard of Captain Kidd . . . has become as legendary as the dream of the pot of gold at the end of the rainbow." It has also proved just as elusive. Many people have searched for Kidd's buried treasure over the years, spending dearly in both money and time, but they have found nothing. Undoubtedly there will be more searches in the future, and, while I wish them well, they, too, will almost certainly be gravely disappointed because there is no evidence that Kidd, or any pirates during the Golden Age, buried their treasure. Why would they? Pirates wanted to keep and spend their treasure, not secret it away. If they buried it in some out-of-the-way place, who knows when, or whether, they would have had a chance to return to retrieve it; even if they had that chance, there was the possibility that somebody else would get there first.

But there is pirate treasure to be found, under the waves, and Barry Clifford proved it. As a boy on Cape Cod, he heard the legendary story of Sam Bellamy and the wreck of the *Whydah* numerous times, most often from his uncle Bill, a jack-of-all-trades who knew how to weave an engrossing tale. Dreams of finding the *Whydah*'s treasure captured young Clifford's imagination, and when he grew up he decided to pursue his dream. In the early 1980s, he began combing through historical records to find clues as to where the ship might have sunk. A key focus of his search was Cyprian Southack's writings and his map of the Cape, which very roughly marked where the *Whydah* went down. An expert salvager and diver, Clifford next

---

* Famed writer, and master of the macabre, Edgar Allan Poe used the legend of Kidd's buried treasure—in this case near South Carolina's Sullivan's Island—as the central plot element in his short story *The Gold Bug*, written in 1843.

put together a team, backed by eager investors, to scour the waters off Wellfleet's Marconi Beach for the ultimate prize.

In the centuries since the *Whydah* sank, plenty of tangible evidence that treasure lay hidden just offshore had come to light. Writing in 1793 about the wreck, minister Levi Whitman noted, "At times to this day, there are King William and Queen Mary's coppers picked up [along Wellfleet's and Eastham's beaches], and pieces of silver, called cob money," which were crude coins produced by Spain's American colonies. An enterprising Cape Codder who visited those beaches after every nor'easter in the early 1900s was rewarded with a stash of nearly six hundred pieces of eight. There were even occasional sightings of what was thought by some to be part of the wreck peeking above the water during unusually low tides, or when storms churned up the ocean floor, rearranging the coastal topography.

These hints and whispers potentially coming from the *Whydah*, along with the oft-told tale of the ship's crash and all the booty it had onboard, led historian Edward Rowe Snow to mount a recovery effort in the late 1940s. His divers, constantly batted about by the rough seas, spent many hours searching and sifting through the sand, but found only a few silver and gold coins, some cannonballs, and pieces of wood, all of which, it was later discovered, belonged to another ship. Given the considerable amount of money Snow had invested in the venture, and the meager returns, he ruefully concluded, "It will be a very lucky treasure hunter who ever does more than pay expenses while attempting to find the elusive gold and silver still aboard the *Whydah*." In the end, Clifford's team, using remote sensing and recovery technology, proved to be "very lucky" indeed.

On July 20, 1984, the cry came up from one of the divers of a find of cannons deep in the sand. It was the beginning of a torrent of artifacts drawn from the sea in subsequent years, including vast numbers of gold and silver coins, as well as gold dust, guns, cannonballs, plates, tea kettles, rings, gaming pieces, cufflinks, candlesticks, remnants of clothes, and actual wooden pieces of the ship. The item that proved beyond a shadow of a doubt that all of these artifacts came from the *Whydah* was the ship's heavily encrusted bell, which was brought to the surface in the late summer of 1985. Once the concretions fell off or were gingerly chipped away, the writing on the bell's shoulder was plain to see—The ✠ Whydah ✠ Gally ✠ 1716. Clifford and his team had made history, unearthing the first authenticated pirate ship and treasure ever found.*

How much the recovered treasure is worth is not exactly clear. Estimates range from an unreasonably low $200,000 to a wildly improbable $400 million. It doesn't matter to Clifford, however—as of this writing, he's not selling. Instead, he and his investors have decided to continue searching, documenting what they find, and keeping all the artifacts together in order to preserve an important part of our cultural heritage.†

The *Whydah* find is not the only exciting pirate discovery to be made off the American coast in recent years, which has brought the Golden Age of Piracy squarely back into the public eye. In November 1996, salvagers from Intersal, Inc., located an eighteenth-century shipwreck in the relatively shallow waters of Beaufort Inlet. A little more than twenty feet down, they found a debris field that included two massive anchors and nine cannon tubes. On the very first day of the dive, they brought to the surface a bronze church or ship's bell dating back to 1705, the barrel of a blunderbuss, and two cannonballs. These artifacts were, many thought, part of the remains of Blackbeard's flagship, the *Queen Anne's Revenge*. At a press conference in March 1997, former North Carolina governor James B. Hunt shared news of the find. "It looks as if the graveyard of the Atlantic yielded one of the most exciting and historically significant discoveries ever located along our coast. . . . We look forward to the

---

* In 2009, a group of American treasure hunters found pirate Joseph Bannister's ship, the *Golden Fleece*, along with some treasure, in the waters off the Dominican Republic. The story of the find is well told in Robert Kurson's *Pirate Hunters: Treasure, Obsession, and the Search for a Legendary Pirate Ship* (New York: Random House, 2015).

† Anyone who wants to learn more about the *Whydah* and see what has thus far been uncovered can visit the *Whydah* Pirate Museum, which opened its doors in West Yarmouth in the summer of 2016.

day when all North Carolinians can see these exciting artifacts for themselves."

Since that time, archaeologists from the North Carolina Department of Natural and Cultural Resources have overseen efforts to recover hundreds of thousands of artifacts from the site. In addition to more than a dozen cannons, they have retrieved grenades, a sternpost, pewter flatware, liquor bottles, beads, gold dust, ballast stones, belt buckles, a gilded hilt of a sword, fragments of paper from an early eighteenth-century book, and brass scale weights, as well as a urethral syringe manufactured in Paris, which was used to administer mercury, the recommended treatment for syphilis and other venereal diseases in the early 1700s. While there is no single artifact that proves the identity of the wreck, as was the case with the *Whydah* and its bell, North Carolina state archaeologists and officials are convinced, based on the preponderance of circumstantial evidence, that they indeed found the *Queen Anne's Revenge*. Thus, it is likely that the syringe was part of the medicine chest that Blackbeard demanded from Charleston during his blockade of the city.*

THE PIRATES DEPICTED IN this book blazed a fiery and unforgettable path through the history of colonial America. For centuries, their turbulent, destructive, and fascinating lives have beguiled, horrified, and entertained us, leaving an indelible and unique mark on our culture. Undoubtedly, there will be more pirate movies, books, and television shows in the future, many of which will perpetuate myths, or create them anew. But, in the end, there is no need to embellish the history of these pirates, for what they actually did was amazing enough.

---

* Governor Hunt's hope has been realized. The North Carolina Maritime Museum in Beaufort, which is the official repository for the state's *Queen Anne's Revenge* project, displays a wide selection of artifacts from the ship, which visitors from around the world can now enjoy.

Acknowledgments

THIS BOOK'S ORIGIN STORY BEGINS WITH MY KIDS. AFTER I finished *Brilliant Beacons: A History of the American Lighthouse*, I began searching for a new book topic. I asked Lily and Harry, who were then in their teens, what I should write about. When I raised the possibility of pirates, their eyes lit up, both of them saying, "That's it, you have to write about pirates." Lily even threw out two possible titles for the book: "Swords, Sails, and Swashbucklers;" and "Argh"—or, perhaps more emphatically, "Arrrgh"—which, I had to tell Lily, much to her chagrin, is a word that probably was never uttered by a Golden Age pirate, and is more likely a creation of movies in which pirates dispense *arghs* with relish.

My kids' excitement about the pirate theme is not surprising. Lily and Harry were weaned on the *Pirates of the Caribbean* movies and love them. They had also read and seen other things about Golden Age piracy and thought pirates were "cool." My children's strong support is, of course, not the only reason I wrote this book. But the fact that they were early adopters of the pirate idea, gives me hope that they will read this book. And, who knows, they might even think it's "cool."

Great credit is also due to Bob Weil, the editor-in-chief and publishing director at Liveright, and Bill Rusin, the former sales director at W. W. Norton. When I was searching for a topic, I submitted a number of potential options for their consideration. I had a few ideas I thought were very good, and which were unlike any other book that had come out in recent years. I also included the pirate book as a possibility, because I knew I would greatly enjoy writing it, but I downplayed it, saying that there had been so many pirate books as of late, I wasn't sure there was room for another. So, when we had a conference call to discuss the ideas, I was very surprised when they said they liked the pirate idea the best. I reiterated my concern, and they said, "Well, there has never been an Eric Jay Dolin book about pirates." I couldn't disagree, and that was how the book was officially born. I thank Bob and Bill for their confidence in me, and I believe that this book proves that it wasn't misplaced. Despite my initial concern, the book ended up being different from any other, and it is a unique contribution to the literature.

Marie Pantojan, Bob's assistant editor, and the first line editor for *Black Flags, Blue Waters* did a wonderful job, improving the book by cutting unnecessary material and offering insightful suggestions as to how I could enliven the text to make it flow more smoothly. Not only did she improve the book, but she also shepherded it through the process from manuscript submission to the finished product you are holding in your hands. It was an added bonus that she performed all of these tasks with patience, consideration, and good humor. She is a pleasure to work with. Copyeditor Charlotte Kelchner also helped polish the text with her careful eye.

All of my books with Norton have been beautifully designed. *Black Flags, Blue Waters* continues this trend, due to the careful attention and creative touch of Anna Oler, Liveright's production director. Don Rifkin, associate managing editor at Norton/Liveright, was his usual tireless and keen-eyed self, repeatedly checking the text and layout for errors and inconsistencies. Kudos for the dramatic cover, which captures the drama, menace, and deep history of pirates, goes to Steve Attardo, the art director at Liveright. Without dedicated people working to promote a new title to bookstores, online sellers, and potential readers, an author's work would fail to find a good audience, and for such promotion I am heavily indebted to Deirdre Dolan, assistant sales director at Norton; Peter Miller, director of publicity at Liveright; and Cordelia Calvert, Peter's assistant.

My longtime agent, Russ Galen, as always, was at once trusted advisor, confidante, sounding board, friend, and a most valuable supporter. He has a direct, yet agreeable, way of putting things into perspective, especially when I am lacking in that department. I couldn't imagine a better companion to have on my travels through the ups and downs of the often-mystifying world of publishing.

I want to thank Jim Nelson, Gregory Flemming, Bruce and Ann Belason, David Kane, and Ruth Rooks, all of whom gave me valuable feedback on the manuscript. While they can claim to have made many improvements, they have absolutely no responsibility for any errors that might have crept into the book. Those are mine. Jim, who looks more like a stereotypical pirate than anyone I know, deserves even more of my gratitude because of his willingness to answer numerous questions about a variety of nautical topics with accuracy and a sense of humor.

I also want to extend my thanks to all the people, alive and dead, whose names you see in the endnotes and the select bibliography. Their books and articles were essential sources, without which I couldn't have written this book. Like any writer of nonfiction, to reach my goal, I stood on the shoulders of those storytellers and scholars who preceded me.

The following people have also helped me in various ways, and I thank them: Penny Allen, Matthew Aumiller, Joe Barricella, Karen Bridges, Patricia Keenan-Byrne, Brandon Clifford, Anna Clutterbuck-Cook, David Cordingly, David Dobson, Penny Dolin, Paul Fontenoy, Ian Graham, Andrea Green, Donna Kelly, Angus Konstam, Jessa J. Krick, Neel Lattimore, Douglas Mayo, Kelly McAnnaney, Lauren McCormack, Laura Nelson, Stephanie A. Nelson, Allison Nicks, Libby Oldham, Molly Bruce Patterson, Pam Peterson, Betty Raynor-Davis, David Rumsey, Dale Sauter, John Schoonover, Dan Small, Richard Zacks, Nickolas Urquhart, Cindy Vallar, Samuel H. Williamson, Vicken Yepgarian, and the wonderful librarians at Harvard's Widener Library, The National Archives (London), the Caird Library & Archive at The National Maritime Museum (Greenwich), Abbot Public Library, and Salem State University Library.

My father, Stanley, died while I was writing this book, and I miss him greatly. He loved hearing about my projects, and he would have enjoyed reading this book. My mom, Ruth, has been, and continues to be, one of my biggest supporters. Thanks to both of them for everything they have provided throughout the years.

Harry and Lily were not only the earliest supporters of this book, but they also remained engaged throughout, often asking if I had uncovered any particularly gruesome pirate stories. As for Jennifer, my wife, I would run out of superlatives trying to describe her. She is not perfect, of course, but I don't see her flaws (well, maybe a few!). She is my first reader, and the first person I share both good and bad news with. I trust her judgment more than anyone else's, and without her unwavering support, I could never have pursued my dream of becoming a writer. Now, if I could only adopt her relentlessly upbeat disposition, I'd be all set.

Notes

ABBREVIATIONS USED IN THE NOTES

ADM   High Court of the Admiralty

BNL   *Boston News-Letter*

CO   Colonial Office Records

NAL   National Archives, London

CSPC   Calendar of State Papers Colonial, America and West Indies. Her Majesty's Stationary Office published this multivolume set, which spans 1574–1739. The volumes cited in this book were published from the late 1800s to the early to mid-1900s, and were edited by a number of editors, including W. Noel Sainsbury, J. W. Fortescue, and Cecil Headlam. They are available in hard copy, or via Proquest (http://www.proquest.com/), or at British History Online (http://www.british-history.ac.uk/search/series/cal-state-papers--colonial--america-west-indies). The following endnotes will include the title of the correspondence, item number, volume number, and page numbers for the *CSPC* documents cited.

ix   **"Ships are but":** William Shakespeare, *The Merchant of Venice*, in *The Works of William Shakespeare*, ed. Edmond Malone, vol. V (London: Printed for the Proprietors, 1816), 16.

INTRODUCTION

xviii   **Jamaica's vast. and lucrative . . . grind to a halt:** Trevor Burnard, *Planters, Merchants, and Slaves: Plantation Societies in British America* (Chicago: University of Chicago Press, 2015), 64–69; James D. Rice, "Jamaica," in *The Historical Encyclopedia of World Slavery*, vol. I, ed. Junius P. Rodriguez (Santa Barbara: ABC-CLIO, 1997), 374; Gilder Lerhman Institute for American History, "Facts About the Slave Trade and Slavery," https://www.gilderlehrman.org/

history-by-era/slavery-and-anti-slavery/resources/facts-about-slave-trade-and-slavery, accessed on November 22, 2017; Alan Taylor, *American Colonies* (New York: Viking, 2001), 217–18; and W. J. Gardner, *A History of Jamaica* (London: Elliot Stock, 1873), 155–56.

xviii   **"bad usage . . . like dogs"**: Cotton Mather, *The Vial Poured Out Upon the Sea: A Remarkable Relation of Certain Pirates Brought Unto A Tragical and Untimely End* (Boston: T. Fleet for N. Belknap, 1726), 1, 21.

xviii   **William Fly**: Background information for Fly's exploits comes from Joel H. Baer, ed., "Tryals of Sixteen Persons for Piracy etc." (Boston: Joseph Edwards, 1726), in *British Piracy in the Golden Age: History and Interpretation, 1660–1730*, vol. 3 (London: Pickering & Chatto, 2007); 231–58; Mather, *Vial Poured Out*; and Benjamin Colman, *It is a fearful thing to fall into the Hands of the Living God: A Sermon Preached to Some Miserable Pirates, July 10, 1726, The Lords Day* (Boston: Philips and Hancock, 1726).

xviii   **"Damn you"**: Baer, "Tryals of Sixteen Persons," 249.

xviii   **"For God's sake . . . upon my soul"**: Ibid.

xix   **"Come out . . . save my life"**: Ibid., 257.

xix   **"He should go . . . me a rope"**: Ibid., 256.

xix   **"Gentlemen of Fortune"**: Ibid., 254.

xix   **plundered three**: Ibid., 254. See also "New York, June 20," *Boston Gazette* (June 20–27, 1726); and "Philadelphia, June 23," *American Weekly Mercury* (June 23, 1726).

xx   **"blow his brains"**: Baer, "Tryals of Sixteen Persons," 254.

xx   **"humor"**: Mather, *Vial Poured Out*, 3.

xxi   **"have a fleet"**: Colman, *It is a fearful thing*, 34.

xxi   **"he was a dead"**: Ibid., 34–35.

xxii   **"cursed himself . . . away with the ship"**: Ibid., 35–36.

xxii   **On June 29**: "Yesterday came in here," *BNL* (June 23–30, 1726).

xxii   **gloomy stone edifice**: "Petition of Poor Prisoners in Boston Jail, 1713," in *Bulletin of the Boston Public Library* (January–March, 1919), 82.

xxii   **"escape the"**: Mather, *Vial Poured Out*, 11.

xxii   **"he would not have"**: Ibid., 47.

xxii   **"go out of"**: Ibid., 19.

xxiii   **"sullen and raging"**: Ibid., 47.

xxiii   **"Fly briskly"**: Colman, *It is a fearful thing*, 37.

xxiii   **"a brave . . . his trade"**: Mather, *Vial Poured Out*, 47.

xxiv   he **"would advise . . . judgment to come"**: Ibid., 48.

xxiv   **"hung up"**: "On Tuesday the 12th Instant," *BNL* (July 7–14, 1726).

xxv   **"to attempt, attack"**: "Pirate," *The Oxford English Dictionary*, 2nd ed., vol. XI, ed. J. A. Simpson and E. S. C. Weiner (Oxford: Clarendon Press, 1989), 898–99. See also Ricardo Gosalbo-Bono and Sonja Boelaert, "The European Union's Comprehensive Approach to Combating Piracy at Sea: Legal Aspects," in *The Law and Practice of Piracy at Sea: European and International Perspectives* (Oxford: Hart Publishing, 2014), 81.

xxv   **"sea-wolves"**: Homer, *The Odyssey*, translated by Robert Fagles (New York: Penguin, 1996), 28. For more on the great antiquity of piracy, see Daniel Heller-Roazen, *The Enemy of All: Piracy and the Law of Nations* (New York: Zone Books, 2009), 31–39.

xxvi **"As in all":** John Smith, "The Bad Life, Qualities and Conditions of Pyrates; And How They Taught the Turks and Moores to Become Men of Warfare," in *Capt. John Smith, Works, 1608–1631*, ed. Edward Arber (Birmingham: Privately published, 1884), 913.

xxvi **"There was never a time":** Dio Cassius, *Dio's Annals of Rome*, translated by Herbert Baldwin Foster, vol. II (Troy: Pafraets Book Company, 1905), 16.

xxvi **"licensed":** See, for example, William Barton, *A Dissertation on the Freedom of Navigation and Maritime Commerce and Such Rights of States, Relative Thereto, as are Founded on the Law of Nations* (Philadelphia: John Conrad, 1802), 294; and Angus Konstam, *The World Atlas of Pirates* (Guilford, CT: Lyons Press, 2010), 174.

xxvii ***hostis humani generis*:** William Blackstone, *Commentaries on the Laws of England*, 9th ed., vol. 4 (London: Printed for W. Strahan, T. Cadell, and D. Prince, 1783), 71. Sir Edward Coke did not come up with the appellation *hostis humani generis*, or the "enemy of mankind," on his own. Its roots reach back all the way to Roman politician Marcus Tullius Cicero (106–43 BCE), who referred to pirates as *communis hostis omnium*, or the "common enemy of all." See Daniel Heller-Roazen, *The Enemy of All: Piracy and the Law of Nations* (New York: Zone Books, 2009), 16.

xxviii **"under the banner":** Marcus Rediker, "'Under the Banner of King Death': The Social World of Anglo-American Pirates, 1716 to 1726," *William and Mary Quarterly* (April 1981), 204.

CHAPTER I — SMALL BEGINNINGS

2 **"been advised":** Philip III, King of Spain, letter to the Duke of Medina Sidonia, July 29, 1608, MS 2010.5, John D. Rockefeller Jr. Library, Colonial Williamsburg Foundation. See also Mark G. Hanna, *Pirate Nests and the Rise of the British Empire: 1570–1740* (Chapel Hill: University of North Carolina Press, 2015), 68; and *The Genesis of the United States*, vol. I, ed. Alexander Brown (Boston: Houghton, Mifflin and Company, 1890), 119–21.

2 **killed the Incan emperor:** Mark Cocker, *Rivers of Blood, Rivers of Gold: Europe's Conquest of Indigenous Peoples* (New York: Grove Press, 1998), 9; and Kim MacQuarrie, *The Last Days of the Incas* (New York: Simon & Schuster, 2007), 95–96, 123, 133–34.

2 **"to be rich as":** Kenneth Pomeranz and Steven Topik, *The World that Trade Created: Society, Culture, and the World Economy, 1400 to the Present* (Armonk, NY: M.E. Sharpe, 2006), 154.

4 **"first truly":** Niall Ferguson, *The Ascent of Money: A Financial History of the World* (New York: Penguin Press, 2008), 25–26.

4 **3,000 tons:** Neil MacGregor, "Pieces of Eight," in *A History of the World in 100 Objects* (New York: Viking, 2011), 518.

4 **"mountain that eats men":** Patrick Greenfield, "Story of Cities #6: How Silver Turned Potosi into 'the First City of Capitalism,'" *Guardian* (March 21, 2016), accessed on November 9, 2017, https://www.theguardian.com/cities/2016/mar/21/story-of-cities-6-potosi-bolivia-peru-inca-first-city-capitalism.

5 **Manila Galleons:** David Cordingly, *Spanish Gold: Captain Woodes Rogers and the Pirates of the Caribbean* (London: Bloomsbury, 2011); and Patricio N. Abi-

nales and Donna J. Amoroso, *State and Society in the Philippine*s (Lanham, MD: Rowman & Littlefield, 2005), 63.

5 **"the prize":** Glyndwr Williams, *The Great South Sea: English Voyages and Encounters, 1570–1750* (New Haven, CT: Yale University Press, 1997), 233.

5 **While this influx . . . biggest prizes:** Taylor, *American Colonies*, 63–65.

5 **Treaty of Tordesillas:** H. Michael Tarver and Emily Slape, "Overview Essay," in *The Spanish Empire: A Historical Encyclopedia*, vol. I, ed. H. Michael Tarver and Emily Slape (Santa Barbara, CA: ABC-CLIO, 2016), 61–62.

7 **Raised in the company . . . Crown's annual income:** Kelsey, *Sir Francis Drake*, 11–39, 75–82, 137–70, 210–19; Hanna, *Pirate Nests*, 43–45; Robert C. Ritchie, *Captain Kidd and the War against the Pirates* (Cambridge, MA: Harvard University Press, 1986), 12; Henry Walter, *A History of England*, vol. III (London: J. G. & F. Rivington, 1832), 588–89; and David Cordingly, *Under the Black Flag: The Romance and the Reality of Life among the Pirates* (Orlando: Harvest Book, 1995), 28–31.

8 **"diverse injuries":** Harry Kelsey, *Sir Francis Drake: The Queen's Pirate* (New Haven, CT: Yale University Press, 1998), 76.

8 *Cacafuego,* **or "Shitfire":** Kenneth R. Andrews, *Trade, Plunder, and Settlement: Maritime Enterprises and the Genesis of the British Empire, 1480–1630* (Cambridge: Cambridge University Press, 1984), 154.

9 **"no man is a** *pirate***":** Samuel Taylor Coleridge, *Specimens of the Table Talk of the Late Samuel Taylor Coleridge*, vol. II (New York: Harper & Brothers, 1835), 16.

9 **"sea dogs":** William Wood, *Elizabethan Sea-Dogs: A Chronicle of Drake and His Companions* (New Haven, CT: Yale University Press, 1921).

10 **self-professed privateers:** Ritchie, *Captain Kidd*, 13; and Mark St. John Erickson, "Spain Feared Jamestown for Harboring English Pirates," *Daily Press* (June 1, 2012).

10 **Instead of spying:** James Horn, *A Land as God Made It: Jamestown and the Birth of America* (New York: Basic Books, 2005), 200–203.

10 **"his majesty":** "Letter of Don Diego De Molina, 1613," *Narratives of Early Virginia, 1606–1625*, ed. Lyon Gardiner Tyler (New York: Charles Scribner's Sons, 1907), 218.

11 **In early 1619 . . . including the Spanish:** W. Frank Craven, "The Earl of Warwick, A Speculator in Piracy," *The Hispanic American Historical Review* (November 1930), 463–64; Hanna, *Pirate Nests*, 76–77; John Donoghue, *Fire under the Ashes: An Atlantic History of the English Revolution* (Chicago: University of Chicago Press, 2013), 26–27; Horn, *A Land as God Made It*, 244; James Oliver Horton and Lois E. Horton, *Slavery and the Making of America* (Oxford: Oxford University Press, 2005), 27–29; Engel Sluiter, "New Light on the '20 Odd Negroes' Arriving in Virginia, August 1619," *William and Mary Quarterly* (April 1977), 395–98; "The First Africans," Jamestown Rediscovery, Historic Jamestowne, accessed on November 9, 2017, http://historic-jamestowne.org/history/the-first-africans/; Bernard Bailyn, *The Barbarous Years: The Peopling of British North America; The Conflict of Civilizations, 1600–1675* (New York: Alfred A. Knopf, 2013), 174–75; and Clive Senior, *A Nation of Pirates: English Piracy in its Heyday* (London: David & Charles Newton Abbot, 1976), 8.

11 **several had been brought to Bermuda:** Horn, *A Land as God Made It*, 286–87.

12 **"lewd and ill":** *James I, By the King. A Proclamation Against Pirats* (January 8, 1609) (London: Deputies of Robert Barker, 1609).

12 **"severely punished":** "Virginia Company Instructions to the Governor and Council of State in Virginia (July 24, 1621)," in Samuel M. Bemiss, *The Three Charters of the Virginia Company of London* (Williamsburg: Virginia 350th Anniversary Celebration Corporation, 1957), 110.

12 **Dixie Bull:** Background for Dixie Bull comes from Jim McClain, *A Brief Account of the Wicked Doings of Dixie Bull, Reportedly the First Pirate in New England Waters* (New York: Court Printers, 1980); C. E. Banks, "Pirate of Pemaquid, 1631," *The Maine Historical and Genealogical Recorder*, vol. I (Portland, ME: S.M. Watson, 1884), 57–61; John Winthrop, *Winthrop's Journal, "History of New England,"* 1630–1649, vol. I, ed. James Kendall Hosmer (New York: Charles Scribner's Sons, 1908) 82, 95–96, 101–2; Roger Clap, *Memoirs of Captain Roger Clap* (Boston: David Carlisle, 1807), 18–19; and George Francis Dow and John Henry Edmonds, *The Pirates of the New England Coast, 1630–1730* (New York: Sentry Press, 1968, facsimile of the 1923 edition), 20–22.

12 **Gathered by the Indians . . . voyage to America:** Eric Jay Dolin, *Fur, Fortune, and Empire: The Epic History of the Fur Trade in America* (New York: W. W. Norton, 2010), xv, 21–22, 37–73; and James Truslow Adams, *The Founding of New England* (Boston: Atlantic Monthly Press, 1921), 102.

14 **Established in 1630:** Harry Gratwick, *The Forts of Maine: Silent Sentinels of the Pine Tree State* (Charleston, SC: History Press, 2013); and J. Wingate Thornton, "Ancient Pemaquid, An Historical Review," *Collections of the Maine Historical Society*, vol. V (Portland, ME: Published for the Society, 1857), 197.

14 **£500:** "John Winter to Robert Trelawny" (July 11, 1633), *Documentary History of the State of Maine*, vol. III, ed. James Phinney Baxter (Portland, ME: Hoyt, Fogg, and Donham, 1884), 23.

14 **this at a time when:** William B. Weeden, *Economic and Social History of New England, 1620–1789*, vol. II (Boston: Houghton, Mifflin and Company, 1890), 877–78.

14 **"filled with fear":** Clap, *Memoirs*, 18.

14 **"any further expedition":** Winthrop, *Winthrop's Journal*, vol. I, 95.

15 **"They had been . . . than be taken":** Ibid., 96.

15 **Anthony Dicks:** Sidney Perley, *The History of Salem Massachusetts*, vol. I (Salem, MA: Sidney Perley, 1924), 223.

15 **"that they were afraid":** Clap, *Memoirs*, 18.

15 **"a pinnace":** Winthrop, *Winthrop's Journal*, vol. I, 101–2.

16 **"fled eastward . . . wretched man":** Clap, *Memoirs*, 18–19.

16 **Others believe:** Perley, *History of Salem*, 223.

17 **Around 1630 . . . half a man's share:** Alexander O. Esquemelin, *The Buccaneers of America*, translated by Alexis Brown, and introduction by Jack Beeching (Mineola, NY: Dover Publications, 2000 [this is a reprint of the 1969 Penguin Books translation, which was originally published in Dutch in 1678]), 8–10, 29, 47, 70–72; Violet Barbour, "Privateers and Pirates of the West Indies," *American Historical Review* (April 1911), 536–39; James Burney, *A Chronological History of the Voyages and Discoveries in the South Sea or Pacific Ocean*, vol. IV

(London: Luke Hansard & Sons, 1816), 47–51; and Cordingly, *Under the Black Flag*, xviii.

19   **"Brethren of the Coast":** James Burney, *History of The Buccaneers of America* (London: Swan Sonnenschein, 1891, reprint of 1816 edition), 41.

20   **"his eyes":** Esquemelin, *Buccaneers*, 147.

22   **"ripped open":** Ibid., 107.

22   **Not long after:** Ibid., 117.

22   **Over time, buccaneers . . . Crown's coffers:** Hanna, *Pirate Nests*, 102–114; Douglas R. Burgess Jr., *The Pirates' Pact: The Secret Alliances between History's Most Notorious Buccaneers and Colonial America* (New York: McGraw Hill, 2008), 47–50; Stephen Talty, *Empire of Blue Water: Captain Morgan's Great Pirate Army, the Epic Battle for the Americas, and the Catastrophe that Ended the Outlaw's Bloody Reign* (New York: Crown, 2007), 20–23; and Dudley Pope, *The Buccaneer King: The Biography of the Notorious Sir Henry Morgan, 1635–1688* (New York: Dodd, Mead, 1977), 121–25.

23   **"no peace beyond":** Lennox Honychurch, *The Caribbean People*, Book 2 (Cheltenham, UK: Thomas Nelson & Sons, 1995), 45.

24   **Arguably the wealthiest:** Michael Pawson and David Buisseret, *Port Royal Jamaica* (Barbados: University of the West Indies Press, 2000), 135; Mathew Mulcahy, "'that fatall spot': The Rise and Fall—and Rise and Fall Again—of Port Royal, Jamaica," in *Investing in the Early Modern Built Environment*, ed. Carole Shammas (Leiden: Brill, 2012), 196; and Mathew Mulcahy, *Hurricanes and Society in the British Greater Caribbean, 1624–1783* (Baltimore: Johns Hopkins University Press, 2006), 120.

24   **"wickedest city":** Hamilton Mabie and Marshal H. Bright, *The Memorial Story of America, Comprising the Important Events, Episodes, and Incidents Which Make Up the Record of Four Hundred Years* (Philadelphia: John C. Winston, 1892), 119.

24   **"Sodom of the":** Carl and Roberta Bridenbaugh, *No Peace beyond the Line: The English in the Caribbean, 1624–1690* (New York: Oxford University Press, 1972), 367.

24   **"Whenever they have":** Esquemelin, *Buccaneers*, 81–82.

24   **"A stout figure":** Diana and Michael Preston, *A Pirate of Exquisite Mind: Explorer, Naturalist, and Buccaneer—The Life of William Dampier* (New York: Walker, 2004), 28.

24   **Once in Jamaica, Morgan . . . what might have been:** Talty, *Empire of Blue Water*, 101–128, 199–252; Patrick Pringle, *Jolly Roger: The Story of the Great Age of Piracy* (New York: W. W. Norton, 1953), 67–75; Hanna, *Pirate Nests*, 103–114; Esquemelin, *Buccaneers*, 180–204; Pope, *Buccaneer King*, 62–67, 216–49; and Cordingly, *Under the Black Flag*, 45–53.

26   **"thus was consumed":** Henry Morgan's Account of an Expedition Against the Spaniards (April 20, 1671), in "America and West Indies: April 1671," *CSPC*, item 504, vol. 7, 203.

27   **Estimates of the treasure:** Talty, *Empire of Blue Water*, 251.

27   **Morgan was warmly . . . raucous than it once had been:** Pope, *Buccaneer King*, 248–82; Talty, *Empire of Blue Water*, 253–82; Patrick Pringle, *Jolly Roger*, 75–78; Hanna, *Pirate Nests*, 115–42; "King Charles II to Thomas Lynch" (March 10, 1671), CO 137/11, fol. 111, NA; and Burgess, *Pirates' Pact*, 67–77.

28 **"Merry Monarch"**: Anna Keay, *The Magnificent Monarch: Charles II and the Ceremonies of Power* (London: Continuum, 2008), 2–3.

28 **"This cursed"**: "Sir Thos. Lynch to Joseph Williamson" (January 13, 1672), *CSPC*, item 729, vol. 7, 315–17.

CHAPTER 2 – WELCOMED WITH OPEN ARMS

30 **Colonial merchants . . . next voyage:** Hanna, *Pirate Nests*, 150–58, 167.

31 **"common seaman":** John Winthrop, *Winthrop's Journal, History of New England, 1630–1649*, vol. II, ed. James Kendall Hosmer (New York: Charles Scribner's Sons, 1908), 272.

31 **"lusty":** William Bradford, *History of Plymouth Plantation*, ed. Charles Deane (Boston: Privately Published, 1856), 441.

31 **"like mad . . . and orderly":** Ibid.

31 **"gave freely . . . comfort and help":** Winthrop, *Winthrop's Journal*, vol. II, 272.

31 **"are now full":** "Sir Thomas Lynch to the Lords of Trade and Plantations" (February 28, 1684), *CSPC*, item 1563, vol. 11, 592–98.

31 **"the common":** John Romeyn Brodhead, *History of the State of New York*, vol. II (New York: Harper & Brothers, 1871), 524.

31 **To get an idea of the magnitude:** William B. Weeden, *Economic and Social History of New England, 1620–1789*, vol. I (Boston: Houghton, Mifflin and Company, 1890), 334; and Weeden, *Economic and Social History of New England*, vol. II, 887.

31 **"at least half":** Hanna, *Pirate Nests*, 171. See also Shirley C. Hughson, "The Carolina Pirates and Colonial Commerce (1670–1740)," in *Johns Hopkins University Studies in Historical and Political Science*, ed. Herbert B. Adams, Twelfth Series, V-VI-VIII (Baltimore: Johns Hopkins Press, 1894), 249–50; and John Fiske, *Old Virginia and Her Neighbours*, vol. II (Boston: Houghton, Mifflin and Company, 1897), 362.

31 **In addition . . . knives, and spoons:** Hanna, *Pirate Nests*, 96–98, 169–70; Thomas Hutchinson, *The History of the Colony of Massachusetts-Bay* (London: M. Richardson, 1760), 177–78.

32 **"encouraged pirates":** "Edward Randolph to the Lords of Trade (May 29, 1689)," in *Documents Relative to the Colonial History of the State of New-York*, ed. John Romeyn Brodhead, vol. III (Albany, NY: Weed, Parsons and Company, 1853), 582.

32 **Pirates also brought . . . African slaves:** Hanna, *Pirate Nests*, 91, 167–72.

33 **"several . . . £1,500 a man":** "Edward Randolph to William Blathwayt (October 19, 1688)," in *Edward Randolph, 1678–1700*, vol. VI (Boston: The Prince Society, 1909), 275.

33 **"a good substantial":** Abiel Holmes, *American Annals; or A Chronological History of America*, vol. I (Cambridge: W. Hilliard, 1805), 444n2.

33 **Captain Thomas Paine:** Background for Paine comes from Howard M. Chapin, "Captain Paine of Cajacet," *Rhode Island Historical Society Collections* (January 1930), 19–32.

33 **"bring in or destroy":** "Thomas Lynch to Leoline Jenkins" (November 6, 1682), *CSPC*, item 769, vol. 11, 318–21.

33   **"time to arm"**: "Relation of T. Thacker, Deputy-Collector" (August 16, 1684), *CSPC*, item 1862ii, vol. 11, 684–86.

34   **"been on a piratical"**: Ibid.

34   **In September 1684 . . . Paine and his ship**: "William Dyre to Leoline Jenkins" (September 12, 1684), *CSPC*, item 1862, vol. 11, 684–86.

34   **"arch-pirate"**: Ibid.

34   **"I observed that"**: Edward Randolph, "A Discourse About Pirates, With Proper Remedies to Suppress Them" (1696), in Philip Gosse, *The History of Piracy* (Mineola, NY: Dover Publications, 2007, reprint of original 1932 edition), 320.

35   **The acceptance of . . . virtually meaningless**: Hanna, *Pirate Nests*, 148n6, 178; "Earl of Craven to Lords of Trade and Plantations" (May 27, 1684), *CSPC*, item 1707, vol. 11, 642–43.

35   **"instead of . . . detriment of trade"**: "King James II to Governor Dongan" (October 13, 1687), in *Documents Relative to the Colonial History of the State of New-York*, vol. III, 490–91.

36   **In August 1684 . . . other establishments**: "Governor Cranfield to Lords of Trade and Plantations" (August 25, 1684), *CSPC*, item 1845, vol. 11, 678–79; and C. H. Haring, *The Buccaneers in the West Indies in the XVII Century* (New York: E. P. Dutton and Company, 1910), 251–52.

36   **"of the first magnitude . . . and cacao"**: "William Dyer to Sir Leoline Jenkins" (September 12, 1684).

36   **other victims**: "William Stapleton to Lords of Trade and Plantations" (January 7, 1685), *CSPC*, item 2042, vol. 11, 759–60.

36   **This was not surprising . . . within their borders**: Curtis Nettles, "British Policy and Colonial Money Supply," in *Economic History Review* (October 1931), 219–33; Bernard Bailyn, *The New England Merchants in the Seventeenth Century* (Cambridge, MA: Harvard University Press, 1979), 182–83; Hanna, *Pirate Nests*, 168–71.

37   **"*Silver in New-England*"**: Cotton Mather, "Some Consideration on the Bills of Credit Now Passing in New-England," in *Tracts Relating to the Currency of the Massachusetts Bay, 1682–1720*, ed. Andrew McFarland (Boston: Houghton, Mifflin and Company, 1902), 17.

37   **Colonial governors valued . . . to step down**: "Edward Randolph to William Popple" (May 12, 1698), *CSPC*, item 452, vol. 16, 211–15; Hughson, "Carolina Pirates," 23; Taylor, *American Colonies*, 286; and B. R. Carroll, *Historical Collections of South Carolina*, vol. I (New York: Harper & Brothers, 1836), 86–87.

37   **Navigation Acts**: Taylor, *American Colonies*, 258.

38   **"even if individual"**: Hanna, *Pirate Nests*, 145–46.

38   **"hardly safe"**: "A Letter to a Member of Parliament Concerning the Suppression of Piracy (March 20, 1700)," in *Letter-Book of Samuel Sewall*, Collections of the Massachusetts Historical Society, vol. I, Sixth Series (Boston: Massachusetts Historical Society, 1886), 222n.

38   **In the summer of 1690 . . . welcome in Newport**: Ibid., 263–70; Chapin, "Captain Paine of Cajacet," 25–29; and Samuel Greene Arnold, *History of the State of Rhode Island and Providence Plantations*, vol. I (New York: D. Appleton, 1874), 520–21.

39 **"a very violent":** Samuel Niles, "A Summary Historical Narrative of the Wars in New-England with the French and Indians, in the Several Parts of the Country," in *Collections of the Massachusetts Historical Society*, vol. VI of the Third Series (Boston: American Stationers' Company, 1837), 269.

39 **"by some means":** Ibid., 270.

40 **Although the number . . . and military force:** "John J. McCusker, "Colonial Statistics," in *Historical Statistics of the United States, Earliest Times to the Present, Millennial Edition, Part E*, eds. Susan B. Carter et. al. (Cambridge: Cambridge University Press, 2006), 5-651–53, 5-655.

41 **By offering all of these:** Philip Alexander Bruce, *Institutional History of Virginia in the Seventeenth Century*, vol. II (New York: G. P. Putnam's Sons, 1910), 209.

42 **Thomas Pound:** The background for this section on Pound comes from John Henry Edmonds, *Captain Thomas Pound* (Cambridge, MA: John Wilson and Son, 1918), 23–84; and Dow and Edmonds, *Pirates*, 54–72. The former source contains many pages of contemporary, transcribed trial records and depositions from the participants in this event, which are only cited when quotes are used.

42 **a rather strange, selfish:** Priscilla Sawyer Lord and Virginia Clegg Gamage, *Marblehead: The Spirit of '76 Lives Here* (Radnor: Chilton Book Company, 1972), 65; and Samuel C. Derby, "The Derby Family," *The 'Old Northwest' Genealogical Quarterly* (January, 1910), 36.

43 **"rogues":** Sylvanus Davis, "Deposition" (August 19, 1689), in Edmonds, *Captain Thomas Pound*, 55.

43 **"good watch":** Ibid.

43 **"came out after":** John Smart, "Deposition" (August 17, 1689), in Edmonds, *Captain Thomas Pound*, 56.

44 **"pirates . . . subdue":** "Governor's Council to Samuel Pease" (September 30, 1689), in Edmonds, *Captain Thomas Pound*, 61.

44 **"there was a pirate":** Benjamin Gallop et al., "Deposition" (1689), in Edmonds, *Captain Thomas Pound*, 36.

44 **"bloody [red] flag . . . give you quarter":** Ibid., and Matthew Mayhew, "Deposition" (August 29, 1689), in Edmonds, *Captain Thomas Pound*, 59.

45 **"women of quality":** "Journal of Benjamin Bullivant" (May 19, 1690), *CSPC*, item 885, vol. 13, 263–65.

46 **"great disgust":** Samuel Sewall, "Diary of Samuel Sewall," vol. I, 1674–1700, in *Collections of the Massachusetts Historical Society*, vol. V, Fifth Series (Boston: Massachusetts Historical Society, 1878), 310.

46 **As if to provide . . . in the world:** R. B., *The General History of Earthquakes* (London: A. Bettersworth and J. Hodges, 1734), 134–40; M. N., "Earthquake at Port Royal in Jamaica in 1692," *The Gentleman's Magazine* (November 1785), 879–80; and Hanna, *Pirate Nests*, 142.

46 **"meat for fish and fowls":** Matthew Parker, *The Sugar Barons: Family, Corruption, Empire, and War in the West Indies* (New York: Walker, 2011), 169.

46 **"terrible judgment . . . debauched people":** "An Account of a Dreadful Earthquake, That Happened at Port Royal in Jamaica, on June the 7th, 1692," in "Two Letters Written by a Minister of that Place," in *Philotheus, True and Particular History of Earthquakes* (London: Printed for the Author, 1748), 57.

CHAPTER 3 — "WHERE THE MONEY WAS AS PLENTY AS STONES AND SAND"

49 **"Almost useless . . . men aboard":** J. Ovington, *A Voyage to Suratt in the Year, 1689* (London: Jacob Tonson, 1696), 102–3.

49 **These pirates were . . . holiest of voyages:** Charles Grey, *Pirates of the Eastern Seas (1618–1723): A Lurid Page of History* (Port Washington, NY: Kennikat Press, 1971, first published in 1933), 12, 89–109; Ovington, *A Voyage*, 103–5; *Piracy Destroyed: Or, A Short Discourse Showing the Rise, Growth and Causes of Piracy of Late; With a Sure Method How to Put a Speedy Stop to that Growing Evil* (London: John Nutt, 1701), 2; and Charles Hill, "Notes on Piracy in Eastern Waters," *The Indian Antiquary* (March 1927), Hill, 89–91.

51 **The first known American ship:** The background for the story of the *Jacob* comes from Robert C. Ritchie, "Samuel Burgess, Pirate," *Authority and Resistance in Early New York*, ed. William Pencak and Conrad Edick Wright (New York: New-York Historical Society, 1988), 117–18; Hannah, *Pirate Nests*, 215; "Deposition of Samuel Burgess" (May 3, 1698), *CSPC*, item 473ii, vol. 16, 224–29; "Deposition of Edward Taylor" (May 7, 1698), *CSPC*, item 473iii, vol. 16, 224–29; "Letter from Peter Delanoy Relative to Governor Fletcher's Conduct" (June 13, 1695), *CSPC*, item 1892, vol. 14, 503–6; Charles Burr Todd, *The Story of The City of New York* (New York: G. P. Putnam's Sons, 1888), 174; and "Council of Trade and Plantations to the Lords Justices of England (October 19, 1698)," *CSPC*, item 904, vol. 16, 480–82.

52 **"a man of strong":** William Smith, *The History of the Province of New-York From The First Discovery to the Year MDCCXXXII* (London: Thomas Wilcox, 1757), 80.

52 **"a poor beggar":** James Grant Wilson, *The Memorial History of the City of New-York, From its First Settlement to the Year 1892*, vol. I (New York: New-York History Company, 1892), 495.

52 **"a particular delight":** "Letter from Peter Delanoy Relative to Governor Fletcher's Conduct" (June 13, 1695), *CSPC*, item 1892, vol. 14, 503–6.

52 **A Rhode Islander by birth . . . and to Benjamin Fletcher:** Burgess, *Pirates' Pact*, 108–12; Dow and Edmonds, *Pirates*, 84–88; Baldridge Deposition, J. Franklin Jameson, *Privateering and Piracy in the Colonial* Period—Illustrative *Documents* (New York: Augustus M. Kelley, 1923), 183; Randolph, "A Discourse About Pyrates," 321; "Secretary to the East India Company to William Popple" (December 18, 1696), *CSPC*, item 517, vol. 15, 259–64; and Daniel Defoe [Charles Johnson], *A General History of the Pyrates*, ed. Manuel Schonhorn (Mineola, NY: Dover Publications, 1999—this is a superbly edited version of some of the earliest editions of the *General History*, from 1726 and 1728), 422–23, 438–39.

53 **"He was free":** "John Graves to Council of Trade and Plantations" (February 19, 1697), *CSPC*, item 744, vol. 15, 379.

54 **recently passed four thousand:** McCusker, "Colonial Statistics," 5-655.

54 **"its hilt set with":** Rufus Rockwell Wilson, *New York: Old & New, Its Story, Streets, and Landmarks*, vol. I (Philadelphia: J. B. Lippincott Company, 1903), 136–37.

54   **At local taverns . . . for £300:** "Copy of a report from the Attorney-General of New York to Governor Lord Bellomont" (May 4, 1698), *CSPC*, item 846 iii, vol. 16, 455–468; and "I. T. South to the Lords Justices of Ireland. Dublin" (August 15, 1696), *CSPC*, item 517, vol. 15, 248–67.

55   **"came as a stranger":** "Governor Fletcher to Council of Trade and Plantations" (June 22, 1697), *CSPC*, item 1098, vol. 15, 517–20.

55   **"a man of courage . . . in value not much":** "Benjamin Fletcher to Council of Trade and Plantations" (December 24, 1698), *CSPC*, item 1077, vol. 16, 583–91.

56   **"highly caressed":** "Letter from Peter Delanoy Relative to Governor Fletcher's Conduct" (June 13, 1695).

56   **"It was public":** "Council of Trade and Plantations to the Lords Justices of England" (October 19, 1698), *CSPC*, item 904, vol. 16, 480–82.

56   **Commission in hand . . . to pay off:** Dow and Edmonds, *Pirates*, 96; Gosse, *History of Piracy*, 321; "Baldridge Deposition," in Jameson, *Privateering*, 184; Defoe, *General History*, 439; Burgess, *Pirates' Pact*, 113–16; and "John Graves to Council of Trade and Plantations" (February 19, 1697), *CSPC*, item 744, vol. 15, 379.

56   **"to go to the Red Sea":** "Nathaniel Coddington Narrative" (November 27, 1699), CO 5/1259, fol. D74, NAL.

57   **£100 each:** "Deposition of James Emott (May 1698) and Deposition of Leonard Lewis" (May 1698), *CSPC*, item 473 vii and ix, vol. 16, 224–29.

57   **"protection":** "Deposition of Leonard Lewis" (May 1698), *CSPC*, item 473 vii, vol. 16, 224–29.

57   **"to prevent":** "Deposition of Samuel Burgess" (May 3, 1698).

57   **hundreds of pirates:** "Mr. Weaver's Statements to the Board of Trade," September 27, 1698, in John Romeyn Brodhead, *Documents Relative to the Colonial History of the State of New York*, vol. IV (Albany: Weed, Parson and Company, 1854), 384.

57   **"It may be":** "Governor Fletcher to Council of Trade and Plantations" (June 22, 1697).

57   **£30,000:** "Letter from Peter Delanoy Relative to Governor Fletcher's Conduct" (June 13, 1695).

58   **The royal customs collector . . . the local sheriff:** P. Bradley Nutting, "The Madagascar Connection: Parliament and Piracy, 1690–1701," *American Journal of Legal History* (July 1978), 210.

58   **And prominent New York:** Gary B. Nash, *The Urban Crucible: Social Change, Political Consciousness, and the Origins of the American Revolution* (Cambridge, MA: Harvard University, 1979), 68.

58   **"an early American":** Ibid.

58   **A Dutchman by birth:** Background for Philipse comes from Jacob Judd, "Frederick Philipse and the Madagascar Trade," *New-York Historical Society Quarterly* (October 1971), 354–57; Aline Benjamin, "From Rags to Riches in 1686," *New York Times* (October 30, 1977); Kevin P. McDonald, *Pirates, Merchants, Settlers, and Slaves: Colonial America and the Indo-Atlantic World* (Oakland: University of California Press, 2015), 48; and Edwin G. Burrows and Mike Wallace, *Gotham: A History of New York City to 1898* (New York: Oxford University Press, 1999), 80.

58   **twelve-foot-tall wall:** John Steele Gordon, *The Business of America: Tales from the Marketplace—American Enterprise from the Settling of New England to the Breakup of AT&T* (New York: Walker Publishing, 2001), 9; and Burrows and Wallace, *Gotham*, 64.

59   **hub of the colonial:** Lillian S. Williams, Amybeth Gregory, and Hadley Kruczek-Aaron, "African Americans," *The Encyclopedia of New York State*, ed. Peter Eisenstadt (Syracuse: Syracuse University Press, 2005), 18; and Leslie M. Harris, *In the Shadow of Slavery: African Americans in New York City, 1626–1863* (Chicago: University of Chicago Press, 2003), 11–12.

59   **reports circulated:** Burgess, *Pirates' Pact*, 96; and "Deposition of Samuel Perkins" (August 25, 1698), *CSPC*, item 771, vol. 16, 403–4.

60   **This wasn't a rash . . . in the Western colonies:** Arne Bialuschewski, "Pirates, Slavers, and the Indigenous Population in Madagascar, c. 1690–1715," *International Journal of African Historical Studies* (2005), 404; McDonald, *Pirates, Merchants, Settlers*, 40–41, 47, 85; and Virginia Bever Platt, "The East India Company and the Madagascar Slave Trade," *William and Mary Quarterly* (Oct., 1969), 549.

60   **By the time Baldridge:** Platt, "The East India Company," 548–50; McDonald, *Pirates, Merchants*, 40–41; and James C. Armstrong, "Madagascar and the Slave Trade in the Seventeenth Century," *Omaly sy anio* (1983), 218.

60   **To ingratiate himself . . . built a modest fort:** "Deposition of Adam Baldridge (May 5, 1699)," in Jameson, *Privateering*, 181.

60   **"King Baldridge":** McDonald, *Pirates, Merchants*, 88–89; and Burgess, *Pirates' Pact*, 95–97.

60   **How Baldridge learned . . . back to America:** Judd, "Frederick Philipse," 357–66. See also Ritchie, *Captain Kidd*, 112–16; Deposition of Baldridge (May 5, 1699)," 182–87; McDonald, *Pirates, Merchants*, 84–89; Nash, *Urban Crucible*, 70; and "Examination of Edward Buckmaster (June 6, 1699)," in Jameson, *Privateering*, 197.

61   **A gallon of rum:** "Earl of Bellomont to the Lords of Trade" (November 14, 1698), in Brodhead, *Documents Relative to the Colonial History of the State of New York*, vol. IV, 532.

61   **"chiefest profit":** Judd, "Frederick Philipse," 358.

62   **fellow New York merchants grew rich:** Cathy Matson, *Merchants & Empire: Trading in Colonial New York* (Baltimore: Johns Hopkins University Press, 2002), 63–64; and McDonald, *Pirates, Merchants*, 51–52.

62   **"notorious as a pirate":** Ritchie, *Captain Kidd*, 38.

62   **Red Sea Men:** "Letter from Peter Delanoy Relative to Governor Fletcher's Conduct" (June 13, 1695).

62   **nearly forty:** Caroline Frank, *Objectifying China, Imagining America: Chinese Commodities in Early America* (Chicago: University of Chicago Press, 2011), 31–32.

62   **"held a [privateering] commission":** Hanna, *Pirate Nests*, 201.

62   **"The vast riches":** "Lord Bellomont to Lords of the Admiralty, Boston" (September 7, 1699), *CSPC*, item 769 xviii, vol. 17, 425–32.

63   **one to two pounds:** Ralph Davis, *The Rise of the English Shipping Industry in the Seventeenth and Eighteenth Centuries* (St. Johns: International Maritime Economic History Association, 2012), 127–34.

63   **"infidels":** "Nathaniel Coddington Narrative" (November 27, 1699), CO 5/1259, fol. D74, NAL. See also *Piracy Destroyed*, 5.

63   **"he had not known":** *The Ordinary of Newgate his Account of the Behavior, Confessions, and Dying-Words of Captain William Kidd, and other Pirates, that were Executed at the* Execution-Dock *in Wapping, on Friday May 23, 1701* (London: Printed for E. Mallet, 1701).

64   **in such high demand:** McDonald, *Pirates, Merchants,* 41; and Hanna, *Pirate Nests,* 197.

64   **"The laws of England":** Bailyn, *New England Merchants,* 157–58; and Taylor, *American Colonies,* 276.

64   **Making it easier . . . these men's actions:** Mark G. Hanna, "Well-Behaved Pirates Seldom Make History: A Reevaluation of the Golden Age of English Piracy," in *Governing the Sea in the Early Modern Era: Essays in Honor of Robert C. Ritchie,* eds. Peter C. Mancall and Carole Shammas (Huntington, CA: Huntington Library, Art Collections, and Botanical Gardens, 2015), 134–45.

65   **"protecting their . . . purchased their goods":** Mark G. Hanna, "A Lot of What Is Known about Pirates Is Not True, and a Lot of What Is True Is Not Known: The Pirate Next Door," *Humanities* (Winter 2017), https://www.neh .gov/humanities/2017/winter/feature/lot-what-known-about-pirates-not-true-and-lot-what-true-not-known, accessed June 12, 2017.

65   **"several privateers":** "Lieutenant-Governor Sir William Beeston to Lords of Trade and Plantations" (June 10, 1693), *CSPC,* item 393, vol. 14, 114.

65   **"are pardoned":** "Lieutenant-Governor Sir William Beeston to the Earl of Nottingham" (July 28, 1693), *CSPC,* item 479, vol. 14, 135–36.

66   **"really zealous to suppress":** "Edward Randolph to William Popple" (May 12, 1698).

66   **"I fear":** "Governor Nicholson to the Duke of Shrewsbury" (June 14, 1695), *CSPC,* item 1897, vol. 14, 510–13.

66   **"commodious harbor":** "From Captain Thomas Warren, of H.M.S. *Windsor,* to the East India Company" (November 28, 1697), *CSPC,* item 115 I, vol. 16, 67–71.

66   **Other accounts:** Ritchie, *Captain Kidd,* 112; and Jane Hooper, "Pirates and Kings: Power on the Shores of Early Modern Madagascar and the Indian Ocean," *Journal of World History* (June 2011), 223.

67   **"head of a":** "Council of Trade and Plantations to the King" (February 26, 1698), *CSPC,* item 265i, vol. 16, 121–22.

67   **built a small . . . ships at night:** Ritchie, *Captain Kidd,* 112; and "Deposition of Samuel Perkins of New England" (August 25, 1698), *CSPC,* item 771, vol. 16, 403–4.

67   **"I have not":** John C. Appleby, *Women and English Piracy, 1540–1720: Partners and Victims of Crime* (Woodbridge, UK: Boydell Press, 2013), 116.

67   **1,300 pieces:** Ritchie, *Captain Kidd,* 119.

67   **"The whole of":** "Deposition of Samuel Perkins of New England" (August 25, 1698).

67   **The bloodiest . . . much as before:** Ritchie, *Captain Kidd,* 116; "Deposition of Baldridge," Jameson, *Privateering,* 186–87; McDonald, *Pirates, Merchants,* 126; and "Governor the Earl of Bellomont to Council of Trade and Plantations" (July 1, 1698), *CSPC,* item 622, vol. 16, 301–14; and "Governor the Earl of Bellomont to Council of Trade and Plantations" (August 24, 1699), *CSPC,* item 740, vol. 17, 402–11.

68   **Edward Randolph:** Background on Randolph comes from Bailyn, *New England Merchants*, 154–59; and Michael Garibaldi Hall, *Edward Randolph and the American Colonies: 1676–1703* (Chapel Hill: University of North Carolina, 1960), 1, 178–82.

69   **"permitting pirates . . . harbored":** Randolph, "A Discourse About Pyrates," 320–21.

69   **"the governor entertains":** "Edward Randolph to the Commissioners of Customs" (November 10, 1696), *CSPC*, item 396i, vol. 15, 212–15.

CHAPTER 4 – CRACKDOWN

70   **The men aboard . . . headed south:** Joel H. Baer, "'Captain John Avery' and the Anatomy of a Mutiny," *Eighteenth Century Life* (February, 1994), 1–15; and "Examination of John Dann" (August 3, 1696), in Jameson, *Privateering*, 165.

71   **"of a gay":** Hill, "Notes on Piracy," 100.

71   **"I am a man":** Baer, "'Captain John Avery' and the Anatomy of a Mutiny," 14.

72   **No doubt feeling . . . Bab-el-Mandeb:** "Examination of John Dann," 165–66; and Defoe, *General History*, 50–52.

72   **"My men . . . Englishman's friend":** "Petition of the East India Company" (July 1696), in Jameson, *Privateers*, 154.

72   **Avery's hope:** Ritchie, *Captain Kidd*, 87.

72   **As soon as . . . certainly suffer:** "Extract, E. I. Co., Letter from Bombay" (May 28, 1695), in Jameson, *Privateering*, 155–65 (quote from this source); John Keay, *The Honourable Company: A History of the English East India Company* (Hammersmith: Harper Collins, 1993), 185–86; and Hill, "Notes on Piracy," 94–95.

73   **In mid-summer . . . sailing for the Carolinas:** "Examination of John Dann" 167–70; "Abstract, E. I. Co. Letters from Bombay" (October 12, 1695), in Jameson, *Privateering*, 156–59; "Affidavit of Philip Middleton" (November 11, 1696), in Jameson, *Privateering*, 171–72; "Narrative of Philip Middleton, of the ship *Charles Henry*, to the Lords Justices of Ireland" (August 4,1696), *CSPC*, item 517 ii, vol. 15, 259–64; Pringle, *Jolly Roger*, 142–43; Ritchie, *Captain Kidd*, 87–89, 130–33; John Biddulph, *The Pirates of Malabar and An Englishwoman in India Two Hundred Years Ago* (London: Smith, Elder, 1907), 26; Hill, "Notes on Piracy," 103; and Cordingly, *Under the Black Flag*, 191.

76   **"All this will":** "Abstract, E. I. Co. Letters from Bombay" (October 12, 1695), in Jameson, *Privateering*, 159.

76   **Despite this wish . . . resumed soon thereafter:** Ibid., 156–59; Keay, *Honourable Company*, 186–88; and Ritchie, *Captain Kidd*, 130–32.

78   **Avery's bloody acts . . . his underlings:** "By the Lords Justices, A Proclamation" (July 17, 1696) (London: Charles Bill, July 1696); and "By the Lords Justices, A Proclamation" (August 10, 1696), *Proceedings of the Council of Maryland, 1693–1696/7*, ed. William Hand Browne (Baltimore: Maryland Historical Society, 1900), 496–98; Ritchie, *Captain Kidd*, 135.

78   **"the first worldwide":** Burgess, *Pirates' Pact*, 144.

78   **In subsequent years:** Baer, "'Captain John Avery,'" 1–2.

79   **more preposterous accounts:** Charles Johnson, *The Life and Adventures of*

Capt. John Avery, and the Successful Pyrate, introduction by Joel H. Baer (Los Angeles: Augustan Reprint Society, 1980).

79 **As for Avery's . . . pirate in prison:** Douglas R. Burgess Jr., *The Politics of Piracy: Crime and Civil Disobedience in Colonial America* (Lebanon, NH: ForeEdge, 2014), 62–63; and Dann, in Jameson, *Privateering*, 171.

79 **"For suffer pirates":** Dr. Newton, "The Trial of Joseph Dawson and Others" (October 19, 1696), *A Complete Collection of State Trials*, vol. XIII, ed. T. B. Howell (London: Longman, Hurst, Rees, etc., 1816), 453.

79 **The government and the East India Company . . . mutiny on the *Charles II*:** Ritchie, *Captain Kidd*, 135–37.

80 **"a nation":** Senior, *A Nation of Pirates*.

80 **"Since foreigners look":** Sir Charles Hedges, "The Trial of Joseph Dawson and Others," 456.

80 **"done very much":** L. C. J. Holt, "The Trial of Joseph Dawson and Others," 481.

81 **"expressed a due":** Hill, "Notes on Piracy," 102.

81 **In Avery's wake:** "Extracts from letters received by the East India Company" (December 21, 1698), *CSPC*, item 115, vol. 16, 61–78.

81 **"So alluring":** "Extracts from letters received by the East India Company" (February 17, 1698), *CSPC*, item 235, vol. 16, 112–14.

81 **Just six months . . . top priority:** Ian K. Steele, *Politics of Colonial Policy: The Board of Trade in Colonial Administration, 1696–1720* (Oxford: Clarendon Press, 1968), 3–23, 42–43; and Ritchie, *Captain Kidd*, 149–50.

81 **the Board of Trade replaced the Lords of Trade and Plantations:** Although the Board of Trade supplanted the Lords of Trade and Plantations, for many years after this change, official documents in England still referred to the Lords of Trade and Plantations, even though the body's official name was the Board of Trade. Subsequent text will refer to the body as the Board of Trade, even when the citations in the endnotes state that a document was either produced by or was sent to or from the Lords of Trade and Plantations.

82 **"do their utmost":** "Board of Trade to Lieutenant-Governor Stoughton" (January 20, 1697), *CSPC*, item 604, vol. 15, 312–14.

82 **Snead, a former carpenter:** Charles P. Keith, *Chronicles of Pennsylvania From the English Revolution to the Peace of Aix-La-Chapelle, 1688–1748*, vol. 1 (Philadelphia: Patterson & White Company, 1917), 312.

82 **"great present":** "Robert Snead to Sir John Houblon" (September 20, 1697), *CSPC*, item 1331, vol. 15, 613–15.

82 **had recently married James Brown:** "Edward Randolph to William Popple" (April 25, 1698), *CSPC*, item 401, vol. 16, 180–81; and Governor the Earl of Bellomont to the Council of Trade and Plantations" (May 30, 1700), *CSPC*, item 466, vol. 18, 266–82.

83 **"over their cups":** "Robert Snead to Sir John Houblon" (September 20, 1697).

83 **"If people came":** Ibid.

83 **"saw plainly that . . . advantage to the country":** "Narrative of Captain Robert Snead" (1697), *CSPC*, item 451i, vol. 16, 211–15.

83 **"informer . . . called an informer":** Ibid.

84 **"a rascal":** Ibid.

85   **"was a very fat gross"**: "Information of Thomas Robinson" (1697), *CSPC*, item
     451ii, vol. 16, 211–15.

85   **"All people see"**: "Robert Snead to Sir John Houblon" (September 20, 1697).

85   **four hundred houses and about 2,500**: Russell F. Weigley, ed., *Philadelphia:
     A 300-Year History* (New York: W. W. Norton, 1982), 11; and McCusker,
     "Colonial Statistics," 5-653. Other sources have Philadelphia's population at
     the time closer to five thousand. I chose to use the numbers in *A 300-Year
     History* because they are based on multiple data points, including tax lists
     and quitrent rolls. Either way, Philadelphia was a relatively small town at the
     time.

86   **"Those [privateers] that were rich"**: John Smith, "The Bad Life, Qualities and
     Conditions of Pyrats," in *The Generall Historie of Virginia, New England & The
     Summer Isles, Together with The True Travels, Adventures and Observations, and
     A Sea Grammar*, vol. II (Glasgow: James MacLehose and Sons, 1907), 202–3.

86   **Although he was appointed . . . reputation for hard work**: William L. Stone,
     "The Earl of Bellomont and the Suppression of Piracy, 1698–1701," *National
     Magazine* (November, 1892), 1–5.

86   **no evidence**: Ritchie, *Captain Kidd*, 179. See also Herbert L. Osgood, *The
     American Colonies in the Eighteenth Century*, vol. I (New York: Columbia Uni-
     versity Press, 1924), 272.

86   **"had not formerly . . . had been done"**: "Minutes of the Council of New York"
     (May 8, 1698), *CSPC*, item 433, vol. 16, 203–4.

87   **"odious practice"**: "Earl of Bellomont At A Council Held at New York" (May
     19, 1698), *Journal of the Legislative Council of the Colony of* New-York, *Began
     the 9th Day of April, 1691; And Ended the 27th of September, 1743* (Albany: Wee,
     Parsons, 1861), 111.

88   **"chief broker"**: "Governor the Earl of Bellomont to Council of Trade and
     Plantations" (June 22, 1698), *CSPC*, item 593, vol. 16 (1697–1698), 279–89.

88   **"the scum"**: Ibid. See also Ritchie, *Captain Kidd*, 170.

88   **Bellomont now took aim . . . lay in tatters**: James S. Leamon, "Governor
     Fletcher's Recall," *William and Mary Quarterly* (Oct., 1963), 538–42; and
     "Heads of Complaint Against Colonel Fletcher, in Brodhead," in *Documents
     Relative to the Colonial History of the State of New York*, vol. IV, 433–34.

88   **"great encouragement"**: "Council of Trade and Plantations to the King"
     (March 9, 1699), *CSPC*, item 167, vol. 17, 95–98.

88   **"a favorer"**: Edward Randolph, "List by Mr. Randolph of all the Proprietors
     of the Plantations That Are Independent of the Government of his Majesty"
     (February 20, 1697), in *The Manuscripts of the House of Lords, 1695–1697* (Lon-
     don: Eyre and Spottiswoode, 1903), 442.

88   **"both foul"**: William Penn, "Mr. Penn's Answer to Mr. Randolph's Paper
     Relating to Pennsylvania," *Manuscripts of the House of Lords, 1695–1697*, 457.

89   **"walk the streets"**: "Col. Quar[r]y to the Council of Trade and Plantations"
     (October 20, 1699), *CSPC*, item 877, vol. 17, 463–82.

89   **"the least aid . . . settling amongst them"**: "Col. Quar[r]y to the Council of
     Trade and Plantations" (June 6, 1699), *CSPC*, item 495, vol. 17, 274–75; and
     Hanna, *Pirate Nests*, 2.

89   **"to use their utmost"**: William Penn, Broadside, "By the proprietary of the

province of Pennsylvania, and counties annexed with the advice of the Council, a proclamation" (Philadelphia: Reinier Jansen, 1699). See also Hanna, *Pirate Nests*, 1–3.

90 **An Act Against:** "An Act Against Pirates and Sea-Robbers," (November 27, 1700), in *The Statutes at Large of Pennsylvania from 1682 to 1801*, vol. II (Philadelphia: Clarence M. Busch, 1896), 100–104.

90 **"Jamaica had not been":** "William Penn to the Council of Trade and Plantations" (April 28, 1700), *CSPC*, item 366, vol. 18, 208–12.

90 **"extremely hard":** "Jeremiah Basse to William Popple" (July 26, 1697), *CSPC*, item 1,203, vol. 15, 563–65.

90 **"You cannot be":** "Jeremiah Basse to William Popple" (July 18, 1697), *CSPC*, item 1187, vol. 15, 557–58.

90 **"suppress these sea-wolves":** "Governor Basse to William Popple" (April 1698), *CSPC*, item 415, vol. 16, 186–87.

91 **"clamor":** "Governor the Earl of Bellomont to William Popple, Postscript" (July 7, 1698), *CSPC*, item 646, vol. 16, 325–26.

91 **"chief-searcher":** "Governor the Earl of Bellomont to Council of Trade and Plantations" (June 22, 1698), *CSPC*, item 593, vol. 16, 279–89.

92 **"they are too well":** "Governor the Earl of Bellomont to Council of Trade and Plantations" (May 3, 1699), *CSPC*, item 343, vol. 17, 191.

92 **"a nest of pirates":** "Governor the Earl of Bellomont to Council of Trade and Plantations" (May 18, 1698), *CSPC*, item 472, vol. 16, 221–24.

92 **"unlawful trade":** "Governor the Earl of Bellomont to William Popple" (October 27, 1698), *CSPC*, item 944, vol. 16, 512–13.

92 **Another step . . . quite a difference:** "Council of Trade and Plantations to the King" (November 9, 1699), *CSPC*, item 943, vol. 17, 514; Ritchie, *Captain Kidd*, 155–59; and Steele, *Politics of Colonial Policy*, 53–54.

92 **governors begged:** See, for example, "Governor the Earl of Bellomont to the Council of Trade and Plantations" (August 24, 1699).

92 *Providence Galley*: The background for the *Providence Galley* and captain James comes from Donald G. Shomette, *Pirates on the Chesapeake: Being a True History of Pirates, Picaroons, and Raiders on Chesapeake Bay, 1610–1807* (Centreville: Tidewater Publishers, 1985), 103–113; Lloyd Haynes Williams, *Pirates of Colonial Virginia* (Richmond, VA: Dietz Press, 1937), 53–62; and Hugh F. Rankin, *The Golden Age of Piracy* (New York: Holt, Rhinehart & Winston, 1969), 64–76.

92 **Its captain was Englishman:** "Account by Richard Burgess, Master of the Maryland Merchant of Bristol" (August 13, 1699), *CSPC*, item 711, vol. 17, 390.

92 **hung gold chains:** "Deposition of Nicholas Thomas Jones, Robert McEllam, Samuel Johns, and William Parker Himarke" (August 4, 1699), CO 5/1411, NAL.

92 **Earlier in the year . . . bottle of gunpowder:** "Governor Day to Council of Trade and Plantations" (September 21, 1699), *CSPC*, item 802, vol. 17, 444–45.

93 **spied an unknown vessel:** "John Aldred to Francis Nicholson" (July 26, 1699), CO 5/1411, NAL.

94 **"I always abhorred":** "Order of the Lords Justices of England in Council" (October 5, 1697), *CSPC*, item 1363, vol. 15, 269.

94   **taken the *Roanoke Merchant*:** "John Martin to Francis Nicholson" (July 29, 1699), CO 5/1411, NAL.

94   **dozens of ships:** "Micajah Perry, Edward Haistwell and John Goodwin to the Council of Trade and Plantations" (November 23, 1699), *CSPC*, item 989, vol. 17, 539–40.

94   **The HMS *Shoreham*:** The background for this section on the HMS *Shoreham*, its fight with *La Paix*, and the aftermath, comes from Shomette, *Pirates on the Chesapeake*, 122–51; "Libel by Captain William Passenger" (May 11, 1700), in Jameson, *Privateering*, 271–72; "Deposition of Joseph Man" (June 11, 1700), in Jameson, *Privateering*, 273–74; "Deposition of William Woolgar and Others" (June 11, 1700), in Jameson, *Privateering*, 272–73; Rankin, *Golden Age of Piracy*, 64–76; "Governor Nicholson to the Council of Trade and Plantations" (June 10, 1700), *CSPC*, item 523, vol. 18, 307–28; *The Proceedings of the Court of Admiralty, by a Special Commission, Being The Tryal of all the French Pirates at the Old-Bailey, on Monday, Tuesday, Thursday, and Friday, Being the 21st, 22nd, 24th, 25th Days of October, 1700* (London: Printed for W.H. Near Fleet Bridge, 1700); and Williams, *Pirates of Colonial Virginia*, 53–62.

95   **"take, sink":** Shomette, *on the Chesapeake*, 131.

95   **"You sail in":** Ibid., 125.

96   **"great ship":** Ibid., 133.

96   **"this is but":** "Capt. Passenger's account of the taking of a French pirate" (June 10, 1700), *CSPC*, item 523ii, vol. 18, 307–28.

96   **"almost beaten":** Ibid.

96   **"tell the commander":** Shomette, *Pirates on the Chesapeake*, 135.

97   **"broil, broil":** Rankin, *Golden Age of Piracy*, 73.

97   **At the same time that the Crown . . . was also compensated:** "An Act for the More Effectual Suppression of Piracy" (1700), *The Statutes Relating to the Admiralty, Navy, Shipping, and Navigation of the United Kingdom*, ed. John Raithby (London: George Eyre and Andrew Strahan, 1823), 86–89; David R. Owen and Michael C. Tolley, *Courts of Admiralty in Colonial America, the Maryland Experience, 1634–1776* (Durham, NC: Carolina Academic Press, 1995), 32–34, 165–66; and Hanna, *Pirate Nests*, 289–90.

97   **A statute reaching back . . . piracy, and hanged:** "Council of Trade and Plantations to the King" (January 11, 1700), *CSPC*, item 29, vol. 18, 26; "Draft of a Letter for His Majesty's Signature" (February 1, 1700), *CSPC*, item 73, vol. 18, 52; and Steele, *Politics of Colonial Policy*, 56–7.

98   **"having in view":** "Council of Trade and Plantation" (April 11, 1700), *CSPC*, item 312, vol. 18, 163–66.

98   **At the same time . . . the colony's charter:** "An Act to Punish Governors of Plantations in this Kingdom, for Crimes By Them Committed in the Plantations," in *Statutes Relating to the Admiralty*, 90; Hanna, *Pirate Nests*, 290; Burgess, *Politics of Piracy*, 193; and Attorney General to the King (June 19, 1700), *CSPC*, item 566, vol. 18, 350–51.

99   **The king's order . . . a Crown priority:** "Council of Trade and Plantations to the King" (January 11, 1700), *CSPC*, item 29, vol. 18, 26; "Draft of a Letter for His Majesty's Signature" (February 1, 1700), *CSPC*, item 73, vol. 18, 52; and Steele, *Politics of Colonial Policy*, 56–57.

99   **Captain William Kidd:** The background for this section on Kidd comes from

"The Trial of Captain William Kidd, at the Old Bailey, for Murder and Piracy Upon the High Seas . . . (May 8, 1701) in *A Complete Collection of State Trials and Proceedings for High Treason and Other Crimes and Misdemeanors*, vol. XIV, ed. T. B. Howell (London: T. C. Hansard, 1812), 123–46; "The Trials of Wm. Kidd, Nicholas Churchill, James Howe . . . (May 9, 1701)", in Howell, *Complete Collection of State Trials and Proceedings*, 147–234; Ritchie, *Captain Kidd*; Richard Zacks, *The Pirate Hunter: The True Story of Captain Kidd* (New York: Hyperion, 2002); Cordingly, *Under the Black Flag*, 180–89; "Deposition of Benjamin Franks" (October 20, 1697), in Jameson, *Privateering*, 190–95; "Narrative of William Kidd" (July 7, 1699), in Jameson, *Privateering*, 205–13; "Examination of Edward Buckmaster" (June 6, 1699), in Jameson, *Privateering*, 197–98; personal communication with historian Richard Zacks, July 11, 2017; Graham Brooks, ed., *Trial of Captain Kidd* (Edinburgh: William Hodge, 1930), 1–50; and ADM, "Captain William Kidd's Deposition, Instance and Prize Courts: Examinations and Answers" (October 15, 1695), 13/81, 313, NAL.

101 **Broadsides announcing . . . former pirates themselves:** Zacks, *Pirate Hunter*, 11–20; "Col. Robert Livingston to Shrewsbury," (September 20, 1696), in Historical Manuscripts Commission, *Report on the Manuscripts of the Duke of Buccleuch & Queensbury*, vol. II, part 2 (London: Mackie, 1903), 405–6; and Pringle, *Jolly Roger*, 158–60.

101 **"One Captain Kidd":** "Governor Fletcher to Council of Trade and Plantations" (June 22, 1697), *CSPC*, item 1098, vol. 15, 517–20; and Hill, "Notes on Piracy," 112–22.

102 **"Come, boys":** "The Trials of Wm. Kidd, Nicholas Churchill, James Howe . . . ," 164.

104 **into the realm of piracy:** Ritchie, *Captain Kidd*, 99–100; and "The Trial of Captain William Kidd, at the Old Bailey, for Murder and Piracy Upon the High Seas . . . (May 9, 1701)," 156–57, 195, 203, 213. For a possible instance of Kidd taking an English ship just before the *Mary*, see "Extract from a Letter From Carwar to Bombay" (August 9, 1697), *CSPC*, item 723, vol. 16, 363–67.

104 **"he was going upon":** "Narrative of William Cuthbert" (July 1699), *CSPC*, item 680, vol. 17, 366–80.

104 **"denied that he had":** "The Trial of Captain William Kidd, at the Old Bailey, for Murder and Piracy Upon the High Seas . . . (May 9, 1701)," 157.

104 **About a week later . . . of a valuable prize:** Ibid., 100–102; and Zacks, *Pirate Hunter*, 134–37.

104 **"being a very lusty man":** Ritchie, *Captain Kidd*, 102.

105 **"a lousy dog . . . You are a villain!":** "The Trial of Captain William Kidd, at the Old Bailey," 134–35.

105 **"I have good friends":** Ibid., 138.

105 **"By God":** "The Trials of Wm. Kidd, Nicholas Churchill, James Howe . . . ," 158.

106 **"was as bad":** Ibid., 160.

106 **"would have my soul":** Ibid., 167.

107 **declaring Kidd and his men:** Benjamin F. Thompson, *The History of Long Island; From Its Discovery and Settlement to the Present Time*, vol. II (New York: Gould, Banks, 1843), 332.

107 **The *Quedah Merchant*, far:** Ritchie, *Captain Kidd*, 127.

108 **By June, the *Saint Antonio* . . . hovered off the coast:** "Memorial of Duncan Campbell" (June 19, 1699), in Jameson, *Privateering*, 202–5; "Narrative of John Gardner" (July 17, 1699), in Jameson, *Privateering*, 220–23; "A Copy of the Earl of Bellomont's Letter to Captain Kidd" (June 19, 1699), *Journals of the House of Commons* (London: House of Commons, 1803), vol. 13, 22; "Declaration of William Kidd" (September 4, 1699), in Jameson, *Privateering*, 236–37; and Ritchie, *Captain Kidd*, 176–77.

108 **as much as £400,000:** Narcissus Luttrell, *A Brief Relation of State Affairs from September 1678 to April 1714*, vol. IV (Oxford: Oxford University Press, 1857), 543–49; Ritchie, *Captain Kidd*, 168; and Hanna, *Pirate Nests*, 297.

109 **In Boston, Kidd met . . . thrown in jail:** "Lord Bellomont to the Board of Trade" (July 8, 1699), in Jameson, *Privateering*, 213–18; Ritchie, *Captain Kidd*, 177–80; "Narrative of William Kidd" (July 7, 1699), in Jameson, *Privateering*, 205–13; "Governor the Earl of Bellomont to the Council of Trade and Plantations" (July 26, 1699), *CSPC*, item 680, vol. 17, 366–79.

109 **"they would rather":** "Narrative of William Kidd" (July 7, 1699), 210.

110 **"ten ounces of gold":** Ibid.

110 **"quickly found":** "Lord Bellomont to the Board of Trade" (July 26, 1699), in Jameson, *Privateering*, 225. See also, "Lord Bellomont to the Board of Trade" (July 8, 1699), in Jameson, *Privateering*, 215.

111 **Even before Kidd . . . controversy to rest:** Ritchie, *Captain Kidd*, 183–92.

111 **"Parliaments are grown":** "Vernon to the Duke of Shrewsbury (September 25, 1697)," *James Vernon, Letters Illustrative of the Reign of William III, From 1696 to 1708*, vol. I (London: Henry Colburn, 1841), 405.

111 **"a very little":** Ritchie, *Captain Kidd*, 192.

112 **"a habitation":** C. Whitehead, *Lives and Exploits of English Highwaymen, Pirates, and Robbers*, vol. I (Philadelphia: Carey, Hart, 1835), 182; and Cordingly, *Under the Black Flag*, 188.

112 **"It was not":** "The Trial of Captain William Kidd, at the Old Bailey," 143.

112 **During the trial . . . voted him down:** "The Trials of Wm. Kidd, Nicholas Churchill, James Howe . . . ," 169–70, 174, and 210.

112 **Kidd's ability to prove . . . and damning:** Ritchie, *Captain Kidd*, 208–9; and "William Kidd to Speaker of the House of Commons" (April 1701), in Jameson, *Privateering*, 250–51.

113 **"My lord":** "The Trials of Wm. Kidd, Nicholas Churchill, James Howe . . . ," 234.

114 **"have the benefit . . . according to":** "William Kidd to Robert Harley, Petition Enclosed" (May 12, 1701), *The Manuscripts of His Grace The Duke of Portland*, vol. IV (London: Eyre and Spottiswoode, 1897), 17.

114 **Kidd's gambit . . . passed by:** *The Ordinary of Newgate his Account*; Zacks, *The Pirate Hunter*, 381–93; Ritchie, *Captain Kidd*, 222–27; *A True Account of the Behavior, Confession and Last Dying Speeches, Of Captain William Kidd*; and Margarette Lincoln, *British Pirates and Society, 1680–1730* (London: Routledge, 2014), 35, 37.

114 **"been instrumental in his":** *A True Account of the Behavior, Confession and Last Dying Speeches, Of Captain William Kidd, and the Rest of the Pirates, That Were Executed at Execution Dock in Wapping, on Friday the 23rd of May, 1701* (London: Bride Lane, 1701).

114   **"expressed [an] abundance"**: Ibid.

114   **"declaring openly that he repented"**: *The Ordinary of Newgate his Account.*

117   **The company used Kidd's**: Ritchie, *Captain Kidd*, 137.

118   **If that trade . . . outside world**: Platt, "The East India Company and the Madagascar Slave Trade," 553–54; Lincoln, *British Pirates*, 127; Bialuschewski, "Pirates, Slavers, and the Indigenous Population," 419; and "The East India Company to Council of Trade and Plantations" (March 7, 1698), *CSPC*, item 279, vol. 16, 126–27.

118   **cluster of business**: Ritchie, *Captain Kidd*, 233; and D. T. Valentine, *Manual of the Corporation of the City of New York* (New York: Charles W. Baker, 1857), 466–68.

118   **"from Madagascar"**: "Governor the Earl of Bellomont to the Council of Trade and Plantations" (November 28, 1700), *CSPC*, item 953, vol. 18, 667–703.

118   **Another East India Company . . . those who did not**: Nutting, "The Madagascar Connection," 208–9; Steele, *Politics of Colonial Policy*, 52–53; and Osgood, *American Colonies*, vol. I, 543.

118   **"We have great reason"**: Steele, *Politics of Colonial Policy*, 53.

118   **slowly diminished**: Hill, "Notes on Piracy," 141, 154; and Woodes Rogers, *A Cruising Voyage Around the World* (London: A. Bell, 1712), 419.

118   **virtually nonexistent**: Arne Bialuschewski, "Between Newfoundland and the Malacca Strait: A Survey of the Golden Age of Piracy, 1695–1725," *Mariner's Mirror* (May 2004), 172–73; McDonald, *Pirates, Merchants, Settlers*, 125–27; and Judd, "Frederick Philipse," 374. There is at least one other known case of an American colonist turning pirate and heading to the Indian Ocean after 1700. John Halsey left Boston around 1706 with a privateering license to capture French ships off Newfoundland, this being during the War of the Spanish Succession, when England was arrayed against France and Spain (there is more on this war in the next chapter of this book). Instead of hunting the French, he led his men to the Indian Ocean to plunder Mughal and other shipping. See Hill, "Notes on Piracy," 138–40.

119   **Finally, Kidd's . . . by the locals**: Ritchie, *Captain Kidd*, 153; and Shawn Antcil, *Order and the Atlantic World: A Study in the British War against the Pirates, 1695–1725* (PhD diss., University of Ottawa, 2008), 61.

119   **The Crown's . . . remedial action**: Ritchie, *Captain Kidd*, 128; and Taylor, *American Colonies*, 296.

119   **a decline**: "Preface," *CSPC*, vol. 18, vii–lxiii; and Steele, *Politics of Colonial Policy*, 42–59.

119   **"all the news"**: "Col. Quarry to the Council on Trade and Plantations" (June 5, 1700), *CSPC*, item 500, vol. 18, 300–301.

119   **"The sea [is] now"**: "Governor Blake to the Earl of Jersey" (June 10, 1700), *CSPC*, item 500, vol. 18, 300–301.

120   **"is in its wane"**: "Governor the Earl of Bellomont to the Council of Trade and Plantations" (November 28, 1700), *CSPC*, item 953, vol. 18, 667–703.

120   **"I don't hear"**: "George Larkin to the Council of Trade and Plantations" (October 14, 1701), *CSPC*, item 945, vol. 19, 576–77. See also, "Mr. Larkin to the Council of Trade and Plantations" (December 30, 1701), *CSPC*, item 1131, vol. 19, 719–20.

120 **"because they were poor . . . in the least":** "Governor the Earl of Bellomont to Mr. Secretary Vernon" (January 3, 1700), *CSPC*, item 8, vol. 19, 1–17.

120 **"These fellows":** "George Larkin to the Council of Trade and Plantations" (December 5, 1701), *CSPC*, item 1054, vol. 19, 658–59.

CHAPTER 5 — WAR'S REPRIEVE

122 **not a salient:** See, for example, Arthur Pierce Middleton, *Tobacco Coast: A Maritime History of Chesapeake Bay in the Colonial Era* (Baltimore: Johns Hopkins Press, 1984), 207; and James G. Lydon, *Pirates, Privateers, and Profits* (Upper Saddle River, NJ: Gregg Press, 1970), 77. Also based on a review by the author of the *CPSC* for the years of the war.

122 **ballooned from:** Christopher Lloyd, *The British Seaman: 1200–1860, A Social Survey* (Rutherford, NJ: Fairleigh Dickinson University Press, 1968), 286–87.

122 **roughly double:** Davis, *Rise of English Shipping*, 129–31.

122 **1,600 privateering:** W. R. Meyer, "English Privateering in the War of the Spanish Succession, 1702–1713," *Mariner's Mirror* (November 1983), 435.

122 **a few scattered:** See, for example, "Governor Dudley to [? the Earl of Nottingham]" (May 10, 1703), *CSPC*, item 673, vol. 21, 408–10; and Hill, "Notes on Piracy," 138–40.

122 **John Quelch:** Background material for this section on Quelch and the *Charles* comes from *The Arraignment, Tryal, and Condemnation of Capt. John Quelch, and Others of his Company* [1705], in *British Piracy in the Golden Age: History and Interpretation, 1660–1730*, vol. 2, ed. Joel H. Baer (London: Pickering & Chatto, 2007), 257–61, 263–88; Clifford Beal, *Quelch's Gold: Piracy, Greed, and Betrayal in Colonial New England* (Washington, DC: Potomac Books, 2008); and *Chapter 47 in The Acts and Resolves, Public and Private, of the Province of the Massachusetts Bay*, vol. VIII, 1703–1707 (Boston: Wright & Potter, 1895), 386–98.

122 **"worse . . . what we can":** Baer, *Arraignment, Tryal*, 286.

123 **"fight, take":** Ibid., 284.

123 **"perfectly fitted":** Ibid., 287.

123 **One of the leading . . . markets throughout Europe:** Samuel Roads Jr., *The History and Traditions of Marblehead* (Marblehead, MA: N. Allen Lindsey, 1897), 26, 46–47; Lord and Gamage, *Marblehead: The Spirit of '76 Lives Here*, 18–35; and Christine Leigh Heyrman, *Commerce and Culture: The Maritime Communities of Colonial Massachusetts, 1690–1750* (New York: W. W. Norton, 1986), 245.

124 **"very weak . . . totally lost":** Heyrman, *Commerce and Culture*, 286.

125 **"which," they said, "makes us":** Ibid., 286–87.

127 **"met with some":** Ibid., 10.

127 **"Arrived in Marblehead":** *BNL* (May 15–22, 1704).

128 **"By what we have":** Baer, *Arraignment, Tryal*, 287.

128 **Povey issued:** *BNL* (May 22–29, 1704).

129 **"from constable":** "Rhode-Island May 26," *BNL* (May 22–29, 1704).

129 **On May 29:** *Chapter 47 in The Acts and Resolves*, 389.

129 **three-man commission:** "Marblehead, June 9," *BNL* (June 12–19, 1704).

129 **more than thirty:** Eve LaPlante, *Salem Witch Judge: The Life and Repentance of Samuel Sewall* (New York: HarperOne, 2007), 1.

129 **One other person . . . his last breath:** Ibid., 170–71; Emerson W. Baker, *A Storm of Witchcraft: The Salem Trials and the American Experience* (New York: Oxford University Press, 2015), 37–38; and personal communication with Emerson W. Baker, November 26, 2017.

130 **"blame and shame":** Baker, *A Storm of Witchcraft*, 223.

130 **"first pamphlet":** Mark A. Peterson, "The Selling of Joseph: Bostonians, Antislavery, and the Protestant International, 1689–1733," *Massachusetts Historical Review* (2002), 1. See also LaPlante, *Salem Witch Judge*, 225–29, 300–304.

130 **On their way . . . for the men:** Samuel Sewall, "Diary of Samuel Sewall, 1674–1729," vol. II, 1699–1700–1714, *Collections of the Massachusetts Historical Society*, vol. IV, Fifth Series (Boston: Massachusetts Historical Society, 1879), 103; and "Marblehead, June 9," *BNL*.

131 **"pirates, double-armed":** Sewall, "Diary of Samuel Sewall," vol. II, 104.

131 **"guilty of piracy . . . be gone":** Hanna, *Pirate Nests*, 342.

131 **"five blows":** Ibid.

132 **Discouraged . . . signed on:** "Gloucester, Upon Cape Anne, June 9," *BNL* (June 12–19, 1704).

132 **"three very handsome":** Sewall, "Diary of Samuel Sewall," vol. II, 105.

132 **"the wickedness":** Ibid.

133 **"without [Sewall's men] striking":** Ibid., 106.

133 **"being strangers":** "Gloucester, June 12," *BNL* (June 12–19, 1704).

133 **"attended with":** "Boston, June 17," *BNL* (June 12–19, 1704).

134 **Governor Dudley convened . . . guilty of piracy:** Baer, *Arraignment, Tryal*, 263–88; *Chapter 47 in The Acts and Resolves*, 386–98; and Stephen C. O'Neill, "The Forwardness of Her Majesty's Service: Paul Dudley's Prosecution of Pirate Captain John Quelch," *Massachusetts Legal History*, vol. 6 (000), 29–34.

134 **"piracy, robbery":** Baer, *Arraignment, Tryal*, 266.

134 **"received into":** Ibid., 268.

136 **seemed to agree:** "Governor Dudley to the Council of Trade and Plantations (July 13, 1704)," *CSPC*, item 455, vol. 22, 213–18.

136 **Mather was a highly learned:** Kenneth Silverman, *The Life and Times of Cotton Mather* (New York: Harper & Row, 1984), 29, 129, 194.

137 **"the minister's":** George Bull, *A Companion for the Candidates of Holy Orders* (London: George James, 1714), 8.

137 **"Will our merciful":** Cotton Mather, *Faithful Warnings to Prevent Fearful Judgments* (Boston: Timothy Green, 1704), 37.

137 **"privateering stroke":** Ibid.

137 **"Sermons preached":** Daniel A. Cohen, *Pillars of Salt, Monuments of Grace: New England Crime Literature and the Origins of American Popular Literature, 1674–1860* (Amherst: University of Massachusetts Press, 2006), 3.

137 **388 works during:** Silverman, *Life and Times of Cotton Mather*, 197.

137 **"young and ignorant":** "Governor Dudley to the Council of Trade and Plantations (July 13, 1704)."

137 **Dudley failed . . . currency crisis:** Beal, *Quelch's Gold*, 139, 174, 177, 179, 181, 185.

138 **"rude people":** "Governor Dudley to the Council of Trade and Plantations (July 25, 1704)," *CSPC*, item 1274, vol. 22, 585–93.

139 **"amazed":** Sewall, "Diary of Samuel Sewall," vol. II, 109.

139 **Executions had . . . one another:** Daniel Allen Hearn, *Legal Executions in*

New England: A Comprehensive Reference, 1623–1960 (Jefferson, NC: Mcfarland, 1999); and Ronald A. Bosco, "Lectures at the Pillory: The Early American Execution Sermon," *American Quarterly* (Summer, 1978), 159.

139 **"first continuously"**: "The *Boston Newsletter*, number 1," Massachusetts Historical Society, Collections Online, accessed on January 13, 2017, http://www.masshist.org/database/viewer.php?item_id=186.

140 **"I am not"**: *An Account of the Behavior and Last Dying Speeches of the Six Pirates, That Were Executed on Charles River, Boston Side, On Fryday June 30th, 1704* (Boston: Boone, 1704).

140 **"We [the ministers] have told you . . . So ruin them"**: *An Account of the Behavior and Last Dying Speeches of the Six Pirates.*

140 **Dudley was undoubtedly:** Beal, *Quelch's Gold,* 179.

140 **"Lord, what . . . hanged for it"**: *An Account of the Behavior and Last Dying Speeches of the Six Pirates.*

141 **"When the scaffold"**: Sewall, "Diary of Samuel Sewall," vol. II, 110.

141 **Nobody recorded . . . before expiring:** D. P. Lyle, "What Happens When Someone is Hanged?" Writer's Forensics Blog, accessed on January 15, 2017, https://writersforensicsblog.wordpress.com/2011/03/31/question-and-answer-what-happens-when-someone-is-hanged/.

142 **"the marshal's dance"**: Lincoln, *British Pirates,* 37.

142 **"dancing to"**: Marcus Rediker, *Villains of all Nations: Atlantic Pirates in the Golden Age* (Boston: Beacon Press, 2004), 53.

142 **"dancing the Tyburn Jig"**: Catharine Arnold, *Underworld London: Crime and Punishment in the Capital City* (London: Simon & Schuster, 2012), 106.

142 **"pull the dying"**: Henri Misson, *M. Missons's Memoirs and Observations in his Travels over England* (London: D. Browne, 1719), 123.

142 **"Ye pirates"**: Ralph D. Paine, *The Ships and Sailors of Old Salem* (Chicago: A. C. McClurg., 1912), 42.

142 **"We crave"**: "Humble Address of the Council and Assembly of the Massachusetts Bay to the Queen (July 12, 1704)," *CSPC,* item 451, vol. 22, 212–13.

142 **As for the treasure . . . war debts:** Beal, *Quelch's Gold,* 184, 194, 197–98, 207–08; Dow and Edmonds, *Pirates,* 114–15; and Philip Steele, *Isaac Newton: The Scientist Who Changed Everything* (Washington, DC: National Geographic, 2007), 53.

CHAPTER 6 — INTERLUDE, OR A PIRATE CLASSIFICATION

145 **"It is the opinion"**: "Wm. Bignall to [? Mr. Dummer] Kingston (January 17, 1708)," *CSPC,* item 445i, vol. 24, 270–71.

145 **This fear was . . . to the future:** Francis R. Stark, *The Abolition of Privateering and The Declaration of Paris* (New York: Columbia University Press, 1897), 68–69; Meyer, "English Privateering," 444; and N. A. M. Rodger, *The Command of the Ocean: A Naval History of Britain* (New York: W. W. Norton, 2004), 196–97.

145 **"great complaints . . . infest it"**: "Mr. Dummer to Mr. Popple" (January 17, 1709), *CSPC,* item 301, vol. 24, 201–2.

146 **more that thirty-six thousand:** Lloyd, *British Seaman,* 287.

146 **Such worries . . . would-be pirates:** Davis, *Rise of English Shipping,* 25–26, 129–31; "A Letter from Jamaica to a Merchant in London" (September 22, 1725), in

The Political State of Great Britain for the Month of March, 1726 (London: T. Warner, 1725), 233; Colin Woodard, *The Republic of Pirates: Being the True and Surprising Story of the Caribbean Pirates and the Man Who Brought Them Down* (New York: Harcourt, 2007), 86–7; and Cordingly, *Spanish Gold*, 123.

146 **"No man will be"**: James Boswell, *The Life of Samuel Johnson*, vol. I (London: T. Davison, 1821), 286–87.

147 **"at least thirty-one"**: Rediker, *Villains of All Nations*, 46–47.

147 **"the too great"**: "Letter from an Officer of an East-India Ship," in *Piracy Destroy'd: Or, a Short Discourse Shewing The Rise, Growth and Causes of Piracy of Late* (London: John Nutt, 1701), 12.

147 **"not be too like"**: Mather, *Vial Poured Out*, 44.

147 **"Their reasons for going"**: William Snelgrave, *A New Account of Some Parts of Guinea, and the Slave-Trade* (London: James, John, and Paul Knapton, 1734), 225.

147 **A devastating disaster . . . loot by becoming pirates:** E. Lynne Wright, *Florida Disasters: True Stories of Tragedy and Survival* (Guilford, CT: Globe Pequot, 2017), 7–11; Cordingly, *Spanish Gold*, 123–25; and Woodard, *Republic of Pirates*, 103–6.

148 **"It was so violent"**: Cordingly, *Under the Black Flag*, 125.

148 **"attempt[ing] the recovery:** "Lt. Governor Spotswood to Secretary Stanhope" (October 24, 1715), *CSPC*, item 651, vol. 28, 315–17.

148 **"mad to go . . . not quitted them"**: "Captain Belchen to Josiah Burchett" (May 13, 1716), CO 137/11, fol. 97, NAL.

149 **Another, less obvious, factor . . . the first time:** McDonald, *Pirates, Merchants*, 22–23; Cordingly, *Spanish Gold*, 130; Lincoln, *British Pirates*, 10–11; and Defoe, *General History*, 36.

149 **90 percent:** *The Tryals of Major Stede Bonnet, and Other Pirates* (London: Benjamin Cowse, 1719), 8.

150 **"swore that . . . their articles"**: "Advertisement, James Salter," *Boston Gazette* (November 29–December 6, 1725).

150 **place an ad:** Joel H. Baer, ed., *British Piracy in the Golden Age: History and Interpretation, 1660–1730*, vol. 1 (London: Pickering & Chatto, 2007), 282; "Advertisements, New-York, July 4, 1723," *American Weekly Mercury* (July 4–11, 1723); and "Advertisement," *BNL* (August 1–8, 1723).

150 **"whipped him"**: "Advertisements," *BNL* (August 7–14, 1721).

151 **"In an honest"**: Defoe, *General History*, 244.

151 **eighty men:** Manuel Schonhorn, "Postscript;" Defoe, *General History*, 705.

151 **"go on the account"**: Defoe, *General History*, 487.

151 **"the love of drink"**: Peter Earle, *The Pirate Wars* (New York: Thomas Dunne Books, 2003), 179.

152 **"It appears that"**: Rediker, *Villains of all Nations*, 29–30. One should note, however, that these numbers of pirates in the Atlantic are rough estimates, based on many disparate sources, and the actual numbers might be different. Indeed, earlier estimates by Rediker concluded that the overall number of pirates during this period was 4,500 to 5,500, with there being roughly "1,800 to 2,400" pirates between 1716 and 1718," "1,500 to 2000 between 1719 and 1722, and 1000 to 1,500, declining to fewer than 200 between 1723 and 1726." Nev-

ertheless, the trajectory is the same—a rapid rise in piracy, followed by a dramatic decline. See Marcus Rediker, *Between the Devil and the Deep Blue Sea: Merchant Seamen, Pirates, and the Anglo-American Maritime World, 1700–1750* (Cambridge: Cambridge University Press, 1987), 256.

152 **"suffered more by":** Defoe, *General History*, 26. See also Rediker, *Villains of All Nations*, 33.

152 **"and may well have been far greater":** Davis, *Rise of the English Shipping Industry*, 305.

152 **2,400 merchantmen:** Rediker, *Villains of All Nations*, 33–34.

152 **Of course . . . at least, plausible:** Ibid.

152 **high as seven thousand:** David J. Starkey, *British Privateering Enterprise in the Eighteenth Century* (Exeter, UK: University of Exeter Press, 1990), 100.

153 **lower classes:** Rediker, *Villains of all Nations*, 51; and Schonhorn, "Postscript," 703.

153 **Most pirates . . . European and African nations:** Rediker, *Villains of all Nations*, 42–43, 49–52; and Rediker, *Between the Devil and the Deep Blue Sea*, 258.

154 **Of the latter, none . . . indispensable source:** Defoe, *General History*; Cordingly, *Under the Black Flag*, xix–xx; Lincoln, *British Pirates*, 9n17; P. N. Furbank and W. R. Owens, *The Canonization of Daniel Defoe* (New Haven, CT: Yale University Press, 1988), 100–121; John Robert Moore, *Defoe in the Pillory and Other Studies* (Bloomington: Indiana University Publications, 1939), 126–88; Bialuschewski, "Daniel Defoe, Nathaniel Mist, and the 'General History of the Pyrates'"; and Larry Schweikart and B. R. Burg, "Stand By To Repel Historians: Modern Scholarship and Caribbean Pirates, 1650–1725," *Historian* (February 1984), 228.

154 **just a pen name:** Some authors have argued that "Captain Johnson" is a pen name, not for Defoe, but for Nathaniel Mist, a sailor who became a journalist and printer in London, and published the *Weekly Journal: or, Saturday's Post*. Arne Bialuschewski, "Daniel Defoe, Nathaniel Mist, and the 'General History of the Pyrates,'" *The Papers of the Bibliographical Society of America* (March 2004), 21–38.

154 **"It could be argued":** Cordingly, *Spanish Gold*, 248. For a similar take on the influence of the book, see Moore, *Defoe in the Pillory*, 127.

155 **"banditti":** "Governor Sir N. Lawes to the Council of Trade and Plantations" (January 31, 1719), *CSPC*, item 34, vol. 31, 12–21.

155 **in their twenties:** Rediker, *Villains of all Nations*, 49; and Cordingly, *Under the Black Flag*, 14–15.

155 **Anne Bonny and Mary Read:** Background for these two female pirates, and Rackham, comes from *The Tryals of Captain John Rackham, and Other Pirates* (Jamaica: Robert Baldwin, 1721), 16–18; Defoe, *General History*, 148–65; and "Jamaica, St. Jago de la Vega, Nov. 21," *BNL* (February 20–27, 1721).

155 **"wore men's jackets":** *Tryals of Captain John Rackham*, 18.

156 **"pleaded their bellies":** Defoe, *General History*, 152.

156 **"She was sorry":** Ibid., 165.

157 **For instance, the existence . . . than historical reality:** Cordingly, *Under the Black Flag*, 100–103; Rediker, *Villains of All Nations*, 74–75; James Neill, *The Origins and Role of Same-Sex Relations in Human Societies* (Jefferson, NC; McFarland, 2009), 408.

157 **some to claim:** B. R. Burg, *Sodomy and the Pirate Tradition: English Sea Rovers*

in the Seventeenth-Century Caribbean (New York: New York University Press, 1995).

157   **"The evidence"**: Hans Turley, *Rum, Sodomy, and the Lash* (New York: New York University Press, 1999), 2.

158   **"It seems likely"**: Cordingly, *Under the Black Flag*, 103.

158   **A significant number of black . . . is not clear**: Cordingly, *Under the Black Flag*, 15–16; Rediker, *Villains of all Nations*, 53–55; Marcus Rediker, "Libertalia: The Pirate's Utopia," in *Pirates: Terror on the High Seas—From the Caribbean to the South China Sea* (Atlanta: Turner Publishing, 1996), 132–34; Arne Bialuschewski, "Pirates, Black Sailors and Seafaring Slaves in the Anglo-American Maritime World, 1716–1726," *Journal of Caribbean History* (2001), 143–44; Kinkor, "Black Men," 195–210; Peter T. Leeson, *The Invisible Hook: The Hidden Economics of Pirates* (Princeton, NJ: Princeton University Press, 2009), 157–164; Schonhorn, "Postscript," 705–7; Lincoln, *British Pirates and Society*, 7, 9; Angus Konstam, *Blackbeard: America's Most Notorious Pirate* (Hoboken, NJ: John Wiley & Sons, 2006), 49; Benerson Little, *Pirate Hunting: The Fight Against Pirates, Privateers, and Sea Raiders from Antiquity to Present* (Washington, DC: Potomac Books, 2010), 159–60; Earle, *Pirate Wars*, 171–72; Antcil, *Order in the Atlantic World*, 33; Bolster, *Black Jacks*, 13–15; and Williams, "Nascent Socialists or Resourceful Criminals," 42–43.

159   **"To many white"**: W. Jeffrey Bolster, *Black Jacks: African American Seamen in the Age of Sail* (Cambridge, MA: Harvard University Press, 1998), 15–16.

159   **"suggest[s] that perhaps"**: Kenneth J. Kinkor, "Black Men under the Black Flag," in *Bandits at Sea: A Pirates Reader*, ed. C. R. Pennell (New York: New York University Press, 2001), 200–201.

159   **"it would seem"**: Kinkor, "Black Men," 201.

159   **Not surprisingly, we don't . . . with their contemporaries**: "Deposition of Adam Baldridge" (May 5, 1699), 182; Cindy Vallar, "Pirates and their Clothes," accessed on June 9, http://www.cindyvallar.com/dress.html; Cordingly, *Under the Black Flag*, 8–13; and Benerson Little, *The Golden Age of Piracy: The Truth behind Pirate Myths* (New York: Skyhorse Publishing, 2016), xiii–xxiv.

159   **"This would mean"**: Personal communication with James L. Nelson, June 9, 2017.

161   **the common council**: Rediker, *Between the Devil and the Deep Blue Sea*, 263–64; and Rediker, *Villains of all Nations*, 68–69.

161   **Although the captain . . . as their leader**: Defoe, *General History*, 213–14.

162   **"trustee . . . civil magistrate"**: Johnson, *History of the Pirates*, 213.

162   **He, not the captain . . . position as well**: Rediker, *Villains of all Nations*, 66–68; Rediker, *Between the Devil*, 263; and Defoe, *General History*, 213–214.

162   **"social security"**: Rediker, *Villains of All Nations*, 73.

162   **"The captain shall have . . . in the hold"**: *Tryals of Thirty-Six Persons for Piracy* (Boston: Samuel Kneeland, 1723), reproduced in Baer, *British Piracy in the Golden Age*, vol. 3, 191. See also "Here Follow the Articles," *BNL* (August 8, 1723).

163   **"If at any time"**: Dow and Edmonds, *Pirates*, 316.

163   **"the musicians"**: Defoe, *General History*, 213.

163   **"The lights and candles"**: Ibid., 211.

164   **"Distribution of Justice"**: Peter Linebaugh and Marcus Rediker, *The Many-*

Headed Hydra: Sailors, Slaves, Commoners, and the Hidden History of the Revolutionary Atlantic (Boston: Beacon Press, 2000), 163.

164 **able to exact revenge:** See, for example, Snelgrave, *New Account of Some Parts of Guinea*, 225.

165 **"Most of them . . . of one man":** *Lives of the Most Remarkable Criminals, Who Have Been Condemned and Executed for Murder, the Highway, Housebreaking, Street Robberies, Coining and Other Offenses*, ed. Arthur L. Hayward (New York: Routledge, 2002, first published in 1735), 37.

165 **floating society:** Leeson, *Invisible Hook*, 20, 27, 203.

166 **However pirates . . . maneuverability for size:** Angus Konstam, *The Pirate Ship 1660–1730* (Oxford: Osprey Publishing, 2003), 4–8.

166 **Pirate vessels ranged:** Cordingly, *Under the Black Flag*, 161–62, 206; and Angus Konstam, *The History of Pirates* (Guilford, CT: Lyons Press, 1999), 76.

166 **"main small workhorse":** Konstam, *History of Pirates*, 76.

169 **The favored type:** William Gilkerson and Spencer C. Tucker, "Naval Weapons, Boarding," in *The Encyclopedia of the Wars of the Early Republic, 1783–1812*, ed. Spencer C. Tucker (Santa Barbara: ABC-CLIO, 2014), 468; and David F. Marley, *Daily Life of Pirates* (Santa Barbara: Greenwood, 2012), 131.

169 **"Where the game":** Defoe, *General History*, 5.

169 **To keep their . . . running out:** Rediker, *Villains of all Nations*, 98; Cordingly, *Under the Black Flag*, 114–17; and "Philadelphia, Febr. 22," *Boston Gazette* (March 21–28, 1726); and Hill, "Notes on Piracy," 147.

171 **Although a few . . . attempting to depict:** For a good discussion of the questionable provenance of many pirate flags, see Little, *Golden Age of Piracy*, 16–23. See also Hill, "Notes on Piracy," 147.

171 **"a sable ensign":** Hill, "Notes on Piracy," 146.

171 **By the 1710s . . . a skeletal head:** Cordingly, *Under the Black Flag*, 118; Pringle, *Jolly Roger*, 123; Eric Partridge, *A Dictionary of Slang and Unconventional English* (Oxon, UK: Routledge, 1984), 826; Little, *Golden Age of Piracy*, 23–30; Robert S. Gauron, "Fascinating Flags of Plundering Pirates and Profiteering Privateers," *Raven: A Journal of Vexillology* (2000), 6–7; Hill, "Notes on Piracy," 147–48; and Grey, *Pirates of the Eastern Seas*, 16–19.

172 **"that have made":** "London, March 8," *BNL* (June 16–23, 1718).

174 **battle-ready:** Konstam, *The Pirate Ship*, 13–15.

CHAPTER 7 − TREASURE AND THE TEMPEST

175 **In the early fall . . . make Mary his bride:** Woodard, *Republic of Pirates*, 28–30, 52, 90–95; Barry Clifford, *Expedition Whydah: The Story of the World's First Excavation of a Pirate Ship and the Man Who Found Her*, with Paul Perry (New York: Cliff Street Books, 1999), 4–7, 104–5; Joseph Berger [Jeremiah Digges], *Cape Cod Pilot* (Cambridge, MA: MIT Press, 1969, first published in 1937), 193–97; "Information of Andrew Turbett, Master; and Robert Gilmore, Supercargo, of the ship Agnes of Glasgow before Lt. Governor Spotswood, Virginia. April 17, 1717," CO 5/1318 no.16ii, in *The Whydah Sourcebook*, compiled and edited by Kenneth J. Kinkor (Provincetown: Privately published, 2003), 92; "Last Will & Testament of Mary Hallett," in *Whydah Sourcebook*, 286–87; *Whydah Sourcebook*, 343–45; Rozina Sabur, "Possible Remains of World's 'Rich-

est Pirate' Captain Black Sam Bellamy to Be Compared to English Descendant's DNA," *Telegraph* (February 19, 2018); and Tom Payne, "Carpenter, 33, Gives a DNA Sample to Find Out Whether He Is Related to Infamous Pirate Black Sam Who Plundered Booty Worth £85 Million 300 Years Ago," *Daily Mail* (April 6, 2018).

176 **A married and successful silversmith . . . Block Island:** George Andrews Moriarty, "John Williams of Newport, Merchant, and His Family," *Genealogical Magazine* (December 1915), 4–10.

177 **How and when Williams . . . their efforts:** Woodard, *Republic of Pirates*, 97, 106, 124; Clifford, *Expedition Whydah*, 110–13; and Defoe, *General History*, 585.

177 **Discouraged, but still . . . periaguas and made their escape:** "Deposition of Allen Bernard, Jamaica" (August 10, 1716), JCM fols. 63–68, reproduced in *Whydah Sourcebook*, 57–59; Woodard, *Republic of Pirates*, 122–34; Clifford, *Expedition Whydah*, 136–40; "Deposition of John Cockrane, Jamaica" (August 10, 1716), JCM fols. 68–69, reproduced in *Whydah Sourcebook*, 61–62; and "Memorial of Monsr. Moret [n.d.] Jamaican Council Minutes fols.17–23," reproduced in *Whydah Sourcebook*, 47.

178 **"cut to pieces":** "Deposition of Joseph Eels of Port Royall, Carpenter" (December 20, 1716), *CSPC*, item 411i, vol. 29, 211–15.

179 **Not long after taking flight . . . capture was yet to come:** "Examination of John Brown and Thomas South" (May 6, 1717), *The Trials of Eight Persons Indicted for Piracy* (Boston: B. Green, 1718), 23–25; "Examination of Jeremiah Higgins, Late Boatswain of the 'Mary Anne'" (July 12, 1717), Papers Relating to a Piracy Case, 6/2/1717–7/12/1717, Record Group 21: Records of District Courts of the United States, 1685–2009, National Archives at New York; "Letter of Governor [Walter] Hamilton to the Council of Trade and Plantations," (March 1, 1717), CSPCS 29:#484 (also CO 152/11, nos. #57,57i.)," reproduced in *Whydah Sourcebook*, 88; Woodard, *Republic of Pirates*, 87–89, 112–13, 131–32, 134–36, 140, 144–54; Clifford with Perry, *Expedition Whydah*, 166–69, 221–245; and Defoe, *General History*, 31.

179 **"Flying Gang":** "Deposition of John Vickers" (July 3, 1716), *CSPC*, item 240i, vol. 29, 139–42.

180 **Nassau in 1713:** "Lt. Governor Pulleine to the Council of Trade and Plantations" (April 22, 1714), *CSPC*, item 651, vol. 27, 332–34.

180 **"The Republic of Pirates":** Woodard, *Republic of Pirates*, 1, 3, 7.

180 **"a second Madagascar":** "Deposition of John Vickers" (July 3, 1716).

180 **And like Madagascar:** "[Thomas Walker?] to the Council of Trade and Plantations" (August 1716), CO 5, 1265 no.52, reproduced in *Whydah Sourcebook*, 52.

180 **"The pirates themselves have often":** "Mr. Gale to Col. Thomas Pitt, junr. So. Carolina," (November 4, 1718), *CSPC*, item 31i, vol. 31 (1719–1720), 1–21.

180 **"been almost":** Margarette Lincoln, "Woodes Rogers and the War against Pirates in the Bahamas," in *Governing the Sea in the Early Modern Era*, 111. See also "Lt. Governor Pulleine to the Council of Trade and Plantations" (April 22, 1714), *CSPC*, item 651, vol. 27 (1712–1714), 332–34.

180 **"commit great":** "Deposition of John Vickers" (July 3, 1716).

182 **"kill himself":** "Deposition of Abijah Savage, Commander of the Sloop *Bonetta* of Antigua before His Excellency Walter Hamilton" (November 30, 1716), CO 137/11, no.45iii, reproduced in *Whydah Sourcebook*, 78. See also

Thomas H. Maugh II, "A Pirate's Life for Him—At Age 9," *Los Angeles Times* (June 1, 2006); and Clifford, *Expedition Whydah*, 222, 224.

182 **spotted a large ship:** The background for this section on the *Whydah*, its capture, and its reconfiguration comes from Woodard, *Republic of Pirates*, 156–58, 169–70; Clifford, *Expedition Whydah*, 246–253; "Examination of John Brown and Peter Cornelius Hoof" (May 6, 1717), in *Trials of Eight Persons*, 15, 23, 25; "Examination of Jeremiah Higgins"; "Examination of Richard Caverley (June 15, 1717)," Papers Relating to a Piracy Case, 6/2/1717–7/12/1717, Record Group 21: Records of District Courts of the United States, 1685–2009, National Archives at New York; Herbert S. Klein, *The Atlantic Slave Trade: New Approaches to the Americas* (Cambridge: Cambridge University Press, 2010), 106–7; "Shipping Returns, 1709–1722," Jamaica, CO 142/14, no. 58, NAL; and *Whydah Sourcebook*, 347–48.

182 **twenty thousand slaves:** Robert Harms, *The Diligent: A Voyage through the Worlds of the Slave Trade* (New York: Basic Books, 2002), 159.

183 **"a death's head":** *Trials of Eight Persons*, 24.

184 **"much of . . . his charges":** "Examination of John Brown and Peter Cornelius Hoof," in *Trials of Eight Persons*, 23.

184 **With spring fast . . . some of his wealth:** *Trials of Eight Persons*, 23–24; "Examination of Richard Caverley"; and Woodard, *Republic of Pirates*, 170.

184 **Captain Beer:** "Rhode-Island, May 3," *BNL* (April 29–May 6, 1717).

184 **"I am sorry . . . deck at pleasure":** Defoe, *General History*, 587.

185 **"What thou meanest":** Aurelius Augustine, *The City of God*, trans. Rev. Marcus Dods, vol. I (Edinburgh: T & T Clark, 1871), 140.

185 **was made up:** For an alternate view, that Beer did indeed have this conversation with Bellamy, see Woodard, *Republic of Pirates*, 174.

186 **"pretended to be":** *Trials of Eight Persons*, 11.

186 **lost sight:** "Examination of Richard Caverley."

186 **Over the next . . . not clear:** Thomas Daniels et al., "Deposition, Block Island" (April 28, 1717), *Rhode Island Historical Magazine* (April 1885), 291–92; Examination of Jeremiah Higgins"; and "Deposition of John Lucas, Master of the Ship *Tryal of Brighthelmstone* of Great Britain before John Hart, Governor of Maryland" (April 13, 1717), CO 5/1318 no. 16iii, *Whydah Sourcebook*, 89–90; and Woodard, *Republic of Pirates*, 178–79.

186 **Bellamy didn't fare . . . new captain:** *Trials of Eight Persons*, 23–24; and "Information of Andrew Turbett, Master; and Robert Gilmore, Supercargo, of the ship *Agnes* of Glasgow before Lt. Governor Spotswood" (April 17, 1717), CO 5/1318 no. 16ii, *Whydah Sourcebook*, 92–93.

187 **"Our coast is":** "Anonymous to Council of Trade and Plantations, Rappahannock, Virginia" (April 15, 1717), CO 5/1318 no. 4, *Whydah Sourcebook*, 91. See also "April the 19th, 1717," *Executive Journals of the Council of Colonial Virginia, May 1, 1705–October 23, 1721*, ed. H. R. McIlwaine, vol. III (Richmond: Virginia State Library, 1928), 443–44.

187 **Bellamy set his . . . Long Island:** *Trials of Eight Persons*, 9, 24; and Woodard, *Republic of Pirates*, 180.

187 ***Mary Anne*:** *Trials of Eight Persons*, 9–11, 24; and "Deposition of Thomas Fitzgerald and Alexander Mackonachy" (May 6, 1717), in Jameson, *Privateering*, 296–98.

187   **"armed with muskets"**: *Trials of Eight Persons*, 9.

188   **seven thousand gallons**: Clifford, *Expedition Whydah*, 259.

188   **"green wine"**: "Deposition of Thomas Fitzgerald and Alexander Mackonachy," 296.

188   **With the *Whydah* . . . Bellamy's dilemma**: *Trials of Eight Persons*, 9.

188   **the sloop *Fisher***: *Trials of Eight Persons*, 9; and "Deposition of Ralph Merry and Samuel Roberts" (May 11, 16, 1717), in Jameson, *Privateering*, 301–2.

188   **replied in the affirmative**: "Deposition of Ralph Merry and Samuel Roberts" (May 11, 16, 1717), 301.

189   **"make more haste"**: *Trials of Eight Persons*, 9.

189   **"damn . . . seen her"**: Ibid., 10.

189   **"find liquor"**: Ibid., 9–10.

189   **"through the head"**: Ibid., 10.

189   **"that the king"**: Ibid., 10–11.

189   **"stretch"**: Ibid., 10.

190   **Pochet Island**: "Deposition of Thomas Fitzgerald and Alexander Mackonachy," 297.

190   **"cried out saying"**: *Trials of Eight Persons*, 10.

190   ***Ann Galley* and the *Fisher***: "Deposition of Ralph Merry and Samuel Roberts" (May 11, 16, 1717), in Jameson, *Privateering*, 301.

190   **At about the same . . . torn apart**: "Cyprian Southack to Governor Samuel Shute" (May 5, 1717), in Jameson, *Privateering*, 292; Woodard, *Republic of Pirates*, 183–85; and Clifford, *Expedition Whydah*, 264–65.

191   **130 to 163**: "Samuel Shute, A Proclamation," *BNL* (May 6–13, 1717); Woodard, *Republic of Pirates*, 185; and Clifford, *Expedition Whydah*, 265.

191   **Julian was**: *Trials of Eight Persons*, 24. During the trial, one of Bellamy's men testified that there was an Indian onboard (almost certainly Julian) who was born on Cape Cod. However, historian Kenneth Kinkor argues that more recent research has shown Julian to have been a Moskito Indian from Central America. Since there is doubt as to what type of Indian Julian was, I have left it indeterminate. See *Whydah Sourcebook*, 335.

192   **"they would first"**: Owen Morris, *Trials of Eight Persons*, 19.

192   **Samuel Harding**: "Cyprian Southack to Governor Samuel Shute (May 8, 1717)," in Jameson, *Privateering*, 299.

192   **"mooncussers"**: Jeremiah Digges, *Cape Cod Pilot: A Loquacious Guide* (Provincetown, RI: Modern Pilgrim Press, 1937), 136–37; Rodney E. Dillon Jr., "South Florida in 1860," *Florida Historical Quarterly*, (April 1982), 453; Birse Shepard, *Lore of the Wreckers* (Boston: Beacon Press, 1961), 7–10.

192   **"we pray to thee"**: Cathryn Pearce, *Cornish Wrecking 1700–1860: Reality and Popular Myth* (Woodbridge, UK: Boydell Press, 2010), 86.

193   **"got a great"**: Cyprian Southack to Governor Samuel Shute" (May 8, 1717), 299–300.

193   **"looked very much"**: *Trials of Eight Persons*, 11.

193   **Meanwhile, the *Mary Anne* . . . awaited their fate**: *Trials of Eight Persons*, 10, 12; "Colonel Buffet to Governor Shute, Sandwich, Ma." (April 29, 1717), *Whydah Sourcebook*, 100–101; "Boston," *BNL* (May 6, 1717).

194   **At the same time . . . Bellamy and Williams**: "Deposition of Ralph Merry and Samuel Roberts," 301–2.

194 **Doane didn't . . . offered up:** "Journal of Cyprian Southack at Cape Cod, May 3, 1717," MA (Journals 1695–1767) 38A:16–17, *Whydah Sourcebook*, 103; "Cyprian Southack to Governor Samuel Shute" (May 8, 1717), 299; and Arthur T. Vanderbilt II, *Treasure Wreck: The Fortunes and Fate of the Pirate Ship Whydah* (Boston: Houghton Mifflin, 1986), 64–65.

195 **search their houses:** "Advertisement by Cyprian Southack" (May 4, 1717), MA vol. 38A:18, *Whydah Sourcebook*, 105.

195 **"these people are very":** Cyprian Southack to Governor Samuel Shute" (May 8, 1717), 299.

195 **"money, bullion":** "Samuel Shute, A Proclamation," *BNL* (May 6–13, 1717).

195 **Southack's own . . . on the Cape:** "Minutes of Governors Council (September 19, 1717). MA 6:513–14," in *Whydah Sourcebook*, 166; "Advertisements," *BNL* (June 10–17, 1717); and "Advertisements," *BNL* (July 22–29, 1717).

196 **According to one of their crew . . . to the Caribbean:** "Deposition of Ralph Merry and Samuel Roberts," 302. See also "Piscataqua, May 17," *BNL* (May 13–20, 1717); "Marblehead, May 11," *BNL* (May 6–13, 1717); "Deposition of Paul Mansfield," Salem, Ma. (May 25, 1717). SCF 11945, *Whydah Sourcebook*, 133–34; and "Piscataqua, May 24," *BNL* (May 20–27, 1717).

196 **Richmond Island:** "Examination of Richard Caverley."

196 **After riding out the storm . . . cleaned their ship:** "Examination of Richard Caverley"; and "Deposition of Zachariah Hill, Boston (May 11, 1717), SCF 11945," in *Whydah Sourcebook*, 124; and Woodard, *Republic of Pirates*, 189–92.

196 **Still wondering what . . . for the Caribbean:** Woodard, *Republic of Pirates*, 192; "Deposition of Samuel Skinner, Salem, Ma (May 26, 1717)," in *Whydah Sourcebook*, 134–35; "New-York, June 17," *BNL* (June 17–24, 1717); and "Philadelphia, June 20," *BNL* (June 24–July 1, 1717).

197 **In the aftermath . . . and sailed south:** "Rhode-Island, May 10," *BNL* (May 6–13, 1717); "New-York, May 6," *BNL* (May 6–13, 1717); "Rhode-Island, May 17," *BNL* (May 13–20, 1717); "Piscataqua, May 17," *BNL* (May 13–20, 1717); "Piscataqua, May 24," *BNL* (May 20–27, 1717); "Boston," *BNL* (May 20–27, 1717); "Philadelphia, June 13," *BNL* (June 17–24, 1717); "New-York, June 17," *BNL* (June 17–24, 1717); "Philadelphia, June 20," *BNL*; "New-York, July 29," *BNL* (July 29–August 5, 1717); Richard B. Morris, "The Ghost of Captain Kidd," *New York History* (July 1938), 288, 295–96; and Woodard, *Republic of Pirates*, 191–93, 196.

197 **"guarding our":** "A Proclamation for a Publick THANKSGIVING," *BNL* (November 18–25, 1717).

197 **"two good sloops":** "Rhode-Island, May 10," *BNL* (May 6–13, 1717).

197 **"in quest":** "Philadelphia, June 20," *BNL* (June 24–July 1, 1717).

198 **"surprise and capture":** "Governor Cranston to Governor Shute, Rhode Island (May 31, 1717). MA (Colonial) 2:166," in *Whydah Sourcebook*, 138.

198 **"barbarously beat":** "Philadelphia, June 20," *BNL* (June 24–July 1, 1717).

198 **addressed as "captain":** Snelgrave, *New Account of Some Parts of Guinea*, 258; and Woodard, *Republic of Pirates*, 321.

199 **"horribly *murdered all their*":** Cotton Mather, *Instructions to the Living, from the Condition of the Dead* (Boston: Allen for Boone, 1717), 7.

199 **into slavery:** *Whydah Sourcebook*, 335.

199 **"Enemy of Mankind":** *Trials of Eight Persons*, 6.

200 **"never excuse":** Ibid., 13.

200 **"civil and kind":** Ibid., 14. See also ibid., 9–12.

201 **"long and sad":** Cotton Mather, *Diary of Cotton Mather*, vol. II, 1709–1724 (New York: Frederick Ungar Publishing, 1957), 488.

201 **"Behold, Reader":** Cotton Mather, *Instructions to the Living*, 38.

CHAPTER 8 – THE GENTLEMAN PIRATE AND BLACKBEARD

203 **La Buse struck:** "Piscataqua, July 19th," *BNL* (July 15–27, 1717); and "Boston," *BNL* (July 15–27, 1717).

203 **"We have been":** John F. Watson, *Annals of Philadelphia* (Philadelphia: E. L. Carey & A. Hart, 1830), 465; and Arne Bialuschewski, "Blackbeard off Philadelphia: Documents Pertaining to the Campaign against the Pirates in 1717 and 1718," *Pennsylvania Magazine of History and Biography* (April 2010), 172.

203 **Born into a prosperous:** Background for Bonnet's early life until his departure on the *Revenge* comes from Defoe, *General History*, 95; Lindley S. Butler, *Pirates, Privateers, and Rebel Raiders of the Carolina Coast* (Chapel Hill: University of North Carolina Press, 2000), 51–55; Woodard, *Republic of Pirates*, 197–99; and Christopher Byrd Downey, *Stede Bonnet: Charleston's Gentleman Pirate* (Charleston: History Press, 2012), 19–25.

203 **title of "Major":** How Bonnet got this appellation is not clear. Some accounts contend that it was his rank in the island's militia. Others argue that landowners on Barbados were granted military titles that ascended in rank along with the increase in the size of the acreage they controlled, and Bonnet's four-hundred-plus-acre estate was large enough to earn the right to be called *major*. See, for example, Byrd Downey, *Stede Bonnet*, 22.

204 **"generally esteemed":** Defoe, *General History*, 95.

204 **"a disorder":** Ibid.

204 **"discomforts":** Ibid.

204 **sixty-ton sloop:** Ibid.; and Woodard, *Republic of Pirates*, 198–99.

205 **126 men:** Colin Woodard, "The Last Days of Blackbeard," *Smithsonian* (February 2014), 36.

206 **Being a novice . . . were off the coast of Charleston:** Defoe, *General History*, 95–96; "New-York, May 6," *BNL* (May 6–13, 1717); and "By Letters from South Carolina of the 22nd past," *BNL* (October 21–28, 1717).

206 **Charleston was the . . . it from attack:** Walter J. Fraser Jr., *Charleston! Charleston!: The History of a Southern City* (Columbia: University of South Carolina Press, 1989), 22; and McCusker, "Colonial Statistics," 5–655.

206 **"It was . . . a potpourri":** Ibid.

206 **South Carolina's plantation . . . nearly two to one:** Walter Edgar, *South Carolina: A History* (Columbia: University of South Carolina Press, 1998), 66–67, 78.

207 **Maritime traffic . . . sailed away:** "By Letters from South Carolina of the 22nd past," *BNL* (October 21–28, 1717); Defoe, *General History*, 96; *Tryals of Major Stede Bonnet*, iii; and Woodard, *Republic of Pirates*, 200–201.

207 **"forced to let":** "By Letters from South Carolina of the 22nd past," *BNL* (October 21–28, 1717).

207   **When Palmer reported:** Ibid.

207   **On the way . . . Edward Thatch:** "Philadelphia, October 24th," *BNL* (November 4–11, 1717); and Defoe, *General History*, 96.

209   ***Thatch* as the spelling:** David Moore, "Blackbeard the Pirate: Historical Background and the Beaufort Inlet Shipwrecks," *Tributaries* (October 1997), 31.

209   **also referred to:** Robert E. Lee, *Blackbeard the Pirate: A Reappraisal of His Life and Times* (Winston-Salem, NC: John F. Blair, 1990), 4; and Baylus C. Brooks, *Quest for Blackbeard: The True Story of Edward Thache and His World* (Lake City: Lulu Press, 2016), 127–30.

209   **His birthplace . . . that effect:** Lee, *Blackbeard the Pirate*, 3–4; Butler, *Pirates, Privateers*, 29–30; Defoe, *General History*, 71; David Moore, "Blackbeard the Pirate: Historical Background and the Beaufort Inlet Shipwrecks," *Tributaries* (October 1997), 31–32; Kevin P. Duffus, *The Last Days of Black Beard the Pirate* (Raleigh, NC: Looking Glass Productions, 2008); Brooks, *Quest for Blackbeard*, 143–69; and Charles Leslie, *A New History of Jamaica, From the Earliest Accounts, to the Taking of Porto Bello by Vice-Admiral Vernon* (London: J. Hodges, 1740), 275.

209   **"was a tall":** "Deposition of Henry Bostock" (December 19, 1717), CO 152/12, fols. 219–20, NAL.

209   **"name of Blackbeard":** "Abstract of a letter from Mr. Maynard, first Lieutenant of His Majesty's Ship *Pearl*, the Station-Ship at Virginia, to Mr. Symonds, Lieutenant of His Majesty's Ship the *Phoenix*, the Station-Ship at New York," *Weekly Journal or British Gazetteer* (April 25, 1719).

209   **"assumed the cognomen":** Defoe, *General History*, 84–85.

210   **He is often portrayed:** Ibid., 96.

210   **one other instance:** "Depositions of Henry Bostock"; "New-York, Feb. 24th," *BNL* (March 3–10, 1718).

210   **"In fact . . . the image":** Bialuschewski, "Blackbeard off Philadelphia," 170.

211   **A thirty-two-gun . . . next expedition:** "Capt. Mathew Musson to the Council of Trade and Plantations" (July 5, 1717), *CSPC*, item 635, vol. 29, 338.

211   **Blackbeard, who had . . . of his own ship:** "Capt. Ellis Brand to the Admiralty" (December 4, 1717), ADM 1/1472, NAL; and Woodard, *Republic of Pirates*, 202–3.

211   **The *Revenge* was repaired . . . into the sea:** "From Philadelphia, October 24," *BNL* (October 28–November 4, 1717); "From New-York, Octob. 28," *BNL* (October 28–November 4, 1717); "Philadelphia, October 24," *BNL* (November 4–11, 1717); "New-York, October 28," *BNL* (November 4–11, 1717); "Philadelphia, Novemb. 14th," *BNL* (November 18–25, 1717); Capt. Ellis Brand to the Admiralty (December 4, 1717); "New-York, Novemb. 4," *BNL* (November 4–11, 1717); and "Indictment for William Howard (1717), in Lee, *Blackbeard the Pirate*, 102.

212   **"the pirate sloop":** "Philadelphia, October 24," *BNL* (November 4–11, 1717).

212   **Blackbeard knew Bellamy:** Woodard, *Republic of Pirates*, 134, 145.

212   **"revenge it on":** "Philadelphia, October 31," *BNL* (November 4–11, 1717).

212   ***La Concorde*:** Background for *La Concorde* and its capture comes from David D. Moore and Mike Daniel, "Blackbeard's Capture of the Nantaise Slave Ship *La Concorde*: A Brief Analysis of the Documentary Evidence," *Tributaries*

(October 2001); Woodard, *Republic of Pirates*, 210–12; "Indictment for William Howard (1717), in Lee, *Blackbeard the Pirate*, 103; and Brooks, *Quest for Blackbeard*, 362–63.

213   **"scurvy and":** Moore and Daniel, "Blackbeard's Capture of the Nantaise," 24.

213   **To make it more powerful:** Woodard, *Republic of Pirates*, 212–14; and "Deposition of Thomas Knight (November 30, 1717)," CO 152/12, no. 67ii.

214   **"cut the throats":** Moore and Daniel, "Blackbeard's Capture of the Nantaise," 25.

214   **Sixty-one . . . retain their slaves:** Ibid., 21, 27; and Woodard, *Republic of Pirates*, 215.

214   **As for Dosset . . . Bad Encounter:** Moore and Daniel, "Blackbeard's Capture of the Nantaise," 25.

214   **For months . . . well-seasoned consort:** Woodard, *Republic of Pirates*, 214–15, 240–41; and "Deposition of Henry Bostock."

215   **Captain William Wyer:** Background for Stede's encounter with the *Protestant Caesar* comes from "Boston, on the 31st of May last," *BNL* (June 9–16, 1718).

215   **"telling him":** Defoe, *General History*, 72.

216   **While the pirates . . . of the *Adventure*:** "The Information of David Herriot and Ignatius Pell," *Tryals of Major Stede Bonnet*, 44; and Defoe, *General History*, 72.

216   **"he might not":** "Boston, on the 31st of May last," *BNL* (June 9–16, 1718).

217   **"if they would stand":** Ibid.

217   **"murdered by":** Ibid.

217   **"glad":** Ibid.

217   **"belonged to Boston":** "The Information of David Herriot and Ignatius Pell," 45. See also "Boston, on the 31st of May last," *BNL* (June 9–16, 1718).

217   **The following day . . . were let go:** Ibid.

217   **For more than . . . near Havana:** *Tryals of Major Stede Bonnet*, 9, 45.

217   **blockading the entire city:** Background for this section on the blockade of Charleston comes from *Tryals of Major Stede Bonnet*, iii–iv, 8; "Extracts of several letters from Carolina" (August 19, 1718), *CSPC*, item 660, vol. 30, 336–38; Defoe, *General History*, 74–5, 87–91; and "Governor Johnson to the Council of Trade and Plantations" (June 18, 1718), *CSPC*, item 556, vol. 30, 266–67.

218   **"it struck great":** Defoe, *General History*, 88.

219   **"threatened to come":** "Extracts of several letters from Carolina" (August 19, 1718).

219   **"truly represent":** Defoe, *General History*, 89.

220   **"to and fro":** *Tryals of Major Stede Bonnet*, 8.

220   **"robbers and murderers":** Defoe, *General History*, 74.

220   **stripped them:** "Governor Johnson to the Council of Trade and Plantations" (June 18, 1718), *CSPC*, item 556, vol. 30, 266–67.

220   **"to the northward":** "South Carolina, June 6," *BNL* (June 30–July 7, 1718).

220   **Although the medicine . . . avoid at all costs:** 8; Edward McCrady, *The History of South Carolina Under the Proprietary Government, 1670–1719* (New York: Macmillan, 1897), 591.

221   **"he had got":** *Tryals of Major Stede Bonnet*, 48.

221 **Instead, for six days . . . the chance:** *Tryals of Major Stede Bonnet*, 45; and Moore and Daniel, "Blackbeard's Capture of the Nantaise," 27.

221 **a phrase that indicates:** Woodard, *Republic of Pirates*, 254.

221 **On June 3 . . . Spanish sloop:** *Tryals of Major Stede Bonnet*, 45–46; and "Ellis Brand to the Admiralty" (July 12, 1718), ADM 1/1472, NAL.

222 **According to one . . . nefarious record expunged:** *Tryals of Major Stede Bonnet*, iv, 19; Brooks, *Quest for Blackbeard*, 419–28; "Brand to the Admiralty (July 12, 1718)"; Woodard, *Republic of Pirates*, 254–57; Butler, *Pirates, Privateers*, 38–9, 60; Konstam, *Blackbeard*, 183–84; and Defoe, *General History*, 75.

222 **"It was generally":** *Tryals of Major Stede Bonnet*, 46. See also, "Philadelphia, July 10," *BNL* (July 14–21, 1718).

223 **Right after the two . . . returning to piracy:** *Tryals of Major Stede Bonnet*, 46; Defoe, *General History*, 75, 96–97; Butler, *Pirates, Privateers*, 39, 60; and Baylus, *Quest for Blackbeard*, 530–33.

223 **capital of the colony:** Herbert R. Paschal, *A History of Colonial Bath* (Raleigh, NC: Edwards & Broughton, 1955), 9–14, 38.

223 **Act of Grace:** "By the King, A Proclamation for Suppressing of Pirates," *BNL* (December 2–9, 1717).

224 **Governor Eden granted . . . join their venture:** *Tryals of Major Stede Bonnet*, 11, 19, 46–47; "Brand to the Admiralty" (July 12, 1718); Butler, *Pirates, Privateers*, 60–61; and Defoe, *General History*, 97–99.

226 **On July 29 . . . surged to action:** *Tryals of Major Stede Bonnet*, iv, 7, 13, 21–23, 30, 48; and Hughson, *Carolina Pirates*, 90.

226 **"fell to beating":** *Tryals of Major Stede Bonnet*, 23. See also "Philadelphia, August 7," *BNL* (August 11–18, 1718).

226 **"be merciful . . . stomach to eat":** *Tryals of Major Stede Bonnet*, 13. See also "Philadelphia, August 7," *BNL* (August 11–18, 1718).

226 **"that if any":** *Tryals of Major Stede Bonnet*, 50.

226 **wages for a carpenter at the time:** United States Department of Labor, *History of Wages in the United States from Colonial Times to 1928*, bulletin no. 604 (Washington, DC: United States Government Printing Office, 1934), 51.

228 **Rhett had earned his military . . . South Carolina and beyond:** *Tryals of Major Stede Bonnet*, iv, 8–9; Hughson, *Carolina Pirates*, 90–93; Defoe, *General History*, 136–37; "Rhode-Island, October 10," *BNL* (October 13–20, 1718); Butler, *Pirates, Privateers*, 64–65; and "Governor and Council of South Carolina to the Council of Trade and Plantations" (October 21, 1718), *CSPC*, item 730, vol. 30, 366–67.

228 **A famously courageous:** Edward McCrady, *The History of South Carolina under The Proprietary Government, 1670–1719* (New York: Macmillan, 1897), 369.

228 **"continually alarmed":** "Governor Johnson to the Council of Trade and Plantations" (June 18, 1718), *CSPC*, item 556, vol. 30, 266–67.

229 **After capturing a merchant . . . in his mouth:** "Deposition of Edward North" (May 22, 1718), *CSPC*, item 551ii, vol. 30, 260–64.

229 **into a panic:** Hughson, *Carolina Pirates*, 92.

229 **Meantime, having failed . . . October 3, 1718:** *Tryals of Major Stede Bonnet*, iv–v.

230 **utterly destroy:** Ibid., 50.

231 **"beckoned with their hats"**: Ibid., v.

231 **"If anyone"**: Ibid., 19.

231 **"would die"**: Ibid..

231 **"loved very well"**: Ibid., 25–26.

231 **"much shattered . . . finishing stroke"**: Ibid., v.

232 **Charleston had no . . . reach North Carolina**: Ibid., v, 11; Hughson, *Carolina Pirates*, 99–101; "Mr. Gale of South Carolina to Thomas Pitt" (November 6, 1718), CO 23/1; Brooks, *Quest for Blackbeard*, 455–56; and "Philadelphia, Novemb. 13," *BNL* (November 17–24, 1718).

233 **According to Thomas Hepworth**: *Tryals of Major Stede Bonnet*, 11.

233 **"sent hue and cries"**: Ibid., 9.

233 **This elicited . . . tighter guard**: Ibid., v–vi.

234 **wave of panic**: Background for this section on Moody and Worley comes from Hughson, *Carolina Pirates*, 112–22; Defoe, *General History*, 297–303 (which includes a letter from a Charleston resident on the details of the engagements); and David Duncan Wallace, *The History of South Carolina*, vol. I (New York: American Historical Society, 1934), 228–33.

235 **this battle was viewed**: "Letter from a Charleston resident sent to Charles Johnson," in Defoe, *General History*, 302.

236 **Benjamin Franklin later claimed**: Walter Isaacson, *A Benjamin Franklin Reader* (New York: Simon & Schuster, 2003), 149–51.

236 **In the meantime . . . view of pirates**: L. Lynn Hogue, "Nicholas Trott: A Man of Laws and Letters," *South Carolina Historical Magazine* (January 1975), 25, 28; and Ritchie, *Captain Kidd*, 150.

237 **"heinousness"**: *Tryals of Major Stede Bonnet*, 3.

238 **"for though your sins"**: Ibid., 36.

238 **"Archpirata . . . robber, a pirate."**: Ibid., 9.

238 **Bonnet pleaded . . . where he was hanged**: *Tryals of Major Stede Bonnet*, 37–42; Defoe, *General History*, 111; and David Ramsay, *Ramsay's History of South Carolina* (Newberry, SC: W. J. Duffie, 1858), 116–17n.

238 **"I am sorry . . . family grieves me"**: *Tryals of Major Stede Bonnet*, 39.

239 **"a Christian"**: Defoe, *General History*, 112.

239 **"The execution"**: Wallace, *History of South Carolina*, 232–33.

240 **"reveled night and day"**: Defoe, *General History*, 77.

240 **"some disorders"**: "North Carolina Council Journal" (December 30, 1718), in *The Colonial Records of North Carolina*, vol. II, ed. William L. Saunders (Raleigh, NC: P. M. Hale, 1886), 322.

241 **"married a young . . . his face"**: Defoe, *General History*, 76.

241 **"there is no direct"**: Jane Stubbs Bailey, Allen Hart Norris, and John H. Oden III, "Legends of Black Beard and His Ties to Bath Town," *North Carolina Genealogical Society Journal* (August 2002), 273. See also "Capt. Ellis Brand to the Admiralty" (February 6, 1719), ADM 1/1472, NAL.

242 **"like dogs"**: *Tryals of Major Stede Bonnet*, 11.

242 ***Rose Emelye* and the *Toison d'Or***: The background for this section on the capture of the French ships comes from Colin Woodard, "Last Days of Blackbeard," 32–41.

242 **"thrown them into"**: Ibid., 40.

242   **About the middle . . . the pirates' capture:** "Lt. Governor Spotswood to the Council of Trade and Plantations" (December 22, 1718), *CSPC*, item 800, vol. 30, 425–35; "Lt. Governor Spotswood to the Council of Trade and Plantations" (August 11, 1719), *CSPC*, item 357, vol. 31, 205–14; and Defoe, *General History*, 76–77.

243   **His title notwithstanding:** Leonidas Dodson, *Alexander Spotswood: Governor of Colonial Virginia, 1710–1722* (New York: AMS Press, 1969, reprint of a 1932 edition), 6.

244   **"the dangerous consequences":** "Spotswood to the Lords of the Admiralty" (July 3, 1716), *The Official Letters of Alexander Spotswood*, vol. II, ed. R. A. Block (Richmond: Virginia Historical Society, 1885), 168.

244   **"seize upon some":** "Lt. Governor Spotswood to the Council of Trade and Plantations" (August 14, 1718), *CSPC*, item 657, vol. 30, 332–35.

244   **"unlawful and riotous":** Alexander Spotswood, "A Proclamation Prohibiting the Unlawful Concourse of Such Persons as Have Been Guilty of Piracy," *Executive Journals of the Council of Colonial Virginia*, vol. III, ed. H. R. McIlwane (Richmond: Virginia State Library, 1928), 612.

244   **"disarming and suppressing":** "Lt. Governor Spotswood to the Council of Trade and Plantations" (December 22, 1718), *CSPC*, item 800, vol. 30, 425–35.

245   **"insulting and abusing . . . such prices":** "Brand to Admiralty" (February 6, 1719).

245   **"the insolence of that . . . a general rendezvous":** "Lt. Governor Spotswood to the Council of Trade and Plantations" (December 22, 1718).

245   **Charles Vane had visited:** "Alexander Spotswood to George Gordon" (November 21, 1718), ADM 1826, NAL; and Woodard, *Republic of Pirates*, 287.

245   **"extirpate this nest":** "Lt. Governor Spotswood to the Council of Trade and Plantations" (December 22, 1718). See also "Brand to Admiralty" (February 6, 1719).

246   **the oldest naval officer:** "George Gordon to the Admiralty" (March 10, 1718), ADM 1826, NAL.

246   **two small sloops:** "Brand to Admiralty" (February 6, 1719); and Butler, *Pirates, Privateers*, 43.

247   **many in Virginia who favored:** "Lt. Governor Spotswood to the Council of Trade and Plantations" (December 22, 1718); and "Alexander Spotswood to Lord Cartwright" (February 14, 1719), *The Official Letters of Alexander Spotswood*, vol. II (Richmond: Virginia Historical Society, 1885), 274.

247   **Spotswood had a less-than-charitable view:** Herbert L. Osgood, *The American Colonies in the Eighteenth Century*, vol. II (New York: Columbia University Press, 1924), 229; and Dodson, *Alexander Spotswood*, 16.

248   **"absolutely necessary":** H. R. McIlwaine, ed., *Journals of the House of Burgesses of Virginia* (Richmond: Printed by Virginia State Library, 1912), 223.

248   **Act to Encourage:** Ibid., xl.

248   **invasion of North Carolina had already begun:** The background for the invasion, and its outcome, comes from "Brand to Admiralty" (February 6, 1719); "George Gordon to Adm. Sec. Josiah Burchett" (September 14, 1721), ADM 1/1826, NAL; "Lt. Governor Spotswood to the Council of Trade and Plantations" (December 22, 1718); "Abstract of a letter from Mr. Maynard, first

Lieutenant of His Majesty's Ship *Pearl*"; Lee, *Blackbeard the Pirate*, 115, 137, 227–28; and Butler, *Pirates, Privateers*, 44–47.

250 **"Teach called to"**: "Rhode Island, February 20," *BNL* (February 23–March 2, 1719).

250 **"At our first"**: "Abstract of a letter from Mr. Maynard, first Lieutenant of His Majesty's Ship *Pearl*."

251 **"fought like"**: Ibid.

253 **"Maynard and Teach"**: "Rhode Island, February 20," *BNL* (February 23–March 2, 1719).

253 **"he fell with five"**: "Abstract of a letter from Mr. Maynard, first Lieutenant of His Majesty's Ship *Pearl*."

254 **Maynard's sister, Margaret:** J. A. Leo Lemay, *The Life of Benjamin Franklin: Journalist, 1706–1730*, vol. 1 (Philadelphia: University of Pennsylvania Press, 2006), 62.

254 **"a sailor's song"**: Benjamin Franklin, *Benjamin Franklin's Autobiography*, ed. William B. Cairns (New York: Longmans, Green, and Co., 1905), 13.

255 **"Originally the name"**: Samuel Johnson, *A Dictionary of the English Language*, vol. II (London: Longman, Hurst, Rees, Orme, and Brown, 1818), s.v. "Grub Street."

255 **"Then each man"**: Justin Winsor, *The Memorial History of Boston*, vol. II (Boston: James R. Osgood and Company, 1881), 174n1.

255 **"When the bloody"**: Lemay, *Life of Benjamin Franklin*, 66.

255 **"discouraged me"**: Franklin, *Benjamin Franklin's Autobiography*, 13.

256 **In the aftermath . . . under some hay:** "Capt. Ellis Brand to Admiralty" (February 6, 1719); and "Capt. Ellis Brand to the Admiralty" (March 12, 1718), ADM 1/1472, NAL.

256 **On January 3 . . . in kind:** Cordingly, *Spanish Gold*, 176–77.

256 **on a pike:** John F. Watson, *Annals of Philadelphia, and Pennsylvania, In the Olden Time*, vol. II (Philadelphia: Edwin S. Stuart), 221.

256 **"enlarged with"**: Ibid., 221. See also Lee, *Blackbeard the Pirate*, 124–25.

256 **four years:** Lee, *Blackbeard the Pirate*, 139.

256 **All of the goods:** "Alexander Spotswood to Secretary Craggs" (May 26, 1719), *The Official Letters of Alexander Spotswood*, vol. II, ed. R. A. Brock (Richmond: Virginia Historical Society, 1885), 317; and Butler, *Pirates, Privateers*, 48.

256 **This was a decent, though:** Weeden, *Economic and Social History of New England*, vol. II, 890–91.

257 **Spotswood's invasion . . . Knight not guilty:** Minutes of the North Carolina Executive Council for December 30–31, 1718, April 3 and May 27, 1719; in *Records of the Executive Council, 1664–1734*, ed. Robert J. Cain (Raleigh, NC: Department of Cultural Resources, 1984), 79–91; Lee, *Blackbeard the Pirate*, 143–56; "Capt. Ellis Brand to the Admiralty" (March 12, 1718), ADM 1/1472, NAL; "Capt. Brand to the Admiralty" (July 14, 1719), ADM 1/1472, NAL; "Alexander Spotswood to Secretary Craggs" (May 26, 1719), 316–19; "Alexander Spotswood to the Lords of Trade" (May 26, 1719), in *The Colonial Records of North Carolina*, vol. II, ed. William L. Saunders (Raleigh, NC: P. M. Hale, 1886), 336–38; and "North Carolina Council Journal (May 27, 1719)," in Saunders, *Colonial Records of North Carolina*, vol. II, 341–49.

257   **"it does not seem"**: Defoe, *General History*, 92.

258   **With respect to the case**: Ibid., 93. See also Butler, *Pirates, Privateers*, 49.

258   **The trial of . . . a free man**: Lee, *Blackbeard the Pirate*, 136–38; and "Brand to the Admiralty" (July 14, 1719).

258   **"in London, begging"**: Defoe, *General History*, 84.

CHAPTER 9 – FADING AWAY

260   **The Act of Grace . . . arrests and convictions**: "By the King, A Proclamation," *BNL* (April 13–20, 1719); "Rhode-Island, August 8," *BNL* (August 4–11, 1718); Lincoln, *British Pirates*, 72–73; Cordingly, *Under the Black Flag*, 205–6; and "Mr. Popple to Sir Edward Northey" (August 9, 1717), *CSPC*, item 9, vol. 30, 6.

261   **In 1721, the 1700 Act . . . would be enormous**: "Governor Sir N. Lawes to the Council of Trade and Plantations" (June 21, 1718), *CSPC*, item 566, vol. 30, 270–72; Leeson, *Invisible Hook*, 147–48; and Rediker, *Villains of all Nations*, 27–28.

261   **"unless some effectual"**: "Whitehall, September 15, 1717," *BNL* (December 16–23, 1717).

262   **In subsequent years**: Ibid.; and Cordingly, *Under the Black Flag*, 208–9; and Earle, *Pirate Wars*, 185.

262   **They weren't the navy's . . . successes as well**: Earle, *Pirate Wars*, 185–89.

263   **Bartholemew Roberts**: The background on Roberts and his demise comes from Defoe, *General History*, 5, 194–287; and Cordingly, *Spanish Gold*, 209–28.

264   **Captain Samuel Cary**: This story and all the quotes are from "Boston," *BNL* (August 15–22, 1720).

265   **"made a gallant"**: Defoe, *General History*, 243.

266   **more than four hundred**: Rediker, *Villains of all Nations*, 163.

266   **And for every pirate**: Taylor, *American Colonies*, 297.

266   **Yet another critical setback**: Background for this section on the elimination of pirates from New Providence comes from Cordingly, *Spanish Gold*, 132–66; Woodard, *Republic of Pirates*, 163–68, 232–35, 284–86, 301–4, 311; and "Whitehall, September 15, 1717," *BNL* (December 16–23, 1717).

266   **"Here they [pirates] now reign"**: Lincoln, "Woodes Rogers and the War against Pirates in the Bahamas," 115.

267   **Woodes Rogers, a major booster . . . South American mainland**: Woodes Rogers, *A Cruising Voyage Round the World* (London: Cross Keys and Bible in Cornhil, 1712), 124–31; Cordingly, *Spanish Gold*, 40–42; and Becky Little, "Debunking the Myth of the 'Real' Robinson Crusoe," *National Geographic* (September 28, 2016), accessed on November 19, 2017, https://news.national geographic.com/2016/09/robinson-crusoe-alexander-selkirk-history/.

269   **"I landed and took"**: "Governor Woodes Rogers to the Council of Trade and Plantations" (October 31, 1718), *CSPC*, item 737, vol. 30, 372–81.

269   **returned to piracy**: Ibid.

269   **the two-day trial**: "Trials and Condemnation of Ten Persons for Piracy at New-Providence in December 1718," CO 23/1, no. 28, fols. 75–82, NAL; and Defoe, *General History*, 643–58.

269   **"the son of loyal"**: "Governor Rogers to Mr. Secretary Craggs" (December 24, 1718), *CSPC*, item 807, vol. 30, 424–46.

269   **"he knew a time":** "Trials and Condemnation of Ten Persons," 80.

270   **"marked the end":** Cordingly, *Spanish Gold*, 167.

271   **Adding to the colonies':** Carl Bridenbaugh, *Cities in the Wilderness: The First Century of Urban Life in America, 1625–1742* (New York: Alfred A. Knopf, 1968), 175–82.

272   **Born in London . . . end of 1721:** Defoe, *General History*, 318–19; Dow and Edmonds, *Pirates*, 141–43; Gregory N. Flemming, *At the Point of a Cutlass: The Pirate Capture, Bold Escape, & Lonely Exile of Philip Ashton* (Lebanon, NH: ForeEdge, 2014), 9–11; and "Rhode Island, June 8," *American Weekly Mercury* (June 14–21, 1722).

273   **There, they joined . . . in different directions:** "On the 10th of January," *BNL* (April 23–30, 1722); "Rhode-Island, June 8," *New-England Courant* (June 4–11, 1722); and "Advertisement," *New-England Courant* (June 11–18, 1722); Flemming, *At the Point of a Cutlass*, 13–15; "Boston, July 2," *Boston Gazette* (June 25– July 2, 1722); Defoe, *General History*, 304–14; and Dow and Edmonds, *Pirates*, 134–35, 143–46.

274   **On June 3 . . . looking for Low:** "Newport, Rhode Island, June 7," *American Weekly Mercury* (June 14–21, 1722); "Rhode Island, June 8," *American Weekly Mercury* (June 14–21, 1722); Defoe, *General History*, 319–20; and Flemming, *At the Point of a Cutlass*, 15.

275   **"drums . . . to be beat":** "Newport, Rhode Island, June 7," *American Weekly Mercury* (June 14–21, 1722); and Flemming, *At the Point of a Cutlass*, 15.

275   **Soon after Rhode Island's . . . mantle of publisher:** Lemay, *Life of Benjamin Franklin*, vol. 1, 158; and Parton, *Life and Times of Benjamin Franklin*, vol. I, 87–88.

275   **" 'Tis thought he":** "Newport, Rhode-Island, June 7," *New-England Courant* (June 4–11, 1722).

275   **"a high affront":** James Parton, *Life and Times of Benjamin Franklin*, vol. I (Boston: Ticknor and Fields, 1867), 87.

275   **Despite Franklin's tart . . . Sabbath was over:** "Boston, June 18," *New-England Courant* (June 11–18, 1722); Dow and Edmonds, *Pirates*, 148–49; John Barnard, *Ashton's Memorial: An History of the Strange Adventures, and Signal Deliverances, of Mr. Philip Ashton* (Boston: Samuel Gerrish, 1725), 1–2; and Daniel E. Williams, "Of Providence and Pirates: Philip Ashton's Narrative Struggle for Salvation," *Early American Literature* (1989), 169.

275   **"that the pirates":** "By his Excellency, Samuel Shute," *Boston Gazette* (July 16–23, 1722).

276   **Papillion set sail:** "Boston, July 2," *Boston Gazette* (June 25–July 2, 1722).

276   **A few days later:** Ibid.

277   **"sailing from the Eastward":** Gregory Flemming, "Dangerous Waters: In the Early Days of Whaling on Martha's Vineyard, Foul Weather and Ferocious Whales Were the Least of a Whaler's Worries," *Martha's Vineyard* (May–June, 2014), 4. See also *Tryals of Thirty-Six Persons for Piracy*, in *British Piracy in the Golden Age*, vol. 3, 182; and "Boston," *BNL* (June 25–July 2, 1722).

277   **"from under":** Barnard, *Ashton's Memorial*, 2.

277   **a dozen other:** "Boston, July 2," *Boston Gazette* (June 25–July 2, 1722).

278   **"cried out":** Barnard, *Ashton's Memorial*, 3.

278   **"an uneasiness":** Ibid.

279   **"respect and kindness"**: Ibid., 4.

279   **"new, clean"**: Ibid., 5.

280   **When Low overtook . . . crew of thirty-two:** "Governor Hart to the Council of Trade and Plantations" (March 25, 1724), *CSPC*, item 102, vol. 34, 71–73.

281   **"'Oh! I wish'"**: Barnard, *Ashton's Memorial*, 10.

281   **"thrashed"**: Ibid., 7.

281   **"I soon found"**: Ibid., 7.

281   **On that late winter day . . . pirates might say:** Ibid., 16–18.

282   **"The dog is . . . leave you alone"**: Ibid., 17.

282   **Thus began Ashton's:** Background for Ashton's time on Roatán comes from ibid., 18–40.

283   **"five pound[s]"**: Ibid., 27.

283   **"started back"**: Ibid., 31.

284   **"by their garb"**: Ibid., 37.

284   **"Honest men"**: Ibid., 40.

284   **"was received"**: Ibid., 38.

285   **"whose hearts are"**: Ibid., preface.

286   **"a real-life"**: Flemming, *At the Point of a Cutlass*, 168.

286   **"the most noted"**: "Captain Peter Solgard" (June 12, 1723), ADM, 1/2452, NAL; and Flemming, *At the Point of a Cutlass*, 14.

286   **On March 10, 1723:** "Rhode Island, May 9," *BNL* (May 9–16, 1723); and "Rhode-Island, May 8," *New-England Courant* (May 13–20, 1723).

286   **"all the Spaniards"**: "Rhode-Island, May 8," *New-England Courant* (May 13–20, 1723).

286   **"a greater monster"**: "Governor Hart to the Council of Trade and Plantations" (March 25, 1724), *CSPC*, item 102, vol. 34, 71–73.

286   **"were more civil"**: "Rhode-Island, May 8," *New-England Courant* (May 13–20, 1723).

286   **Over the next . . . Charles Harris:** Flemming, *At the Point of a Cutlass*, 103–5; and *Tryals of Thirty-Six Persons*, 176–77.

287   **One of the ships . . . forcibly retained:** *Tryals of Thirty-Six Persons*, 174–75, 176–77, 188–89.

287   **On June 7 . . . number one:** "Rhode-Island, June 14," *BNL* (June 13–20, 1723); and Flemming, *At the Point of a Cutlass*, 105.

287   **Three days later:** Background for this section on the battle between the Greyhound and the Pirates comes from *Tryals of Thirty-Six Persons*, 177–78; "Captain Peter Solgard (June 12, 1723)"; "Rhode-Island, June 14," *New-England Courant* (June 10–17, 1723); "Postscript," *New-England Courant* (June 10–17, 1723); "From the *Boston Gazette*, June 17," *American Weekly Mercury* (June 20–27, 1723); and "Rhode-Island, June 14," *BNL* (June 13–20, 1723).

288   **"to encourage"**: *Tryals of Thirty-Six Persons*, 178.

288   **"an anatomy [skeleton]"**: "New-port, Rhode-Island, July 19," *BNL* (July 18–25, 1723).

288   **urging his men:** "Rhode Island, June 14," *BNL* (June 13–20, 1723).

289   **"went forward with"**: "Rhode-Island, June 14," *New-England Courant* (June 10–17, 1723).

289   **The trial . . . their black flag:** *Tryals of Thirty-Six Persons*, 171–92; and Cot-

ton Mather, *Useful remarks: An essay upon Remarkables in the Way of Wicked Men: A Sermon on the Tragical End, Unto Which the way of Twenty-Six Pirates Brought Them; at New Port on Rhode-Island, July 19, 1723: With an Account of their Speeches, Letters, & Actions, Before Their Execution* (New London: T. Green, 1723), 29; Dow and Edmonds, *Pirates*, 307–8; "New-port, Rhode-Island, July 19," *BNL* (July 18–25, 1723); Flemming, *At the Point of a Cutlass*, 188–89.

289 **"piratically and feloniously"**: *Tryals of Thirty-Six Persons*, 174–75.

289 **The astounding number:** "An exact account of the vessels taken by the pirates during the time John Waters (one of those lately executed at Rhode Island) was with them." *BNL* (August 1–8, 1723).

290 **"This flag"**: "Postscript," *New-England Courant* (July 22, 1723).

290 **"Never was there"**: *An Account of the Pirates With Divers of Their Speeches, Letters, &c., and A Poem Made by One of Them: Who Were Executed at Newport, on Rhode Island, July 19, 1723* (pamphlet, 1769, location and name of printer unknown, but likely printed in Boston).

290 **"Oh!"**: Mather, *Useful remarks*, 43–44. Mather was not at the execution but had received written accounts from those who were.

290 **"within the flux"**: Arnold Greene, *The Providence Plantations for Two Hundred and Fifty Years* (Providence, RI: J. A. & R. A. Reid, 1886), 439.

291 **"In youthful blooming . . . your welfare tend"**: *An Account of the Pirates, With Divers of Their Speeches*, 11–12.

291 **"Freedom of the City"**: "City of New-York," *Boston Gazette* (September 23–30, 1723); and Minutes of the Common Council of the City of New York, 1675–1776, vol. III (New York: Dodd, Mead and Company, 1905), 321–23.

291 **"The enemies of mankind"**: Personal communications with Stephanie A. Nelson, assistant dean, College of Arts and Sciences, and associate professor of classical studies at Boston University, June 27, 2017; and Mathew Aumiller, classical language teacher, June 26, 2017. Boston College High School.

291 **"about the deck . . . their business"**: "Rhode-Island, June 24," *BNL* (June 27, 1723). See also, "Boston," *BNL* (June 13–20, 1723).

292 **fifty hours:** "A True Lover of Passive Obedience and Non-Resistance, Boston, June 24," *New-England Courant* (June 17–24, 1723).

292 **"slashing and mauling"**: "Rhode-Island, June 24," *BNL* (June 27, 1723).

292 **"He would do"**: *American Weekly Mercury* (June 20–27, 1723); and Flemming, *At the Point of a Cutlass*, 111.

292 **"presenting one at"**: "Canso, August 1, 1723," *BNL* (September 12–19, 1723).

292 **At the end of July . . . came to an end:** Dow and Edmonds, *Pirates*, 213–17; Flemming, *At the Point of a Cutlass*, 114; Robert Francis Seybolt, Jonathan Barlow, and Nicholas Simons, "Captured by Pirates: Two Diaries of 1724–1725," *New England Quarterly* (October 1929), 658–59; "New-York, March 9," *Weekly Journal or British Gazetteer* (May 30, 1724); and "Advertisements," *BNL* (August 1–8, 1723).

293 **John Phillips's piracy:** The background for this section on Phillips comes from John Fillmore, "A Narrative of the Singular Sufferings of John Fillmore and Others, Onboard the Noted Pirate Vessel Commanded by Captain Phillips" (Aurora, NY: A. M. Clapp, 1837), *Millard Fillmore Papers*, vol. I, Publications of the Buffalo Historical Society, vol. X, ed. by Frank H. Severance

(Buffalo, NY: Buffalo Historical Society, 1907), 29–39; "Trial of John Fillmore and Edward Cheesman May 12, 1724," in Jameson, *Privateering*, 323–30; "Trial of William Phillips and Others (May 12, 1724), in Jameson, *Privateering*, 330–38; "Trial of William White, John Rose Archer, and William Taylor" (May 13, 1724), in Jameson, *Privateering*, 338–42; "Trial of John Baptis and Peter Taffery" (May 13, 1724), in Jameson, *Privateering*, 342–44; "Deposition of John Fillmore," *Boston Gazette* (April 27–May 4, 1724); Defoe, *General History*, 341–51; Dow and Edmonds, *Pirates*, 310–27; "Boston, June 3," *BNL* (May 29–June 4, 1724); and Flemming, *At the Point of a Cutlass*, 114–18, 134–38.

294   **"Phillips was completely"**: Fillmore, "A Narrative of the Singular Sufferings of John Fillmore," 36.

294   **"stood in such"**: Ibid., 34.

296   **bit of carpentry:** John J. Babson, *History of the Town of Gloucester, Cape Ann, Including the Town of Rockport* (Gloucester, MA: Proctor Brothers, 1860), 287.

297   **"brought up"**: "Deposition of John Fillmore," *Boston Gazette* (April 27–May 4, 1724).

297   **severed heads:** "Boston, May 4," *New-England Courant* (April 27–May 4, 1724); and "Diary of Jeremiah Bumstead of Boston, 1722–1727," in *New England Historical and Genealogical Register* (July 1861), 201.

297   **"It is almost"**: "On the Lord's Day," *BNL* (April 30–May 7, 1724).

297   **The subsequent admiralty . . . all to see:** "Boston, May 18," *Boston Gazette* (May 11–18, 1724); "Boston, June 8," *New-England Courant* (June 1–8, 1724); and Babson, *History of the Town of Gloucester*, 288.

297   **"Kitchen Stuff" . . . "of the vulgar herd"**: "To Old Father Janus," *New-England Courant* (May 11–18, 1724).

298   **Although most modern readers:** Mary Beth Norton, *Separated by Their Sex: Women in Public and Private in the Colonial Atlantic World* (Ithaca, NY: Cornell University Press, 2011), 120–22.

298   **rushed into print:** Cotton Mather, *The Converted Sinner. The Nature of a Conversion to Real and Vital Piety: and the Manner in Which it is to be Pray'd & Striv'n for: A Sermon Preached in Boston, May 31, 1724* (Boston: Nathaniel Belknap, 1724).

298   **"One of the first"**: Cotton Mather, *Diary of Cotton Mather*, vol. II, 729.

299   **"was drunk"**: Ibid.

299   **"But one wickedness . . . to great temptations"**: Dow and Edmonds, *Pirates*, 325.

299   **"so far protected"**: "By the Honourable William Dummer, Esq., A Proclamation for a General Thanksgiving," *BNL* (October 15–22, 1724).

300   **"Your Lordships"**: "Col. Spotswood to the Council of Trade and Plantations" (June 16, 1724), *CSPC*, item 210, vol. 34, 112–20.

300   **"golden luggage"**: "Philadelphia, March 17," *American Weekly Mercury* (March 17, 1720).

300   **"showed just abhorrence"**: "Alexander Spotswood to the Board of Trade" (May 20, 1720), 338.

300   **"would not spare man"**: Rankin, *Golden Age of Piracy*, 137. See also "Lt. Governor Spotswood to the Council of Trade and Plantations" (May 31, 1722), *CSPC*, item 513, vol. 32, 326–29.

300   **This message was delivered:** "At a Council Held at the Capitol, the 3rd Day of May 1721," *Executive Journals of the Council of Colonial Virginia, May 1, 1705–October 23, 1721*, 542; and Dodson, *Alexander Spotswood*, 220.

300   **Fearing for their safety:** "Lt. Governor Spotswood to the Council of Trade and Plantations" (June 11, 1722), *CSPC*, item 175, vol. 33, 79–99.

EPILOGUE — "YO-HO-HO, AND A BOTTLE OF RUM!"

303   **"There is no theme":** Grey, *Pirates of the Eastern Seas*, vii.

304   **"three crosses of red ink":** Robert Louis Stevenson, *Treasure Island* (London: Cassell, 1883), 51.

304   **"Fifteen men on a dead man's chest":** Ibid., 7.

304   **"Onboard the Derelict":** Young E. Allison, "Onboard the Derelict," *Library of Southern Literature*, ed. Charles Alphonso Smith, vol. 14 (New Orleans, LA: Martin & Hoyt Company, 1907), 6134–36; and Walt Mason, "An Apology and Appreciation," *Seven Seas Magazine* (November, 1915), 8.

305   **"think much of . . . I am a Pirate King!":** W. S. Gilbert and Arthur Sullivan, *The Pirates of Penzance* (New York: J.M. Stoddart, 1880), 7.

307   **"It's fun":** Stephen Totillo, "Does It Say 'Aargh' When You Make a Kill?" *New York Times* (October 29, 2013).

307   **"permanent ambition":** Mark Twain, *Life on the Mississippi* (Hartford, CT: American Publishing Company, 1899), 43.

307   **"It cannot but be":** M.E.S., "Deeds of Pirate Kings: A Romantic Kind of Sailor Now Extinct," *New York Times* (January 24, 1892).

308   **"I have become quite":** Robert C. Ritchie, "Living with Pirates," *Rethinking History* (September 2009), 417.

309   **"The hoard of":** Ralph D. Paine, *The Book of Buried Treasure* (London: William Heinemann, 1911), 9.

309   **Many people have . . . would get there first:** Paine, *The Book of Buried Treasure*, 26–41; Peter Ross, *A History of Long Island From Its Earliest Settlement to the Present Time*, vol. I (New York: Lewis Publishing Company, 1902), 180–81; Cordingly, *Under the Black Flag*, 178–90; Thomas A. Janvier, "The Sea-Robbers of New York," *Harper's New Monthly Magazine* (November 1894), 822; Rebecca Simon, "The Many Deaths of Captain Kidd," *History Today* (July 2015), 7; and W. C. Jameson, *Buried Treasures of the* Mid-Atlantic *States: Legends of Island Treasure, Jewelry Caches, & Secret Tunnels* (Little Rock, AR: August House, 2000), 25–29.

309   **But there is pirate treasure:** The background for this section on the discovery of the *Whydah* and its treasure comes from Clifford, *Expedition Whydah*; Donovan Webster, "Pirates of the *Whydah*," *National Geographic Magazine* (May 1999), 64–77; Great Big Story and CNN Films, "This Explorer Shares Shipwrecked Treasures with the World," https://www.discoverpirates.com/news/, accessed on June 15, 2017; The Whydah Pirate Museum website, https://www.discoverpirates.com/, accessed on June 15, 2017; and Doug Fraser, "Legend of the *Whydah* Pirate Ship Endures," *Cape Cod Times* (April 23, 2017).

310   **"At times to this day":** Levi Whitman, "A Topographical Description of Wellfleet, in the County of Barnstable," (October 26, 1793), in *Collections of the*

Massachusetts Historical Society for the year 1794, vol. III (Boston: Apollo Press, 1794), 120.

310 **An enterprising . . . coastal topography:** Vanderbilt, *Treasure Wreck*, 121–22; and Edward Rowe Snow, *True Tales of Buried Treasure* (New York: Dodd, Mead, 1951), 57–59.

310 **"It will be a very":** Snow, *True Tales of Buried Treasure*, 59.

311 **In November 1996 . . . his blockade of the city:** Background for the discovery of the *Queen Anne's Revenge* comes from North Carolina Department of Natural and Cultural Resources *Queen Anne's Revenge* Project website, http://www.qaronline.org/, accessed on June 17, 2017; Moore, *Blackbeard the Pirate*, 31–39; David D. Moore, "Blackbeard's *Queen Anne's Revenge*: Archaeological Interpretation and Research Focused on the Hull Remains and Ship-Related Accoutrements Associated with Site 31-CR-314," *Tributaries* (October 2001), 49–64; Mark Wilde-Ramsing and Charles R. Ewen, "Beyond Reasonable Doubt: A Case for Queen Anne's Revenge," *Historical Archaeology* (June 2012), 110–33; Samir S. Patel and Marion P. Blackburn, "Blackbeard Surfaces," *Archaeology* (March/April 2008), 22–27; Willie Drye, "Blackbeard's Ship Confirmed off North Carolina," National Geographic News (August 29, 2011, and updated on July 24, 2017), http://news.nationalgeographic.com/news/2011/08/110829-blackbeard-shipwreck-pirates-archaeology-science/, accessed July 25, 2017; Kristin Romey, "Chance Blackbeard Discovery Reveals Pirate Reading Habits," *National Geographic* (January 4, 2018), https://news.nationalgeographic.com/2018/01/blackbeard-pirate-book-cannon-revenge/; and personal communication with Paul Fontenoy, Curator of Maritime History, North Carolina Maritime Museums, July 11, 2017.

311 **"It looks as if":** Mark U. Wilde-Ramsing and Charles R. Ewen, "Beyond Reasonable Doubt: A Case for 'Queen Anne's Revenge,'" *Historical Archaeology* (2012), 110.

Select Bibliography

THIS BIBLIOGRAPHY CONTAINS BUT A SMALL FRACTION OF the sources cited in this book. It is intended as a starting point for the general reader who wants to learn more about the history of America's pirates, and piracy in general. For additional information about specific topics and particular pirates covered in the text, please refer to the endnotes.

Appleby, John C. *Women and English Piracy, 1540–1720: Partners and Victims of Crime*. Woodbridge, UK: Boydell Press, 2013.

Baer, Joel H., ed. *British Piracy in the Golden Age: History and Interpretation, 1660–1730*, 4 vols. London: Pickering & Chatto, 2007.

Beal, Clifford. *Quelch's Gold: Piracy, Greed, and Betrayal in Colonial New England*. Washington, DC: Potomac Books, 2008.

Bialuschewski, Arne. "Between Newfoundland and the Malacca Strait: A Survey of the Golden Age of Piracy, 1695–1725." *Mariner's Mirror* (May 2004), 167–86.

Brooks, Baylus C. *Quest for Blackbeard: The True Story of Edward Thache and His World*. Lake City: Lulu Press, 2016.

Burgess, Douglas R., Jr., *The Pirates' Pact: The Secret Alliances between History's Most Notorious Buccaneers and Colonial America*. New York: McGraw Hill, 2008.

Butler, Lindley S. *Pirates, Privateers, and Rebel Raiders of the Carolina Coast*. Chapel Hill: University of North Carolina Press, 2000.

Clifford, Lindley S. *Expedition Whydah: The Story of the World's First Excavation of a Pirate Ship and the Man Who Found Her*. With Paul Perry. New York: Cliff Street Books, 1999.

Cordingly, David. *Under the Black Flag: The Romance and the Reality of Life among the Pirates*. Orlando: Harvest Book, 1995.

———. *Spanish Gold: Captain Woodes Rogers and the Pirates of the Caribbean*. London: Bloomsbury, 2011.

Defoe, Daniel [Charles Johnson]. *A General History of the Pyrates*, ed. Manuel Schonhorn. Mineola, NY: Dover Publications, 1999.

Dow, George Francis, and John Henry Edmonds. *The Pirates of the New England Coast, 1630–1730*. New York: Sentry Press, 1968. First published in 1923.

Downey, Christopher Byrd. *Stede Bonnet: Charleston's Gentleman Pirate*. Charleston: History Press, 2012.

Earle, Peter. *The Pirate Wars*. New York: Thomas Dunne Books, 2003.

Esquemelin, Alexander O. *The Buccaneers of America*. Translated by Alexis Brown, and introduction by Jack Beeching. Mineola, NY: Dover Publications, 2000.

Flemming, Gregory N. *At the Point of a Cutlass: The Pirate Capture, Bold Escape, & Lonely Exile of Philip Ashton*. Lebanon, NH: ForeEdge, 2014.

Gosse, Philip. *The History of Piracy*. Mineola, NY: Dover Publications, 2007. First published in 1932 by the University of North Carolina Press.

Grey, Charles. *Pirates of the Eastern Seas (1618–1723): A Lurid Page of History*. Port Washington, NY: Kennikat Press, 1971. First published in 1933 by S. Low, Marston & Co.

Hanna, Mark G. *Pirate Nests and the Rise of the British Empire: 1570–1740*. Chapel Hill: University of North Carolina Press, 2015.

Jameson, J. Franklin. *Privateering and Piracy in the Colonial Period, Illustrated Documents*. New York: Augustus M. Kelley, 1923.

Konstam, Angus. *The History of Pirates*. Guilford, CT: Lyons Press, 1999.

———. *The Pirate Ship: 1660–1730*. Oxford: Osprey Publishing, 2003.

———. *Blackbeard: America's Most Notorious Pirate*. Hoboken, NJ: John Wiley & Sons, 2006.

Lee, Robert E. *Blackbeard the Pirate: A Reappraisal of His Life and Times*. Winston-Salem, NC: John F. Blair, 1990.

Leeson, Peter T. *The Invisible Hook: The Hidden Economics of Pirates*. Princeton, NJ: Princeton University Press, 2009.

Lincoln, Margarette. *British Pirates and Society, 1680–1730*. London: Routledge, 2014.

Little, Benerson. *The Golden Age of Piracy: The Truth behind Pirate Myths*. New York: Skyhorse Publishing, 2016.

McDonald, Kevin P. *Pirates, Merchants, Settlers, and Slaves: Colonial America and the Indo-Atlantic World*. Oakland: University of California Press, 2015.

Moore, David. "Blackbeard the Pirate: Historical Background and the Beaufort Inlet Shipwrecks." *Tributaries* (October 1997).

Pringle, Patrick. *Jolly Roger: The Story of the Great Age of Piracy*. New York: W. W. Norton, 1953.

Rankin, Hugh F. *The Golden Age of Piracy*. New York: Holt, Rhinehart & Winston, 1969.

Rediker, Marcus. "'Under the Banner of King Death': The Social World of Anglo-American Pirates, 1716 to 1726," *William and Mary Quarterly* (April 1981).

———. *Between the Devil and the Deep Blue Sea: Merchant Seamen, Pirates, and the Anglo-American Maritime World, 1700–1750.* Cambridge: Cambridge University Press, 1987.

———. *Villains of all Nations: Atlantic Pirates in the Golden Age.* Boston: Beacon Press, 2004.

Ritchie, Robert C. *Captain Kidd and the War against the Pirates.* Cambridge, MA: Harvard University Press, 1986.

Senior, Clive. *A Nation of Pirates: English Piracy in its Heyday.* London: David & Charles Newton Abbot, 1976.

Shomette, Donald G. *Pirates on the Chesapeake: Being a True History of Pirates, Picaroons, and Raiders on Chesapeake Bay, 1610–1807.* Centreville, MD: Tidewater Publishers, 1985.

Williams, Lloyd Haynes. *Pirates of Colonial Virginia.* Richmond, VA: Dietz Press, 1937.

Woodard, Colin. *The Republic of Pirates: Being the True and Surprising Story of the Caribbean Pirates and the Man Who Brought Them Down.* New York: Harcourt, 2007.

———. "The Last Days of Blackbeard." *Smithsonian* (February 2014).

Zacks, Richard. *The Pirate Hunter: The True Story of Captain Kidd.* New York: Hyperion, 2002.

Illustration Credits

Page 73: Courtesy Library of Congress

Page 75: Charles Ellms, *The Pirates Own Book, or Authentic Narratives of the Lives, Exploits, and Executions of the Most Celebrated Sea Robbers* (Boston: S. N. Dickinson, 1837). Courtesy Houghton Library, Harvard University

Page 87: Courtesy The Miriam and Ira D. Wallach Division of Art, Prints and Photographs: Print Collection, The New York Public Library

Page 89: Courtesy John Carter Brown Library at Brown University

Page 100: Courtesy Art and Picture Collection, The New York Public Library, Astor, Lenox and Tilden Foundations

Page 103: Courtesy National Maritime Museum, Greenwich, London

Page 109: Courtesy John Carter Brown Library at Brown University

Page 113: Courtesy Library of Congress

Page 115: Charles Ellms, *The Pirates Own Book, or Authentic Narratives of the Lives, Exploits, and Executions of the Most Celebrated Sea Robbers* (Boston: S. N. Dickinson, 1837). Courtesy Houghton Library, Harvard University

Page 124: Courtesy Library of Congress

Page 130: Courtesy Library of Congress

Page 135: Courtesy Library of Congress

Page 136: Courtesy Library of Congress

Page 141: Map reproduction courtesy of the Norman B. Leventhal Map Center at the Boston Public Library

Page 144: Courtesy Houghton Library, Harvard University

Page 156: Courtesy John Carter Brown Library at Brown University

Page 157: Courtesy John Carter Brown Library at Brown University

Page 158: Charles Ellms, *The Pirates Own Book, or Authentic Narratives of the Lives, Exploits, and Executions of the Most Celebrated Sea Robbers* (Boston: S. N. Dickinson, 1837). Courtesy Houghton Library, Harvard University

Page 167 (top): Courtesy John Carter Brown Library at Brown University

Page 167 (bottom): Courtesy Library of Congress

Page 170: Courtesy Åland Maritime Museum /Ålands sjöfartsmuseum, Åland, Finland

Page 175: Courtesy John Carter Brown Library at Brown University

Page 176: Courtesy Metropolitan Museum of Art, the Jefferson R. Burdick Collection, Gift of Jefferson R. Burdick

Page 179: Courtesy Library of Congress

Page 196: Courtesy Library of Congress, Geography and Map Division

Page 202: Courtesy John Carter Brown Library at Brown University

Page 204: Courtesy John Carter Brown Library at Brown University

Page 205: Courtesy Library of Congress

Page 206: Courtesy John Carter Brown Library at Brown University

Page 208: Courtesy John Carter Brown Library at Brown University

Page 213: Courtesy Angus Konstam

Page 222: Courtesy John Carter Brown Library at Brown University

Page 227: Courtesy Library of Congress

Page 236: Courtesy © Eric Holch, from one of his silkscreen prints (www.ericholch.com)

Page 237: Courtesy Library of Congress

Page 239: Courtesy John Carter Brown Library at Brown University

Page 241: Courtesy Library of Congress

Page 243: Courtesy Miriam and Ira D. Wallach Division of Art, Prints and Photographs: Print Collection, The New York Public Library

Page 246: Charles Ellms, *The Pirates Own Book, or Authentic Narratives of the Lives, Exploits, and Executions of the Most Celebrated Sea Robbers* (Boston: S. N. Dickinson, 1837). Courtesy Houghton Library, Harvard University

Page 249: "New and Correct Map of the Province of North Carolina," by Edward Moseley (1733). Courtesy Joyner Library, East Carolina University

Page 252: Charles Ellms, *The Pirates Own Book, or Authentic Narratives of the Lives, Exploits, and Executions of the Most Celebrated Sea Robbers* (Boston: S. N. Dickinson, 1837). Courtesy Houghton Library, Harvard University

Page 254: Charles Ellms, *The Pirates Own Book, or Authentic Narratives of the Lives, Exploits, and Executions of the Most Celebrated Sea Robbers* (Boston: S. N. Dickinson, 1837). Courtesy Houghton Library, Harvard University

Page 259: Courtesy John Carter Brown Library at Brown University

Page 263: Courtesy John Carter Brown Library at Brown University

Page 265: Courtesy Houghton Library, Harvard University

Page 268: Courtesy John Carter Brown Library at Brown University

Page 270: Courtesy Stack's Bowers Galleries

Page 272: Courtesy Metropolitan Museum of Art, the Jefferson R. Burdick Collection, Gift of Jefferson R. Burdick

Page 274: Courtesy John Carter Brown Library at Brown University

Page 276: Courtesy Library of Congress

Page 278: Courtesy NOAA National Marine Fisheries Service

Page 280: Charles Ellms, *The Pirates Own Book, or Authentic Narratives of the Lives, Exploits, and Executions of the Most Celebrated Sea Robbers* (Boston: S. N. Dickinson, 1837). Courtesy Houghton Library, Harvard University

Page 283: Courtesy David Rumsey Map Collection, www.davidrumsey.com

Page 285: John Barnard, *Ashton's Memorial: Or An [sic] History of the Strange Adventures, and Signal Deliverances, of Mr. Philip Ashton*. Courtesy Houghton Library, Harvard University

Page 290: Courtesy Library of Congress

Insert

2. Courtesy Stack's Bowers Galleries
3. Courtesy Angus Konstam
4. Courtesy David Rumsey Map Collection, www.davidrumsey.com
6. Courtesy Library of Congress
7. Courtesy David Rumsey Map Collection, www.davidrumsey.com
9. Courtesy Library of Congress

10. Courtesy Gibbes Museum of Art / Carolina Art Association
11. Courtesy National Maritime Museum, Greenwich, London
12. Courtesy © Eric Holch, from one of his silkscreen prints (www.ericholch.com)
13. Frank E. Schoonover Manuscript Collection, Helen Farr Sloan Library & Archives, Delaware Art Museum
14. Courtesy Library of Congress
15. The Jon B. Lovelace Collection of California Photographs in Carol M. Highsmith's America Project, Library of Congress, Prints and Photographs Division
16. Courtesy Center for Historic Shipwreck Preservation
17. Courtesy William Curtsinger, National Geographic Creative
18. Courtesy William Curtsinger, National Geographic Creative
20. Courtesy Library of Congress.
21. © Lily Dolin

Index

ERIC JAY DOLIN is the author of *Leviathan: The History of Whaling in America*, which was chosen as one of the best nonfiction books of 2007 by the *Los Angeles Times*, *Boston Globe*, and *Providence Journal*, and also won the 2007 John Lyman Award for U.S. Maritime History; and *Fur, Fortune, and Empire: The Epic History of the Fur Trade in America*, which was chosen by the *Seattle Times* as one of the best nonfiction books of 2010, and also won the James P. Hanlan Book Award, given by the New England Historical Association. He is also the author of *When America First Met China: An Exotic History of Tea, Drugs, and Money in the Age of Sail*, which was chosen by *Kirkus Reviews* as one of the 100 best nonfiction books of 2012; and *Brilliant Beacons: A History of the American Lighthouse*, which was chosen by *gCaptain* and *Classic Boat* as one of the best nautical books of 2016. A graduate of Brown, Yale, and MIT, where he received his PhD in environmental policy, Dolin lives in Marblehead, Massachusetts, with his family. For more information on his background, books, and awards, please visit his website, ericjay dolin.com. You can also follow Dolin's posts on Facebook on his professional page, @ericjaydolin, or on Twitter, @EricJayDolin.